NORDIC PATHS TO MODERNITY

NORDIC PATHS TO MODERNITY

Edited by

Jóhann Páll Árnason and Björn Wittrock

berghahn
NEW YORK · OXFORD
www.berghahnbooks.com

Published in 2012 by

Berghahn Books

www.berghahnbooks.com

©2012, 2015 Jóhann Páll Árnason and Björn Wittrock
First paperback edition published in 2015

All rights reserved. Except for the quotation of short passages
for the purposes of criticism and review, no part of this book
may be reproduced in any form or by any means, electronic or
mechanical, including photocopying, recording, or any information
storage and retrieval system now known or to be invented,
without written permission of the publisher.

Library of Congress Cataloging-in-Publication Data
Nordic paths to modernity / edited by Jóhann Páll Árnason and Björn Wittrock.
  p. cm.
  Includes bibliographical references and index.
  ISBN 978-0-85745-269-6 (hardback : alk. paper) – ISBN 978-1-78238-684-1 (paperback
  : alk. paper) – ISBN 978-0-85745-270-2 (ebook)
  1. Scandinavia–History–21st century. 2. Scandinavia–Social policy–History–21st
  century. 3. Scandinavia–Civilization–21st century. I. Árnason, Jóhann Páll, 1940-
  II. Wittrock, Björn.
  DL87.N66 2011
  948–dc23

2011020291

British Library Cataloguing in Publication Data
A catalogue record for this book is available from the British Library.

Printed on acid-free paper.

ISBN: 978-0-85745-269-6 (hardcopy)
ISBN: 978-1-78238-684-1 (paperback)
ISBN: 978-0-85745-270-2 (ebook)

Contents

Acknowledgements　　vii

Introduction　　1
Jóhann Páll Árnason and Björn Wittrock

1. Nordic Modernity: Origins, Trajectories, Perspectives　　25
   Bo Stråth

2. The Danish Path to Modernity　　49
   Uffe Østergård

3. Denmark 1740–1940: A Centralized Cultural Community　　69
   Niels Kayser Nielsen

4. The Making of Sweden　　89
   Björn Wittrock

5. History and Ethics in Pre-revolutionary Sweden　　111
   Peter Hallberg

6. The Metamorphoses of Norwegian Reformism　　143
   Rune Slagstad

7. Alternative Processes of Modernization?　　167
   Gunnar Skirbekk

8. Nordic and Finnish Modernity: A Comparison　　191
   Risto Alapuro

9. Paradoxes of the Finnish Political Culture　　207
   Henrik Stenius

10. Icelandic Anomalies 229
    Jóhann Páll Árnason

11. Icelandic Modernity and the Role of Nationalism 251
    Guðmundur Hálfdanarson

    Notes on Contributors 275

    Index 279

Acknowledgements

This book has been in the making for a long time, and contributions to it have benefited from several rounds of discussion. The first published installment was a special Nordic issue of the journal *Thesis Eleven* (no. 77, published in 2003). Thanks are due to Sage Publications for permission to republish the papers by Rune Slagstad and Uffe Østergård, with minor revisions, as well as more extensively revised versions of the chapters by Jóhann P. Árnason and Björn Wittrock. Risto Alapuro and Bo Stråth have reworked their contributions in a much more radical way.

The other papers, previously unpublished, grew out of a workshop at the Swedish Collegium for Advanced Study in Uppsala in April 2005, but their final versions also reflect later and less formal discussions between the authors and interested colleagues.

Thanks are due to Karl Smith for copy-editing work, and to Sara Grut and Sophie Sköld for helping to get the manuscript into presentable shape.

Introduction

Jóhann Páll Árnason and Björn Wittrock

The Historical Background

This is a book about five independent states which are commonly included in definitions of the Nordic region (and now formally associated through membership in various organizations): Denmark, Finland, Iceland, Norway and Sweden. These countries are characterized by a high, and in a European context arguably unique, degree of commonality in terms of traditions, cultural habits, institutional structures, languages and closeness of cooperation.

At various points in time from the late medieval era to the period after the Second World War, there have been advanced plans for the creation of a common political entity. In the course of the fourteenth century, at least from 1319 onwards, there was a sequence of efforts, partly successful, to join two or all three of the main Scandinavian countries in a union. This occurred to a large extent in reaction to the extension of influence by various rulers and constellations from the German lands south of the Baltic. The most long-lasting and successful of the Scandinavian unions was the all-Scandinavian united state, the so-called Kalmar Union (1397–1523). This entity constituted the largest country in Europe, extending from Greenland in the west to what is now Western Russia in the east, and from North Cape to what is now Northern Germany.

In the mid- and late nineteenth century, in an age of increasing nationalism, there was a strong movement of Scandinavianism, also promoted by the royal houses of Denmark and Sweden. A main focus of this movement was opposition to German nationalism and the threat it posed to the then Danish-ruled province of Schleswig-Holstein (Slesvig/Sleswig-Holsten). The movement, however, rapidly lost momentum in the wake of the Danish defeat in the war against Prussia in 1864. Furthermore, in 1873, Sweden and Denmark concluded a currency union with the use of the monetary unit of the crown having equivalent value in both countries. Two years later Norway joined this currency union which officially dissolved only in 1924 in the wake of the economic turbulence after the First World War.

In the period after the Second World War, plans for a Scandinavian defence union failed. However within the framework of the Nordic Council, founded in 1952, a uniquely close collaboration evolved that by decades antedated what the European Union has relatively recently achieved or is about to achieve in terms of a common labour market, exemption from the needs to carry passports at crossings of national boundaries and extensive rights, not only social but also political, being preserved beyond national boundaries. In the contemporary period the Nordic countries have often appeared, and presented themselves, to the outside world as a group of small, peaceful and socially concerned parliamentary democracies, independent but operating within a framework of a shared political culture. This image still has considerable validity. However there is also another side to Nordic history.

For three centuries from the early sixteenth to the early nineteenth centuries, that is, during what is normally referred to as the early modern period in European historiography, the Nordic countries were divided by a chasm between on the one hand the conglomerate monarchy of Denmark, including Norway, Iceland, the Faroe Islands, Greenland and a range of other possessions, not least in Northern Germany, and on the other hand the Central-Eastern Swedish Realm that had today's countries of Sweden and Finland at its core and with Baltic and German possessions attached to it. This chasm was a persistent feature of Northern European history and has shaped institutional and political legacies of relevance up to the present day. It was also deep enough to lead to some of the most bloody military conflicts in European history.

At a few points in time in this period, it seemed as if one of the contenders, most notably so the Swedish Realm, was about to achieve a violent reunification of all the Nordic countries. The late summer of 1659, when, in the words of the Danish historian Uffe Østergård, Denmark was reduced to Copenhagen inside the walls, is the most obvious case in point. It does not require an excessive use of counterfactual history to envisage the possibility of radically different trajectories of the history of the North-Eastern half of Europe, should something analogous to that have occurred. However the Baltic region was at the time becoming ever more part of a wide nexus of trade routes of an increasingly trans-regional and indeed global reach. The Western seafaring powers of Britain and, as in 1659, the Netherlands, strenuously tried to safeguard their interests and see to it that the Baltic did not become entirely controlled by one of the land powers along its shores and did not hesitate to intervene, whether by pressure or sheer force, to try to secure these objectives.

This feature of Western interest in access to the Baltic was a persistent one in Nordic history at least from the sixteenth century, through the events of the Great Northern War of 1700–1721 and the so-called Crimean War, originally planned as a Baltic War, up until the contestations of the Cold War. It was paralleled by Russian efforts, from the failed efforts of Ivan IV in the Livonian war of 1558–1564 and including the successful ones of Peter I in the war of 1700–1721, and of Alexander I in the war of 1808–1809, and up until the dramatic changes of the present period, of gaining, extending and maintaining access to the Baltic.

Thus to use a conventional map, embracing the five core countries of the Nordic region, is not to deny that further qualifications may be needed for various purposes. Observers of the contemporary scene might suggest that the autonomous parts of the Danish state (the Faroe Islands and Greenland), now in all probability embarking on a more independent history, deserve more attention, and together with Iceland they are sometimes seen as a North-Western periphery of the Nordic world, marked by – or at least open to – trans-Atlantic connections in a way that the Scandinavian countries, more narrowly conceived, are not. Furthermore, a long-term perspective links the core of the Danish kingdom to continental neighbours and suggests that its history cuts across the divide between Northern and Central Europe (if the latter region is further divided between east and west, Denmark is an obvious candidate for inclusion in West Central Europe). The Schleswig-Holstein/Slesvig/Sleswig-Holsten connection is perhaps the most striking reminder of this cross-regional dimension. It goes back to the twelfth century and culminated in nineteenth-century military conflicts between Denmark and Prussia (at the time in alliance with Habsburg Austria) which led to the loss of a third of the continental part of the Danish realm. Indeed, the pre-1864 Danish realm extended into the suburbs of Hamburg.

Another historical overlap is the blurred frontier between the Nordic and the Baltic world, important enough in modern times for some scholars to construct North-Eastern Europe as a historical region including what are now Sweden, Finland and the Baltic countries. Indeed in the post-Soviet era, the ministers of the member states of the Nordic Council now regularly meet with their peers from the Baltic countries, and there is a preponderant Swedish and Finnish presence in the economies of Estonia and Latvia. Present Nordic perceptions of regional boundaries still allow for some flexibility: at a minimum, Estonia, a country linked to Finland and Sweden in historical, cultural and linguistic terms, can claim the status of a particularly close neighbour. But the most massive trans-regional link, and the only one to be extensively discussed here, was the Finnish experience of integration – on special terms – into the Russian Empire between the Napoleonic Wars and the First World War. As the dates indicate, this episode is also an example of European geopolitics affecting the course of Nordic history. The results were crucial to the making of modern Finland.

Regional and National Patterns

With the exception just mentioned, the contributions to this book will nevertheless focus on relatively clear-cut Nordic patterns of history and approach them from the perspective of the units that emerged as nation-states in the modern phase of development. The well-founded emphasis in much contemporary scholarship on regional, European and global perspectives should not lead to a complete disregard for the nation-state frame of reference, especially not in cases where processes of nation formation and national settings of modernization have been as central as in the Nordic countries. And as will be seen, national variations in the way of relating to the common Nordic domain are still of considerable importance.

If the arguments of individual authors are thus geared to the national level of analysis, the introduction will foreground some basic features of the regional context as such, and situate the approaches represented in this book in relation to other perspectives. Since the 1930s, international interest in *Norden* (see 'Note on Terminology' at the end of this chapter) – both scholarly and political – has tended to focus on the regional record of the welfare state, including the strategies of adaptation to global capitalism in the closing decades of the twentieth and at the beginning of the twenty-first century, and on the political projects of the parties most directly involved in its development. Scandinavian, and more specifically Swedish and Norwegian Social Democracy have often been presented as the most authentically successful branch of the socialist movement. These aspects of the Nordic experience have, most recently, figured in the debate on multiple modernities. If we distinguish the category of alternative modernities from the more general notion of multiple modernities, and reserve the former for cases of explicit ambition to contest and replace established models on a global scale, the Nordic way appears as one of the intermediate types.

There is no doubt about its status as a distinctive pattern of modernity; it did not emerge as an alternative with global claims or aspirations, even if some of its architects were guided by ideological orientations defined in an international context. Most of them were also acutely aware that this international context at the time was characterized by waves of transitions from parliamentary democracy to various forms of authoritarian regimes. With both the Soviet Union of Stalin and Nazi Germany in close geographical proximity, it was inevitable that the Nordic welfare states had to position themselves vis-à-vis these explicitly alternative modernities. Thus some of the architects of the Nordic welfare states sought to articulate a vision of society that would deny any lure among their own population of policies embraced by these large and powerful alternative modernities next door. These efforts of the Nordic welfare states must, in a comparative perspective, be deemed highly successful – see for instance the minor modern classic (Lindström 1985) for a comparative analysis of fascism, or rather the relative weakness of it, in Scandinavia in the interwar period.

It is also true that from an early stage, observers of the model in the making included those who wanted to spell out its message for a more global audience. Marquis Childs's book on the Swedish 'middle way', first published in the aftermath of the Great Depression (Childs 1936), set an example later followed by many others. This line of interpretation was sometimes also embraced by representatives of the parties in power. At the time of the inception of this debate, outside interpreters and internal representatives alike were aware of the context and the antinomies that characterized the emergence of a specifically Scandinavian model of a modern state. Two such prominent features were, especially in the Norwegian and Swedish cases, the fact that there occurred a transition from a situation in the early part of the interwar period with very high levels of labour conflicts and strikes, to one characterized by a remarkable degree of peaceful accommodation in the labour market. The strong labour movements in these countries were clearly reformist in their orientation but there existed relatively strong radical leanings in both movements; in the Norwegian case the majority of the Norwegian Labour Party had even briefly joined the Third, Communist International. Similarly it was certainly not a foregone conclusion that it would be possible to successfully forge an alliance between the labour parties in these countries and parties representing the peasantry. In much of the rest of Europe, agrarian strata had often come to form the backbone of fascist political movements, but in Scandinavia this did not occur.

With the passage of time, however, the context of emergence of the model became less prominent and its contemporary achievements tended to become more directly linked to the policy choices of leading political parties. As a result, contingencies existing at various earlier points fell into relative oblivion, and imaginations about Nordic welfare states took on features sometimes of an account of a story of political wisdom and heroism. With the growth, in Scandinavia itself but largely in major universities and research institutes in the United States, in Britain, and, somewhat later in Germany, of quantitative studies of welfare regimes from the 1960s onwards, interpretations of the experiences of the Nordic states once more became strongly comparative but now within the framework of a large scholarly discussion and also close research collaboration between Scandinavian sociologists, political scientists and economists and their peers abroad, not least in leading British and American universities. At roughly the same time, there was a growth of interest in social history and conceptual history (*Gesellschaftsgeschichte, Begriffsgeschichte,* to use the German terms of origin) among Scandinavian historians, some of them being represented in this volume, which also prompted an interest in long-term patterns of social development and state formation in Scandinavia in a broad comparative analysis (with Torstendahl 1991 as one of its towering achievements). Still these different debates have coexisted with little or no interaction. Nor have they led to a more comprehensive stocktaking of the different Nordic paths to modernity.

This book, in contrast, seeks to examine precisely the key issues concerning Nordic modernity in a broader historical-sociological context than that which has dominated the policy interpretations from the 1930s onwards. Thus a main emphasis of this book is on long-term historical processes. To put it another way, with reference to the title of the book, our concern is with 'paths to' rather than 'patterns of' modernity. One particularly important outcome of the developmental trends to be analysed is the consolidation of features of political culture across the region, but certainly not without significant differences between countries. The Social Democratic movements and governments, more important in some states than in others, implemented their projects in the context of a much older and broader political culture. This is not to belittle the stature or the achievements of these political actors, but their actions were less self-contained and less sovereign than analysts of the Nordic experience have sometimes tended to assume.

The stress on long-term dynamics should, as already emphasized, not be mistaken for a one-sided construction of continuity. It is definitely not the intention of the present group of authors to argue for a vision of Nordic history prefiguring and inexorably ushering in the twentieth-century version of Nordic modernity. As will be seen, there are surprising turns to the story, and contingent events unfolding in a larger arena affected the regional trajectory. A long-term perspective must take note of changing balances between continuity and discontinuity, of the different twists to such constellations in particular countries, and of the trans-regional entanglements, which also vary from one case to another.

Geopolitics and Transformations

A historical sociology of the region should make at least a passing reference to medieval beginnings. The major European regions are to a great extent (but not exclusively, and not all to the same degree) defined by the historical circumstances in which they became parts of the civilization of Western Christendom (see also Árnason and Wittrock 2004). That seems eminently applicable to the Nordic world, where the formation of Christian monarchies in Denmark, Norway and Sweden (as well as the more marginal non-monarchic Christianization of Iceland) during the High Middle Ages set the stage for regional history. The medieval phase will not be discussed at length in this book (although more so in the Icelandic case than the others, due to the particular importance of the medieval legacy for the Icelandic pattern of nation formation).

Let us however note that some of the most interesting current debates on Nordic history have to do with this period and with comparative perspectives on its characteristics. The comparison with another peripheral part of Western Christendom, taking shape at roughly the same time, the Central Eastern European cluster of Christian monarchies, is a key theme of a long-term research project organized by the Centre of Medieval Studies in Bergen; these two extensions of the European world beyond its Roman and Carolingian core areas are particularly revealing cases of civilizational expansion, as distinct from the military conquests that led to enlargement on other frontiers during the same period. Nordic echoes and ramifications of the twelfth-century developments that transformed Western Christendom – the 'first European revolution', as R.I. Moore (2000) described it – have also become the subject of scholarly controversies. Denmark was closest to the centres of change, and the most divergent interpretations have focused on its twelfth-century experience: one school of thought stresses commercial dynamism and even the formation of an early capitalist spirit (Carelli 2001), thus aligning itself with the most modernistic accounts of twelfth-century Europe, while another insists on the continuity of kinship-based aristocratic domination (Hermanson 2000). On the cultural level, the debate revolves around the 'twelfth-century renaissance', to use the classic term coined by C.H. Haskins, and its analogies and/or influences in the Nordic world; here the main theme is the flowering of a vernacular literary culture in Iceland (Johansson et al. 2007).

It is, of course, one of the most basic facts about Nordic history that the original geopolitical constellation did not remain unchanged. In that sense, claims to regional continuity must be qualified. The high medieval monarchies (including the thirteenth-century enlarged version of the Norwegian realm) were absorbed into a late medieval composite state, centred on Denmark but operating on a new geopolitical scale. Here too, a comparison with East Central Europe is instructive. In both cases, monarchic states (or, as in Iceland, a non-monarchic polity) of medieval origin disappeared from the scene, but cultural memories of them contributed to the building of states with a more clear-cut or at least more explicitly claimed national identity centuries later, although in East Central Europe the rupture of continuity came later and took a different turn. The main intra-regional candidate for an imperial role, the Polish kingdom (reunified in the fourteenth century and then expanded into a Polish-Lithuanian Union), failed to realize its ambitions, and the historical states were in the end absorbed by empires built up from outside the region, none of which achieved uncontested domination within it (the failure of the Habsburg Empire to do so was of momentous importance for European history).

The Nordic composite state mentioned above, commonly known as the Kalmar Union (1397–1523), is for many reasons a noteworthy chapter in the history of the region. Its record in the two Scandinavian parts of the realm was strikingly different. In Sweden, it was troubled by periodic revolts with both aristocratic and peasant support, and by intermittent de facto restorations of Swedish independence, whereas control over Norway was more stable and became a prelude to tighter integration into the Danish kingdom after the Reformation. In addition to this uneven reach, the union was plagued by dynastic instability; even so, some progress was made towards a more effective mode of administration, and the mere fact that some kind of authority was exercised over the most far-flung European territory ever claimed by a single state (from Greenland to the western marches of today's Russia) was not insignificant. Last but not least, the late medieval period saw a massive growth of German influence, largely due to the activities of the Hanseatic League, and as can be seen in retrospect, this created preconditions for the particularly rapid and successful spread of a new religious culture coming from Germany.

Reformation brought about radical changes to the relationship between state and church, as well as to the broader complex of relations between state and society. This break was more conclusive in the Nordic world than anywhere else in the contested domains of Western Christendom, but a historical account of its dynamics must also take note of conditions resulting from earlier developments, even when there is clearly no immanent evolutionary logic at work. Even if reformation eventually came to be thoroughly implemented in the Nordic countries, its implementation was, as in Britain, a protracted process with many contingent features. In the late sixteenth century it also became entangled with immediately political and dynastic affairs. In the case of the Swedish Realm, it entailed the legitimate king of this protestant country and also of Catholic Poland-Lithuania, Sigismund/Zygmunt Vasa, being deposed in a short but bloody civil war in Sweden proper. During the ensuing century the main line of international contestation in the northeastern half of Europe became focused on these two parts of what for a brief period was a Swedish–Polish confederation ruled by a single king. The great Northern War of 1700–1721 led to a dramatic weakening of both of these contenders, eventually ushering in three partitions of Poland and the disappearance of this country as an independent state. The war was also linked to the rise of two new regional hegemonic powers that were to dominate North-Eastern Europe for the next quarter of a millennium, namely, Russia, claiming the status of an empire, and Prussia, being officially formed as a state at this time. The events of the years 1989–1991 mark the end of this nearly tercentennial period in the history of a large part of Europe beyond the Atlantic seaboard.

In the Nordic world, early modernity began with a geopolitical and religious mutation that paved the way for further social and political changes, with significant differences between countries. The period was also conducive to more pronounced regional affinities that came to be of lasting importance. In particular an earlier pattern of somewhat different cultural orientations between the southern and western parts of the Nordic world and the central and eastern ones was being reinforced through the emergence of two dominating, more or less absolutist, regimes, a western Scandinavian composite monarchy under the Danish king and a more unitary east-central state with Sweden–Finland as its core, locked in rivalry and intermittent warfare, but also involved in power struggles in the larger European arena.[1]

As already highlighted, for three centuries these states were the main protagonists of Nordic history. Their record is crucial to the understanding of later developments, but also – as Bo Stråth stresses in his synoptic essay – provides a warning against reading too much continuity and logical progression into the regional trajectory. These regimes, with their strongly militaristic orientations, do not fit into narratives of old traditions maturing into democratic forms of political and social life. As elsewhere in Europe, the Nordic paths to modernity were shaped by absolutist backgrounds as well as by cultural, political and social forces developing in opposition to these; regional variations to this general pattern are still reflected in more recent turns of Nordic history.

Aspects of this complex process will be discussed in several papers. But there were also differences between the two states, their roads to absolutist rule and their ways of institutionalizing it. One of the most frequently noted contrasts has to do with the much stronger presence of burghers in the Danish and peasants in the Swedish version of the estate order, but in both cases these forces made royal-popular coalitions against the aristocracy possible. The Danish model of absolutism has rightly been singled out as the most uncompromisingly consistent one among European regimes of the same kind. The Swedish 'age of freedom', a return to estate rule with a severely curtailed monarchy between two phases of absolutism, was a notable deviation from the dominant European pattern. Nothing comparable happened in Denmark, but reform projects emerged from within the absolutist framework.

Finally, the exits from absolutism also differed in timing and texture of events. In the Swedish case, it was an improvised coup from within the very centre of the political elite that put an end to absolutism in 1809; it is all the more striking that the new rules of government were at once codified in a mature and, by international comparison, very long-lived constitution of 1809, which at the time of its replacement in 1974 was arguably the second oldest in the world (after the American constitution). In the Danish case there were two exits: the Norwegian secession in 1814, characterized by a high level of mobilization and quasi-revolutionary overtones, and then, in 1848, an unspectacular but irreversible self-cancellation of absolutism – one of the few liberal success stories of that year.

As will be seen below, the differences between the modern trajectories of individual Nordic countries – both the heartlands of the two absolutisms and the dependent regions that became separate states – go far beyond these early signs of divergence. It is nevertheless difficult to deny that commonalities of political culture, especially those involved in the construction of welfare states (and thus in the achievements most frequently presented as models for wider use), have been more pronounced than historical evidence might have given ground to expect. This observation raises questions about long-term effects and echoes of both socio-economic and cultural forces active in the early modern mutation. It is often argued, if sometimes with some exaggeration, that much, if not most, of the Nordic world, except the continental heartlands of Denmark, had comparatively speaking far fewer feudal traits than much of the rest of Europe, and that at least in large parts of the Nordic world there existed a degree of local self-governance by free-holding peasants with few direct analogies. As for cultural developments, there can be little doubt about the overriding importance of Lutheranism.

The Nordic world is not the only part of Europe where Lutheran influences have counted for something in modern history, but it seems to be the region where this version of the Reformation played the most decisive and durable role. Lutheran doctrines and practices helped to consolidate the early modern state, but their socio-cultural potential went far beyond these beginnings. There are for instance immediate links, not least via the growth of universities and their role in the training of a new and disciplined Lutheran clergy in the seventeenth century, and the enhancement of state capacities in this period. Later developments are discussed in several papers, and the relationship between Lutheran religious culture and social movements emerges as a particularly important issue. Lutheranism, which for a long time supplied the moral backbone of an absolutist or semi-absolutist state, also came to serve as a source of reading, critical thinking and movement in the course of the nineteenth century. There were, of course, differences between individual countries: the state Church was strongest in Sweden, whereas a Grundtvigian people's Church played a more significant role in Denmark and Norway.

If the concept of the composite state is defined as historians of early modern Europe have done, that is, not just in terms of ethnic, cultural or regional diversity, but with a more specific reference to different political traditions and constitutional or quasi-constitutional arrangements, it is clearly applicable to the Danish monarchy during its absolutist as well as its post-absolutist phases (this is discussed in contributions by Uffe Østergård and Niels Kayser Nielsen). It is less clear how far it can be taken on the Swedish side of the early modern divide. The territory lost to Russia in 1809, which now had become the main part of the Grand Duchy of Finland,[2] had been an integral and long-standing part of the Swedish kingdom. Indeed, the grand old man of Swedish twentieth-century historiography, Erik Lönnroth, has described these events as the 'First Partitioning of Sweden'. In fact both Finnish and Swedish historians use analogous terms today when the events of 1809 are being commemorated. In late eighteenth- and early nineteenth-century Sweden, the fate of Poland and its three divisions were a recurring theme in public discourse. It was also invoked by the Swedish king, Gustavus III, as justification for his coup d'état of 1772, putting an end to the remarkable period of parliamentary rule, but also extensive foreign involvement in this process, and for his further strengthening of power in 1789.

The expanded realm of the seventeenth and early eighteenth centuries – Sweden's 'great power period' – was in many ways an entity with some composite features but also with uniquely developed integrative forces in institutional terms. Step by step – and in reaction to the anticipation and eventual reality of large-scale and protracted war – this state engaged in efforts to overcome the limitations of its resource base by way of finding means of more efficient organization and indeed mobilization. In its later stages, it came to take on features of statehood and warfare that were not to be seen in Europe until some two centuries later and which still do not easily fit into prevalent analytical frameworks. By the same token, the conventional label 'empire' seems doubtful. In the early modern European context, the latter concept is, in any case, an essentially contested one: even its applicability to the Habsburg monarchy has recently been questioned.

There is one more Nordic example of a composite state that should be of particular interest to comparative historians: the Swedish–Norwegian union that lasted from 1814 to 1905. In this case, the two constituent countries were, through a mixture of conquest and negotiation, brought together under a monarchic government; this happened after constitutional transformations on both sides, but they differed in regard to the social context as well as to the levels of innovation (the Norwegian one was more radical). As Bo Stråth's recent and comprehensive history of the union (Stråth 2005) shows, the development, crisis and disintegration of this composite state can only be understood in light of the complex, unequal and in part divergent modernizing processes that affected the two national societies as well as the common political framework.

Although the monarchy was obviously more Swedish than Norwegian, it also represented a third force in relation to the two countries which it strove to keep together. The whole process unfolded within a constitutional order and in connection with an increasingly articulate public sphere; this makes it a very instructive experience of a kind relevant to broader comparative issues. Most of all it is perhaps instructive in terms of the peaceful nature of its dissolution in 1905 at a time when much of the rest of Europe, from the sequence of horrendously bloody contestations over land in the Balkans to the imaginaries of future imperial and oceanic contestations between Germany and the Anglo-Saxon powers in the West, seemed inexorably to be moving towards the catastrophe which occurred only nine years later. The felicitous course of events in the Nordic case, contrary to that of European history at large, was undoubtedly related to a sense of pragmatism among leading politicians but also to one of the curious antinomies of the Nordic world. Thus on the one hand, there was, and is, a sense of commonality and relatedness that warded off the worst in terms of pronouncements of the evil nature of the adversary – 'the other' was simply a bit too much like oneself for that to be possible. On the other hand the many centuries of separate institutional development led, on the Swedish side, to a somewhat more dispassionate view of what was at stake in the event of a dissolution of the personal union than might otherwise have been the case.

Modernity and its Variations

Before moving closer to concrete themes in Nordic history, let us briefly return to the issue of modernity and its variations. Although both editors have been deeply involved in the international discussion on the understanding of modernity, extensive comments on the theory of modernity would be out of place in this book. However, a brief indication of alternative perspectives may help to clarify the background of individual arguments that appear in the volume. Basically, there seem to be three main answers to the question of modernity's defining characteristics.

An influential but far from homogeneous school of thought has explained modernity in terms of a rationalizing dynamic, expanding across the whole spectrum of social life and moving beyond every particular embodying structure. This view was already adumbrated by the modernization theorists who were – as they saw it – dealing with the sum total of changes brought about by the sustained growth of applicable knowledge. Later approaches have been more inclined to stress differences between regimes or cultural models of knowledge; as will be seen, such distinctions have a significant bearing on the history of reformist policies in the Nordic region.

Another interpretation of the link between rationality and modernity focuses on a supposedly epoch-making reflexive turn. A well-known example is Anthony Giddens's conception of reflexivity as the essence of modernity. But the Habermasian model of an increasingly articulate distinction between instrumental, expressive and communicative types of rationality (not *ipso facto* translating into balanced development) should also be included in this category; echoes of Habermasian themes and ideas will be noticeable in several contributions to the book.

If the first kind of theory goes in search of a highly abstract common denominator, the second attributes historical or structural primacy to more specific factors. A strong tendency to equate modernization with industrialization and its social consequences was for some time characteristic of mainstream sociological discourse, and is still of some importance. In relation to the Nordic region, this point of view has always seemed less plausible than in many other places. Not that industrialization was a minor aspect of the overall modernizing process. However this occurred within a broader societal context that shaped the contours of long-term outcomes. In this regard, there were major differences between individual countries.

More recent scholarship has placed a stronger emphasis on the modern state, with its bureaucratic organization and its mobilization of cognitive resources. The Foucaultian theme of 'governmentality' is an offshoot of this approach, and like the interpretations highlighting statehood in a more conventional sense, it has proved suggestive and fruitful relative to the Nordic record. Finally, growing interest in nations and nationalism during the last decades has in some cases resulted in constructions that put this long-neglected problematic at the very centre of modernizing transformations. Ernest Gellner's work is the most representative example. There is no doubt about the importance of nationalism for Nordic paths to modernity. But there are also – as argued by several authors – good reasons to stress the complex nature of processes of nation formation. The arguments of these authors suggest that these processes of nation formation were, interestingly but perhaps not surprisingly, much less derivative and less functionally determined than Gellner's analyses of nationalism suggest.

A third perspective projects the pluralism signalled by 'multiple modernities' into the very idea of modernity, a concept articulated by S.N. Eisenstadt and drawing on projects in which both editors have been involved. The common denominator now appears as a cluster of multiple factors or forces, capable of combining in different ways and thus giving rise to divergent patterns of modernity. An obvious way to articulate this view is to distinguish between economic, political and cultural components. The economic sphere can then be seen as the field of capitalist development through industrialization, together with the socio-political correctives and counterweights that affected its historical forms, and the critical responses that can translate into visions of non-capitalist alternatives. In the political sphere, the process of modern state formation and the new forms of power which it generates intertwine with the long-term dynamics of democratic transformations. In the cultural sphere, this line of analysis can begin with the interconnected but at the same time polarizing currents of enlightenment and romanticism, both defined in a broad sense: the former as institutionalized cognitive progress, especially in its scientific form, the latter as a quest for meaning responding to the challenges inherent in that progress. In all the different spheres it is also possible to discern antinomies and inherent tensions that should be analytically spelt out rather than glossed over within all-embracing processes of modernization.

S.N. Eisenstadt himself has consistently highlighted that complex interplay between institutional and cultural programmes of modernity, and also the degree to which such programmes, all of them with their own tensions and antinomies, are still formulated against the background of the cosmological heritage of the different great world civilizations. This, of course, to some extent resounds in our own interest in the perennial debate in ancient and medieval Scandinavian studies on the interpretation of Norse civilization and its traces across time, and its role for later institutional and cultural paths of development.

In the present context, however, the idea of a Nordic model is not interpreted against the background of the most long-term trajectories. Rather it is seen to be based on a distinctive way of balancing the demands of capitalism and democracy, of economic, political and cultural tendencies in a broad comparative perspective. Such balancing, however, takes place within a nexus of diverse cultural programmes that bring out a variety of differently articulated relationships between enlightenment and romanticism, between rationality and critique, between horizons of expectation and sites of the familiar and local. In fact, such cultural programmes of modernity seem to have contained greater antinomies than those in most other countries. In this respect the Nordic countries do not only exemplify a successful search for a middle way. In some respects, different cultural and institutional programmes of modernity may have been more successfully, if contingently, balanced, and more thoroughly, if not completely, implemented in the Nordic countries than in virtually any other countries in Western Europe or North America. The Nordic countries have, in different ways and to different degrees, been both more nostalgically backward-looking and more decisively forward-looking than other European countries. In fact, at crucial points in time, not least as exhibited by the great exhibitions in Stockholm in 1897 and in 1930, these two tendencies have coexisted locally so as to mutually enhance and reinforce each other.

The following essays contain references, allusions and implicit connections to all the metatheoretical images of modernity mentioned above. But ways of ranking or synthesizing them are not on the primary agenda of this book. At the present stage of the debate, it seems, more useful to allow for pluralism also on a basic conceptual level. Even so, it is clear that comparative sociological and historical analyses have enriched our general understanding of modernity as an epoch and as a socio-cultural condition. That result can certainly be expected from more sustained reflection on the Nordic experience and its distinctive features.

Examples and Interpretations

At this point, coming to specific questions about more recent phases, it seems best to turn to summaries of the arguments developed in individual contributions.

Bo Stråth's synoptic essay surveys the complex process of economic, social and political modernization in the Nordic region. The trajectory that led from militarized absolutist regimes to the twentieth-century welfare states went through several successive phases; detailed historical analyses do not support the idea of predetermined progress, and alternative lines of development seem to have been possible at various critical junctures. The results were nevertheless coherent and uniform enough to constitute the core of a regional profile. The social forces involved in the process are comparable to those known from the history of other Western European countries, but their interplay took a specific turn, and the coalitions that decided the outcome were unique to the region. As Stråth notes, the political orientation of the peasantry differed from the typical cases of continental Europe, and this was reflected in epoch-making alliances with labour movements led by Social Democrats. It was also important that the reformist coalitions included sections of the liberal bourgeoisie. The notion of a clear-cut and central conflict between labour and capital is, generally speaking, not an adequate key to nineteenth- and twentieth-century history, but in the Nordic context it would be particularly misleading. As for ideological aspects, it is noteworthy that themes often associated with conservative currents in European history were adapted to more left-leaning strategies in the Nordic countries. The classic example is the appropriation of the idea of a 'national home' (*folkhem*) by the Swedish Social Democrats. Stråth's essay finishes with sceptical reflections on the prospects of the Nordic model. The inroads of neo-liberal ideology and rhetoric since the 1980s, the strong influence of an international environment dominated by financial capitalism, and the divergent responses of the Nordic countries to European integration are good reasons to conclude that the region faces an uncertain future.

Uffe Østergård discusses the Danish path to modernity, with particular emphasis on changing relations between statehood and nationality. Danish nationalism stands out as one of the cases that do not fit easily into the dichotomy of Eastern/ethnic and Western/civic models: it obviously combines features of both types. The explanation is to be found in the history of the Danish kingdom and its position on the receiving end of European geopolitics. The lost war against Prussia in 1864, which brought the victor closer to the goal of a unified Germany, also changed the character of the Danish composite state. For its self-understanding and its European profile, its remaining North Atlantic dependencies mattered less than the Schleswig-Holstein bridgehead into Central Europe. A national framework of modernization prevailed, and it was characterized by a remarkably strong economic, political and cultural position of the peasant farmers. The dominant ideology that grew out of this constellation and set the course for further development was marked by a combination of libertarian and solidaristic elements, and a strong emphasis on consensus among the people, in Danish *folk*. A distinctive kind of populism – *folkelighed* – came to be shared by all political parties. The long-term outcome was an industrialized agrarian capitalism with a nationally homogeneous face.

Niels Kayser Nielsen proposes a somewhat different perspective on the same process. His main emphasis is on the centralizing drive that shaped the course of modern Danish state-building, and on its interaction with social and civic movements. Both factors were crucial, and the peculiar turn taken by their interplay had much to do with an evolving religious culture. The Grundtvigian movement is one of the decisive forces of modern Danish history. Together with a high level of popular education (which it helped to further), it was instrumental in fusing the notions of *demos* and *ethnos*, and thus in reconciling democracy and nationalism. Against this background, the later rise of Social Democracy can be seen as a sustained and successful effort to bring a third notion, oikos, into the synthesis. The care of family and household was integral to the model of the welfare state; at the same time, the working class became an important and equal part of the hegemonic social coalition. All these trends converged in the making of one of the most centralized and culturally homogeneous societies of Europe. It is of course true that the underlying reality is rather more complicated than the codified self-image, but any critique along those lines must recognize the latter as a reality in its own right.

Björn Wittrock traces the making of Sweden back to medieval origins and stresses two cultural fault lines that mark Nordic history, thus setting the region apart from its neighbours to the east and south: the differences between Western and Eastern Christendom, and between feudal and non-feudal societies. The Swedish state was constituted as a Christian kingdom somewhat later than the Danish and Norwegian ones, and re-established after a brief and unruly union with them at the beginning of the period. This state was neither a feudal nor a composite one. It ruled over one of the largest but also least populated countries in Europe, and its relative lack of resources gave rise to unusual but effective techniques of statecraft, demonstrated most strikingly in two periods when Sweden was prominent on the European scene: first as a great power (1620–1720), when it developed characteristics that did not appear elsewhere in Europe until the twentieth century, and then during the rapid modernization that began around 1870. This latter period and its key junctures are analysed in some detail, with particular emphasis on the social democratic breakthroughs that in turn led to the antinomies of present-day Sweden.

Peter Hallberg's paper deals with an episode that represents – in comparison with the other Nordic countries – a distinctive aspect of Swedish history. The 'Age of Freedom' during the middle decades of the eighteenth century is perhaps more memorable because of its role in the formation of a Swedish public sphere than because of short-lived constitutional arrangements. This period gave a new meaning to cultural contacts between Scandinavia and continental Europe, and its legacy was important for later developments. The efforts to build a public sphere drew on an intensive appropriation of Enlightenment discourses and the accompanying ideas of civil society. Hallberg discusses this cultural flowering with particular reference to history writing and its expected contribution to the elaboration of modern social norms. Historical reflection was understood as a social practice that creates civic bonds between individuals and groups, bonds that are crucial for the creation and prosperity of civil society and, more broadly speaking, the institution of modernity. The paper concludes with an analysis of texts that articulated the notion of history as a teacher of life and a source of exemplary behaviour, especially through two different media: statues and biographies.

Rune Slagstad's analysis of Norwegian reformism, in its successive nineteenth- and twentieth-century incarnations, focuses on the question of changing knowledge regimes. In the Norwegian case, shifting political frameworks have to a remarkable extent been accompanied by shifting knowledge discourses. More specifically, and regardless of whether the ideological principles invoked have been liberal or socialist, the reformist projects have been grounded in different versions of social science. The nineteenth-century state, dominated by civil servants, relied on a legal knowledge regime. Towards the end of the century, this was replaced by a democratic-pedagogical knowledge regime. When the Labour Party gained control over the political centre in 1945 (after a less conclusive episode during the 1930s), it did so in coalition with the new economists. Following the setbacks suffered by the Labour Party in the 1980s (seen by some as a demise of the Social Democratic state), some features of a new knowledge regime have become visible. A critique of instrumentalism, with moral and political implications, has been developed, but its relationship to an emerging depoliticized market regime of economic knowledge is still a matter of dispute.

Gunnar Skirbekk links his analysis of the Norwegian case directly to the debate on multiple modernities. Divergent interpretations of modernity are amply attested by the disagreements that began to develop within classical modernization theory and became more radical during the closing decades of the twentieth century; the question of different modernizing processes in various historical settings is less straightforward, but comparative studies have now built up a strong case for a pluralistic approach; the most crucial issue is whether, or to what extent, we can distinguish multiple versions of basic cultural orientations, including in particular the core ideas of the Enlightenment. With this problematic in mind, Skirbekk focuses on nineteenth-century Norwegian developments. The story begins with a bid for independence and an attempt to establish a new political regime, remarkably advanced in the European context of the time; the results were scaled down but far from obliterated by the enforced union with Sweden. Within the Norwegian part of the unified state, the decisive factor was the interplay between Lutheran state officials on the one hand, and popular movements and their elites on the other. Skirbekk concludes that the changing constellation of political agents, with their distinctive versions of Enlightenment ideas, was at the centre of a modernizing process that sets Norway apart from more familiar models based on Anglo-American, French or German experiences.

Finland differs from the Scandinavian countries in many significant ways, and there is wide scope for disagreement on its Nordic identity. Risto Alapuro discusses this question in light of nineteenth- and twentieth-century historical experience. He first notes that compared to the core Nordic countries, the Finnish trajectory has obviously been massively more affected by external factors. The pan-European upheaval that followed the French Revolution separated Finland from Sweden and linked its destiny to a very different kind of great power. More dramatically, the revolution that destroyed the czarist regime had an instant and decisive impact on Finnish history, and the consequences unfolded in two steps. The first was a rapid completion of the democratizing process that had already been more advanced in Finland than in other parts of the empire before the war. But the crisis in Russia continued to affect the course of events in Finland, and the result was a polarization that culminated in civil war. This event remains the most potent reminder of Finland's unique path to modernity, and still confronts historians with unsettled questions. However, its aftermath, and more specifically the road to national reconciliation, testifies to enduring institutional and cultural similarities with the other Nordic countries. Alapuro concludes that in the long run, this deeply rooted affinity has prevailed over the external forces that seemed more conducive to divergence. The decline and dissolution of the Finnish Communist movement, whose strength had long been one of the conspicuously non-Scandinavian features, can be seen as a final twist to this re-converging process.

Henrik Stenius focuses on the experience of the Finnish Grand Duchy (1809–1917) as a politically privileged part of the Russian Empire, and on the significance of this period for the maturing of a political culture based on foundations laid during the preceding early modern phase. As he argues, the 'Finnish way of being Nordic' goes back to the comprehensive cultural repatterning brought about by the Lutheran Reformation. His interpretation agrees with Alapuro's in stressing the pervasiveness and resilience of a common regional pattern, but he places a stronger emphasis on a Finnish paradox: it was precisely the separation from the rest of the region, with safeguards of partial statehood and guarantees against complete absorption into the Russian Empire, that enabled Finland to develop an almost paradigmatic version of the more general model. A statist culture with universalistic solutions to societal problems achieved an unusually solid hegemony. But against this background, the civil war looms very large indeed. How did a society characterized by a strong emphasis on civic loyalty and obedience to the law, together with a remarkable capacity to mobilize support for social and cultural projects, lapse into the vicious circle of violence? On the social and political level, the legacy of the civil war may have been successfully overcome, but the intellectual challenge has not been laid to rest.

The other country frequently seen as an atypical case in the Nordic region is Iceland. Jóhann Páll Árnason reflects on this case and begins with the observation that two very different perspectives on Iceland have emerged in comparative studies. On the one hand, Iceland, and more precisely its medieval experience, has been a key theme for those who defend the idea of a distinctive Nordic civilization. On the other hand, it has been suggested – most forcefully by Richard Tomasson, who drew on the work of Louis Hartz – that Iceland's affinities with the Nordic region are less important than its similarities to other 'new societies' created by European settlers overseas. Both approaches are problematic (although the short and in the end self-destructive neo-liberal episode raises new questions about settler society characteristics that might account for Iceland's receptivity to this ideology), but their common kernel of truth has to do with the importance of the medieval heritage. It is crucial to Icelandic national identity, but not a sufficient explanation of later nation-forming processes. The nationalist turn in the early nineteenth century began as a response to changes at the centre of the Danish composite monarchy, but led to demands for separate statehood. Convergence on this point did not prevent the emergence of different forms of nationalism, which continued to influence Icelandic politics after final separation from Denmark.

Guðmundur Hálfdanarson is more sceptical about medieval inputs into the process of nation formation and takes issue with nationalistic accounts of Icelandic modernization. There has been a pervasive tendency, dominant in political discourse and strongly represented in traditional historiography, to depict the radical transformation of Icelandic society in the late nineteenth and early twentieth centuries as being a direct result of the regained self-determination and independence of the Icelandic nation. There are several fundamental problems with this view. Icelandic modernization has, to a very high degree, been an externally induced process; it has entailed a particularly marked break with socio-cultural patterns that had, until the late nineteenth century, been remarkably resistant to change; and the result has been a rapid assimilation to trends exemplified by capitalist and democratic modernity in Western Europe. To the extent that nationalist narratives presuppose continuity, or at least indigenous directions of change, they are manifestly inadequate. But if nationalism is not a good guide to explanations, it is a large and lasting part of the story to be explained. As the twentieth-century record shows, nationalist ideology, rhetoric and imagery have proved adaptable to a wide range of strategies from different parts of the political spectrum. The rise and fall of neo-liberalism added another chapter to this story.

Note on Terminology

Since the authors of this book do not always use the same labels to describe the geographical field of inquiry, some clarifying remarks may be useful.

The term *Norden*, commonly used in Danish, Norwegian and Swedish to refer to the five countries mentioned at the beginning of the introduction, is now often adopted by anglophone writers on the subject and may be regarded as synonymous with the 'Nordic region' or the 'Nordic area' (the areas dealt with in area studies are more or less identical with historical regions). Sometimes the term 'Nordic countries' has also been used in public discourse in anglophone countries to refer to *Norden*, a translation that is reasonable in terms of denotation but less than ideal in terms of connotation. 'The North' has vaguer connotations and is best avoided in this context. As noted above, the boundaries of the region are blurred, but no more so than in comparable cases, and the covering label will sometimes be stretched to include borderline territories.

By contrast, 'Scandinavia' tends to refer to a more narrowly circumscribed heartland, but it is not always demarcated in exactly the same way. The most common usage refers to Denmark, Norway and Sweden only.

Finland has sometimes, more often so in the past than the present, been described as not being part of Scandinavia with reference to the fact that the majority language of the country does not belong to the family of Scandinavian languages. Nowadays, however, Finland is often labelled a 'Scandinavian' country although this tends to occur less in terms of the comprehensive term 'Scandinavia' and more often in the linguistic guise of the 'Scandinavian countries', a term then being used as a synonym for the 'Nordic countries', and with reference to the cultural, political, institutional and religious heritage that Finland shares with its Western neighbours, in particular with Sweden.

In Iceland, by contrast, the term 'Scandinavia' often denotes only the Scandinavian peninsula, that is, Norway and Sweden. If the three core countries are grouped together, Finland and Iceland stand out as more specific cases, but not in a way that would suggest a common category.

There is one other perennial terminological problem that should be mentioned at the outset. That is the problem of how to deal in an analytically and historically satisfactory way with the relationship between shifting geographical boundaries and linguistic denotations. One possible strategy is to utilize only linguistic denotations that were dominant or at least prevalent in the period at hand by the rulers or inhabitants of a particular region or country. In many ways this is an attractive and justifiable strategy. It has, however, two obvious problems.

Firstly, there are ruptures in terminological usage that may have to be highlighted in order to make clear to readers that different terms are actually referring to the same geographical region or site although in a new political or linguistic context. Can it be safely assumed that most readers immediately grasp that the terms Christiania and Oslo refer to the same urban agglomeration or that the same is true of Viborg, Viipuri and Vyborg? Different authors in the volume have addressed this problem in different ways, but they all try to highlight shifts in usage as well as the non-contemporaneous nature of political and linguistic transitions. Obviously one simple way to do so is to indicate parallel or competing linguistic denotations of a region, for example the Danish versus the German names for the borderline provinces of the two countries, namely, Slesvig/Sleswig and Holsten versus Schleswig and Holstein.

Secondly, there is a natural, perhaps an inevitable, tendency on the part of most readers to adopt the linguistic perspective of the present day and implicitly to read the denotations of present-day terms backwards into history. One obvious case in point is the area now covered by the two countries Sweden and Finland, an area that used to form a comprehensive political entity for more than six centuries. If the term Sweden–Finland is used to describe this area in historical perspective a terminology is being imposed that was alien at the time. Furthermore such seemingly neutral usage cannot avoid the fact that it enters a contested discursive landscape. In this case it might risk being identified as signalling the adoption of a particular, and somewhat old-fashioned and nationalistic, position in the context of Finnish historiography. However, if the area is described in an historical account as simply 'Sweden' many present-day readers might grossly misunderstand the text. In this particular case, the easiest solution might simply be to use the term

'Swedish Realm' to refer to the political entity for the period until 1809 and then use the term 'Sweden' for the remaining post-1809 'Rump-Sweden' or the Western part of the separated historical entity.

Similar problems abound, although this particular case may be the hardest one since it involves a rapid and deep rupture of an entity of very long duration. Again the most viable strategy in this and similar cases appears to be to signal by way of both terminology and narration the contingent and shifting nature of the boundaries of geography and language.

Notes

1. The choice of terms in referring to political entities in historical context poses inevitable problems (see the above note on terminology). It is not only a matter of transmitting a relevant idea of what geographical area a term may refer to but also of the nature of relationships within this area. We have tried to solve these problems not only by being as explicit as possible about geographical designations but also by indicating in terms familiar to early twenty-first century readers some rough outlines of the nature of a given political entity. In some cases and for the sake of abbreviation it is, however, convenient also to use short-hand descriptions even if they were not used in the given historical context itself. In this sense a term such as the Swedish Realm, with present-day Sweden and Finland at its core, is a label used at the time but also one that highlights the strong integrative nature of that entity, in contrast to other areas of the realm, in this case, in particular the Baltic and German provinces.
2. The Grand Duchy was constituted not only by areas lost in 1809 but also by some areas of Eastern Finland, most notably Carelia, which had been lost by Sweden already as a result of defeat in the failed war of revenge of 1741–1743.

References

Carelli, Peter (2001) *En kapitalistisk anda: Kuturella förändringar i 1100-talets Danmark.* Stockholm: Almqvist & Wicksell International.

Childs, Marquis W. (1936) *Sweden: The Middle Way.* New Haven: Yale University Press.

Hermanson, Lars (2000) *Släkt, vänner och makt: En studie av elitens politiska kultur i 1100-talets Danmark.* Göteborg: Göteborgs Universitet.

Johansson, Karl G. (2007) *Den norröna renässansen. Reykholt, Norden og Europa 1150–1300.* Reykholt: Snorrastofa.

Lindström, Ulf (1985) *Fascism in Scandinavia, 1920–1940.* Stockholm: Almqvist & Wiksell International.

Moore, R.I. (2000) *The First European Revolution.* Oxford: Blackwell.

Torstendahl, Rolf (1991) *Bureaucratization in Northwestern Europe, 1880–1985: Domination and Governance.* London: Routledge.

CHAPTER 1
Nordic Modernity: Origins, Trajectories, Perspectives

Bo Stråth

The Military and Absolutist Point of Departure

Nordic modernity is often understood in terms of enlightened and progressive welfare politics and social equality. There is a more or less implicit association with images of a Social Democratic model. The aim of this article is twofold: to discuss the historical preconditions and construction of that model of progressive politics, and to discuss its relevance today and its future prospects.

Concerning the first aim, there is nothing historically predetermined about a progressive development path. Nordic modernity should not be understood as teleology or as given by a natural state of egalitarian peasant communities. On the contrary, until the Napoleonic turmoil at the beginning of the nineteenth century, Denmark-Norway, to which Iceland belonged, and Sweden-Finland had a long history of military involvement in the European wars. Sweden was ruled by royal absolutism until 1809, Denmark until 1848. The series of military defeats in the eighteenth century changed the preconditions of the warlike disposition, but in Sweden the nobility continued to play an important political, cultural and economic role. The king based his power on a popular royalism built up not least in conflict with the nobility. King, gentry and people were involved in a triangular power struggle (*kungamakt, herremakt, folkmakt, monarchical power, aristocratic power, people's power*) from the seventeenth through to the nineteenth century. In Finland many of these structures remained after 1809 when it was transferred to a grand duchy under the Russian tsar, but they were more complex due to the language issue and the cultural struggle between the *svekomans* and the Fennomans. In Denmark-Norway the king based his absolutist regime from 1660 on a strong popular support under elimination of the political role of the nobility. Iceland is the exceptional case in this warlike and absolutist history. As a sparsely populated (less than sixty thousand inhabitants around 1850) and remote island in the Atlantic, it never developed any military or feudal structures, and distance always ensured a certain degree of autonomy within the absolutist (until 1848/1849) Danish state.

Popular royalism was in particular based on the mobilization of politically strong freeholder peasants and urban middle classes. Here it must be noted that the North, until the end of the nineteenth century, was rural, and the degree of urbanization was less than in continental Europe. Political mobilization in the nineteenth century took a nationalistic turn. Nationalistic rhetoric frequently invoked a heroic military past. In Denmark nationalism was used against the growing power of Prussia during the decades after 1848. In Sweden the perceived threat was Russia, and nationalistic activism was linked to hopes of reconquering Finland. A third variation of the nationalistic theme was Scandinavianism, which tried to unify the threats of the Danes in the South and the Swedes in the East into one *Denkfigur* where a common Nordic past since the Viking Age was invoked. Scandinavianism as a dynastic and nationalistic programme failed in the end because few Danes were prepared to die for Sweden in the East, and the Swedes were not prepared to die for Denmark in the South. Norway developed a specific left-oriented nationalism in the framework of the union with Sweden. It claimed more autonomy and equality for Norway in the union and turned against the dangerous military activism associated with Swedish claims of national superiority and hopes for the reconquest of Finland. Again, Iceland is an exception. Nationalism there emerged also in the 1840s, but it only slowly developed into a political programme for independence, and a target for hostility was less identifiable. However, Finland also deviated from the Scandinavian pattern of centrifugal nationalisms and the vain attempts to overcome the lack of cohesion through Scandinavianism as an alternative nationalist ideology. After 1809, Finland searched for a position as a new nation that acknowledged a certain Swedish heritage even while adapting to the Russian presence. This search provided the framework for a language struggle that intensified throughout the nineteenth century, although it always remained subordinated to the shared struggle for national autonomy.

Authoritarian versus Democratic Options

There were also factors underpinning a more progressive and egalitarian development in the North, in particular the strength of the peasant freeholders and of the (numerically small) urban middle classes. The argument in this article is that these forces in the end broke through, but not until the 1930s in response to the Great Depression. Everywhere in *Norden*, red-green Social Democratic–Farmers' Party reform coalitions emerged in attempts to cope with the economic crisis. Extreme political alternatives of both the right and left were marginalized. The Social Democrats were, with the exception of Iceland, the larger party in the coalitions. In that sense there is a Scandinavian *Sonderweg* but, again, there was nothing teleological in that breakthrough. In Iceland, a predominantly peasant society, these forces had, in a sense, always been stronger.

In the introduction to the revised (1981) edition of *The Crisis of German Ideologies*, George Mosse noted that while his book appeared to have left the impression among some readers that *völkisch* thought must inevitably lead to Nazism, this was not his intention. Not only were 'moderate', mainstream conservatives in pre-1933 Germany deeply infected with *völkisch* thoughts, but there also existed the non-authoritarian *völkische* socialism of Gustav Landauer which drew on the ideal of the Volk as a democratic community of equals (Mosse 1981). Eugene Lunn (1973) has suggested that Landauer's *völkische* socialism could provide an antidote to the tendency among historians to teleologically link *völkische* romanticism with the triumph of Hitler's version of *völkische* ideology. (For a discussion of the concept of *völkisch* in a comparative European perspective, see Hettling 2003.) The argument in this article is that the North fits well into this alternative scenario that Mosse drafted.

Mosse contended that socialists of all countries made efforts to combine *völkisch* and socialist thought, and speculated that if such a blend had been successful, National Socialism might not have triumphed so easily. Lars Trägårdh has taken up and developed this idea in a comparison of *völkische* ideologies in two 'Germanic' countries, Sweden and Germany, taking 1933 as the point of departure for the analysis. The same year as Germans voted their way to *völkische* Nazi dictatorship, a new coalition government headed by the Social Democrats came to power in Sweden. Founded by men inspired by Lassalle, Marx, Kautsky and other luminaries of the German socialist movement, the Swedish party was in many ways modelled on the German SPD. However, by the end of the 1920s the Swedish Social Democrats began to integrate *völkische* and socialist themes. They redefined their party from a workers' class-based party to a people's party, bent upon the idea of a *folkhem*, a home for the people. Class alliances replaced the class struggle as the dominant strategy for achieving the socialist dream of the classless society (Trägårdh 1999). The Swedish Social Democrats appropriated the political priority of interpretation of the *folk* concept after a protracted discursive struggle with the conservatives who had, at the turn of the century, used the concept to develop a strategy that one of the protagonists (Rudolf Kjellén, who later became known for his geopolitical theories) labelled 'national socialism', an ideological instrument designed to ward off the threats of class-struggle socialism. Rudolf Kjellén was uncompromising in his opposition to class-struggle socialism as the basis for political discourse. From his conservative perspective he argued for national socialism, portraying the country as a whole in which all of the people should be involved in society. The country was supposed to be a home for the whole population. The integrative idea of the '*folkhemmet*', in which society was organized as a family, with the home as a metaphor, subordinated the class struggle to national welfare.

When Kjellén talked about the concept of *folkhemmet*, *folk* had a different connotation from *Volk* in Germany. *Volk* was a more holistic notion inspired by Herder's philosophy and Romanticism. *Folk* connoted rather the empirically derived view of a union of all social classes. Both varieties of the concept connected visions of future potential to past achievements, but *Volk* had more utopian and *folk* more empirical connotations (for the German case, see Jansen 1993).

The Swedish Social Democrats were attracted to the *folkhemmet* concept from an early stage, but wanted to give it another content. They rejected the conservative version as 'the fortified poor-house', a reference to the priority of military over social state expenditures in the conservative programme. They gradually found themselves involved in a discursive struggle about the definition of the *folk*. When, in the 1930s, the Social Democrats took over the *folkhemmet* metaphor and made it their symbol, they argued that the happiness of the lower classes, of which the working class was just one part, was based on their efforts to contribute to the *folkhemmet*. As expressions of traditional values, *folk* and *folkhem* were mobilized as linguistic instruments for modernization (Stråth 1996).

The Swedish case could be seen, in ideal typical terms, as representative of a broader Nordic pattern of development. The point is not only the outcome in the 1930s, but the long period of contention and social conflict about the shaping of the future before the breakthrough.

Freeholder Peasants, Education and Religion: Modernity as Individualism with Solidarity

The Enlightenment was not retarded in the Nordic peasant communities, as sometimes has been argued. However, there was a specific kind of enlightenment. The enlightenment tradition in the North contained a pragmatic, empirical and fact-finding dimension, which sometimes – in its modern and bureaucratic version – seems to come close to Max Weber's idea of permanent disenchantment, and which was underpinned by the social sciences and by beliefs in politics for social improvement. The term social engineering has been used to describe this ethos (Marklund 2008).

In Scandinavia the tension between freedom and equality in the political culture was contained better than elsewhere. The peasant figure created by the intellectuals and the clergy in *Norden*, with a view to reducing the tension between freedom and equality, was not merely a romantic fiction with no relation to the real world, but was rather an increasingly active participant in economic and political processes. In most other parts of Europe, the peasant had been effectively eliminated from the political processes and was invoked as a rhetorical, even utopian, figure. The inherent tension between the concepts of freedom and equality was better controlled in the North by means of the peasant myth. The Nordic peasant was too conservative to be radical but too radical to be conservative (Witoszek 1997; cf Aronsson 1993; Karlsson 2000). The concept of freedom was less practised in the sense of Isaiah Berlin's term 'negative freedom' than in terms of positive liberty connected to virtues of responsibility for co-citizens. Freedom contained a solidaristic dimension and individualistic ideals were interwoven with ideas of collective performance.

In Sweden the peasants had been represented by their own Estate in the Diet since the fifteenth century. In Denmark the last remnants of serfdom were not abandoned until 1788, but the mythical historical construction of a free peasantry with roots in the Viking Age began soon thereafter and proved successful.

Given this framework of peasant-oriented foundation myths, Nordic Romanticism was pragmatic and individual-oriented, in contrast to the more holistic community produced by the *Sturm und Drang* movement in the German-speaking territories. In the North the Protestant Romantic produced a specific version of the protestant ethic. The Nordic people's, rather than populist movements, which emerged in the nineteenth century as protest movements criticizing the old society, expressed specific educational ideals. The message they mediated expressed an individual-oriented protestant responsibility and ethics rather than holistic collectivism. This individualist orientation constitutes an important element of the Nordic culture (Trägårdh 1997). The influence of the Enlightenment in the North must be seen in the context of the social communication capacity developed through the people's movements. Education (*bildning/dannelse*) was a key instrument for self-realization and, in contrast to the German *Bildungsbürgertum* for example, was seen very much as a bottom-up process. Here we must draw attention to the development of a communicative skill of the peasantry, whose training ground was the parish meeting, and which gradually paved the way for a constructive dialogue between social democracy and a liberalism with a social rather than economic emphasis (see below). The commitment to people's self-education, *folkbildning/–dannelse* within the people's movements provided growing articulateness and ability of the peasant freeholders to negotiate their agenda. Self-education was a school of politics (Sørensen and Stråth 1997). (The argument is developed in the discussion of Grundtvig below.)

The emerging patterns of social organization merged hierarchy and centralized state authority with local community as the basis of government, alongside state church norm-setting of religious authority and pietist individualization of transcendental experiences. Over time the local farmer cooperatives ended in state corporatism, as Niels Kayser Nielsen demonstrates in this volume. Also Gunnar Skirbekk, in his contribution, emphasizes the inter-dynamics between Lutheran state officials and the people's movements (*folkbeve/æ/gelser/folkrörelser*), and the connection between monoreligious cultures and religious tolerance of difference.

Social democracy as a continuation/transformation of Lutheranism and parochial political culture, and of social liberalism, as well as reform conservatism, could be seen as a particularly Scandinavian expression of how to handle the inherent tensions contained in the freedom and equality ideals. The question of whether this applies to Finland, which had gone through a civil war and had been on the brink of a fascist coup in the 1930s, must, according to Risto Alapuro's convincing argument in this volume, be answered affirmatively. For Alapuro, the language struggles and the cultural conflict between the Swedish-speaking and the Finnish-speaking populations in the nineteenth century were less important than their shared national aspirations. Under the Grand Duchy of the Russian Empire, the Finnish-speaking free-holding peasantry and the Swedish-speaking economic and political elite combined to lay the foundations for a common political culture that paralleled the rest of *Norden*. This common culture embraced two competing approaches, the Fennomans emphasizing an ethnic nation and the elite emphasizing a liberal constitution. Together they contributed to the consolidation of the Grand Duchy as a separate political entity within the Russian Empire. The people's movements in several respects bridged the oppositions. At the end of the nineteenth century, Scandinavian-type administrative and political institutions, a national economy and a small armed force confirmed the entity's existence, adjusting to the flexible geopolitical situation in the

Baltic. The Finnish destiny at the moment of independence was determined outside the country, where its historical experiences and institutions were of limited value. The civil war was a consequence of a specific political conjuncture in the wake of the Russian Revolution and the collapse of the two Baltic empires. The full force of the tensions that had been developing between Russia and Germany since the early 1890s hit Finland at the moment of independence. The clash between white guards and red guards on Finnish ground was a continuation of the violent conflict between empire and communism. The civil war made it impossible to reconcile class and nation as in the rest of *Norden*. Finland after 1918 was a nation opposed to class, a configuration that endured until the end of the Cold War. It was particularly distinct in the 1930s with the Lappo movement. The experiences of two wars against the Soviet Union (1939–1944), a strong Communist Party and the shadow from the East over the autonomous republic dampened flagrant expressions of autonomy. However, the wars also promoted steps towards reconciliation between nation and class, and reconnection to the Scandinavian institutional and normative pattern which had marked Finland during the nineteenth century (Alapuro in this volume; cf. Alapuro 1988).

Alapuri's analysis of how Finland fits into a broader Nordic pattern of a long-term coming to terms with the tension between authoritarianism and democracy, between national homogeneity/collectivist approaches and individual freedom demonstrates how open the Scandinavian developments were and how close the authoritarian alternative was.[1] Seen as a part of that broader Nordic pattern, the case of Finland shows how close alternative developments were and how contingent the actual development really was in, for instance, Sweden (cf. the Ådalen example in end note 1).

Therefore, the Nordic developments should not be conceptualized in terms of path dependency, because dependency on the past for future developments always comes with a degree of indeterminacy and contingency, in the sense of not necessary yet not impossible, only visible in retrospect.[2]

The Nordic nineteenth century, as modernization combined with a permanent peasant revolt (the people's movements), may be seen as an alternative development both to the French, British and American standard of Enlightenment modernization, and to what Theodor Adorno and Max Horkheimer, with reference to German and Soviet developments, called the Dialectic of Enlightenment. The peasant was not only a historically derived construct. He was also a political actor and provided cohesive mortar in the processes of national integration. The core of the Nordic peasant myth is a figure which does not correspond to the more continental notion of the peasant, which connotes subordination in a feudal order. The Nordic peasant is instead between a yeoman and a freeholder in the English context, mutating into a farmer around 1900.

Nor did the peasant icon lead to peasant populism as in Central Europe. Social criticism in the wake of enlightenment was not transformed into the antithesis of enlightenment. The conservative integration of the class into the nation in Sweden around 1900, when the conservatives suggested national socialism as an alternative to class-struggle socialism, was a careful response to social protests under the metaphoric symbol of *folkhemmet*, the people's home, a response which in the long run transformed both the conservatives and the Social Democrats. In Norway there was more of a merger between people's peasant nationalism and class struggle.

The peasants were not only carriers of freedom and equality but also of education. They were the core of the ambitious enlightenment programme of Danish clergyman N.F.S. Grundtvig in the nineteenth century. It is difficult to exaggerate his influence not only in Denmark but all over Scandinavia. His programme must be seen in the framework of a Danish popular mobilization against a perceived threat of a militarily and culturally expansive Germany. Grundtvig's programme of education, moulding (*dannelse*), was both far-reaching and widespread. In the perspective of an imagined Christian community based on the Holy Communion and baptism, his scheme embraced the establishment of farmers' producers' cooperatives and a farmers' political party for political reforms. Against the artificial Latin-based scholarship at the universities, he put the 'real' *dannelse* as an emancipative instrument in the hands of the peasants. *Folkehøjskolen*, the people's high school, became a veritable movement which spread from Denmark to the other Nordic countries. They became formation and education centres, where the popular thirst for knowledge was satisfied. The peasants as carriers of education stand in marked contrast to stereotypes current elsewhere.

A comparison between Grundtvig and the father of the modern university Wilhelm von Humboldt is instructive. Both were influenced by English liberalism and utilitarian ideas. They embraced both enlightenment and romanticist ideas. They considered education (*dannelse/Bildung*) as an emancipative instrument. Education and freedom were closely interrelated in their perspective. However, with freedom they did not mean the same thing. While von Humboldt required that the state both guarantee the academic freedom and pay for it, Grundtvig argued that education had to be organized independently of the state and in conscious opposition to the mandarins of the universities. Humboldt's academic freedom paved the way for the emergence of the German *Bildungsbürgertum* under state control, a social formation which never emerged in *Norden* to the same extent as in Germany. The concept of *dannelse/bildning* connoted much more the people's (revivalist, temperance, labour), not populist, movements, which all had study circles and local libraries as organizational cornerstones. The role of the peasants and the people's movements as carriers of education gave the modernization of the North its specific shape. This is particularly valid for the way in which national romanticism developed in a much more common sense and Enlightenment-oriented direction than in Germany, for example. It is true that the civil servants and the bourgeois society were sceptical about the cultural and political maturity of the peasants, but this scepticism never resulted in the emergence of a bourgeois education alternative such as the German *Bildungsbürgertum* (Sørensen and Stråth 1997).

We can thus compare two opposite patterns of the integrative role of education, from above and from below respectively (Stråth 1988). These alternative integrative processes were not in a simple way 'caused' by the different approaches to the education issue, of course. The different solutions to the question of *dannelse/bildning/Bildung* reflect deeper cultural differences between the Scandinavian/Nordic and the German societies. Not least the role and the social self-esteem of the peasants are important in this connection.

Religion was nationalized in *Norden* in the sixteenth century when Lutheran state churches were established. Lutheran orthodoxy and state orientation provoked pietism and religious revivalism. Revivalism has often been interpreted as a popular reaction to enlightenment and modernization. It can also be seen as a movement which broke the unity of premodern agrarian society, created new social forms and stood for modernity (Thorkildsen 1997). Pietism and revivalism meant individualization and dehierarchization of religion with a long-term secularizing impact when religion moved from the public arena to the private room, and from confessional and religious unity guaranteed by the state to personal conviction. The world-view was religious but the emphasis on individual emotions and experiences represented modernity. The long-term impact of the criticism within and outside the Lutheran state churches meant the abandoning of religious hierarchies and the emergence of the doctrine of the priesthood of all believers. On the other side, the Lutheran Protestant doctrine of society promoted the maintenance of political hierarchies and social order.

The people's movements are difficult to imagine without their revivalist element. The people's movements were much more than the labour movements and the rising working class. The labour movements took form and content from this religious ambience and were lastingly influenced by them. This is similar to the case of Britain. The difference between the two lies in the fact that the protest in *Norden* was to a considerable extent canalized early on through independent labour parties, while in Britain the political affiliation of the protest with the conservative and liberal parties lasted much longer.

Mainstream liberalism in *Norden* from the 1880s onwards was a social liberalism. The early Nordic liberalism at the beginning of the nineteenth century had a more economic focus, with claims for freedom of trade and the separation of the rights of possession from birth privileges. However, this economic liberalism never appeared as a laissez-faire liberalism but was from the beginning state-oriented. The state was seen as an instrument of liberal politics aiming at modernization. There was a high degree of continuity from this classical state-oriented liberalism to the emergence of the Social Democrats and a successful form of capitalism a hundred years later.

The late nineteenth-century social reorientation of liberalism reflected the growing weight of the working class. Early twentieth-century developments in Sweden exemplified this trend. Many of the liberals among the employers abandoned the liberal leader Karl Staaff after his orientation of the party in a more social direction; they went over to the conservatives, who, in turn, under their new leader Arvid Lindman, were modernized from a rather anti-modernizing agricultural-based party to a progressive industry-promoting party. The transfer from the liberal to the conservative camp did not mean that the employers changed their mind, but rather that the party terrain changed. In Denmark the liberal *Venstre* split in 1905. The old party became a major spokesman for agrarian economic interests whereas *Radikale Venstre* developed in a social-liberal direction. In Norwegian liberalism the social dimension was obvious already from the start of *Venstre*. It began as a progressive 'little-people' (*småfolk*) party through a coalition of peasants and intellectual radicals against taxes and bureaucracy which gradually came to be identified with the Swedish supremacy in the union. *Venstre* became the rallying point against the union.

This Scandinavian social liberalism was full of contradictions between rural and urban interests and between puritanistic and dogmatic Christian moralism and atheistic value relativism. In Sweden the liberal party split in the early 1920s, and farmers' parties were established in Sweden and Norway during the period 1913–1920 in response to these tensions. However, the decisive point is that the social-liberal profile went beyond the contradictions to such an extent that the liberal parties were capable of coalition with the Social Democrats until around 1920 (in Denmark, until the Second World War). In Norway and Sweden after 1920 the farmers' parties gradually emerged as the more attractive coalition partners for the Social Democrats in search of a parliamentary majority. Red–green coalitions emerged as parliamentary majorities in the three Scandinavian countries in response to the Great Depression. The same happened in Finland, although under greater fascist and communist pressure, and in Iceland, except there the farmers' party was the dominant partner.

This social-liberal mainstream trend was progressive in a sense that differed from the Marxian one. From the latter perspective, liberalism was the ideology of the bourgeoisie confronting feudal society and state. In the North, liberalism merged with the state into an ideology of modernity, and, later on, petty bourgeoisie and the small farmers, guided by a socially oriented liberalism, merged with the workers against mighty economic interests. Interest conflicts and social divisions did not result in the kind of antagonism predicted by Marxist theory, nor the historical polarization that prevailed in other countries, such as Germany.

In Finland, after introduction of universal (male and female) suffrage in 1906 in the wake of the first Russian revolution in 1905, the Social Democrats emerged as the big party with eighty of the two hundred seats in Parliament. The liberals, closer to classical economic liberalism, drew support from the Swedish-speaking 'bourgeoisie'.[3] The Finnish wood-manufacturing industry was spread throughout the rural districts and the Social Democrats received 90 per cent of their votes in rural districts. The farmers' party was a coalition partner equivalent to social liberalism in Scandinavia. Civil war split the nation immediately after its independence in December 1917. A strong Communist party emerged and the farmers' party drifted towards the extreme right. In the 1930s, Finland came close to a Fascist coup, but the farmers saw the risks and again approached the Social Democrats. With the Fascist threat averted, the preconditions for a political development along social democratic-centre lines returned (Alapuro 1988).

In terms of the role of the peasant, Iceland was the most pronounced Nordic case since the society was more or less exclusively rural and there was no nobility (which is not to say that there was no social difference, of course). The typical pattern of self-organization and social protest movements was the same as in the rest of the North. Revivalism was strong and emphasized individual responsibility. The labour movement broke through during the 1910s and emphasized collective responsibility and solidarity. In that respect the strength of the cooperative movement must be mentioned. The cooperation movement assembled consumers as well as producers in small agricultural and fishing enterprises. The difference to the rest of the North concerns education, which occurred much more in the framework of the family than in the people's movements as elsewhere (Karlsson 2000).

During the first decades of the twentieth century, the three Scandinavian countries and Iceland developed a parliamentary order with a stable party system. This order was based on Social Democratic parties dominating conservative or right-wing parties, which had lost a considerable part of their nineteenth century power, as well as one or more rather small agrarian liberal-centre parties, and small and rather isolated Communist parties. Finland, with a stronger Communist party and – during the 1920s and 1930s – a more authoritarian farmers' movement, gave a polarizing twist to the same pattern.

Empirical Social Sciences and the Quest for the Perfect Society

Francis Sejersted, Göran B. Nilsson and Rune Slagstad have analysed the early merger between state planning and liberalism in Norway and Sweden in depth (Sejersted 1993, 2001a, b, c; Nilsson 2001; Slagstad 1998, 2000). During the second half of the nineteenth century, the merger contributed to the development of economic and communicative infrastructures; in the twentieth century it continued as social engineering. They have demonstrated that visions of modernity had a political centre and were based on an ability to find compromises between competing definitions of the common good. These compromises, in turn, were based on social contention and bargaining, not on any kind of general consensus given by nature or specific social structures.

The outcome of these processes was never predetermined. Francis Sejersted has emphasized the tension between law and politics, constitutionalism and democratization, *Rechtstaat* and *Sozialstaat*, positive law and natural law. In the Nordic countries law lost much of its universal connection in the nineteenth century and became positive law, a human contextual convention for specific political purposes. Peter Hallberg in this volume shows how Swedish historiography since the eighteenth century had social utility as its aim, outlining a close relationship between knowledge about the past and value production around concepts like civility, virtue and patriotism. He makes a crucial observation when he describes how the emerging language of civil society, in the first formulations, in the translations of Locke, were *borgerlig* or *verldslig* – opposed to the religious but not to the state. Locke talked not only about civil society but also about civil government, and it was this latter connection that won through. Progress was seen as the ascent from the lawless state of nature to the rule of law, governing the relations between individuals and larger collective aggregates. Society was law, and law was the state.

Society, in Swedish *samhälle*, from the verb *hålla samman* (to keep together), does not connote degradation like in Ferdinand Tönnies distinction between *Gemeinschaft* and *Gesellschaft*, but political pragmatism without utopian or ideological overtones. *Samhälle* is a key concept in the organization of politics. Until the 1980s *samhälle* was more or less synonymous with the state. (When, in the 1980s, the synonymous combination split up, under pressure from the neoliberal rhetoric, the anglicism *civilsamhälle* was introduced to express a view in which state and society were separated.) Before the 1980s, the Social Democrats spoke about *det starka samhället*, the strong society, when, in defence of the welfare state, they meant the strong state, for instance. At the same time *samhälle* connoted the local organization of politics such as *stationssamhället*, where the railway meant the connection to the wider world, or *lokalsamhället*. A connected concept, which more specifically addresses the local level of social organization is *samfällighet*, with an original meaning of 'join together' (from the verb *falla samman*, fall together). The concept is used for resources, as for instance water, shared by local landowners or authorities transcending borderlines between private and public ownership and reorganizing them in new practical arrangements. This Swedish conceptual landscape transcended the distinction made by Tönnies bewteen *Gemeinschaft* and *Gesellschaft* and joined them into one figure. Or, rather, *samhälle* contained both of the meanings of the German dichotomy (Stråth 2003).

In the same vein, Uffe Østergård in this volume refers to the Danish merger of patterns from East European integral nationalism typical of smaller, recently independent nation states, and the patriotic term citizenship in the older West European state nations. He refers in particular to the importance of the concept of *folk* in this merger (cf. the discussion of *folk/Volk* above).

Rune Slagstad, in his article in this volume, demonstrates how the priority of the political was connected to the social sciences, which, in turn, can be connected to the specific Nordic people's education paradigm. Democratic-pedagogical knowledge regimes emerged where the social sciences were mobilized in an empirical fact-finding mission with a utilitarian quest for social improvement (Wagner and Wittrock 1992). Slagstad demonstrates for Norway the early merger between social scientists and reform-oriented policy-makers based on a transformation of the role of the intellectual from distant and critical observer to participating policy designer. This model of social engineering by a scientifically informed elite had a more general breakthrough in Europe in the 1930s, a century after it broke through in Norway.

Björn Wittrock emphasizes three kinds of knowledge interest in modern Sweden: the socio-political aiming at politics for social and economic progress, the heroic-narrative, and the civilizational, the latter two underpinning a belief in being a selected people but at the end resulting in empirical pragmatism for autonomy-based progress rather than in overstretched utopian Romanticism, which was and is often the case when national foundation myths mediate a great past and a destiny beyond individual influence.

The belief in education and science was a belief in progress and in the future as makeable. The belief in theoretical and empirical knowledge triggered a great development optimism, which also transformed what was probably the poorest of the Nordic countries, Iceland, as Guðmundur Hálfdanarson demonstrates in his contribution in this volume. For the Norwegian case, in the same vein, see Slagstad in this volume.

The social-democratic political breakthrough in the 1930s meant the intensification of the model. Scientific language went hand in hand with government practices. Economics and sociology became the parade disciplines, which in the 1950s and 1960s were supplemented by political sciences. Ragnar Frisch and his disciple Erik Brofoss represented in Norway the academic and the political dimension of this model; Gunnar Myrdal in Sweden combined the two roles. The old utopian image of a final society without classes was replaced after the Second World War by a not less teleological but less utopian image of state guarantee of welfare and social justice.

Empirical utilitarianism and pragmatism could – up to a point – combine with puritanism and fundamentalism, most evidently in the revivalist movements, but not only there. Amidst the empiricism and the positivist ideals of the education movement there was a quest for social perfection. The belief emerged that collective welfare could be organized through social engineering. Public ordering of private life would perfect the *folkhemmet*. This quest for social engineering was most evident in Sweden and Norway (Hirdman 1989; Marklund 2008). However, everywhere in *Norden*, as well as elsewhere, the national idea of the nations as selected peoples, phrased in a biologistic race language, was a general dimension of the interpretative framework until the 1950s. There was in *Norden* a racial discourse connected to Protestant ideas of progress (Stokholm Banke 1999; Arvidsson, Berntsson and Decik 1994). The Swedish State Institute for Race Biology, founded in 1921 with Herman Lundborg as its founding Director, and the sterilization programme are cases in point.[4] The total separation between biological-race theories and Social Democratic welfare politics occurred after the Second World War in the wake of the insights that not only the German horror but also, later, the consequences of biological racism in the form of eugenics had given.[5]

The development towards the social-democratic political breakthrough in the 1930s with the intensification of the democratic knowledge regime can be seen in a more general framework of capitalist modernity. With the development of industrial capitalism from the 1830s emerged the corresponding social issue about the responsibility for the side-effects ('collateral damages') of capitalism, which became increasingly evident over time. There was a growing agreement that above and beyond the individual level someone had to take responsibility. However, before the 1930s it was difficult to discover social organs accepting this responsibility. The state, local government, employers' associations and the trade unions each tried to shift the responsibility to one another.

The great question in these bargaining processes, after areas of responsibility had been identified, was: who is responsible for old-age pensions, for guaranteeing incomes in cases of sickness or disability, for unemployment insurance, and so on? Such issues distinguished and confronted different social interest groups. The precise outcome of the complex struggles of the nineteenth century varied from country to country according to specific power relationships and historical heritages. However, in more general terms, the answer that emerged out of the turmoil of the 1930s massively assigned social responsibility to the state. In the wake of the collapse of labour markets, governments intervened in most countries on an unprecedented scale to quieten or exploit social unrest. State intervention took very different forms: in the name of national socialism in Germany; of the *front populaire* in France; of social democracy and red-green labour-farmer coalitions in *Norden*; and of the New Deal in the United States. It is important to see the Nordic modernity and the focus it got in the 1930s, not only in relation to its own specific historical conditions but also to the more general European developments. There was nothing predetermined in the Nordic response to the Great Depression, but the growing military threats in the South and the East, and the prospects of a clash between them on Nordic territory, promoted domestic consolidation and the search for social peace. The search involved the interpretation and activation of the historically given. In the process, the interpretation of the historically given was used to provide *ex post* legitimatization to political action.

In the 1950s and the 1960s the state's responsibility was legitimized and confirmed by economic theory. Keynes was a leading figure when ideas emerged that the economy ('the market') was governable through politics. This insight had grown not least by the experiences acquired during two world wars. Economic theory explained the connections between employment, investments and money value, and told that these connections were politically manageable. Political economy, mixed economy, *soziale Marktwirtschaft* and economic planning were among the key concepts as various thinkers talked about a long-term convergence between socialist and capitalist systems based on a belief in political management of the economy. In the North, the particular form of Social Democratic–social liberal political government that had been established in the 1930s continued, promoting domestic consolidation and social peace in the framework of the Cold War.

There is one shared element in the historically shaped preconditions of the five Nordic countries. Social protest and claims for increased democracy originated in a broader people's coalition in which the labour movement was, or rather became, the driving force, though not to the exclusion of others. Farmers also formed an integral part of this coalition. The conflict was not exclusively between labour and capital, the working class and 'the bourgeoisie', but had a more complex cultural-discursive embedding. The lines of division in the construction of community and the demarcation between 'us' and 'them' were detected within the so-called bourgeoisie and within the farmer class, between high and low bourgeoisie, large and small farmers or crofters, which increased the potential for the formation of coalitions with the labour movement. This cultural construction of social community resulted in a less polarized society with a higher capacity for communication than one that follows a Marxian scheme opposing capital and labour (Stråth 1988 and 1990). Finland deviated to a certain extent from this Nordic pattern of community construction from the Civil War of 1918 to the 1950s, due to its more exposed geopolitical location rather than to domestic factors.

The national question was crucial in Norway, Finland and Sweden, although it oriented action in very different directions in these three countries. In Denmark this question had been removed from the national agenda after the defeat by Prussia in 1864. In Norway the national question became the symbol of a people's mobilization against union with Sweden which involved farmers, large parts of the 'bourgeoisie', and the labour movement. In Finland the national question leads to a contrary policy when the conservative economic and political elite appropriated the question during and after the Civil War. There the question implied national polarization rather than unification until 1939. In Sweden the break-up of the union with Norway in 1905 promoted a Conservative reform strategy with the purpose of unifying the nation. This constituted a particular language, which attracted the Social Democrats per se, although they hoped to fill it with an alternative content. The discursive struggle between the conservatives and the Social Democratic–social liberal coalition about what content to give the *folk* concept worked until 1930 despite opposing alternatives in a unifying and nationally consolidating direction. It also demonstrated considerable continuity when the Social Democrats redefined themselves around 1930 from a class to a people's party, thus taking over the agenda from the reform conservatives. In Iceland the national question dealt with the independence from Denmark. The independence movement was pragmatic with a step by step approach from its emergence in the 1840s until it achieved its aim in 1918/1944 (Karlsson 2000).

Visions of modernity and of a better future are often connected to ideas of economic expansion, which, in turn, are connected to ideas of justice and to the question of legitimacy for economic concentration. The legitimacy of economic power in Norway was based on a low degree of economic concentration. The degree of economic concentration was much higher in Sweden, but through a skilfully developed image of thrift, diligence, industry and assiduity, and with the Wallenberg family as a model, the economic elite still managed to comply with the pietistic criteria for legitimacy, which emphasized individual freedom in combination with radical claims for equality. (For a development of this point, see several of the contributions in Sørensen and Stråth 1997. See also Sejersted 2001a, b , c and Stråth 2001.)

The framework of the corresponding Danish debate on economic concentration and justice was less Social Democratic and more 'bourgeois' than in Norway and Sweden. The people's movement tradition in Denmark was different, more heavily influenced by Grundtvig's ideas about farmer education and the farmers as the core of the people than by the puritan moralism of the Norwegian and Swedish people's movements. The moral rejection of economic concentration did not develop as it had in Norway. In addition, the mobilization pressure from below on conservative power centres did not develop as it had in Norway during its union with Sweden, or in Sweden itself. The value basis of Social Democratic power in Denmark was smaller, giving a different economic elite formation. Industry employers, in one sense, were made stronger by the more general 'bourgeois' framework and did not face the same challenge from a unified and centralized trade union movement as in Norway and Sweden. In another sense, they were also weaker because of the stronger concentration of capital in the commercial sector, and because of their role as spokesmen for the domestic market rather than for export interests (although the aliment and beverage industry modified this domestic orientation). Capital concentration did not predominately occur in the manufacturing industry. The commercial sector continued to play a leading role, to which the banks significantly contributed. As opposed to Norway, but similar to Sweden and Finland, a system of large commercial banks emerged as an indication of social acceptance of economic concentration.[6]

The normative basis of the legitimatization of economic power varied in all three of the Scandinavian countries. Finland, in this respect, can be placed between Denmark and Sweden but is, in fact, probably closer to Sweden. These criteria, however, were not sufficient to supply a more general legitimacy to capital ownership. Legitimacy was never stable over longer periods of time but was repeatedly challenged. The first massive challenge in all of the four countries was the general radicalization of the political language around 1920. The second challenge was the Great Depression in the 1930s, where red-green coalition governments through state intervention and state responsibility for crisis management re-established confidence and legitimacy. After the Second World War the next challenge to legitimacy occurred when the Social Democrats in Sweden and Norway wanted tighter political and trade union control over the economy in order to guarantee investments and full employment. Legitimacy was restored after the Social Democrats renounced many of their claims. Compromises were negotiated in the framework of the emerging Cold War, which did not allow for political polarization. Social Democrats guaranteed legitimacy, and industry guaranteed economic growth for political redistribution. However, this new equilibrium was also fragile since the Social Democratic guarantee was repeatedly challenged from the Left. This was obvious in Sweden, Norway and Denmark, when the protests against economic concentration and economic power grew dramatically in the 1960s. The legitimacy crisis was less obvious in Finland which must be understood in the framework of the Cold War and its geographical proximity to the Soviet Union, but the difference should also be referred to the historically shaped more traditional leadership styles and to the fact that Finland had long had a Communist movement and, through this, was accustomed to a more militant language long before the crisis of the 1960s.

The fact that the economic elite, riding on the back of the Social Democratic guarantee of the market economy, acquired a high degree of legitimacy in Scandinavia during certain periods did not imply that they became Social Democrats. The degree of legitimacy for private economic concentration within this Scandinavian pattern varied considerably, being strongest in Sweden and Denmark and weakest in Norway. The economic elites did maintain their own substantial norms and value-orientations, and the political debate was occasionally polarized by the repeated presentation of competing alternatives. The concept of consensus, in this respect, is not very relevant when considering Scandinavian political culture. A high degree of successful compromise achieved over and above opposing positions is more characteristic. The Finnish pattern deviated from the Scandinavian pattern. Although it developed in a more Scandinavian, not to say Swedish, direction during the 1950s, a few legitimizing structures of the authoritarian period remained, such as the fact that questions of unemployment played a relatively less important role in relation to the 'general economic requirements' that served as a mobilizing force, that is, a preparedness to accept economic constraints by the electorate for the sake of long-term growth. Iceland is special, with a much lower degree of economic concentration and therefore also of legitimacy problems. This was true until the breakdown of the financial market in the wake of the Wall Street collapse in the autumn of 2008. The Icelandic participation in the build-up of the bubble transgressed historically established standards and norms. The consequences in terms of legitimacy deficit were obvious when the dimensions of the fiasco became clear.

There is thus not only a Scandinavian pattern of Social Democratic–social liberal reform coalitions since the 1930s, but also a pattern of recurrent challenges to legitimacy and democracy. Due to the conditions during the Cold War this latter pattern was less obvious in Finland. When, at the end of the 1960s, there was a challenge from the rapidly growing criticism of the Left, something new occurred. The employers re-established their legitimacy during the 1980s in the framework of a neo-liberal rhetoric emphasizing values and characteristics such as nearness, smallness, flexibility and individualism. A key concept in this new language was 'co-worker'. This neo-liberal language exposed the Social Democratic–social liberal reform coalitions to fundamentally new challenges. These challenges grew with the globalization theory in the 1990s, which underpinned the neo-liberal approach. The idea of government was transformed into ideas of governance. The confidence in state capacity to guarantee social justice decreased.

The Future Prospects of the Model

What is the Nordic model – with all its variety – based on manufacturing industry and economic growth worth today? Although cultural patterns and value orientations are relatively stable, it is worth remembering that economics have changed dramatically since the 1970s, with a decrease in political control over economies and much larger opportunities for capital evasion from state control. After all, speculation in portfolios and in foreign currencies, with managers compensating themselves through bonus rewards of dramatically new dimensions and for bad performance through 'parachute agreements' with capital owners, whether it be a state or private owner, do not provide the same kind of legitimacy for economic concentration as the ownership of a manufacturing enterprise with thousands of employees. Political control of the economy was a precondition for the political guarantee of legitimacy. This control is no longer as it was. It has become more difficult to attach legitimacy to economic power, and to combine economic concentration with democratization. Both political and economic legitimacy are eroding today and it is not easy to find value criteria on which a new legitimacy might be built. What the banking crisis will mean in the long run in terms of legitimacy is very much an open question.

A rather disintegrative factor for the image of a specific Nordic welfare model and path to modernity is the European attempt to respond to globalizing forces and re-establish political legitimacy and economic growth. In Norway, with a strong oil economy base, and Iceland a majority of the populations are negative or sceptical about this European attempt. The support is rather strong in Finland, although it has declined considerably recently against the backdrop of the euro crisis. In Sweden and Denmark the European commitment is not questioned per se, but it is nevertheless difficult to mobilize a majority for a full commitment. There is less responsibility for a shared problem and more of an interest in picking the fruits. Nationalism and populism are growing all over *Norden*.

The issue at stake is one of value transformation and the extent to which the political imagination is sufficient to transfer old virtues like equality, freedom and solidarity into new patterns of economic organization where terms like growth and profit mean new things. Or, rather than transformation as such, the issue at stake is what direction the transformation will go. This is very much an open question for which historical experiences do not offer much guidance. They do not, in any case, predict the direction of the development.

The crucial question in the present and future challenges transcends the Nordic framework and opens up a global dimension of the debate. With few exceptions the contributions of this volume analyse Nordic modernity from within the Nordic societies. Of course, there are in all contributions references to the world outside *Norden*, which is seen in its international context. However, the contributors who most systematically thematize the different relationships between internal and external determinants are Jóhann Árnason and Risto Alapuro. It might well be that the emerging view beyond the nation states in time and space, imposed by the challenges of the present, requires a new interpretative framework, which would – like Árnason and Alapuro – analyse *Norden* much more in terms of internal–external entanglements and inter-dynamics. Such new interpretative frameworks require more complex theories about time and space, problematizing teleologies, path dependencies and national action units, and emphasizing contingency and openness. The requirements of new interpretative frameworks to cope with the legitimacy problems in the wake of the challenges of the present might need a new kind of Nordic history with more emphasis on fluidity and on the interdependencies between the Nordic societies and their international environment.

Notes

1. See, for instance, for Sweden the events in Ådalen in 1931 when a military troop opened fire on a procession of demonstrators against strike-breakers and killed five unarmed people (Johansson 2001).
2. For a development of this argument, see Stråth 2009.
3. 'Bourgeoisie' is put within quotation marks because *borgerlighet* is a much vaguer concept in the North and more diluted with agrarian elements than bourgeoisie or *Bürgertum* in Germany, for instance. The verbatim translation of the German concept would be *borgardöme*, and this word does not exist in the Scandinavian languages.
4. Lundborg was a race biologist, medical doctor and professor. He examined military conscripts and the same population in the North, and published several books. *Rasbiologi och rashygien* in 1914 was important for the establishment of the government institute. In this book Lundborg tried to demonstrate the superiority of the Nordic race. He had excellent connections to the German academic community and was awarded an honorary doctorate at Heidelberg University in 1936. Although the differentiation from the increasingly overstretched German biological-race discourse became more distinct among Swedish political and intellectual elites from the 1930s, biological-race theories continued to inform ideas of public welfare.
5. The compulsory sterilization in Sweden in the 1930s is a case in point. The discourse on modernity, enlightenment and welfare informed by a Darwinian development language in several academic disciplines, perhaps did not determine but nevertheless facilitated the sterilizations. It was indeed the visions to create a new and better society that motivated the sterilizations. The Swedish sterilizations should not be called genocide because they did not aim at a group. Neither had the sterilizations much to do with ethnical racism. The biological logic behind them makes it more justified to talk about eugenic racism. The idea was to prevent the birth of people who would potentially be a burden to the new welfare society as it was designed in the 1930s, and unfit or unwilling to partake in that project. The idea was not to get rid of a certain race but to reinforce one (Frykman 2000; cf. Hirdman 1989).
6. The biggest name in the Danish financial world up to the 1890s was C.F. Tietgen. This astute businessman had built up his *Privatbanken* during the 1870s and the

1880s, first establishing a steam shipping company which targeted the emigration to America as its key market. He invested in tramways, railways, telephone communications and lime-works, amalgamated a considerable proportion of the Danish alcohol production in *De Danske Spritfabriker*, and merged a great number of Copenhagen breweries to *De Forenede Bryggerier*, which was later joined by Tuborg. At first glance Tietgen resembles a Danish Wallenberg. However, appearances can be deceiving. Tietgen never managed to build industrial development blocs of strategic importance for the Danish economy as a whole as the Wallenberg family had for Sweden. A large proportion of financial outflows from Danish banks had gone to trade and shipping whereas Tietgen had a weakness for breweries. Through a number of less successful investments he failed to accumulate a private fortune. He also had a weakness for keeping up appearances by throwing big parties and banquets, with himself as the principle protagonist. In fact, his control over the enterprises where he had placed capital was not very tight. He delegated much of his owner responsibility to the company management. The Wallenberg family was very different on most of these points. The Wallenberg family made a point of seeing but of not being seen. They held a firm grip over their investments through the loyal managers they placed to oversee their capital who were expected to make the most of their talent. The family was discrete rather than ostentatious in its behaviour. Although they accumulated an overwhelming wealth they did not flaunt it, preferring to radiate virtues such as moderation and responsibility. This attitude penetrated the management style of their entire empire and coloured their relations to the Social Democrats and trade unions.

Tietgen was no Wallenberg and would probably have failed in a Swedish context. In Sweden the same degree of egalitarian moralism as in Norway did not work as an obstacle against the development of a modern banking system. The preparedness to accept economic concentration was higher in Sweden. The puritan framework of the people's movements was there, however, and the key to economic success was to understand how to cope with the dictates of this morality. In Denmark the same type of moralistic barrier against economic concentration as in Norway, or against spectacular manifestations of economic power as in Sweden, did not exist. In his own Danish environment Tietgen was nevertheless one of the people, or one of 'Us', in a culture where the Burghers had represented a popular force joined with the king against the nobility since the seventeenth century.

References

Alapuro, Risto (1988) *State and Revolution in Finland*. Berkeley: University of California Press.
Aronsson, Peter (1997) 'Local Politics: The Invisible Political Culture' in Øystein Sørensen and Bo Stråth (eds), *The Cultural Construction of Norden*. Oslo: Scandinavian University Press.
Arvidsson, Håkan, Lennart Berntsson and Lars Decik (1994) *Modernisering och välfärd*. Stockholm: City University Press.

Frykman, Elin (2000) 'The Cutting Edge: A Sterilisation Campaign in Sweden' in James Kaye and Bo Stråth (eds), *Enlightenment and Genocide: Contradictions of Modernity*. Brussels: PIE-Peter Lang.

Hettling, Manfred (2003) *Volksgeschichten im Europa der Zwischenkriegszeit*. Göttingen: V&R.

Hirdman, Yvonne (1989) *Att lägga livet till rätta. Studier i svensk folkhemspolitik*. Stockholm: Carlsson.

Jansen, Christian (1993) 'Deutsches Wesen, "deutsche Seele", "deutscher Geist". Der Volkscharakter als nationales Identifikationsmuster im Gelehrtenmilieu' in Helmut Kuzmics, Reinhard Blumert and Annette Treibel (Hg), *Transformationen des Wir-Gefühls. Studien zum nationalen Habitus*. Frankfurt/Main: Suhrkamp.

Johansson, Roland (2001) *Kampen om historien. Ådalen 1931. Sociala konflikter, historiemedvetande och historiebruk 1931–2001*. Stockholm: Hjalmarsson & Högberg.

Karlsson, Gunnar (2000) *History of a Marginal Society: Iceland's 1100 Years*. London: Hurst & Company.

Lunn, Eugene (1973) *Prophet of Community: The Romantic Socialism of Gustav Landauer*. Berkeley: California University Press.

Marklund, Carl (2008) 'Bridging Politics and Science: Social Engineering in Sweden and the USA from Depression to Cold War'. Ph.D. thesis, European University Institute, Florence.

Mosse, George L. (1981) *The Crisis of German Ideology*. New York.

Nilsson, Göran B. (2001) *Grundaren. André Oscar Wallenberg*. Stockholm: Carlsson.

Sejersted, Francis (1993) *Demokratisk kapitalisme*. Oslo: Universitetsforlaget.

—— (2001a) *Den vanskelige frihet. Norge 1814–1850*. Oslo: Pax.

—— (2001b) *Demokrati og rettsstat*. Oslo: Pax.

—— (2001c) 'Capitalism and Democracy: A Comparison between Norway and Sweden' in Haldor Byrkjeflot et al. (eds), *The Democratic Challenge to Capitalism: Management and Democracy in the Nordic Countries*. Oslo: Fagbokforlaget.

Slagstad, Rune (1998) *De nasjonale strateger*. Oslo: Pax.

—— (2000) *Kunnskapens hus*. Oslo: Pax.

Sørensen, Øystein and Bo Stråth (1997) 'Introduction' in Øystein Sørensen and Bo Stråth (eds), *The Cultural Construction of Norden*. Oslo: Scandinavian University Press.

Stokholm Banke and Cecilie Felicia (1999) *Den sociale ingeniørkunst i Danmark. Familie, stat og politik fra 1900 til 1945*. Ph.D. Diss, Roskilde University.

—— (ed.) (2001) *Folk og fællesskab*. Working Report Nr 2 from Dansk Center for Holocaust- og Folkedrabstudier, Copenhagen.

Stråth, Bo (ed.) (1988) *Democratisation in Scandinavia in Comparison*. Gothenburg University.

—— (ed.) (1990) *Language and the Construction of Class Identities*. Gothenburg University.

—— (1996) *The Organisation of Labour Markets: Modernity, Culture and Governance in Germany, Sweden, Britain and Japan*. London: Routledge.

—— (2001) 'Nordic Capitalism and Democratisation' in Haldor Byrkjeflot et al. (eds), *The Democratic Challenge to Capitalism: Management and Democracy in the Nordic Countries*. Oslo: Fagbokforlaget.

―――― (2003) 'Hembygd as a Pragmatic Concept: The Alternative Case' in Ron Robin and Bo Stråth (eds), *Homelands Poetic Power and Politics of Space*. Brussels: PIE-Peter Lang.

―――― (2009) 'Path Dependency versus Path-breaking Crises. An Alternative View' in Lars Magnusson and Jan Ottosson (eds), *The Evolution of Path Dependence*. Cheltenham (UK): Edward Elgar.

Thorkildsen, Dag (1997) 'Religious Identity and Nordic Identity' in Øystein Sørensen and Bo Stråth (eds), *The Cultural Construction of Norden*. Oslo: Scandinavian University Press.

Trägårdh, Lars (1999) *The Concept of the People and the Construction of Popular Political Culture in Germany and Sweden: 1848–1933*. Diss 1993. Ann Arbour: University Microfilms International.

―――― (1997) 'Statist Individualism: On the Culturality of the Nordic Welfare State' in Øystein Sørensen and Bo Stråth (eds), *The Cultural Construction of Norden*. Oslo: Scandinavian University Press.

Wagner, Peter and Björn Wittrock (1992) 'Policy Constitution through Discourse: Discourse Transformations and the Modern State in Central Europe' in Douglas E. Ashford (ed.), *History and Context in Comparative Public Policy*. Pittsburgh: University of Pittsburgh Press.

Witoszek, Nina (1997) 'Fugitives from Utopia: The Scandinavian Enlightenment Reconsidered' in Øystein Sørensen and Bo Stråth (eds), *The Cultural Construction of Norden*. Oslo: Scandinavian University Press.

Österberg, Eva (1993) 'Vardagens sträva samförstånd. Bondepolitik i den svenska modellen från vasatid till frihetstid' in Gunnar Broberg, Ulla Wikander and Klas Åmark (eds), *Tänka, tycka, tro. Svensk historia underifrån*. Stockholm: Ordfront.

CHAPTER 2
The Danish Path to Modernity
Uffe Østergård

In a comparative context, Danish national identity and political culture combine features of what is often referred to as East European 'integral nationalism', typical of smaller, recently independent nation-states and the 'patriotic concept of citizenship' in the older West European state nations (Brubaker 1992). The explanation of this apparent paradox is that Denmark belongs to both families. A former multinational, composite state was cut down to a size that enabled a class of about sixty thousand peasant-farmers to establish an ideological hegemony in the diminished and nationalized, yet still fully legitimate, state.[1]

Until the loss of the Norwegian part of the realm in 1814, the name 'Denmark' referred to a composite state, typical of the European era of territorial states.[2] The official name of this mid-sized sovereign power in Northern Europe was the 'Danish Monarchy', or the 'Oldenburg Monarchy'. Today, to the extent that this entity is remembered at all, it is known by such politically correct terms as 'the Dual Monarchy', 'Denmark-Norway', or 'the Twin Kingdom'. However, these polite terms are so imprecise as to be misleading. Following the loss (to Sweden) of Skåne, Halland, Blekinge, Bohuslen, Herjedalen and Gotland in 1658, the Danish king in 1660 became the absolute ruler of the kingdoms of Denmark and Norway and the duchies of Sleswig and Holstein, which comprised the State geographically. Holstein was part of the Holy Roman Empire (in Latin, *Sacrum Imperium*), which complicated the constitutional situation considerably: as duke of Holstein, the Danish king formally was subordinate to the German-Roman emperor. The situation was further complicated by the fact that in 1460 in Ribe the knights of the two duchies had compelled Christian I to recognize that the two regions should 'always' be ruled together.

In addition to the four main realms, the composite state comprised the three North Atlantic territories of Iceland, the Faroe Islands and Greenland. Originally affiliated with Norway, these three countries in the course of the seventeenth and eighteenth centuries gradually came under direct rule from Copenhagen. Finally, the Danish monarchy in this period acquired a number of colonies in the West Indies (St Croix, St John and St Thomas), West Africa (the Christiansborg fortress in today's Ghana), and India (Frederiksnagore, today Serampore outside Calcutta, and Tranquebar). By virtue of this colonial empire, Denmark played a role, however small, in the Atlantic trade triangle between a European centre, the slave-producing West Africa, and the sugar-growing West Indies (Degn 1974), complemented by a part in the East Asian trade (Feldbæk & Justesen 1980). The multinational character of the realm is evidenced by the fact that by the end of the eighteenth century the biggest cities of the composite state were Copenhagen in Denmark proper, Altona and Kiel in Holstein, Flensburg in Sleswig, and Bergen in Norway, while the seaports of Charlotte Amalie in St Thomas and Frederiksnagore were second and sixth, respectively, as measured by trade volume.

Customs duties on traffic to and from the Baltic through the Øresund contributed significantly to the relatively large revenue of the Danish state. In general, the monarchy owed no small part of its strong position to its location at the entrance to the Baltic. In 1420–25, Erik of Pommern built a castle at Elsinore. Frederik II rebuilt it as a spectacular Renaissance castle, which was sufficiently well known in Europe that Shakespeare used the place as the setting for his famous play *Hamlet*. For more than four hundred years until the mid-1600s, the Danish monarchy, due to its geopolitical position, ruled a dominion in Northern Europe that was formalized in the Kalmar Union from 1397 to 1523. The loose union of three crowns, plus dependencies, revolved around a range of issues, but long after the dissolution of the Union in 1523 the quest for maritime control of the Baltic, *Dominium Maris Baltici*, remained the principal theme of the history of Northern Europe (Østergård 1998: 231ff.).

The Oldenburg Monarchy in Europe

Defeat in the war with Sweden led to the introduction of the Absolutist monarchy in 1660 which implied an administrative reorganization or 'modernization' of the state. At the same time began a geopolitical reorientation towards Sleswig and Holstein, which were now gradually incorporated into the core of the kingdom as the competing state-nation project in Northern Europe of the Gottorp family in parts of

Sleswig-Holstein (1490–1720/73) gradually lost out to the Oldenburg family. This realignment was almost of the same magnitude as the simultaneous transformation of Sweden from an East–West to a North–South axis. The Law of Succession of 1665 (*Lex Regia*) was later extended to the whole of Sleswig. Administratively, however, Sleswig was to remain together with the royal portions of Holstein, both of which were to be administered by the German Chancellery (since 1523 situated in Copenhagen), which functioned as the 'Ministry of Foreign Affairs' for the whole state in the Absolutist period.

All in all, the multinational monarchy still ranked as a medium-sized European power at the level of Prussia and Sweden (with present-day Finland). Thanks to Norway it possessed the third largest navy in Europe at the end of the eighteenth century. In 1767, after a major military crisis with the Russian Empire (Østergård 1999), an agreement with the Gottorp heirs who had married into the Russian ruling dynasty was reached. According to this agreement the Danish king gained unchallenged possession of all of Holstein. Thus, the foundations were laid for the great reform process in the various parts of the multinational state from 1784 to 1814. These reforms were initiated primarily by representatives of the German-speaking aristocratic elite within the composite state. This elite, however, saw no reason to make any adjustments to the administrative division of the realm, so that the Danish-speaking regions in Sleswig were to continue to be administered together with Holstein, as was stipulated in the earlier mentioned 'Treaty of Ribe' of 1460.

Even after the loss of the eastern third of the realm in 1658 the composite state was geographically large. The Danish king ruled over vast, thinly populated territories stretching from the North Cape to Hamburg, a distance equal to that between Hamburg and Sicily. Add to that the far-flung North Atlantic parts of the realm. The military, technological and political backbone of the empire was the fleet, manned to a large extent by fishermen from Norway and the North Atlantic islands. This fleet was big enough to fight a growing Swedish rival in the Baltic and to protect the extensive possessions for more than 150 years. However, after exhausting its resources, the realm suffered a series of humiliating defeats by the fast-rising Swedish competitor which established a vast Baltic Empire in Northern Europe that lasted until 1720 (Roberts 1979). Nevertheless, the Danish fleet proved capable of inflicting massive losses among the Swedes in the Scanian War of 1675–79.

The price of this position was a higher degree of militarization of the relatively poor and sparsely populated Danish and Swedish lands than was necessary in more affluent and densely populated European states (Ladewig Petersen 1984). It is, then, rather remarkable that the geographically far-flung and economically overburdened Danish state succeeded in modernizing itself through a kind of revolution from above at the end of the seventeenth century and once again in the late eighteenth century (Horstbøll and Østergård 1990). The Danish kingdom underwent a revolution akin to the French through a timely self-reformation between the years 1784 and 1814. In many respects this northern European monarchy personified the ideals of the Enlightenment thinkers. Thus, from Venice to London the political system of the state was eagerly debated among political observers – not always in flattering terms, as we know from Montesquieu's excoriation in *De l'ésprit des lois* (1748), which in 1753 provoked Holberg to publish a fierce response in French. The fact remains that the state was an object of discussion in intellectual circles all over Europe (Østergård 1995).

Theoretically, the political system was the most autocratic in Europe, formalized, even, in a kind of absolute 'constitution' (*Kongeloven* or *Lex Regia* from 1665). But the political reality was far from despotic, a state that the Norwegian historian Jens Arup Seip somewhat paradoxically has termed 'opinion-governed autocracy' (Seip 1958). This tradition of consulting public opinion is the main reason that the Danish monarchy succeeded in revolutionizing itself from above through a series of relatively continuous reforms of the agrarian system, civil rights, customs, trade, education, and emancipation of the Jews between 1784 and 1814 (Løfting et al. 1989). In contrast, the French king lost legitimacy among the tax-granting assembly of the States General, triggering an incontrollable democratic revolution that was subsequently hailed by much of French history writing as the revealed meaning of history despite the enormous cost and the brutal terror it also involved.

The foundations of this tightly organized state were laid in the 1670s and 1680s, when the Absolutist monarchy reformed itself on the pattern of the France of Louis XIV.[3] The all-encompassing bodies of laws, the *Danske Lov* of 1683 and the *Norske Lov* of 1687, modernized, systematized and made uniform the many varying medieval provincial laws, introducing a chancellery in the European mould (Horstbøll and Østergård 1990). A completely new survey of the productivity of the arable land and other natural resources enabled the state to collect taxes on a fairer basis than before. The central administration was rebuilt on the Swedish-European model of specialized colleges somewhat similar to today's ministries. The administration of the army and navy was the first to be modernized; then followed the administration of finance, with a collegium made up of four nobles and four burghers. That the path to a government career was opened up in this way to persons of non-noble birth was something quite new. The old regional administration of state territories in the Danish and German chancelleries, respectively, was incorporated into the college system as 'domestic' and 'external' administration, and by the end of the seventeenth century the territorial state had gradually been replaced by a tax-based 'Machtstaat' (power-state, cf. Ladewig Petersen 1984).

In a brief episode from 1770 to 1772, Johann Friedrich Struensee (1737–72), physician to King Christian VII, tried to revolutionize the entire state by introducing radical reforms from above of the type recommended by Enlightenment philosophers. Though born in Altona, in other words within the borders of the multinational monarchy, most of Struensee's career had been spent outside Denmark, and he was thus perceived by the majority of the population as a foreigner. His reforms quickly fell into disrepute when he was exposed as an adulterer and the queen's secret lover. His arrest and subsequent execution provoked some anti-German sentiments among Danish-speaking middle classes who hoped to profit from the expulsion of the so-called 'Germans' (Feldbæk 1991: I). In an attempt to forestall further criticism, the government, in 1776, passed a law reserving government jobs for those born inside the realm, the 'Indfødsret'. This law was backed by a whole series of well meant – but futile as it turned out – attempts to build a common patriotic feeling in the whole of the realm in general and for the king in particular (Feldbæk 1991: I–II and Rasmussen 1995: 28–29).

The Enlightenment reforms of the late eighteenth century were based upon reform of the civil laws, which ended the personal dependency of peasants upon landowners, a reform of the system of cultivation comprising abolition of the common field system and enclosure of the individual holdings, establishment of a comprehensive school system (1814), and liberalization of the customs as the most important changes. In 1805, serfdom in Holstein was abolished, a move which alienated the German landed aristocracy of this province and made them the embittered opponents of the monarchy they had been supporting, or at least accepted as legitimate. In 1806, after the abolition of the Holy Roman Empire, Holstein was incorporated into the Danish monarchy. Between 1720 and 1807, the Danish monarchy enjoyed a hitherto unparalleled prosperity, based on rising prices for its agrarian products and huge profits in neutral trading during the repeated European and colonial wars. In the early nineteenth century, however, Denmark-Norway overplayed its hand and ended up an adversary of Britain in the Napoleonic wars. The battle of Copenhagen in 1801, the British bombardment of the capital in 1807, the subsequent loss of the navy and final defeat at the hands of the anti-Napoleon coalition led to bankruptcy of the state in 1813 and the loss of Norway to Sweden in 1814.

From Composite State to Peasant-Farmers' Democracy

In 1800, the Danish king ruled over a vast, though thinly populated, realm, stretching from Greenland, Iceland and Norway to the suburbs of Hamburg – in distance half the total European coastline. According to the reliable census of 1801, the total population of the kingdom was 2.5 million. Denmark and Norway had 1.8 million, 51 per cent of whom lived in Denmark proper; Sleswig-Holstein had six hundred thousand inhabitants, of which 54 per cent were in Holstein; other German possessions counted for some ninety thousand people and the North Atlantic islands some fifty thousand. No reliable census for the colonies exists, as their status was different (Rasmussen 1995: 25). Thus the three major linguistic and national groups in the multinational state balanced each other; that is the economically more advanced German-speaking parts were balanced by a much larger number of Danish and Norwegian (very similar to Danish) speakers.

The loss of Norway in 1814 completely altered the balance between the German and Nordic elements in the composite state. The number of German speakers rose from less than 20 per cent to 35 per cent, and nationalist sentiments began to tear the state apart (Rasmussen 1995: 26). As mentioned above, in 1806 the Duchy of Holstein was annexed to Denmark as a consequence of the disintegration of the Holy Roman Empire. However, with the establishment of the German Confederation in 1815, Holstein was re-established as an independent duchy, which implied that the Danish king participated in the Federal Assembly in his capacity as Duke of Holstein. As punishment for the alliance with France, the Danish king was compelled to cede the kingdom of Norway to Sweden, 'in return' for which he received the tiny Duchy of Lauenburg. Although reduced, this state was still a composite state in legal terms, and it retained a multinational character. It consisted of the Kingdom of Denmark proper (North Jutland to the Kongeåen plus the islands) and the duchies of Sleswig, Holstein and Lauenburg. The latter, no larger in size than the minor Danish island of Lolland, retained its independent status and its particular institutions. Furthermore, the realm comprised the dependencies of Iceland and the Faroe Islands, and the colonies of Greenland, the Danish West Indies, Tranquebar and Guinea. In short, it was still a multi-nation polity in the mould of the Austro-Hungarian monarchy, only smaller. As was the case with the Habsburg Empire, however, the multinational state was soon to be torn apart by two antagonistic, national programmes, a 'Danish' (either the Danish-Danish or the Scandinavianist, that is Danish-Swedish, variant) and a 'German' (either the Sleswig-Holsteinian or the pan-German or *grossdeutsche* variant).

The demand for the creation of a national state with a written constitution was first formulated in minority liberal circles in the first half of the nineteenth century, primarily among students and younger civil servants. In Denmark and Holstein, the move from international or supranational liberalism to national liberalism took place between 1836 and 1842. Until then the liberal movements in Copenhagen and Kiel had been allied in their resistance to the almost unlimited power of the 'absolute monarchy', which continued to prevail even after the introduction of the consultative assemblies in 1830/34. The bourgeoisie alone was so small in numbers that it was in no position to shake the despotic regime. Had this not been apparent before, it certainly became so after the accession of Christian VIII to the throne in 1839. The liberals had believed that Christian VIII would transfer the free Norwegian constitution, the shaping of which he had overseen in 1814, to Denmark. Astute as he was, however, Christian VIII nourished no desire to curtail his own powers and deliver himself into the hands of the increasingly nationalistic liberals. Under these circumstances, the two liberal reform groups in the capitals of Copenhagen and Kiel each established their own strategic alliances. In Denmark, the liberals allied themselves with the peasant farmers, an alliance which in 1846 was capped by the establishment of a political party, *Bondevennerne* (Friends of the Peasant). In Holstein, a more informal alliance was established with the landed aristocracy that later developed into the Sleswig-Holsteinian movement (hyphenated to indicate the long unity of the two historic provinces). The confrontation of 1848 was not the only possible result of the national confrontations in Sleswig as it has been depicted in nationalist historiography from both sides. But neither of the two national liberal groups was able to gain power without a 'national' polarization over an abstract ideology (Wåhlin and Østergård 1975). Thus nationalism came to tear apart the relatively well-functioning composite state, *Helstaten*.

The nationalistic radicalization of the language employed eventually led to war and ended with the dismemberment of the Danish monarchy after the self-inflicted defeat of 1864. Denmark survived as a sovereign nation-state only by the skin of its teeth, and only with help from outside. Again it was the interests of the great powers, this time first and foremost Russia and Britain, in maintaining a neutral power at the entrance to the Baltic that saved Denmark as a sovereign state. Had this not been the case, the country would have become either German or Swedish (the latter eventuality being termed Scandinavianism). Today we have grown used to considering this development as both inevitable and positive. This view reflects the swift exploitation by popular movements of the exceptional situation of a whole sovereign state having been rendered so weak that it allowed the peasant movement and subsequently, the workers movement, to gain control over the state (Østergård 1992). Such popular movements were not altogether uncommon in an international context, but it was quite unique for such movements to gain cultural, economic and eventually political hegemony within a sovereign state. This is what the slogan 'Outward losses must be made up by inward gains' came to mean for the Danes in the period following 1864.

The programme for a romantically, ethnically and historically motivated definition of the nation was, as previously noted, formulated by the National Liberal 'party' – party here being placed in inverted commas because the liberals in principle did not recognize political parties at all, only representatives of the whole nation, 'the nation's finest and best', motivated only by their own convictions (Lehmann 1861). This conception, however, was out of tune with the political and social realities. The years 1830–1848 saw the rise of modern political ideas in Denmark (Wåhlin and Østergård 1975). As a result, the lower classes began to organize themselves from the bottom up. According to the liberals, members of society ought to organize on the basis of their own ideas and compete for political power through free elections – although the liberals meant that only those who understood how to govern should vote: 'the best', 'the brightest' and 'the educated' in the words of one of the leading National Liberal politicians, Orla Lehmann (1861). But this was all theory.

In practice, it was to become apparent already prior to the political upheaval of 1848 and the subsequent civil war between 'Danes' and 'Germans' (the Danish version of a bourgeois revolution, cf. Østergård 1998) that the dividing lines ran parallel with social or class-based affiliations. Liberal academics, officials and other pillars of the liberal community sought to conceal these class cleavages by shrewdly elaborate appeals in the name of 'the people'. The means for creating this alliance across class divisions was the so-called 'national revival' (or more aptly, nationalistic incitement) concerning the status of the Duchy of Sleswig within the national framework. The strategy worked well for a number of years, but ended with the abortive attempt to annex Sleswig in November 1863 and the National Liberals' subsequent collapse. Stubborn and intransigent quibbling by Danish National Liberal politicians and their misjudgement of the international situation enabled Bismarck to establish a united Germany, without Austria, and under Prussian dominance. The international political climate and international agreements notwithstanding, the National Liberals demanded a Danish nation-state within the 'historical' framework, that is all of Sleswig to the river Ejder, regardless of the opinion of the inhabitants. This move would have resulted in a large German-speaking minority within Denmark. Instead

Prussia and Austria took all of Sleswig and Holstein, with a large Danish population in Northern Sleswig (Østergård 1996a).

Eventually a new united German Empire was proclaimed in 1871. The presence in the middle of Europe of this unstable and all too domineering major new power provoked in its turn a national unification in Denmark, as well as in other neighbouring countries. In Denmark, this was achieved in a quite exceptional manner by means of a combination of outside pressures and initiatives from below, primarily from the class of peasant farmers. On the basis of this conscious demarcation from Germany and all things German, the modern, popular and democratic Denmark emerged, that is, everything Danes today celebrate as being particularly Danish about Denmark and the Danes (Østergård 1984).

In the 1870s the agrarian liberals successfully engaged in a virtual *Kulturkampf* (Cultural War) with the conservatives and the urban liberals over control of the schools and the congregations. The struggle over the schools was to have far greater importance for the establishment of cultural hegemony than the better-described conflict of literary cultures in the 1880s (Østergård 1984). The latter has always been the subject of attention from social-liberal intellectuals owing to the quality of the contributions from the critic and politician Edvard Brandes (1847–1931), the literary historian Georg Brandes (1842–1927), the journalist and politician Viggo Hørup (1841–1901) and other so-called 'European' intellectuals. Despite their intellectual brilliance and apparent victory with the founding of the newspaper *Politiken* in 1884, the cultural hegemony they wanted never materialized. The religious and social movements of the Grundtvigians and their opponents in the Pietist 'Inner Mission', however, were more successful. Their efforts led to a hegemony which in the twentieth century subsequently even came to include the Social Democratic workers movement who ruled in alliance with the successors to the Europeanist left, the so called 'Radikale Venstre'.

With social unification, however, came a high degree of national mobilization among the rural masses and in the rest of the nation. This nationalism, in its turn, made it extremely difficult for the responsible government to strike the necessary compromises with the rising German power next door. Only the defeat of the German Reich in the First World War provided an opportunity for Denmark to retrieve the Danish speakers in North Sleswig. Because of clumsy attempts to Germanize them, the Danish-speaking Sleswigers had become ardent Danish nationalists, organizing a sort of parallel society (Japsen 1983). Yet it took almost superhuman efforts on the part of courageous and far-sighted representatives of the Danish minority in Sleswig, such as H.P. Hansen Nørremølle (1862–1936) to bring about the necessary change in the

Danish political line and obtain a vital national compromise with its great neighbour (Østergård 1996a).

One of the prerequisites was building new self-confidence within the population. An important element in this process was a reorientation away from Europe and towards the North (Østergård 1996b). Whether the shift from a European to a Nordic orientation has been worth the cultural price is a matter for debate. However, it is incontestable that in the short run, the reorientation involved major political advantages in terms of a homogeneous and self-important nation-state that was able to hold together, even after having surrendered to German forces almost without firing a shot on 9 April 1940.

The Peasant-Farmer Roots of Danish National Identity

Thus, in the wake of military and political disasters, a middle-sized, multinational, composite state was reduced to the small, linguistically and socially homogeneous nation-state we know as Denmark today.[4] After the loss of Sleswig and Holstein in 1864 many among the dominant elite thought Denmark too small to be likely to survive as an independent state. It did, however. Competing elites invented different programmes for the survival of the state. Parts of the national liberal intelligentsia favoured a union with Sweden and Norway, who had already joined a union together. This programme went by the name of Scandinavianism and would have implied a de facto Swedish hegemony (Stråth 1980; Østergård 1997). While a minority favoured an alliance with the new Germany, the great majority preferred neutrality towards Germany, combined with an economic orientation towards the British Empire. As farmers gradually won political, cultural and economic influence, this programme prevailed as a successful national democracy. In the twentieth century this national democracy became a social democracy as a result of the rise of the workers movement, and the Social Democratic party became the largest party before the First World War. Thus, the Danish rump state became the quintessential 'smaller state', as envisaged by the American sociologist Moore in his introduction to one of the most influential works of comparative historical sociology, *The Social Origins of Dictatorship and Democracy*.[5]

However, although we usually refer to them both as Denmark, it is important to distinguish between this extremely homogeneous nation state and the older composite state. Conflating them would be as misleading as confusing today's Russia with the Soviet Union or Serbia with Yugoslavia. Obvious continuities notwithstanding, the breaks and differences are more important in many respects, most significantly the complete misunderstanding of the role of the composite state in international politics. When innumerable historiographies of Denmark refer to both states as 'Denmark', we conflate a multinational medium-sized power with a small national welfare state in the twentieth century, though as state types they share little but a certain geographic continuity in Denmark proper, that is, the two Jutland provinces of North and South Jutland (Nørrejylland and Sønderjylland), as well as Sealand, Funen and other islands. The logical implication of this disregard for other parts of the monarchy is the denial of differences within the nation-state. Denmark ended up as an extremely centralized state, disguised as local government. This outcome was not given. As Steen Bo Frandsen convincingly has demonstrated in a close analysis of the 'Jutland question', no analysis of nineteenth century Denmark can ignore the attempts to transform this multinational monarchy into a federal state (Frandsen 1993, 1996). But one continuity is too obvious to disregard: the relationship between the remaining parts of the vanished multinational state – the Faroe Islands, Greenland and Denmark proper. Neither the constitution of 1849 nor the redrafted version of 1953 have arrived at a good definition of the relationship between the different parts of the kingdom, hence the continual demands for recognition of other parts of the realm as independent nations – denied by a bipartisan Danish political system which understands the concept of a state only as a nation-state and which, with a knee-jerk reaction, rejects any suggestion of a federation.

Contrary to the situation in most other nineteenth century nation-states, the small size of the amputated Danish state allowed a numerous class of relatively well-to-do 'peasants turned independent farmers' via the reforms of the late eighteenth century to assume economic and political hegemony. This did not occur without opposition, but through the latter part of the nineteenth century the middle peasants gradually took over from the despairing ruling elites. The latter were recruited from the tiny urban bourgeoisie, the civil servants of the state trained at German-style universities both within and outside of the Monarchy, and the manorial class. After the debacle of 1864 and the subsequent establishment of a strong united Germany next door, they lost faith in the survival of the state. Some even played with the thought of joining this neighbouring state which already dominated the culture of the upper classes.

In this situation, however, an outburst of so-called 'popular' energy proclaimed a strategy of 'winning inwards what had been lost to the outside'. The slogan was turned into a literal strategy of retrieving the lost agrarian lands of Western Jutland, now deserted because of the deforestation of the sixteenth and seventeenth centuries. It also took the form of an opening up of 'Dark Jutland' in an attempt to turn the economy of the peninsula away from Hamburg and redirect it towards Copenhagen. This movement, provocatively called 'the Discovery of Jutland' (Frandsen 1995, 1996), entailed the exploitation of Jutland by the capital Copenhagen, situated on the far eastern rim of the country as a remnant of the former empire, much like Vienna in present-day Austria. This battle between metropolis and province is not yet over, as demonstrated in the heated controversies about whether or not to build a bridge between the islands of Fyn and Sjœlland or to connect Sweden and Copenhagen directly with Germany over the gulf of Fehmern (Østergård 2000a, b). The attempt to hold the Danish nation-state together and keep Jutland away from Hamburg won out, as the former bridge has now been completed. The decision, however, was achieved only by a very narrow margin.

More important, however, is the cultural, economic and political awakening of the middle peasants who became farmers producing for the world market precisely in this period. The basis for their success was the relative weakness of the Danish bourgeoisie and the country's late industrialization. The take-off happened only in the 1890s, and the final breakthrough as late as the 1950s (Hansen 1970). The middle peasants developed a consciousness of themselves as a class and understood themselves to be the real backbone of society. Their ideology supported free trade, not surprising as they were beginning to rely heavily on the export of food to the rapidly developing British market. Trade links to Britain were so important that Denmark, economically speaking, was de facto a part of the British Empire from the middle of the nineteenth to the middle of the twentieth century. More surprising is the fact that their ideology also contained strong libertarian elements because of their struggle with the existing urban and academic elites. The peasant-farmers' movement achieved hegemony because it succeeded in establishing an independent culture with its own educational institutions. This was in turn possible because of the unique organizational form of the agrarian industries: the cooperative.

Basic agrarian production remained individual production on independent farms, albeit somewhat larger on average than is usual in a European context. However, the processing of dairy and meat produce into exportable products took place in local farm industries run on a cooperative basis. The cooperative associations were run democratically on the basis of equality, regardless of the initial investment. The cooperative movement formulated this in a slogan of votes being cast 'by heads instead of heads of cattle' (in other words, one man, one vote, regardless of the initial investment). This pun (in Danish *hoveder* and *høveder*) is less true when one starts investigating the realities of the cooperatives. Yet the myth remained, producing a sense of community, which by means of various political traditions has been transformed into a long-lasting hegemony that laid the ground for a national consensus. This consensus, while hard to define, until very recently enabled members of the Danish community to communicate across class differences – through words, symbols and actions. Humour and understatement thrived on common understandings that precede the spoken words.

The libertarian values, though, were not originally meant to include other segments of the population. The agrarian system was based on crass exploitation of agricultural labourers by the farmers. The latter, along with the urban elites, were often not even considered part of 'the people' by the peasant-farmers. However, in an interesting and surprisingly original ideological manoeuvre, the rising social democracy adapted its ideology to the unique agrarian–industrial conditions in Denmark and developed a strategy very different from the Marxist orthodoxy of the German mother party. The Danish Social Democrats even agreed to the establishment of a class of very small farmers called *husmænd* (cottagers). Thus, the Social Democrats fulfilled the expectations of their landless members among the agricultural labourers but at the same time undermined the possibility of ever obtaining an absolute majority in the parliament, as did their sister parties in Sweden and Norway.

This apparently suicidal strategy, as well as subsequent compromises in housing policy, ruled out any position of a virtual Social Democratic monopoly of power, as was the case in Norway and Sweden (Esping-Andersen 1985). Yet as far as we can judge, they did so knowingly and on purpose. During the First World War, it became clear to the Social Democratic leadership that the party would never be able to achieve an absolute political majority. Under Thorvald Stauning's thirty-two years of charismatic leadership (1910–1942), the party restructured its line from a class-based to a more all-embracing strategy. The consensus line was first openly formulated in 1923, and later on adopted in slogans such as 'the people's cooperating rule' and, somewhat less clumsily, 'Denmark for the people' (1934). The platform resulted in a stable governing coalition, from 1929 to 1943, of the Radical Liberals (*Det Radikale Venstre*) and the Social Democratic Party. The Social Democratic leaders apparently accepted the ultimate check on the influence of their own movement in the interests of the society at large. Perhaps they did not distinguish between the two. Developments might have turned out differently in Germany had the Social Democrats in that country in the 1920s adopted a policy directed towards the people as a whole and not just the working class in the Marxist sense.

The eminent German socialist theoretician Karl Kautsky (1854–1938) never really understood the role of agriculture in modern societies. He saw it as something of the pre-capitalist past, which would be better run according to the principles of mass-industrialization as happened in the Soviet Union with the collectivizations of the 1930s (Kautsky 1899). The Danish Social Democrats in their practical policies had a better understanding of agriculture, but proved unable to turn this understanding into a coherent theory. At the level of doctrine, the party stuck to the formulations in the 1913 programme (Lahme 1982). These formulations reflected the international debates in the Second International rather than the Danish reality and the practical policy of the party. The very fact that the programme of 1913 remained unchanged until 1961 testifies to the lack of importance attributed to theory in this most pragmatic of all reformist Socialist parties. Danish Social Democracy was never strong on theory, but the labour movement, in contrast, has produced an impressive number of capable administrators and politicians.

This lack of explicit strategy enabled remnants of the libertarian peasant ideology to take root early on within the party and in the labour movement as such. The Social Democrats embarked upon a policy for all people, and not just for the working class. This testifies to the importance of the liberal-popular ideological hegemony dating back to the peasant-farmers' ideological hegemony in the last third of the nineteenth century. The leaders realized that they would never gain power on their own. The farmers proper constituted only a fragment of the total population, but small-scale production permeated the whole society then as it still does today. Ironically, the Marxist who understood Denmark best was Lenin. In a discussion of the Agrarian Program of the Social Democracy, Lenin (1907) discussed at length the Danish cooperatives, which he had studied on the spot (in the Royal Library in Copenhagen). Lenin turned out to be rather positively disposed towards such a self-reliant strategy but refused to endorse it for Russia for a number of reasons. Maybe he should have done so. That a strategy directed towards the majority of the people would turn out more rewarding seems pretty obvious from today's point of view. Yet a sophisticated socialist party such as the German Social Democrats embarked on this strategy only as late as 1959 in Bad Godesberg; the British Labour and the French Socialist Party took even longer to make up their minds; and what will happen in the former Eastern Europe still remains to be seen.

The main reason why a libertarian ideology of solidarity ended up dominating a whole nation-state was the small size of this particular state. Danish historians and sociologists have eagerly discussed whether the peasant ideological hegemony resulted from a particular class structure dating back to the 1780s or even further back to the early sixteenth century, when the number of farms was frozen by law, or whether it was this ideology that created the particular class structure of nineteenth-century Danish society (Paludan 1995). Constructed in such terms, the discussion is almost impossible to solve, as both positions reveal some truth. My own view is that the outcome can best be explained in terms of the existence of a particular form of populism or 'popular' ideology (*folkelighed*) stressing the importance of consensus among the people. This status was first and most coherently formulated by the important Danish philosopher, historian, priest and poet (virtually untranslated and untranslatable) Nikolaj Frederik Grundtvig (1783–1872).

Depressed by the defeat of Denmark by Great Britain in the war 1807–1814, Grundtvig as a young priest took it upon himself to re-establish what he took to be the original 'Nordic' or 'Danish' 'mind'. He translated the Icelandic Sagas, the twelfth century historian Saxo Grammaticus, the Anglo-Saxon poem *Beowulf* and many other sources of what he considered to be the true but lost core of 'Danishness'. His sermons attracted large crowds of enthusiastic students. His address on *The Light of the Holy Trinity*, delivered in 1814 to a band of student volunteers willing to fight the British, inspired a whole generation of young followers, including the priest Jacob Christian Lindberg (1791–1857), who later organized the first Grundtvigian movement. When Grundtvig embarked upon a sharp polemic with his superiors in the church on matters of theology, he was banned from all public appearances and publishing. This drove him into what he called his 'inner exile' in the 1830s. This inner exile, however, gave him time for reflection where he formulated a programme for the revival of the stagnant official religion. When the ban was lifted in 1839, he burst out in a massive production of sermons, psalms and songs, a literary legacy which, until at least a few years ago, formed the core of the socialization of most Danes.

Grundtvig then formulated an all-embracing view of nature, language and history. In 1848, after the outbreak of the civil war over Sleswig, he produced a refined definition of national identity, which helped set the tone for a nationalism less chauvinistic than most in the nineteenth century. What is particular for the Danish Grundtvigism is its emphasis on the unity of land, country, God and people (*folk*). It has turned out to be virtually impossible to export this particular synthesis. Grundtvigism even played a negligible role among Danish immigrants to the American Midwest. 'Grundtvigism' is thus to be understood as a shorthand for all the revivalist ideologies of self-reliance thriving in Denmark at the time, regardless of their precise teachings. These are the 'peasant roots of Danish modernity' or the 'peculiarity of the Danes'. They help explain many of the apparently paradoxical features of Danish political and social life, including its anarchistic party political system. Real national values are at stake in the present process of European integration, and many Danes fear that they will disappear when society, nation and state are no longer coterminous, as they have been for the last hundred years or so. This is why Danes have been so reluctant to participate fully in 'the construction of Europe'. What they have failed to realize is how recent this identification of society, nation and state is, and how precarious the geopolitically exposed situation is in the centre of Europe at the entrance to the Baltic Sea. When the Baltic region opened up to the rest of Europe with the fall of the Iron Curtain, old tensions dating from before the rise of the nation-states re-emerged and put the need to choose between different international options back on the table. Denmark can no longer have it both ways, as she did during the Cold War.

The Hegemony of Peasant Values in a Modern Nation-State

The peculiarity of Denmark is thus twofold. First, the country has two pasts, so to speak: a somewhat older one of a relatively large composite state in the general West European mould and a more recent one as a small, relatively homogeneous nation-state, sometimes referred to as a typical small state. Secondly, the peasant farmers successfully established an ideological hegemony over the rest of the population in the nineteenth century. In the last decades of the nineteenth and at the beginning of the twentieth century, the working class successfully organized itself as Social Democratic and quickly became the largest political party, which from the mid-1920s came to dominate the organization of the universalist welfare state. Yet, this successful Social Democracy never won the kind of absolute majority enjoyed by its sister parties in Sweden and Norway and thus always had to govern in coalition with others, primarily the social liberals in the so called *Radikale Venstre*. Thirdly, the workers movement modelled itself heavily on the core values of liberalism, social harmony and nationalism promoted by the peasant farmers. In my analysis, these peasant values together with the particular Lutheran version of Protestantism dating back to the Reformation from above in 1536 constitute an ideological hegemony across party lines, a hegemony which still exists today and in combination with later historical experiences helps explain the particularities of the Danish path to modernity (Østergård 2003a).

Today's national identity, mainly born out of the 1864 defeat, depends more heavily on a nominally sovereign state with roots in the composite state of the previous centuries than did the French and even British identity project. This dependence on the state explains the apparent contradictions in Danish collective mentality when confronted with the prospect of European integration. In an ever more closely collaborating Europe with state characteristics dispersed at more levels, the ethno-cultural concept of nation seems to exhibit a series of relative advantages over the exclusively state-based concept we find in the traditional British identification of national sovereignty, with the sovereignty of Parliament and unlimited parliamentarianism (Clark 1991). The French notion of republican, state-based national identity, on the other hand, might eventually come to grips with the new European-wide dispersal of sovereignty, provided the definitions are clear cut. The great loser, eventually, will be the peculiar Danish conflation of nation and state. It is therefore not surprising to see a majority of the Danish populace, for different reasons, rejecting the loss of national sovereignty, although this sovereignty, in real terms, is hard for hard-headed external observers to detect.

To sum up, the major problem is that the 'Denmark' referred to is far from unequivocal. On the one hand the name refers to a typical multinational state-nation with a long-standing role in European politics; on the other hand, this very same name refers to an atypical homogeneous small nation-state. This duality is nicely reflected in the use of two national anthems (cf. Knudsen 1992). The first is *Kong Christian* ('King Christian') written by Johannes Ewald in 1779; this martial song praises the warrior king who defeats the enemies of the country – and politely forgets how he lost everything in the end. The other song is *Der er et yndigt land* ('There is a lovely land') written in 1819 by the romanticist poet Adam Oehlenschläger, praising the beauty of the friendly and peaceful country and its national inhabitants. This latter is the one sung at national football games, regardless of the result. Denmark, Danes and 'Danish' national consensus are caught between competing and at times even antagonistic notions of Danishness.

Notes

1. This article is a rewritten and much shortened version of 'Danish National Identity: Between Multinational Heritage and Small State Nationalism' in H. Branner and M. Kelstrup (eds), *Denmark's Policy towards Europe after 1945*, Odense University Press, 2000, 139–84.
2. The concepts 'composite state' and 'conglomerate state' today have become accepted as technical terms for the territorial states in Early Modern Europe. A definition is proposed by J.C.D. Clark in Østergård (1991a). The features of the British composite state are pursued in Clark (1989); for an examination of the phenomenon in a European context, see H.G. Koenigsberger (1989) and J.H. Elliot (1992). Early attempts to apply these terms in Danish and Nordic history include Ole Feldbæk 1992, Jens Rahbek Rasmussen 1995, and Harald Gustafsson 1994 and 1997.

3. According to the highly original research by Gunner Lind and others, the structural foundations for these legal innovations actually date back to the wars between 1614 and 1660, the Danish version of the European-wide military-political revolution of the seventeenth century (cf. Lind 1994, 1992).
4. That is, if we leave out the problem of the relations between Denmark, the Faroe Islands and Greenland. Their status is unclear in the Constitution of 1953. The Faroe Islands and Greenland enjoy varying forms of Home Rule within the Danish *Rigsfællesskab* (Commonwealth), but both demand some kind of national autonomy or even independence. The main reason for not treating this question is the relative size of the three parts of the state with 5.3 million Danish citizens confronted with fifty thousand Faroese and sixty thousand Greenlanders. For a fuller treatment, see Østergård 2002.
5. According to Barrington Moore, comparative studies may ignore small states because of their lack of originality and influence (Moore 1966: x). His use of the term 'small state' is a historical-sociological description rather than an expression of contempt for small countries, though it has often been perceived as such in the Netherlands and Scandinavia.

References

Brubaker, Rogers (1992) *Citizenship and Nationhood in France and Germany*. Cambridge, MA: Harvard University Press.

――― (1996) *Nationalism Reframed. Nationhood and the National Question in the New Europe*. Cambridge University Press.

Clark, J.C.D. (1991) 'Britain as a composite state', in U. Østergård (ed.), *Britian – Nation, State, Decline*, Special Issue of *Culture and History*. Copenhagen, 55–84.

Degn, Christian (1974) *Die Schimmelmanns im atlantischen Dreieckshandel. Gewinn und Gewissen*, Neumünster: Karl Wachholtz Verlag.

Elliot, J.H. (1992) 'A Europe of Composite Monarchies', *Past and Present* 137: 48–71.

Esping-Andersen, Gösta (1985) *Politics against Market. The Social Democratic Road to Power*. Princeton University Press.

Feldbæk, Ole (ed.) (1991–92) *Dansk identitetshistorie* I–IV, Kbh.: C.A. Reitzels Forlag.

―――(1992) 'Clash of Culture in a Conglomerate State: Danes and Germans in 18th Century Denmark' in C.V. Johansen et al. (eds), *Clashes of Culture*. Odense University Press, 80–93.

Feldbæk, Ole and Ole Justesen (1980) *Kolonierne i Asien og Afrika*. Kbh.: Politikens Forlag.

Frandsen, Steen Bo (1993) 'Jylland og Danmark – kolonisering, opdagelse eller ligeberettiget sameksistens?', U. Østergård (ed.), *Britian – Nation, State, Decline*, Special Issue of *Culture and History*. Copenhagen, 103–29.

――― (1995) 'The Discovery of Jutland: The Existence of a Regional Dimension in Denmark' in N.A. Sørensen (ed.), *European Identities, Cultural Diversity and Integration in Europe since 1700*. Odense University Press, 111–26.

――― (1996) *Opdagelsen af Jylland. Den regionale dimension i danmarkshistorien 1814–64*. Århus Universitetsforlag.

Gustafsson, Harald (1994) *Political Interaction in the Old Regime. Central Power and a Local Society in the Eighteenth-Century Nordic States.* Lund: Studentlitteratur.

—— (1997) *Nordens historia. En europeisk region under 1200 år.* Lund: Studentlitteratur.

Hansen, S.Å. (1970) *Early Industrialization in Denmark.* Kbh.: Academic Press.

Horstbøll, H., and U. Østergård (1990) 'Reform and Revolution. The French Revolution and the Case of Denmark', *Scandinavian Journal of History* 15: 155–79.

Japsen, Gottlieb (1983) *Den fejlslagne germanisering.* Åbenrå: Historisk Samfund for Sønderjylland.

Kautsky, Karl (1899) *Die Agrarfrage. Eine Uebersicht über die Tendenzen Landwirtschaft und die Agrarpolitik der Sozialdemokratie.* Stuttgart.

Knudsen, Tim (1992) 'A Portrait of Danish State-Culture: Why Denmark Needs Two National Anthems' in Morten Kelstrup (ed.), *European Integration and Denmark's Participation.* Copenhagen Political Studies Press, 262–97.

Koenigsberger, Helmut Georg (1989) 'Composite States, Representative Institutions and the American Revolution', *Historical Research* 62: 135–53.

Ladewig Petersen, Erling (ed.) (1984) *Magtstaten i Norden i 1600-tallet og dens sociale konsekvenser.* Odense Universitetsforlag.

Lahme, Norbert (1982) *Sozialdemokratie und Landarbeiter (1871–1901).* Odense University Press.

Lehmann, Orla (1861) 'For Grundloven. Tale ved en politisk Fest i Vejle 1861', *Efterladte Skrifter* IV, Kbh. 1874, 85ff.

Lenin, V. I. (1907) 'The Agrarian Program of the Social Democracy', in *Works* Vol. 13, Moscow 1964.

Lind, Gunner (1994) *Hæren og magten i Danmark 1614–1662.* Odense University Press.

Løfting, C., H. Horstbøll and U. Østergård (1989) 'Les effets de la révolution française au Danemark' in M. Vovelle (ed.), *L'image de la révolution française* I. Oxford: Pergamon Press, 621–42.

Moore Jr., Barrington (1966) *The Social Origins of Dictatorship and Democracy.* Boston: Beacon Press.

Østergård, Uffe (1984) 'Hvad er det danske ved danskerne?', *Den Jyske Historiker* 29–30, 85–134 (reprint 'Ydmyg selvhævdelse – en dansk kunstart', Thorkild Borup Jensen (red.), *Danske tilstande. En antologi af danske essays.* Kbh.: Schønbergs kulturelefanter 2000, 76–85.

—— (ed.) (1991) *Britain – Nation, State, Decline,* special issue of *Culture and History.* Copenhagen.

—— (1992) 'Peasants and Danes', *Comparative Studies in Society and History,* 5–31, reprinted in G. Eley and G. Suny (eds), *Becoming National. A Reader.* Oxford University Press 1996, 179–222.

—— (ed.) (1993) *Dansk identitet?* Århus Universitetsforlag.

—— (1995) 'Republican Revolution or Absolutist Reform?' in G.M. Schwab and J.R. Jeanneney (eds), *The French Revolution of 1789 and Its Impact.* Westport, CO: Greenwood Press, 227–56.

—— (1996a) 'Danmark og mindretallene i teori og praksis', J. Kühl (red.), *Mindretalspolitik.* Kbh.: DUPI, 44–105.

―― (1996b) 'The Nordic Countries: Roots of Cooperation and Early Attempts' in Péter Bajtay (ed.), *Regional Cooperation and the European Integration Process. Nordic and Central European Experiences*. Budapest: Hungarian Institute of International Affairs, 13–50.

―― (1997) 'The Geopolitics of "Norden" – States, Nations and Regions' in B. Stråth and Ø. Sørensen (eds), *The Cultural Construction of Norden*. Oslo: Scandanavian University Press, 25–71.

―― (1998) *Europa. Identitet og identitetspolitik*. Kbh.: Rosinante 1998/2000.

―― (2000a) 'Regions and Regionalism in Denmark', *Newsletter* 2. Århus: Jean Monnet Center, 4–13.

―― (2000b) 'Wie klein und homogen ist Dänemark eigentlich', *Ästhetik und Kommunikation* 107: 25–32.

―― (2002) 'The State of Denmark – Territory and Nation', *Comparare. Comparative European History Review* 2002: 200–19.

―― (2003a) 'Lutheranismen, danskheden og velfærdsstaten' Klaus Petersen (ed.), *13 historier om den danske velfærdsstat*. Odense: Syddansk Universitetsforlag, 27–36.

―― (2003b) 'For konge og fædreland. Universiteterne i den multinationale dansk-norsk-slesvigsk-holstenske Helstat', *Rubicon* 11(2): 17–41.

Rasmussen, Jens Rahbek (1995) 'The Danish Monarchy as a Composite State' in N.A. Sørensen (ed.), *European Identities, Cultural Diversity and Integration in Europe since 1700*. Odense University Press, 23–36.

Seip, J.A. (1958) 'Teorien om det opinionsstyrte enevelde', (norsk) *Historisk Tidssktift* 38: 397–463.

Simonsen, Henrik Bredmose (1990) *Kampen om danskheden. Tro og nationalitet i de danske kirkesamfund i Amerika*. Århus Universitetsforlag.

Sjøquist, Viggo (1966) *Danmarks udenrigspolitik 1933–1940*. Kbh.: Gyldendal.

Sørensen, N.A. (ed.) (1995) *European Identities, Cultural Diversity and Integration in Europe since 1700*. Odense University Press.

Stråth, Bo (1980) 'Illusory Nordic Alternative to Europe', *Cooperation and Conflict* 15: 103–14.

Wåhlin, Vagn, and Uffe Østergård (1975) *Klasse, demokrati og organisation. Politiserings- og moderniseringsprocessen i Danmark 1830–48 I–VI*, Aarhus Universitet.

CHAPTER 3
Denmark 1740–1940: A Centralized Cultural Community

Niels Kayser Nielsen

Every evening at about 6.20 P.M. – when the advertisements are over – TV 2, Denmark's second national and, in principle, public service-oriented television channel, broadcasts a weather report. The scenography is peculiar: placed out in the North Sea, the speaker hides the western part of Jutland most of the time, so that the viewers in this area are kept from seeing what the weather will be like the following day. The speaker's gaze is directed towards Zealand and the capital, Copenhagen. The situation is further complicated when the speaker is a woman: because of her position out in the North Sea, her bosom, depending somewhat on its size, covers most of Ringkøbing Fjord. It may be a pretty sight, but in this case the scope of the national weather forecast is further diminished.

The inhabitants of this part of Denmark and those who, like permanent tourists, live there about half the year view this with a degree of indulgence because they are so used to it. And so far, protests have not been heard over this obvious negligence either. The lack of protest can be regarded as implying that they do not perceive themselves, nor are they perceived as either an ethnic or a national minority entitled to special attention. They are, after all, part of the Danish population, but must accept playing second fiddle. This is a centuries-long tradition.

Still, this can very well raise a number of questions, for what is the reason that Danes from western Jutland do not object to the fact that their weather is left unmentioned? Is it a sign of inferiority or is it due to other circumstances? How did it come about that they accept themselves without hesitation as part of Denmark and the Danish nation even though they are neglected on the weather map?

Further complicating matters is the fact that down through Jutland runs one of the most radical linguistic dividing lines in all of Europe, namely, the differentiation between the preceding and the succeeding definite pronoun. In the Jutland dialect, 'the dog' is *æ hund,* just as in German it is *der Hund.* On the islands the pronoun is placed after the noun, as in Norwegian, Swedish, Icelandic, Romanian and Bulgarian, so that 'the dog' is *hunden.* Still, this linguistic difference has never given rise to demands of national differentiation. This may seem surprising considering, for instance, the long-lasting Norwegian struggle that started in 1850 over which language was the most legitimate one in Norway: the west Norwegian language mostly spoken by peasants and fishermen, or the east Norwegian, which was spoken by other, more trendsetting groups. This lack of protest also seems surprising if we recall the same conflict between the Swedish and Finnish languages in Finland, which has been a contributory factor in both culture and class struggles in Finland. In other words, we are left with the problem that a substantial part of the western Jutland population must tolerate being neglected, and the Danish public accepts this. Let us therefore attempt to find some possible explanations for the tolerance.

Absolute Nationalism – and Some Theses

The formative period of Danish nationalism belongs in the transitional phase between absolute monarchy and democracy, in that as an '-ism' it was constructed in the decades on both sides of the watershed year of 1850. On the other hand, there is no doubt that Danish national identity, viewed as a sense of domicile, loyalty to the crown and continuity in life conduct, goes several centuries back and probably has roots in the Middle Ages. However, nationalism does not arise from this sense of identity alone. Something else is necessary. In this connection it may be helpful to distinguish between nationalism *für sich* and nationalism *an sich.* By these concepts I am referring to the both cognitive and structural objective factors that encouraged and shaped nationalism. Nationalism *an sich* can be said to be nationalism that takes place without an actual master plan, and without nationalism being written above the entrance to these objective factors (Jansson 1994: 195).

I shall argue that by virtue of the Nordic countries' highly centralized governments and powerful armies, they had entirely different prerequisites for nationalism *an sich* than in the rest of Europe – apart from France and Prussia. I also shall argue that the preconditions were even stronger in the Danish-Norwegian monarchy, and that they were strongest in the most royal part of the composite state, that is the part constituted by the islands of Denmark and Jutland. Furthermore, it is in this uncommonly strong centralized hold on the population that we find the reason why the European linguistic division running down through Jutland never had national let alone federal consequences in Denmark. In addition, the absolute monarchy's creation of nationalism *an sich* was too strong. Finally, I argue that this precondition, in the form of nationalism *an sich* in all its structural objectivity, was in massive need of subjectivization, which is why a pronounced emphasis on cultural nationalism is evident in the construction of Danish nationalism, to the detriment of political nationalism. It is thus characteristic that the concept of citizenship that is such an integral part of the political culture of Sweden and Finland has never been quite as important in Denmark. In Denmark we also see a radically different development of democratic participation in decision making at the local level compared to the other Nordic countries. Denmark is a much more highly centralized country and is without the kind of civic participation found, for instance, in Sweden and Finland.

The World of Patriarchalism – and Pietism

Patriarchalism was the fundamental social ideology in traditional peasant society, and throughout more than two hundred years this ideology characterized all Nordic people from the king to the simplest peasant in both their personal conduct of life and their view of society and public authorities. The pivotal point in this ideology was Luther's lesson about the three estates: the church, the state and the household. It received its shortest and most significant expression in the *Haustafel* in 'Luther's Small Catechism' and was accessible to everyone in the Lutheran psalm book. In Denmark-Norway it was supposed to hang in every home. Ultimately, it expresses a theological world and social order (Bregnsbo 1997: 103). However, it says something about the theological world order's all-encompassing strength that it also had its social implications: the head of the family was the highest authority for his household, the king was the highest authority for all households, and God was the highest authority in relation to everyone, including the kings. Everyone was without rank and status, subject in respect to God as the supreme head of the family.

It was the clergyman's task as teacher of the other classes to guarantee the right faith. He was to inculcate the right faith upon the population, but also had to ensure that the householder complied. To help him with this, the householder could draw support from the service. Sunday after Sunday, from the pulpit, the clergyman had to explain the right moral norms and power relations to his congregation, and the householder could then receive his weekly influence (Korsgaard 2004: 62). In addition, the population became aware of this mode of thought through confirmation instruction, which became obligatory in Norway and Denmark in 1736. In the peasant schools that State Pietism introduced in both countries in 1739, Pontoppidan's exposition of Luther's Little Catechism was obligatory reading.

Both of these initiatives were part of a pietistic complex of reforms launched in and around 1740 which involved an 'in-depth Christianization' of society which eventually weakened the old religious norm for private life and society (Korsgaard 2004: 92; Kayser Nielsen 2009: 47–91). The aim was double. In part an internalization of faith was to occur and in part the state was to be under more surveillance, which required a greater degree of centralism. The local variety should be replaced by uniformity and a sense of community. In addition, central to Pontoppidan's explanation was an 'enlightenment of the heart' that aimed towards nothing less than a revival of mankind. That is to say, state centralism and homogenization should go hand in hand with an individualized internalization of faith. Moral self-reflection, rather than complaisance and subjection, was the goal. The Christian individual should learn to relate to himself as a morally self-regulating human being. A subjectivization was occurring (Korsgaard 2004: 101). It has also been said that a privatization and individualization of religion was taking place (Bregnsbo 2004: 105). The reborn, reflective human being should not be a product of the clergyman's discipline and dogma, but of his own choice and responsibility. Important to Pontoppidan was the idea of 'selfishness', which does not mean egoism, but rather self-responsibility and the ability to stand on one's own two feet (Horstbøll 2003). As early as the 1730s, the contours of the nineteenth century's self-reliant individual are faintly visible: a person who blossomed in the Free Church revivals, the self-organized associations and organizations as well as in liberalism. There was no doubt about the main tendency. Patriarchalism gradually disappeared as the dominant ideology, and beginning in the 1730s it was replaced by a field of conflict and interaction between state and individual. Besides religion, the agrarian reforms also contributed to changing things.

Social and Economic Atomization

The Nordic countries were very different in respect to their systems of government and economic conditions at the beginning of the nineteenth century. The most pronounced deviations existed at the outer limits, namely, in what has been referred to as 'the aristocratic republics' in Schleswig-Holstein and in so-called Gamla Finland in Eastern Finland and Karelia. If we content ourselves with looking at Denmark, the peninsula of Ejderstedt in western Schleswig was characterized by an almost capitalistic approach to territory and property. The peasant aristocracy traded family property easily and was not particularly disturbed by dutiful care for either family or their subordinates (Venborg Pedersen 2004: 173). Hence, Schleswig-Holstein accommodated both the most reactionary and economically the most modern parts of the composite state. But also in other parts of the composite state there were movements in a liberal direction.

In the course of the eighteenth century, the cooperative farming system gradually ended in the Danish corporate state, similar to what happened in Sweden and Finland. As a result, the individual farmer now had to manage on his own. In particular the peasants in the very rural areas were acutely aware of the fact that they were left to themselves and their own decisions. While individual independence increased, so did the risks that had to be taken. The atomization had begun: for better and for worse. At the same time, this meant an increase in class and social differentiation: the strong became stronger and the weak failed. This brought along with it considerable pride and self-assurance in those who did well. A large farmer from Løjt in northern Schleswig wrote in his diary in the 1740s: 'On the fifth of June the king was here at the castle; I was there too' (Fink 1955: 123). Around the middle of the eighteenth century, the system of cooperative farming was basically terminated in the area between Kolding and Aabenraa fjord and in parts of Angel and most of northern Frisland (Gregersen 1981: 406). These private measures were then followed up by the state, which through ordinances in 1768 and 1776 promised strong support for additional private initiatives, just as in 1771 an ordinance was issued on the enclosure of the royal areas of Holstein.

At this point the way was paved for the major reforms of the 1780s and 1790s in the remaining part of the composite state, reforms which contained operational aspects and a considerable socio-political element. Protection of the farmers so as to protect the interests of the peasantry was one of the leading issues of the absolute monarchy. Of course, this was not done for the sake of the peasant's well-being alone, nor was it based on a fundamental consideration for the right to private property, but very likely on a fiscal social consideration; the state was, among many other things, also interested in a solid taxation base. The general aim was sustainable agriculture, primarily based on a farming class with a class of agricultural labourers as support. This is evident from the special small-holdings legislation (Jensen 1975: 206). It is at the same time characteristic that in the Land Commission's view of the smallholder it now left the patriarchal principles behind to instead surrender itself to ideas of freedom. The contract between great landowner and smallholder should be a voluntary contract between free contracting parties. In other words, the smallholders found themselves in the modern liberal no man's land, where they were neither legal farmers nor employed farmhands. The duties of the smallholder were neither fixed by law nor controlled according to local custom, but should precisely be characterized by modern working conditions similar to those characterizing salaried work. The smallholders had become part of the agricultural labourers and were no longer peasantry. Atomization and uniform national rules were starting to penetrate through state intervention. This applied not only to the labour market but also in educational matters. In itself it had nothing to do with achieving national solidarity, but was largely an expression of a centralization and a homogenization that could later be filled with a significant national cultural content. State centralism and individual subjectivization went hand in hand.

Alphabetization

In 1721 Frederik IV issued provisions concerning the establishment of the so-called *rytterskoler*, Danish primary schools for the children of peasants who served in a royal house regiment, on the royal estates. The primary schools were succeeded by Christian VI's ordinance of 1739, which established parish peasant schools. The cost of this should be defrayed by the parish *hartkorn*, which was the Danish unit of land evaluation. As a result, the school matter was dependent on the individual landowner's point of view. But, paradoxically enough, it was precisely 'the leased state' (Løgstrup 1985), in the form of the power of the landowners, that along with Europe's new pedagogical ideas paved the way for a new departure. Following up on the agricultural reforms, progressive landowners like the brothers Reventlow, for example, took the initiative to establish new schools, while at the same time the state itself – in the framework of the system of poor relief – initiated teaching and schooling in the so-called 'spinning schools'. Both gathered momentum in the last couple of decades up to 1800 and continued into the nineteenth century. At the same time, it should be noted that J.L. Reventlow primarily had a limited target group in mind: the farmers' children. In his reform schools the children were divided according to 'vocational group'; greater demands were made on the children who were to become future landowners than on the future farmers, and more was expected of them than of the future day labourers. Children of farm labourers and cottagers did not need to learn anything about arithmetic or crops. Christian teachings were enough for them.

His brother Chr. D. Reventlow, in close cooperation with his vicar P.O. Boisen in Vesterborg on northern Lolland, had control of a third kind of teacher training in the enlightenment project of rationalism in 1780–1800: the so-called rectory seminaries that were launched with Vesterborg Seminary in 1801 (Markussen 1988). The aim of this kind of education was, beyond patriotism and Christianity, to develop the pupils' sense of diligence and enterprise. Boisen's seminary inspired a series of seminaries that saw the light of day after 1800: Brønd-byvester in 1802, Skårup in 1805, Borris in 1806, Besser on Samsø in 1812, Snedsted in 1812, Lyngby on Djursland in 1813 and Nylars in 1816. Later the seminary in Jonstrup was established, as well as Jelling in 1841 and Gedved in 1862, while Snedsted was transferred to Ranum in 1848. To a great extent, these rectory seminaries enjoyed the favour of the state. The teacher training they offered was considerably different from that offered by the rationalistic and philanthropic colleges of education established in the 1790s (Kayser Nielsen 2009: 104). With the rectory seminaries it was demonstrated that teacher training was a state matter, and that children belonged to the state. Important educationists and politicians were educated at these rectory seminaries. Thus, Christen Kold, who became a prominent Grundtvigian educationist, graduated from Snedsted in 1836, while Rasmus Sørensen, who played a major role both in the religious revivals and as a peasant politician, received his education at Vesterborg in 1816–18.

Nationalism 'an sich' – and the Need for New Ties

The state's various initiatives as regards national policies such as religious unification, schooling, improved infrastructure, improved communications, countrywide statistical surveys and private initiatives like the national newspapers did not have 'nationalism' as an explicit programme; even so, everywhere in Scandinavia they contributed to creating horizontal, nationally integrative and identity-building relations to replace the vertical estate society (Höjer 1999). In Denmark public statistics were resumed in the 1830s under the leadership of Jonas Collin; the most visible results were the censuses in 1834 and a new registration from 1844. From 1844 to 1853 Adolph Frederik Bergsøe issued *Den danske Stats Statistik* in four closely printed volumes that mapped monarchical society in detail (Bjørn 1998). Denmark became visible on maps and in terms of numerical size. The nation began to take shape here by virtue of economic, social and communicative processes that created a de facto nation without it being called a nation for that reason. These processes were more nationally integrative than the estate society's many small localities, but also more impersonal and abstract than the estate society's face relations and 'communalism' with particularistic special privileges.

On the other hand, the weakening of the traditional social and economic forms of affinity raised demands for new linkages which ultimately concerned a popularization of life. This popularization in itself involved the idea of close interdependence and at the same time more impersonal integration which was no longer traditionally cultural, but new, national and political. In order for this to take place it was necessary for the people to discover themselves and be educated as a people. In the first place, an sich by way of a certain standardization; secondly, this standardization and homogenization was to promote people's sense of being a nation.

The failure of the feudal corporations marked the rise of a 'personality principle' which progressively expanded within the framework of an increasingly homogenized nationalism *für sich*. This new 'personality principle' was expressed in two ways: in school and through the culture of associations and societies; in other words, inside both a state sphere and a civil society sphere. Both of these factors – the training received in the abstract notion of community and the standardization of knowledge and behaviour – paved the way for the nationalism that also reached the general public after initially having rattled as an '-ism' in the minds of philosophers and politicians, as well as in literature, in the first decades of the nineteenth century.

It may be provisionally concluded that nationalism is what finally links the peasantry as a people that had been atomized as a result of the agricultural revolution, pietism and the first revivals, but this nationalism does not appear as a *deus ex machina*. Next to the sense of national identity rooted in a connection with place and territory, which had already been in play for several centuries, it was promoted as an '-ism' by objective factors like education and agricultural reorientation. Without their actual impact nationalism would hardly have broken through as significantly and rapidly as it did in the decades leading up to and following 1850. In both cases it was a question of the state receiving a useful contribution from the population itself. The actors in the form of lay preachers and idealistic schoolteachers played a not insignificant role. The integrative function of education and the school also had driving forces from below. It was not Kant and Rousseau, Herder and Fichte who made the Nordic people national, but rather renewal, religion and school. The peasant school of 1814 was not introduced as a national school, but as a state school (Kayser Nielsen 2009: 93), and was an extension of the norm for compulsory school attendance that was introduced with the reform package in the 1730s. In the north the state came before the nation and the state furthered the nation – which then in return had to be pumped all the more with a cultural-national content. It was Grundtvigianism with the farmer as the focal point that became responsible for this task.

Popularization of Democracy

Contributing to paving the way for the breakthrough of Grundtvigian cultural-national general education in the second half of the nineteenth century was evening school instruction, which was a side benefit of the School Act of 1814. The result of this initiative was that more students attended evening schools than the otherwise so trendsetting Grundtvigian folk high schools (Gjelstrup 1979: 66). One can hardly ignore the fact that the evening schools established the necessary basis to be able to understand the folk high schools' more lofty national rhetoric later in the century. Again, we are dealing with a unifying educational prototype of nationalism which was supported by the book collections that were established around the parishes, for which the monarchical Royal Danish Society for Peasant Education, among other organizations, served as the prime mover. By 1844, over 440 collections like this had already been established, and more were set up after 1850; it is estimated that additionally almost 500 saw the light of day (Gjelstrup 1979: 76).

At the same time, when the peasants started being taxed and included in the state administration as a logical extension of the agricultural reforms, it was difficult to ignore the demand for influence. In Denmark, just like everywhere in the Nordic countries, this meant that in the period between 1850 and 1900 the peasant was mobilized in part on the municipal level and in part via the strong popular movements which branched off all the way down to civil society's culture of associations at the parish level. But the peasant was also capable of acting on his own.

Denmark witnessed a peasant movement in the 1840s. Next to Lolland-Falster and Langeland, Zealand was the part of the country where the copyhold system was still the most widespread, and Holbæk County was clearly in the lead, followed closely by Præstø County. Manors and estates with counts, barons and entailed property with large collections of farms characterized these counties and influenced them both economically and socially. It is thus no coincidence that the peasant movement originated in this part of the country. While other parts of the country became private property after the abolition of adscription, this had not occurred to the same extent on Zealand and Langeland. In Holbæk County in 1844 there were only 751 freeholder farms and inherited copyholds, and all of 3,647 copyholds (Larsen 1980: 16). Such an out-of-date phenomenon as villeinage also occurred in this county (Bjørn 1988: 112). Therefore, it cannot come as a surprise that a peasant movement arose here that advanced the peasants' cause in the assembly of the Estate Diet for the Islands of Denmark and initiated propaganda and organizational work. It was so pervasive that Holbæk County led the country in peasant politics in the 1840s. The growth in politicization was also furthered by the peasants (cf. below) having gained access to influence in the rural district councils. Holbæk County's peasant organization was thus established in 1843, which defied the squires and landowners at the general assembly of the Estates of the Realm and at popular meetings. The mass meeting at Ulkestrup Mark near Aamosen in 1845 gathered eight thousand participants. With Rasmus Sørensen and I.A. Hansen's weekly *Almuevennen* (peasant friend), which began in 1842, as the leading organ, people united around the demands for a common conscription policy – and thus not only the conscription of peasant lads – better popular education and the elimination of privileged *hartkorn* and the copyhold system. In addition to this was a liberal demand for freedom of trade for city and country, which naturally aroused the interest of the National Liberals. In May 1846 *Bondevennernes Selskab* (the Society of Friends of the Peasants) was established as a political organ whose function was to fight for these demands.

Holbæk County became a county heavily influenced by the Liberal Party. I.A. Hansen, the first great leader of the political party called *Venstre*, or the Left, had solid backing here. The Grundtvigians, on other side of the popular revival, albeit in a conflicting relationship of sorts with *Bondevennernes Selskab*, also had a strong foothold here. After 1864 *Bondevennernes Selskab* slowly withdrew from Danish politics, but after 1870 it was politically integrated in *Det forenede Venstre*, the United Left, and culturally overtaken by Grundtvigianism and its popular ideology. They had nonetheless been a lever for the successful struggle for the Constitutional Act and democracy in about 1850. The cooperation between the national-liberal metropolitan middle classes and *Bondevennernes Selskab* gave the democratic struggle popular support and political clout at the subsequent elections. The peasants could stand tall and declare that they had contributed to fighting for the Constitutional Act and democracy.

Municipal Mobilization – Differences and Similarities in Democracy

Highly contributory to the political mobilization of the peasant in the middle of the nineteenth century was the involvement of the peasant in the municipal administration that took place in these years. Those who primarily carried the costs of society, namely, the independent or farming peasants, should also have a certain influence – or, less positively perceived, assist the state officials who in the empty space between landowner administration and municipal government had enough to do and were pressed to the extreme (Christensen 1991: 16). But at the same time there were significant differences between the Nordic countries.

In Denmark, as in Norway, municipal self-governance involved administration on behalf of the state more than local involvement. The situation was radically different in Sweden and Finland with their *sockenstämmorna*, or municipal assemblies, which may be regarded as part of an interaction between state and local society (Österberg 1987, 1994). In other words, we see a double image where in the two Nordic countries with a history of absolutism – Denmark and Norway – it was a matter of filling an empty space after the demise of the absolute local administration, of renewing the official apparatus, which had reached the limit of its capacity, and of 'popularizing' the landowner administration of the locals; while in Sweden and Finland it was largely a matter of enhancing the efficiency of, and homogenizing, the particularistic patchwork quilt of *sockenstämmor*. Here it was necessary to set limitations and exercise financial restraint. The task of Norway and Denmark was to build out.

In 1814 Norway adopted a national democratic constitution that guaranteed a certain degree of national self-government, but it did not get a Constitutional Act for local government until 1837. Sweden had widespread local government with democratic features at the parish level and an Estate Diet. Finland had the same system of local government, but no national assembly between 1809 and 1863.

Thus, the Nordic countries displayed both similarities and differences as regards local government. In Denmark and Finland the state had greater control than was the case in Sweden and Norway. In Sweden, the state traditionally respected local government; in Norway, the peasants succeeded in wresting the power from the government officials in local communities (Fladby 1967; Døssland 2003). Wilfulness was a high priority in Norwegian local communities. In all the Nordic countries, however, it was primarily the peasants, and in particular the farmers, who were in control at the local level. This occurred in Sweden and Finland on the basis of broad support that advanced local government, while no arrangement like this existed in Denmark.

This can give rise to an additional comparison that is not without significance for the gradual development in the direction of democracy at the borderline between the administrative and self-government aspects. This is where the reorientation of the organizational structure of local administration with the relationship between 'everyone' and 'elite' enters the picture in the years 1840–1870. *Sockenstämman* in Sweden and Finland, which could comprise up to one hundred landed or affluent members of the local community, may be regarded as a general assembly. After 1842 and 1862 it was expanded with a *sockennämnd* as a kind of board of governors that nevertheless characteristically enough were placed under *stämman*, or the general assembly (Jansson 1987: 148). This naturally eased the transition to civil society's structure of voluntary associations and popular movements that became so dominant in Sweden and, albeit more state controlled, in Finland. In Denmark, however, the *stämman*, or general assembly, never ended up playing any role; starting in 1841, everything was taken care of by the parish council, the head of which was a mainly executive element – while Norway, with its double 'general assembly', constituted a middle position between the two extreme positions: administration on behalf of the state, and self-government. In Denmark local government was controlled in part by the county council and in part by the Ministry of the Interior. The ministry had no confidence in the abilities of the periphery and the province to manage the issues themselves. The dominance of the capital was alive and well after the formal abolition of absolute monarchy. The extreme centralism continued to prevail as a Danish characteristic; Norway had its distinct western Norwegian policies and its West Norwegian teachers, and Sweden and Finland had strong and independent parish-based self-government, a legacy from *sockenstämmorna*. This created space for a strong popular civil society with a highly diversified culture of associations out in the provinces. This culture of associations was not a Grundtvigian invention, as is sometimes claimed, but the Grundtvigians gave voice to it and interpreted it as an expression of national solidarity (Kayser Nielsen 2009: 239).

That a need arose for alternative forums in the shape of voluntary associations and popular movements as a result of disparities in the local community's economic, social and cultural interests can to a certain degree also be explained from the inadequately democratic feature in the landowner-dominated municipal administration of the local community. In Denmark this was quite extreme in the sense that the local administration was formed in such a way that the governing body was too predominant and the general assembly too scarce. It therefore became necessary – in particular during the 'constitutional struggle' when important socio-economic areas at the national level could not be managed as a result of the general 'policy of obstruction' – to address the self-organized organization of civil society through a culture of associations. That Denmark appears to be a country with a tradition of associations is in other words first of all determined by a democratic insufficiency and the political standstill in the final quarter of the nineteenth century. The state did not interfere in the autonomous economic organizations that arose from this. On the other hand, from its start in 1861, when the rifle clubs saw the light of day, the cultural and national association tradition was supported by the state, as were the Grundtvigian folk high schools which arose in the second half of the nineteenth century. In these forums political nationalism – or state citizenship, as it was also called – ceded its place to cultural nationalism. State power and cultural nationalism went hand in hand – in spite of surface ideological differences.

The Grundtvigian Culture of Associations and Centralism at the Local Level

In the Nordic countries cultural nationalism was most clearly expressed by Grundtvigianism and Fennoman popular heritage (Alapuro 1987, 1999; Stenius 1980, 1993), which received an incredibly strong organizational platform in rural Finland starting in about 1890 in the shape of a youth association movement, which is a Finnish hallmark (Åkerblom 1935; Kayser Nielsen 2004b). In both cases, it was a question of a politically uninterested popular spirit that exclusively set its stakes on a cultural nationalism with the farmer as the lever. Comparing Danish and Swedish folk high school culture, a head of a Grundtvigian folk high school has self-critically pointed out that this resulted in the sailor, symbolizing far-sightedness and contact with the surrounding world, being forgotten as a Danish cultural icon. The country closed in on itself and its own determined, industrious self-sufficiency. Denmark was portrayed as an idyll with the peasant playing the role of custodian (Jensen 1959: 96).

For this very same reason neither the Danish folk high school movement nor the Finnish youth association movement cared about the central circles of power. Neither of them contested the economic power of the Copenhagen merchant middle class's economic power or the elite role of the academic middle class in Finland (Klinge 1996). On the other hand, they held considerable power in the local community, most clearly in Denmark by means of the almost matter-of-course political power of the farmers in the parish councils. In Denmark, a stay at a folk high school could be the ticket to a seemingly apolitical career as parish king, where, after having demonstrated the ability to say a couple of nice words at a party in the community centre or at a general assembly, it was possible to secure influence as a patriarchically minded parish council member. In the world of the folk high school, people learned the power of the word, which later became a major advantage on the home court.

Just as the universities educated the government officials who administered state power, so the folk high schools educated the farmers who took power locally. The folk high schools were run by a couple of handfuls of families who knew each other privately and who were intermarried. People whose surnames were Appel, Boisen, Trier, Begtrup or Dahlerup cast long shadows. The university-educated middle class had one area of influence, and the folk high school-educated farmers had another. The world of the folk high school did not think twice about renouncing centralized power and the universities if only they could guarantee themselves patriarchal power at the local level. Political democracy and state citizenship were renounced in recognition of their strong influence on cultural nationalism and on the interpretation of nationalism as a peasant nationalism.

However, this patriarchal local power was always kept at bay by the culture of associations at the local level, which was of prime importance in local life at the parish level. Even the greatest parochial magnate could not deny the importance of the community centre and the activities that went on there. The state government also needed to have its legitimacy in the local community by virtue of a culture of associations based on respect for democratic opinion. This was much stronger in Norway and Sweden, but was also present in Denmark and Finland. In the latter it turned out that the concept of people, in spite of the risk of a patronizing interpretation of it, was after all a double-edged sword.

A contributory reason for this democratic emphasis all the same was, besides the base of support in the associations, that Grundtvigian peasant culture was also based on the idea of free and equal peasants. Grundtvigian historical narrative operated according to the so-called 'u model', where the peasants were first free and equal in the Middle Ages, then cowed by the squires for several centuries, and finally acquired power and honour once more in the course of the nineteenth century. However historically imprecise this myth might be, its historical effect was incredibly strong. It put an effective damper on possible attempts at establishing far too strong a concentration of power at the local level. The Grundtvigian myth of history had its own core conducive to democracy.

Local civil society was thus not, as the Grundtvigian tradition of history often presents it, influenced by a 'rebellious urge', 'strategy from below' or idea of self-administration, but rather mediated, though not determined by, the particular development of local administration in a Denmark that carried on the monarchical tradition of centralism. The culture of associations is not an expression of a particularly Danish tradition; rather it was created by the circumstances: a rigidly organized tradition of local administration. When the need arose in the second half of the nineteenth century, this administration, which emphasized a parish council as a 'board without a general assembly', had to be supplemented by an association-based civil-society structure that placed emphasis on the general assembly and its choice of governing body. With its structure of associations, Denmark became a Nordic country to a much greater degree than before. The institution of the parish council had certainly incorporated itself in the Nordic tradition of local government, but in a particularly un-Nordic way. Not until the introduction of the culture of associations was the Nordic identity of Denmark complete.

The formally civic structure of associations and the essentially Grundtvigian culture of associations as regards content supplemented the characteristic state control of the administrative structure, and as a result Denmark acquired what Henrik Stenius has referred to as a Danish 'dual public', which he considers a Danish characteristic (Stenius 1993). It goes without saying that this characteristic is not a Grundtvigian invention, but that Grundtvigians have been prominent administrators of one half of it, just as these circles, when it was first established, were good at ensuring it state support so that it could survive.

In spite of being strongly characterized by national culture, this civic culture of associations has nevertheless also been characterized by strong democratic forces. It would turn out to be significant since the anti-democratic forces appeared on the political scene in the interwar period. At this point the symbiosis between centrally supported state citizenship and a Grundtvigian version of cultural nationalism crystallized with Social Democracy (Kayser Nielsen 2009: 441–447).

Heritage and New Challenges

In spite of the failings discussed above as well as attacks from both left and right, Danish democracy enjoyed considerable legitimacy until the interwar period. But this legitimacy was measured in respect to a different sociality from that which characterized the 1930s with its economic and social crises and fascistic solutions to political governance in large parts of Europe. The major problem in the Nordic countries in this period consisted of adjusting and updating. They had to prevent the crises from leading to political instability and to ensure the modernization of their democracy. Key in this situation was the notion of *folk*.

The problem was that at the beginning of the 1930s a political culture had not yet been developed that was well-suited to mobilizing the masses and combining mass politics and the sense of *folk*, and not at all in a modern defence of democracy and parliamentarism. The major task was in other words to give the concept of *folk* a political dimension – beyond its cultural and national concept. It was therefore an important task for the apologists of democracy to create a combination of mass and *folk*. It was not enough to safeguard democracy as a formal system. Social and cultural backing was also necessary. The civic concept of 'demos' and the national cultural concept of 'ethnos' had to be united – not as they were in the nineteenth century, but in a new version for the masses (Kayser Nielsen 2002, 2004a).

In this light it is probably worth considering whether the Nordic countries' modernization programmes in the last half of the 1930s and again after 1945 in fact provide evidence that they not only took exception to fascism and Nazism but also learned from them. In the fascistic welfare states the democrats learned that individual freedom is not enough to ensure the loyalty of the population in the era of mass politics. People do not live on freedom alone. Mass loyalty could also be guaranteed by beating the drum for an organic sense of national solidarity (ethnos) with emphasis on tradition, language and culture. Fascism and Nazism offered a particular combination of modernism and anti-modernism that provided inspiration far beyond Italy and Germany. Fascism was by no means an impossibility in the Nordic countries in the 1930s. Certain forces in agriculture and in the urban middle classes probably felt its attraction. This is evident for one thing from the reactions in the daily press when Niels Bukh returned from Germany in 1933 and praised Nazism in high tones (Bonde 2001: 265). The opinions about his acclamation were strongly divided. The middle class press and parts of the *Venstre* press had difficulty standing aloof from Nazism. On the whole, people were not necessarily blamed for expressing thoughts critical of democracy (Nissen and Poulsen 1963). Decisive in this connection was the Grundtvigian attitude. With its national pathos and its emphasis on cultural nationalism, Grundtvigianism might have been tempted by fascism.

Cultural Nationalism – a Necessary Evil?

The 1930s witnessed a highly charged polemic within the folk high school movement between 'the humanists', that is, the circles that involved science as a legitimate collaborator, and 'the mythologists' who did not care for science in the slightest, but championed the Grundtvigian interpretation of Nordic mythology as truth (Ægidius 1992). This final viewpoint had proponents like Anders Nørgaard and Aage Møller. Aage Møller had established Rønshoved Folk High School at Flensborg Fjord in 1921 as a national bridge towards the south. His high school was established on the idea that the school should be led by a single important personality around whom a series of specialist teachers arrayed themselves. Aage Møller wrote an article entitled 'Vaarbrud' (the first awakening of spring) in the high school yearbook of 1933, in which he enthusiastically praised the new times south of the border. Descent and blood and right of citizenship were also discussed (Ægidius 1992: 89). In the same yearbook there was an article by Frede Bording, who under the heading 'Heritage and Race' also reflected a certain flirtation with Nazi thoughts. However, Aage Møller and Frede Bording never did become Nazis. Nationalism prevented them from this. Their opposition to Germany was greater than their enthusiasm for fascism. The same was true for the majority of their supporters.

The non-fascistic Grundtvigian movement, the fascistic Niels Bukh and the real Nazis all used a bombastic 'Nordic' rhetoric. Much of the same vocabulary and inventory of symbols recurred in all three circles. All three referred often to Nordic mythology and the heroic past. The use of Nordic history – not least the Viking Age and the rich Middle Ages – was also common property. The same was true for an idealistic world view and an idealistic view of mankind with an explicit criticism of any kind of materialism. An additional common characteristic was pronounced nationalism, although while fascists and Nazis underlined the national bond of blood, the Grundtvigians regarded language and history as the basis of the national principle. A certain fascination with irrationalism, based on myths and rituals as a contrast to 'breathless' rationalism and science, was also clear among the Grundtvigians, along with the view of society as an organism and the idea that the individual should submit to the community. This final characteristic was especially evident in the enthusiasm for rallies and large turnouts where songs, flags and mythological signs and symbols were frequently used as a contrast to modern urban civilization's 'culture of reason', which characterized both Marxism and liberalism.

But there were also crucial differences. One crucial difference was probably the attitude to war and the use of violence. This did not appeal to the Grundtvigians, in that most of them harboured a distinct sense of opposition to and disdain for physical force by virtue of influence from the popular democracy in which they were imbibed with the dialogical principle of the culture of associations and community centres. Verbal fights were acceptable, but not physical ones. Dialogues, and in the worst case, arguments, should lead to conflict resolution, not bodily 'speech'. A strong man should be able to talk rather than beat people into place. The fact that Grundtvigianism had always valued cultural nationalism and the nation higher than political civic nationalism made it, as a kind of irony of history, well-suited to function as a bulwark against the fascistic threat. Furthermore, its close connections to the culture of associations of Danish civil society had largely made it impermeable to anti-democratic influences. The national cultural community stood its democratic test – in spite of everything.

Notwithstanding shared ideals, shared vocabulary and symbols, and shared enemies in socialists, liberalists and breathless materialists, an actual political collaboration between Grundtvigians and fascists never came about. The Grundtvigians as a movement never gave away democracy – in spite of certain reservations. At a big meeting in Odense in April 1934, with an audience of one and a half thousand, matters were settled: freedom and democracy should be the ideal, people should beware and not let themselves be fooled by the enemies of freedom (Nissen 1994: 183). This basically involved a defence of democracy, albeit the view of parliamentarism was more hesitant. Paradoxically enough, it was the fact that Grundtvigians and fascists spoke the same symbolic language that prevented fascism from gaining a political foothold. The position was already occupied, but by people with an entirely different goal from that of making Denmark fascist. As John T. Lauridsen has put it, the Danish Nazis could not offer potential sympathizers anything in the area of culture that they could not already find elsewhere. The cultural conception of the party was in agreement with large segments of the population, and its view of art and culture was largely shared by rural constituencies and the conservative party, and in part the social-democratic public (Lauridsen 2002: 208). And as concerns the outer form of politics, the Conservative Youth also had something to offer. By emphasizing *folk* as ethnos, cultural nationalism made sure that it took care of all the 'dirty' work.

Conclusion

It is therefore not a question of a conflict of interests between state centralism and Grundtvigianism, the two biggest '-isms' in Danish history during the last couple of centuries. Grundtvigian ideology has certainly been characterized as seeing itself as a civic anti-state movement, but in reality it was a relationship of complementation. It was thus also relatively easy for Social Democracy in the 1930s to link these two '-isms' together. Initiated by the party programme of 1934, which included a shift from a class-struggle party to a national popular party, they harmonized the two traditions with the smallholder and schoolteacher party, *Det Radikale Venstre*, the Danish Social-Liberal Party, as a faithful attendant. In this way, Denmark also got its version of the common Nordic redgreen cooperation, but with a centralistic heritage that is so strong and so long-lasting that it is hardly visible, and has always been presented as a feeling of national solidarity. People are so used to this combination of centralism and national solidarity, and to the province playing second fiddle, that not even the otherwise so cantankerous fishermen on the west coast grumble about being offered a peripheral position. They content themselves with shaking their heads.

References

Alapuro, Risto (1987) 'De intellektuella, staten och nationen', *Historisk Tidskrift för Finland*, 72(4).
―――― (1999) 'Social Classes and Nationalism: The North-East Baltic', in Michael Branch (ed.), *National History and Identity*. Helsingfors: Finnish Literature Society. Studia Fennica Ethnologica 6.
Bjørn, Claus (1988) 'Landbruget 1830–1860 – socialstruktur og landbopolitik', in Claus Bjørn (ed., in collaboration with Troels Dahlerup, S.P. Jensen and Erik Helmer Petersen), *Det danske landbrugs historie*, vol. 3. Copenhagen: Landbohistorisk Selskab.
―――― (1998) 'Den danske stat ved indgangen til 1848', in Claus Bjørn (ed.), *1848 – det mærkelige år*. Copenhagen: Museum Tusculanum.
Bonde, Hans (2001) *Niels Bukh. En politisk-ideologisk biografi*. Copenhagen: Museum Tusculanum.
Bregnsbo, Michael (1997) *Samfundsorden og statsmagt set fra prædikestolen*. Copenhagen: Museum Tusculanum.
―――― (2004) Præster under pres. – Den danske statskirkegejstligheds reaktioner på udfordringen fra Oplysningstiden i 1790'erne, *Den jyske Historiker* 105.
Christensen, Harry (1991) 'De unge kommuner 1837/41–1867/68', in Per Boje et al. (eds), *Folkestyre i by og på land. Danske kommuner gennem 150 år*. Herning: Poul Kristensen.
Døssland, Atle (2003) 'Bønder, bøker og politikk. Sammenheng mellom skriftkultur og politisk mobilisering i Noreg på 1800-talet', *Norsk Historisk Tidsskrift* 2.
Fink, Troels (1955) *Rids af Sønderjyllands historie*. Copenhagen: Schultz.
Fladby, Rolf (1967) 'Bønder og embetsmenn i lokalstyringen etter 1837', *Norsk Historisk Tidsskrift* 1.
Gjelstrup, Ejnar (1979) *Veje til livslang uddannelse*. Esbjerg: Sydjysk Universitetsforlag.
Gregersen, Hans Valdemar (1981) *Slesvig-Holsten før 1830*. Copenhagen: Politiken.
Höjer, Henrik (1999) 'Snabbätning, siffror och samhällsförändring. Något om statistikens roll i det svenska nationsbygget', in Lars Pettersson (ed.), *I nationens intresse. Ett och annat om territorier, romaner, röda stugor och statistik*. Uppsala: Opuscula Historica Upsaliensia 29.
Horstbøll, Henrik (2003) 'Læsning til salighed, oplysning og velfærd', *Fortid og Nutid* 2.
Jansson, Torkel (1987) *Agrarsamhällets förändring och landskommunal organisation. En konturteckning av 1800-talets Norden*. Uppsala: Studia Historica Uppsaliensia 139.
―――― (1994) 'Samhälle – stat – nation. En af 1800-talets integrationsprocesser. Eksempel från Balto-Skandinavien', in *Det 22. nordiske historikermötet. Rapport 1 – Norden og Baltikum*. Oslo.
―――― (1995) 'Från stormakt till smånation. En väv av ekonomisk-politiska och socio-kulturella trådar', in Stellan Dahlgren, Torkel Jansson and Hans Norman (eds), *Från stormakt till smånation*. Stockholm: Tiden.

Jensen, Bernhard (1959) *Nordens Kavalerfløj*. Copenhagen: Gyldendal.
Jensen, Hans (1975) *Dansk jordpolitik 1757-1919*, vol. 1. Copenhagen Selskabet for udgivelse af kilder til dansk historie.
Kayser Nielsen, Niels (2002) 'Demos, ethnos, oikos – en nordisk historie', *Scandia* 2, 297-317.
―――― (2004a) 'Demokrati og kulturel nationalisme i Norden i mellemkrigstiden – en realpolitisk højredrejning?', *Svensk Historisk Tidskrift* 4, 581-603.
―――― (2004b) 'Foreningsliv i mellemkrigstidens Sydösterbotten og Midtjylland', in *Historisk Tidskrift för Finland* 89(4): 434-56.
―――― (2009) *Bonde, stat og hjem. Nordisk demokrati og nationalisme fra pietismen til 2. verdenskrig*. Aarhus: Aarhus Universitetsforlag.
Klinge, Matti (1996) *Finlands historia*, vol. 3. Helsingfors: Schildts.
Korsgaard, Ove (2004) *Kampen om folket. Et dannelsesperspektiv på dansk historie gennem 500 år*. Copenhagen: Gyldendal.
Larsen, Helge (1980) *Avis, egn og folk*. Holbæk: Holbæk Venstreblad.
Lauridsen, John T. (2002) *Dansk nazisme 1930-45 – og derefter*. Copenhagen: Gyldendal.
Løgstrup, Birgit (1985) 'Den bortforpagtede statsmagt. Godsejeren som offentlig administrator i det 18. århundrede', in *Bol og By 1*.
Markussen, Ingrid (1988) 'Christian Ditlev Reventlow og skolerne på Christianssæde', in *Lolland-Falster Historiske Samfunds Årbog*.
Nissen, Gunhild (1994) *Udfordringer til højskolen. Danske folkehøjskoler 1844 til 1994*. Foreningen for Folkehøjskolers Forlag.
Nissen, Henrik S. and Henning Poulsen (1963) *På dansk friheds grund. Dansk Ungdomssamvirke og De ældres Råd 1940-45*. Copenhagen: Gyldendal.
Österberg, Eva (1987) 'Svenska lokalsamhällen i förändring ca. 1550-1850. Participation, representation och politisk kultur i den svenska självstyrelsen', *Svensk Historisk Tidskrift* 3.
―――― (1994) 'Vardagens sträva samförstånd. Bondepolitik i den svenska modellen från vasatid till frihetstid', in Gunnar Broberg, Ulla Wikander and Klas Åmark (eds), *Tänka, tycka, tro. Svensk historia underifrån*. Stockholm: Ordfront.
Stenius, Henrik (1993) 'Den politiska kulturen i Nordens ontologi. Modell eller icke? Vara eller icke vara', in Godelieve Laureys, Niels Kayser Nielsen and Johs. Nørregaard Frandsen (eds), *Skandinaviensbilleder*. Gent, Amsterdam and Groningen: TijdSchrift voor Skandinavistiek, Jaargang 14(1).
―――― (1980) 'The Breakthrough of the Principle of Mass Organization in Finland', *Scandinavian Journal of History*, 5.
Venborg Pedersen, Mikkel (2004) *Ejderstedt. Skitser fra et landskab 1650-1850*. Copenhagen: Frilandsmuseet.
Ægidius, Jens Peter (1992) *Bragesnak 2. Den mytologiske tradition i dansk folkeoplysning i det tyvende århundrede (1910-1985)*. Odense: Odense Universitetsforlag.
Åkerblom, K.V. (1935) *Johannes Klockars. En folkbildningens banérförare*. Vasa: Finlands svenska nykterhetsförbund.

CHAPTER 4
The Making of Sweden

Björn Wittrock

Sweden in the Early Twenty-First Century

In 2003 two events in Sweden, beside the tragic murder of the young foreign minister, stood out in the stream of events. First, it was the year commemorating the seven hundredth anniversary of the birth of St Birgitta, the only saint of Scandinavia properly canonized by the Pope, and one of three patron saints of Europe and the European Union. Second, in a referendum a clear majority of the Swedish people rejected the third step of European Monetary Union and the acceptance of the Euro as the new currency.

The first event underscored the fact that in the course of the twentieth century the sentiments of earlier ages with a more or less openly expressed distrust of Catholicism had come to an end. Sweden had of course been part of Western Christendom for a millennium, but now it made it clear to the world that it had left behind the earlier self-image of Sweden as a country that in a harsh environment represented more genuine virtues than those of superficially cultured but dubious European elites. As late as the 1960s leading social democratic intellectuals still spoke of the three 'c's that provided grounds enough for Sweden not to join the European Economic Community, namely the fact that this community stood for a Europe that was capitalist, conservative and Catholic. In 2003, such vocabulary would have been utterly incomprehensible. Nor would it have occurred to many people in 2003 to disturb the sequence of celebrations of St Birgitta by pointing out that her role was not only religious but also political, and that she acted in a context of, and to some extent as a spokesperson for, a fierce aristocratic opposition to King Magnus Eriksson of Sweden and Norway, a King who with meagre resources was trying to hold together – against Russians in the east and Danes and Germans in the south – the largest kingdom in Europe, stretching from Lake Ladoga in the east to Greenland in the west.

The second event occurred nine years after Sweden had joined the European Union and two years after Sweden had exercised the presidency of the Union in a way that stood out as an epitome of competence, efficiency and commitment to the Union and its eastern enlargement. It meant the largest defeat of any Social Democratic prime minister in the history of the nation and opened up a chasm of distrust in a country which had for decades, not to say centuries, been characterized by the loyalty of its people towards its governments. It also made clear that at the beginning of the twenty-first century Sweden was the only country in the European Union where the overwhelming majority of the left wing of the Social Democratic Party, including five cabinet ministers, and all of the rest of the left, including the postcommunist party and the Greens, were joined in opposition to full membership in the EMU.

Knowledge Interests and Narratives

If the first event signals a rapprochement with the mainstream, the second suggests that Sweden is still in many respects a country apart. Taken together, they thus raise questions about its position in Europe. Reflections on that subject have mostly been guided by one of three knowledge interests, all of which apply to Nordic countries in general as well as to Sweden in particular.

First, since the second half of the twentieth century by far the most prominent focus has been on the virtues of an enlightened and efficient form of society that is taken to combine an extensive and generous welfare state with economic and technological performances second to none. Let us call this knowledge interest – which appears in a range of varieties, mostly social democratic or left socialist but sometimes also liberal and even conservative – 'socio-political'.

Second, there has always been a knowledge interest that might be termed a 'heroic narrative' one. The focus here has normally not been on the modern era but on two other epochs when achievements in the high North were extraordinary, one of them being the hundred-year-long period between 1620 and 1720 when Sweden was a European great power. The political tone of works on this era has varied from the Enlightenment voice of Voltaire in his biography of Charles XII, to national conservative literature at the turn of the nineteenth century, to late twentieth century meticulous historical scholarship that has made clear the immense human suffering inherent in the deeds figuring in the heroic narratives of earlier times.

This genre of knowledge interest has also had a focus on the era around the turn of the first millennium AD when the Vikings, whether West Scandinavian Norsemen or East Scandinavian 'Varangians', were exploring a world of trade and conquest that eventually came to link Central Asia, the Russian rivers, the Baltic, the North Sea, the British Isles, Iceland, Greenland and even the eastern coastline of North America. Sometimes literature in this second category borders on a third knowledge interest that may be called cultural or even 'civilizational'. This interest is ultimately premised on a notion that the Northern lands embody a different type of deep-seated cultural patterning. Interestingly, this idea is taken up in perhaps the most famous work on the history of civilizations ever written, namely in Arnold Toynbee's magnum opus, *A Study of History*.

The 'Abortive' Norse Civilization

In his monumental work Toynbee traced the development of global history in terms of the rise and decline or survival of twenty-one different civilizations. In outlining the history of Europe, the history of Scandinavia presented Toynbee with a problem. Scandinavia had undeniably come to be part of the world of Western Christendom. In its early history, however, it constituted something of a civilization of its own, an 'abortive' civilization in Toynbee's terminology. In the centuries around the turn of the first millennium AD these Northern peoples came, in Toynbee's view, to exert a more significant influence on European and indeed global history than the Germanic tribes south of the Baltic, which through their conquest of and assimilation to the mores of the Latin lands of Europe had dealt a final blow to the Roman Empire.

In Toynbee's vivid prose, 'Scandinavian expansion in the eighth to eleventh centuries after Christ surpassed the Celtic expansion of the fifth to third centuries BC both in extension and intensity'. However, this period of expansion ended with Christianization:

> In the Scandinavian kingdoms of Russia, Denmark and Norway the formal act of conversion to Christianity was imposed upon the people wholesale by the arbitrary fiat of three Scandinavian princes who reigned contemporaneously by the end of the tenth century ... Thus Scandinavian society was not only conquered but was partitioned, for Orthodox Christendom, which had borne its share of the Viking onslaught, shared also in the religious and cultural counter-offensive.

With the benefit of hindsight the Christianization of the Northern Isles and peninsulas and of the Northern forest areas of what are now the Nordic countries and Russia may appear as the inevitable evolution of historical progress. The Christianization of the Northern lands, however, was an uneven and complex process, full of advances and setbacks and with century-long stretches of time that saw the coexistence of Christian and Norse religion. It was also a process that occurred in different forms in different parts of Scandinavia. In the end it came to mean the replacement of Norse cosmology with a Christian one, though pieces of the old cosmology, itself a complex and layered mythology with different roots, remained in customs and tales. In the Scandinavian context the memory of pre-Christian religion and beliefs was for a long time a more recent and living reality than in most other parts of Europe. One small sign of this was the fact that conversion to Christianity did not necessarily entail the adoption of a Christian name, and traditional Norse names continued to be used. But Christianity entailed a new type of historical consciousness and the repression of an earlier one, the richness of which we can now only catch glimpses of in the Icelandic Sagas, many of them referring to Scandinavian events.

Toynbee's work suggests that in the years around the turn of the first millennium AD the Northern lands become more clearly demarcated from neighbouring polities. The lasting effects of the differences, a kind of cultural fault-line, became visible in the course of the twelfth and thirteenth centuries. They came to mean that despite the geographic proximity to the German lands and despite the web of close interactions between the North and these lands, there remained a cultural distance that was never to be fully bridged. At a time when in the rest of Western continental Europe feudal relationships became institutionalized, this did not occur on anything like a similar level, even in Denmark, the southernmost Scandinavian country.

Another deeper fault-line that opened up was the one distinguished by Toynbee, namely the fact that Scandinavia proper was Christianized from the south and the west, but for the Scandinavian Rus in Kiev, Novgorod and along the great rivers, the Dnepr and the Volga, it was from the southeast. At the time of Christianization, the difference between Latin and Byzantine Christendom was hardly of decisive importance. More importantly, extensive networks of trade, exchange and also princely intermarriage, which had linked (not only during Viking times but probably for several centuries before) Western and Central Asia via the rivers in what is now Russia and the Ukraine to the Baltic and the North Sea (Bolin 1953), broke up under pressure from states which took control of exchange routes in their domains. Once this had occurred, rivalry between the incipient Scandinavian and Russian states, particularly Sweden and Novgorod, and later Muscovy, crystallized into a pattern of conflicts that was to last for most of the rest of the second millennium AD. In contrast, relations to the West during most of the rest of the millennium were – for most of Scandinavia, including Sweden – characterized not only by the absence of armed conflict, but by a sense of distant familiarity.

Cultural Crystallization and State Formation in a Non-Feudal Context

Scandinavian history, after the period of European-wide cultural crystallization in the eleventh to thirteenth centuries, evolved within the broad parameters set by this process. Within this framework Scandinavian and Swedish history is to a large extent a history of the complex and to some extent unique ways in which state formation and state contestation were shaped in a context of rather particular forms of class division and political representation.

The Swedish state that was constituted in the thirteenth century also, from that period and until the early nineteenth century, included present-day Finland as an integral part of the realm. It was, together with a small number of other political entities in Europe, including England, France, Poland and Denmark, among the states in Europe that had the longest continuous histories, and that early on acquired features of a proto-national character. It was, however, a state that operated within the constraints set by its economic foundations and the cultural faultlines indicated, and by ongoing interstate conflicts along those lines.

The country was one of the largest but also one of the least populated in Europe. The rulers were time and again faced with the dilemma that they confronted external enemies from considerably more populous, and often also economically better endowed, countries. In contrast to the situation in most of the rest of Europe they also had to deal with an aristocracy that was relatively small and lacking in wealth, and a substantial free-holding peasantry with some degree of political representation. This meant first of all that the more or less normal European – but also Japanese and Iranian – solution to the problem of rulership and warfare in a situation of extensive territory and limited capacity for the central control and mobilization of the means of violence – the 'feudal alternative' – was not a viable option. There was simply not a sufficiently strong aristocracy, with a sufficiently large resource base to draw from, to whom these powers could be devolved.

Second, strict limits were also set to the other standard solution to the problem of resource mobilization for war and political control, namely centralized despotic or semi-despotic rule. The basic reasons for this are that such a strategy presupposes first, a relatively large resource base; second, sufficient manpower to enable the establishment of a relatively large internal apparatus of control and repression; and third, relatively low costs of such repression, having a population sufficiently subjugated for a sufficiently long historical period. In the Swedish context, none of these three conditions was satisfied to a sufficient degree.

Thus, from the constitution of the realm until the early nineteenth century, a state developed through unusual but rather efficient techniques for the extraction of economic resources, the mobilization of human manpower and their transformation into means of control and of violence. In the first half of the millennium, this state was still in a process of gestation. In the course of the sixteenth century, however, an early modern, distinctly Swedish state was consolidated, and the Reformation helped to secure its financial basis.

During this phase of state transformation, Sweden played a unique role in an all-European perspective, particularly in the so-called Great Power period of 1620–1720. Despite many points of resemblance to absolutist states of the time, it had some characteristics that were only to be seen in other states in Europe during the twentieth century and some which still remain unique.

Swedish Exceptionalism: From Total Mobilization to the Freest Country in Europe

The early stages of the rise to Great Power status are to be found in developments during the 1610s and 1620s at a time when Sweden had been involved in a succession of wars against Denmark and Poland, and when Russia, during the Time of Troubles, became an arena for internal conflicts and external aggression. In Sweden in this period the king and his council made a series of strategic decisions with long-term consequences. One was the decision not to decommission parts of the army after the conclusion of peace treaties with former enemies, but rather to increase its strength. Other decisions pertain to the training of a new and more competent civil service, and of a new Lutheran clergy loyal to the state and capable of transmitting a message of obedience and belief to the population at large. This led to the resurrection of the old University of Uppsala and the creation of new universities in other parts of the realm (Dorpat 1632, Åbo 1640, Lund 1668). The country thus acquired a very capable administrative elite as well as one of the most efficient war-machines, and a population to which the same message, written in the Chancellery in Stockholm, could be transmitted by being read in all churches of the realm at the same time.

The decision, in 1628, to enter the Thirty Years' War was construed as a preventive measure that would pre-empt efforts by the Habsburg Empire to establish hegemony in Germany and eventually in the Baltic. Swedish participation in this war was to last for twenty years and end with the Westphalian peace treaty that confirmed the new status of the country and made the Baltic into something of a Swedish sea. Further wars against Poland and Denmark in the following decade confirmed the territorial gains and brought new ones in the southern parts of the Scandinavian peninsula. In the latter half of the century, when the monarchy became ever more absolutistic, policies were basically aimed at securing the territorial gains made and preparing for expected wars of revenge.

Under the reign of Charles XI (1660–97), ceaseless efforts were made to increase the size of the army – by delegating a steady provision of soldiers to local decisions by groups of farmers all across the country – and to improve its training, motivation and supplies, not least through the build-up of a domestic armaments industry at the many new rural industrial sites and foundries close to iron-ore mines and waterworks (often established with the help of Dutch capital in a belt stretching across central Sweden). The simultaneous reform of the administration, relying on competence rather than inheritance, changed the character of the whole aristocracy.

The fiscal basis of the state was broadened – not least by the so-called reduction, an extensive re-nationalization of land that had been appropriated by the aristocracy. Even if such measures provoked some opposition, they could nevertheless be effectively carried through in the heartlands of the realm proper – the area administered as a unitary political entity that in broad terms encompassed what today constitutes the countries of Sweden and Finland. In the German provinces the Swedish king was, in formal terms, a prince within the Holy Roman Empire and thus bound by traditional German laws. The situation in the Baltic provinces was in a grey zone between these two situations. The central government in Stockholm strove to treat these provinces in a manner analogous to the core realm so as to be able to draw on their resources more efficiently. In practice this entailed a confrontation with the German-Baltic landed aristocracy that rightly saw its position threatened – in many cases coming to the conclusion that its privileges, and its hold on the indigenous rural population, would be better safeguarded under the Russian tsar than under the Swedish king.[1]

The Great Northern War broke out in 1700 with a joint attack by Denmark-Norway, Saxony-Poland-Lithuania and Russia against the Swedish Realm (an area covered by present-day Sweden and Finland at its core and with adjacent Baltic and German provinces). It was to last for twenty-one years and its end would also mark the end of the era of Swedish Great

Power status. In the course of this war, the Swedish state came to develop features that were not to be seen elsewhere in Europe until the twentieth century. Thus the central government was able to mobilize resources on a scale previously unheard of in Europe and – despite very heavy losses – to continue the war in a way that ran counter to the established Westphalian-era doctrine of carefully limited warfare. In so doing, the state developed means of intervention and control that gradually also came to pose a threat to traditional class structure, notwithstanding the fact that the Swedish aristocracy had already been transformed from a class of landowners into a class of civil servants and military officers.

In the 1720s and 1730s, this state, designed for warfare and total mobilization, yielded to a state with the most parliamentary and – as it was often described by foreign observers – the freest political system of Europe. During the next half century, Sweden had a fully-fledged parliamentary system, the most extensive protection of the freedom of the press of any country, and a vibrant public sphere, full of contention, efforts to reconstruct and reinterpret social identities and demands for a wider political representation (for a recent overview of Swedish culture and public life in this period, see Christensson 2006). In 1772, this period, sometimes seemingly on the verge of a revolutionary upheaval, ends with the coup d'état of Gustavus III and his reign of enlightened absolutism, often justified in official propaganda as an event that saved Sweden from sharing the fate of Poland.

The war with Russia in 1808–9 – in the wake of the temporary Franco-Russian alliance – ended with the loss of Finland, an event described by a leading Swedish twentieth-century historian, Erik Lönnroth, but echoed by Finnish and Swedish historians at the time of the bicentennial of the separation, as the first partitioning of Sweden. It left a rump Sweden, linguistically and ethnically more or less homogeneous (for the first time in many centuries) but in search of a new identity. This began with the national romantic backward-looking literature of the early-nineteenth-century Gautic revival. Later, towards the end of the century, the national imaginary was refocused on future horizons of a modern Sweden that had finally abandoned martial dreams in favour of peaceful (but sometimes equally ambitious) efforts in the fields of science, agricultural innovation, social reform and industrial expansion at home and abroad.

Narratives of Modern Sweden

Most historical accounts of modern Sweden tend to have one of three foci (for an excellent overview see Allardt 2000). If they deal with 'economic transformations', they normally centre on the industrial breakthrough. Industrialization took off relatively late in the nineteenth century but then proceeded quite rapidly. Already at the turn of the nineteenth century Sweden had a number of large industries with vast international connections. However, in 1920, 44 per cent of the workforce was engaged in agriculture and it is only in the late interwar period that Sweden became a fully industrialized country. In the period 1870 to 1950 Sweden had exceptionally fast and continuous economic growth. Growth rates were high but not internationally exceptional in the period 1950–70. Thereafter the relative position of Sweden declined somewhat (which happened to coincide, without necessarily involving any causal connections, with an exceptionally rapidly expanding public sector), and it is only from the early 1990s onwards that Sweden has once again compared favourably with other Western European countries.

Most social accounts highlight the fact that whereas some social policies had already been introduced before the First World War, and although there were intense debates about the social question in late-nineteenth- and early-twentieth-century Sweden, the main expansion of social policies did not occur until after the Second World War. One significant event was a long controversy – involving the split of the Social-Democratic-Agrarian coalition government (1951–57) and a referendum in 1958 – about the introduction of an extensive scheme of so-called supplementary pensions (an income-related and state-administered system above the flat-rate old-age pensions). Another controversy involved a major expansion of publicly funded child care in the 1980s and 1990s, parallel to growing participation of women in the labour market.

Sweden's position as a country with one of the largest public sectors and an unusually generous supply of social services, but also with the heaviest tax burden in the developed world and a very high percentage of females in the workforce, crystallized from the mid-1960s onwards. During this period, there was also a profound transformation of the administrative and judicial state apparatuses in Sweden. It was premised on a belief in the possibility of extending hyper-rationalistic instruments of planning and management. This grew out of two different traditions. On the one hand, there were efforts to copy the successful use of interventionist – and politically closely monitored – public agencies in the early years of Social Democratic rule, mainly in the field of labour market policy where a new kind of political-cadre-like agency replaced older forms. On the other hand there was the influence of the whole movement towards rationalistic planning techniques, which emerged out of operations analysis and systems analysis in the military sector in the United States in the 1950s, and which were then subsequently exported across the whole range of Western nations under the umbrella of the OECD; they carried labels such as programme budgeting, social indicators, and management by objectives. The confluence of these traditions meant that the Swedish bureaucracy from the mid-1960s onwards expanded at the local level – under the control of local politically elected government – and to a smaller extent at the central level, while being transformed from a traditional judicial orientation towards both a more political and a more technocratic one. This development happened to coincide with two other processes.

First, there occurred a rapid urbanization and a decline in the number of independent farmers, as well as a concentration of industry. The latter development was partially inherent in processes of capital accumulation in a country where large export-oriented industries dominated their respective sectors. However, government and trade union policy in the form, originally proposed by trade union economists, of so-called solidaristic wage policy strengthened these processes of accumulation and centralization, the idea being that trade unions should try to enforce centrally bargained wage levels that could be sustained by the most dynamic and successful companies but might force others out of operation, a process that would essentially mean that the most dynamic sectors grew further and increased the general standard of living, if at the cost of considerable regional mobility.

Second, parallel to this there occurred comprehensive educational reforms and an expansion of the public sector. Put crudely but not entirely inaccurately, these developments jointly meant that the position of a traditional *Bildungsbürgertum* (educated middle class) – which had always been a precarious and not very large social stratum in Sweden – was fundamentally undermined, at the same time as other independent and semi-independent middle-class groups in the countryside but also in the towns were disappearing and to some extent replaced by the public employees of a growing public sector of a more explicitly political nature than earlier. None of this entailed any threat to private ownership of large enterprises that had always been favoured in terms of taxation and technology policies.

Finally, accounts with an explicit focus on political transformations have tended to focus on one of two breakthroughs: either that to parliamentary democracy and universal suffrage (around the First World War), or the period from 1932 onwards when the Social Democratic party was not only the largest in parliament – that position it had achieved already with the autumn election of 1914 and never lost – but became the only or the dominant government party (with the exception of a few years in the late 1970s, early 1980s and early 1990s) for the rest of the twentieth century and the beginning of the twenty-first. In these accounts the pivotal moment is 1932–33.

In fact, the Social Democrats first entered government in a coalition with the Liberals in 1917, and then became the sole governing party in 1920, in 1921–23, and in 1924–26. It is no exaggeration to say that the Swedish political scene has been dominated by social democracy for the past eighty-six years. At least since the mid-1940s this dominance involved an ideological hegemony. Since at least the mid-1960s, the Social Democrats also enjoyed what might be termed a social hegemony in the sense that the party not only represented large parts of society, it also shaped a society in its own image and created a logic of needs and demands in terms of both employment and public consumption patterns that made it difficult for any political opposition to challenge its policies without alienating large sections of the population. In this respect, Swedish social democracy, which for a long time in the interwar and immediate post-Second World War period developed analogously to that of Norway and Denmark, achieved a position in the last third of the twentieth century – when the Danish and Norwegian parties shrunk to a size similar to that of the larger non-socialist parties and with no hope of gaining a majority of their own – which was probably unparalleled by that of any other political party in a European democracy. Even if the Nordic countries were still similar in terms of basic cultural orientation and a large welfare state, developments at the end of the twentieth century were different enough to justify caution in generalizations covering all of the Nordic countries.

Rethinking Modern Swedish History

The uniquely strong position of Swedish social democracy in the latter half of the twentieth century has been reflected in 'Whig' interpretations of history, with social democracy assigned the Whig role. There have, however, also been inversions of this narrative as was often the case in the 1970s and 1980s when an alternative left-wing narrative emphasized the degree to which the triumph of social democracy in the 1930s and onwards had involved far-reaching concessions to the leading private companies as well as measures designed to curb left-wing oppositional groups within the trade unions.

Both the master-narrative of the growth of a Swedish welfare state, and critical varieties of it, have yielded vast amounts of valuable empirical insights. However, they tended to cast Swedish history in the twentieth century in relatively evolutionary terms and thereby blank out contingency and openness at crucial junctures. There are at least five crucial junctures that should be highlighted. In the present context this can only be done by briefly outlining the nature of the questions that have to be explored.

The Swedish 'Meiji Restoration'

First, there is the take-off period in Sweden's rapid economic development from roughly 1870 onwards. Normally economic historical accounts have, as mentioned, highlighted the fact that industrialization was late but then quite fast; it meant that Swedish industries were already operating on a large international scene by the end of the nineteenth century (see Schön 2007 for a recent overview). There was a correspondingly rapid development of a modern banking system with close ties to leading branches of industry. Engineering education was also expanded and upgraded, and on the whole the Swedish State almost from the start entered into supportive schemes relative to industry. A prominent example of this was the expansion of hydroelectric power early in the twentieth century. The regulation of water rights necessary for such expansion required substantial changes in the legal framework as well as large-scale construction projects, normally at a large distance from population-centres. As a result Swedish industry (ASEA) early on became a world leader in technologies of power transmission over long distances. There are many similar examples which all point to the fact that Sweden in its take-off stage exhibited a pattern of state-industry interaction that is more akin to those that we find in Germany, or for that matter in Japan in the age of the Meiji Restoration and techno-nationalism, than to any ideal-type of a classical liberal market economy.

The Political Order in Flux: Ideological Contestations and Constitutional Transmutations

Second, the whole period from the 1890s to the 1930s is characterized by social and political contestations and conflicts. It is also characterized by the articulation of several competing modernization projects. In the course of this period there was a prolonged struggle about the extension and universalization of suffrage and the shift to parliamentary rule. This struggle occured in a context of social struggle in which the new labour movement – the Social Democratic party (SAP) was founded in 1889 and the trade union congress (LO) in 1898 – came to play an ever more important role.

There is of course also the international context of threats of war – where one line of conflict in Sweden concerned the efforts by the more conservative forces to increase Swedish defence expenditures amidst perceived threats (mostly from Russia) prior to the First World War. In these years, liberal forces, but also several important policy intellectuals on the conservative side, engaged intensely with 'the social question'. In fact, the whole idea of Sweden becoming a home for all its inhabitants, a 'people's home', which became a key Social Democratic metaphor from 1928 onwards, was originally proposed by radical conservatives to highlight their ambitions to unite the whole people across class divides in a situation where industrialization threatened to deepen such divides and where external threats were seen to loom ever larger.

In this context, it is interesting to note that despite the victory of the employers' association (SAF) in the General Strike of 1909, there was no serious effort to push the whole country in a more aggressively conservative direction or to try to suppress the organized labour movement. The answers for this fact have ranged from a reference to traditions of representative government on the national level and wide-ranging local self-government, to an analysis of the strategic position of different groups in the labour market. In the latter perspective, it was important that the rapid Swedish economic development was dependent on groups of skilled labour, not least in the construction sector, which the employers simply could not afford to alienate irreversibly. This was all the more so since Sweden at the turn of the century was a country with a history of one of the highest emigration rates in Europe, and by then emigration had emerged as perhaps the most central theme on the public agenda. The major government commission on emigration (1907–13) acknowledged the need for structural reforms in Sweden and highlighted the long-term dangers to the nation of continued high emigration.

In the same time period, a Conservative government widened suffrage so that it became near-universal for men, but not for women, in elections to the Second Chamber of Parliament. Simultaneously, reform-orientated and nationalist 'young' Conservatives articulated a counter position to that of the labour movement, one element of which was exactly the idea of Sweden becoming a 'people's home'. From the 1910s until the end of the 1930s this broad strand of thinking formed a significant ideological alternative to social democracy and was probably the most prominent ideological position in academic circles.

The complex movement of events may be more clearly seen in a few focal points. One such point is the general strike of 1909, which ended – as noted – with a defeat for the trade unions. Another focal point is the so-called March of the Peasants in the spring of 1914, when tens of thousands of peasants, at the initiative of conservatives, marched through Stockholm to the Royal Palace where the King gave a speech, mainly written by the most famous Conservative public figure, the world-famous explorer Sven Hedin, declaring his sympathy with the peasants and his understanding of their demands. This gave rise to a constitutional crisis which ended with the resignation of the Liberal prime minister and his cabinet and the appointment of a new emergency cabinet, headed by Hjalmar Hammarskjöld (the father of the later UN Secretary General, Dag Hammarskjöld). Apart from peasants, a large number of students had also come to the palace, one of their foremost leaders being Olof Palme the elder (an uncle of the later Social Democratic prime minister), a charismatic figure in the national-conservative youth movement, who four years later was killed in action as a volunteer in the Finnish civil war.

Three years later, in a highly volatile social and political situation, this cabinet was forced to resign, and was replaced by a Liberal-Social Democratic coalition government with a Liberal, the Uppsala history professor Nils Edén, as prime minister. Neighbouring Finland had declared its independence immediately after the Bolshevik revolution but went through a bloody civil war in the spring of 1918, whereas in Sweden suffrage now became truly universal (also for women) and parliamentary rule was hastily introduced in a barely constitutional manner. This dramatic shift occurred virtually without significant change to a single paragraph in the constitution (for a recent analysis of this period see Enzell 2002). For a country that had one of the oldest constitutions in the world and that had always put a high premium on its written constitution, this change meant that the country entered a period of a constitutional limbo that was to last from roughly 1918 to 1974 when a new constitution was promulgated. Entering into this limbo has never been treated as a serious problem by either scholars or politicians – it was seen as a pragmatic expediency. However, one important consequence of this state of what might perhaps even be termed constitutional schizophrenia was to make impossible anything like the emergence of constitutional patriotism. Leading Social Democratic and Liberal politicians could not possibly nourish such public sentiments for a constitution, the first paragraph of which stated: 'The King alone rules the Realm'.

Another result, however, was that even right-wing Conservatives never came to doubt the legitimacy of the political order; even if the prime minister was a socialist in the eyes of conservatives in the civil service, the military or society at large, that did not change the fact that they owed their deepest loyalties to king and country and that the country was precisely the Kingdom of Sweden. Even after the events of 1917–18, the King, although no longer free to choose whomever he wanted as his key advisers in the Cabinet, remained the official head of the administration as well as Commander-in-Chief of the armed forces. The events of 1914 had shown that it was by no means a foregone conclusion that Sweden was bound to become a parliamentary democracy. It is more than likely that with a different development of the course of the war the country would have remained a constitutional monarchy with more or less general suffrage for men but without parliamentary dominance of the executive branch.

The Social Democratic Breakthrough

Third, there is the formative period of the Swedish 'people's home' and 'the Swedish Model', from 1932–33 onwards, which marked the beginning of a period of four and half decades during which there was, except for a brief interlude in the summer of 1936, a Social Democratic prime minister. In its early phases this period was associated with events such as a successful economic and social policy, the end of an earlier era of frequent strikes and conflicts in the labour market, and with the so-called Saltsjöbaden agreement of 1938 between the employers' association and the trade unions. Later historical research has cast doubt on the tendency to unambiguously associate the more notable successes in these years with any particular government policies. However, this is not the case with the 1933 political agreement between the Social Democrats and the Agrarians. This agreement not only entailed a stable parliamentary majority for the government, it also meant that a broad popular coalition was formed that dried up most potential support for any fascist or Nazi party.

Similar developments occurred in the other Nordic countries with the partial exception of Finland and might, together with the longstanding traditions of local self government and representative institutions, help explain the failure of fascist and Nazi parties in playing any significant roles in these countries. Sweden may well have been the country in Europe where such parties were least successful. Not only were they never able to get any representative elected to parliament, but even at the peak of their electoral strength, the parliamentary elections of 1936, their combined vote was less than 2 per cent (and just 0.7 per cent if only the votes for the self-proclaimed Nazi parties are included).

In accounting for this failure of Nazi parties one additional element was the fact that the Swedish Conservatives came to take a relatively early and clear stance against the Nazis. Even those elements in the former youth league, who had been expelled or left the party in the mid-1930s because of their commitment to a radical nationalist ideology and who did not see democracy as being of any particular value, had mostly distanced themselves from Nazi Germany before the Second World War and the ensuing Nazi occupation of Denmark and Norway.

Social Democratic Hegemony

Fourth, the period of strong contention between socialist and non-socialist forces in the immediate post-Second World War period ended with the Social Democrats barely holding on to government power in the wake of the election of 1948 but also abandoning key elements of their radical programme for the postwar period.

Fifth, the period of radical rationalism, technocratic planning and expansion of the public sector from the mid-1960s onwards (and also, one may add, with a substantial immigration significantly greater than in the other Nordic countries) in which, initially, policies were informed by a sense of confidence that this expansion would crown earlier achievements. However, in the wake of the youth revolt of the late 1960s, a growing opposition to the Vietnam War, a series of wildcat strikes, and an emerging concern about global environmental developments, the response of social democracy was an increased emphasis on egalitarian policies, and from the mid-1970s onwards also on new radical economic policies. Some labour economists, associated with the trade unions, launched the idea of so-called wage-earners' funds. The idea was that the vast public pension funds that were building up should be used to buy up shares in companies so that a kind of creeping socialization would be achieved, with an ever growing influence of trade unions as a key characteristic.

The struggle about a programme along these lines played a major part in political debates throughout the 1980s but lost most of its impetus in the latter half of the decade and was definitely buried during the interlude of a non-socialist government in the early 1990s, not to be resurrected when a new Social Democratic government was formed in 1994. Already in the late 1980s, another Social Democratic government had removed most barriers to capital and monetary movements across boundaries and thereby to a large extent set the stage for the rapidly changed stance of social democracy in favour of membership in the European Union.

This leaves Sweden as a country that overtly looks like a normal small European democracy. The outcome of the general elections of 2006 bore further testimony to this. The Social Democratic government was, somewhat unexpectedly given its relatively successful economic policy track-record, replaced by a non-socialist alliance that focused its electoral propaganda on issues of the labour market and unemployment, traditionally the strong points of Social Democracy. This alliance was dominated by the Moderate Party, the liberal-conservative party, which had abandoned most neo-liberal rhetoric and instead presented itself as 'the new labour party'. Conversely, the Social Democratic party, which for decades had been able to control and constitute the cabinet itself, chose to deepen its relationship to two parties it had come to consider its long-term collaborative partners, namely the Green Party, the partner preferred by the social democratic leadership and with a leadership ready to abandon the opposition of the Greens to membership in the European Union, and the Left Party, the former Post-Communists. This meant that the traditional division between two major political blocs became further entrenched. At the same time the centre of gravity in terms of policy choices had become more centrist within both blocs.

In some respects, however, Sweden is still, as indicated initially, distinctly different. To conclude, four antinomies of contemporary Sweden will be outlined.

Antinomies of Contemporary Sweden

First, Sweden has a long legacy of statehood that it is both proud of and tends to deny. It has an even longer cultural legacy that, like its neighbours, it eulogizes when it comes to the life-world of folk customs and holidays, but which it does not deal with reflexively. The concept of Sweden as a 'people's home' (*folkhem*) was a way to bring these different strands together in the early years of Social Democratic dominance. In the last half century, however, political leaders have been unable to articulate any equally encompassing conception of citizenship and collective identity. Official statements may often seem to embrace a notion of constitutional patriotism.

However, with the old 1809 constitution, a position along these lines could not be articulated clearly, and the new 1974 constitution is not written in a language that inspires a sense of emotional commitment. In the absence of constitutional patriotism, a quasi-version of this, with statements about the equal value of human beings, serves as a semi-official ideology, including a strong commitment to gender equality and environmentalism. This quasi-constitutional patriotism of official statements and policies is complemented with a folk-oriented rhetoric often used by politicians as well as authors and artists.

As a consequence, many if not most Swedes feel they are different from other Europeans, and perhaps in some sense more fortunate, but seem to be left without means to articulate this sense of difference. The Swedish Post-Communists, as well as the Greens, have been relatively successful in translating such sentiments into electoral success. To some extent this was so because Sweden entered the EU at a time when an incoming Social Democratic government introduced a strict budgetary policy; this meant that Sweden relatively early became a country with a budgetary surplus and no inflation, but it was also portrayed as something of a betrayal of the traditions of the Swedish welfare state. In the campaign preceding the referendum in September 2003 on the introduction – and rejection – of the Euro in Sweden, a commitment to democracy and egalitarianism and a sense of difference could come together and – except for the 'yes' majority among immigrant voters – the outcome could be presented as a victory of the people against the elites of wealth and political power.

At the same time, there is certainly also evidence of limits to civicness and civility when it comes to the treatment of visible minorities, even if Sweden to date is one of the few countries in Europe, including its western neighbours, where populist more or less xenophobic parties are not, or perhaps not yet, represented in parliament. The series of fires and unrest in some of the most immigrant-dense suburbs in the larger cities in the summer of 2009, small in comparison with analogous events in France and other continental European countries but unfamiliar by Swedish standards, served to further underscore this. These events did not produce an outburst of xenophobic statements by politicians but rather an openly admitted sense of helplessness on the part of social workers, police and politicians alike, a relatively new phenomenon in a country which for decades had been characterized by a belief among decision-makers and administrators that there were no or few problems they could not effectively tackle and solve.

Second, at the turn of the nineteenth century, there were a number of broad popular movements – most prominently the labour movement, the Free Churches (that is free from the State Church of Sweden), and the temperance movement – that engaged vast numbers of people and jointly constituted a civil society as an alternative to and in opposition to the official state and its bureaucracy, its military and its church. With the breakthrough to parliamentary democracy, and even more so with social democracy occupying the governmental peak of a state apparatus that was still largely imbued with very different values, the problem of linking state and civil society became an acute one. Early efforts included the introduction of *Ombudsman* positions both for the civil service and the military. Other measures involved the creation of new loyal administrative apparatuses in key policy areas, mainly the labour market, as well as efforts to further strengthen the old tradition of local self-government. These efforts to both expand and to 'democratize' the state apparatus while maintaining an efficient civil society may have reached some kind of peak in the first decade after the Second World War.

In the era of 'radical rationalism' and technocratic planning ideals, and a concomitant reduction in the number of self-governing local municipalities – some 90 per cent of the municipalities that existed in 1950 had been 'rationalized' away as a result of mergers by the late 1960s

– ever more signs hinted at tensions between a growing governmental penetration of this civil society and the perpetually recurring incantations of the need to 'listen to the movement', as leading Social Democrats expressed it. Increasingly, it seemed that the 'movement' became more and more part of the state apparatus. In parallel, membership in the political parties, and not least their youth associations, which had always been very high by international standards, dwindled dramatically towards the end of the twentieth century.

Third, since the seventeenth century the Swedish state had been characterized by an unusual level of efficiency, in the last instance based less on external control than on the internalization of a strong, partly Lutheran-inspired, moral code. From the mid-twentieth century these features were gradually waning. The radically rationalistic and technocratic conception of public policy in the 1960s and 1970s, and the ensuing move towards a market orientation also of the civil service in the 1980s and 1990s, spelt the demise of these traditional virtues.

Sweden, however, remained a country with low levels of corruption, but in the course of the last two decades there has been a steady and growing stream of 'affairs' which demonstrate that Swedish politicians, civil servants and businessmen behave little better than their counterparts in many other parts of Europe. In a more general sense, one may perhaps even speak of a slow but pervasive cultural shift. Foreign observers of Sweden in the first half of the twentieth century tended to refer to the prevalence of a work-ethic, of a sense of duty and perseverance and, perhaps most notably, a personal demeanour characterized by restraint, not to say humility, across different social strata, including leading politicians. Swedish novels, poetry and films from the period largely reflect this as well (cf. however Gustafsson 2007). It is difficult to discern the connections between this world and these imaginations, and that of unrestrained self-promotion and self-exposure that has come to dominate vast areas of public and private life.[2] Ingmar Bergman died in 2007. Yet his world of silences, probing encounters, self-reflection and anguish now appears as a distant cultural universe.

Fourth, when Sweden in the late nineteenth and early twentieth centuries gradually changed from being a poor rural backwater into a modern industrial nation within a global economy, it trod a careful middle ground between inviting foreign capital in and drawing on the cohesion and loyalty of a sense of Swedish identity among the elite and in the population at large. Neither the development of hydroelectric power, nor of mining, nor of forestry could have been possible without foreign capital. Yet there was always a sense of the risk of selling the country out as it were. In the field of forestry, for instance, large investments were necessary to develop the forest industry in the northern parts of the country, but this provoked resistance from a free-holding class of peasants who owned forests, and in 1906 a law was made that basically froze ownership structure for the rest of the century. In the last decade, Sweden has in many ways overcome the acute economic problems of the 1980s and early 1990s. However, it has done so in an economic environment that is more openly global than before. The succession of earlier Swedish devaluations and the current floating exchange rate have made it relatively inexpensive for foreign capital to buy up Swedish enterprises. This may be a move towards greater efficiency, but there can be little doubt that this has led to the closing down of many Swedish-based strategic and research activities of firms, and made Sweden as a whole somewhat less capable of articulating its own strategic visions.

Postscript

In the early twenty-first century the Nordic countries form a rather unique part of the world, characterized by a sense of common belonging arguably stronger than that which may be found among the other nations of Europe. Paradoxically the different state legacies of these nations, reaching back hundreds of years, still seem able to engender minor, but tangible, frictions between parts of the historical Western Scandinavian realm of Denmark-Norway and of the Central-Eastern Nordic realm comprising the present-day countries of Sweden and Finland at its core. Thus although Sweden and Norway are ideally complementary to each other in terms of industrial structure and populated by people who share common customs and speak a variety of mutually intelligible dialects, they have been less successful in large-scale industrial cooperation than firms and state institutions in Sweden and Finland, who were the two halves of what for most of the previous millennium was one integrated realm.

Similarly, the age-old competition between Denmark and Sweden, two of the oldest continuously existing states in Europe and countries which in the late medieval and early modern period fought more and bloodier wars with each other than most countries in Europe, is a thing of the past. The fact that these feelings of animosity, not to say enmity, were overcome in the course of the nineteenth and twentieth centuries was an achievement, as was the peaceful dissolution of the personal union between Sweden and Norway. Still there is a lingering sense that the potentials of Nordic collaboration have not been fully explored and that they are given clear public expression only in periods of immediate external threat. In consequence, the Nordic countries have not, yet, come to articulate common positions and experiences, for instance, within the European Union but also in other international fora, to the full extent that might have been realistically envisaged.

Sweden is still a prosperous country. However, in relative terms, it is less rich and prominent than half a century or a century ago when it was, as it were, something of a small-scale version of a Gaullist great power economically and even militarily with an incipient Swedish *force de frappe* well underway.

Today Sweden may be content with being a small member of the European Union, or it may again, as a century ago, strive to formulate a compelling vision of its own place in the world whether it chooses Raoul Wallenberg or Dag Hammarskjöld or Olof Palme as an epitome of what such a role might entail. In the year of the second Swedish presidency of the European Union, 2009, these two imaginations of a Swedish past, present and future co-exist. The official rhetoric during the presidency refers to a vision of leadership for the future, not least in the environmental field. Yet the distinctiveness of that vision remains to be articulated.

Notes

1. John Elliott (1992) has analysed the nature of early modern European states as 'composite monarchies'. To some limited extent this notion is also applicable to the Swedish Realm in the sixteenth and seventeenth centuries – and maybe most clearly in the case Elliott points to, namely the brief late-sixteenth-century personal union between Sweden and Poland and, to a lesser extent, in the case of the Swedish German provinces. However, Jonas Nordin (2000) has demonstrated that there were strong tendencies to the formation of a common collective identity, beyond loyalty to the dynasty, in late-seventeenth-century Sweden. There were also clear efforts by the central government in Stockholm – and in this respect the Swedish monarchy differed from the Danish – not only to keep Swedish as the language of the central administration but to replace German with Swedish as the administrative language in the Baltic provinces.
2. Cordelia Edvardson, the famous Swedish-Israeli journalist, daughter of the German legal scholar Herrmann Heller, recently described her interpretation of Swedish culture when she, then a teenager, arrived in the country from Auschwitz at the end of the war and how she came to understand and appreciate its restraint and integrity, but also how utterly alien much of contemporary Swedish culture now appears to her from her present location in Jerusalem (Edvardson 2009).

References

Allardt, E. (2000) 'A Political Sociology of the Nordic Countries', *European Review* 8(1): 129–41.

Bolin, S. (1953) 'Mohammed, Charlemagne and Ruric', *Scandinavian Economic History Review* 1(1): 5–39.

Christensson, J. (ed.) (2006) *Signums svenska kulturhistoria*. Lund: Signum.

Edvardson, C. (2009) 'Vad hände med den svenska integriteten?', *Svenska Dagbladet*, 27 August: 26.

Elliott, J.H. (1992) 'A Europe of Composite Monarchies', *Past and Present* 137: 48–71.

Enzell, M. (2002) *Requiem for a Constitution: Constitutionalism and Political Culture in Early 20th Century Sweden*. Stockholm: Stockholm Political Studies 84.

Gustafsson, T. (2007) *En fiende till civilisationen: Manlighet, genusrelationer, sexualitet och rasstereotyper i svensk filmkultur under 1920-talet*. Lund: Sekel.

Nordin, J. (2000) *Ett fattigt men fritt folk. Nationell och politisk självbild i Sverige från sen stormaktstid til slutet av frihetstiden*. Stockholm: Symposium.

Schön, L. (2007) *En modern svensk ekonomisk historia: Tillväxt och omvandling under två sekel*. Stockholm: SNS Förlag.

CHAPTER 5
History and Ethics in Pre-revolutionary Sweden

Peter Hallberg

Introduction

The purpose of this chapter is to analyse how historians and other writers in eighteenth-century Sweden conceived of the social benefits of history writing within the context of what they considered a modern(izing) enlightened polity.[1] In the 1740s and 1750s the benefits of history were discussed in the context of an ongoing enlightenment discourse on society that stipulated a close relationship between knowledge about the past and values like civility, virtue and patriotism. Virtually all of the speeches that are analysed in this chapter refer to how historical reflection is a social practice that creates civic bonds between individuals and groups, bonds that constitute the premises for the creation and prosperity of a modern civil society and for a collective identity based on civic, as opposed to religious, foundations. The first two sections of the chapter recreate some aspects of the discourse on society in Sweden around the middle of the century, by considering contemporary notions of enlightenment and civil society respectively. The third section shows in more detail how contemporaries argued that moral education was the most powerful instrument to create a community based on fellowship rather than force. A fourth section specifically analyses texts that articulated the notion of history as a teacher of modern sociability, which is then specified in a final section that considers contemporary ideas about the advantages of visual and written historical media – statues and biographies respectively – to engage broader segments of society in the civilizing project.

The Spirit of Liberty and Enlightenment

Ideas about the social function of history were formulated in the context of a modernizing and civilizing mission that formed part of Swedish enlightenment discourse towards the middle of the eighteenth century. In the 1740s and 1750s, the challenges of civil society – particularly the threat of liberty turning into license and of trade as engine of base moral impulses – were discussed on a practical level by individuals that advocated the spread of 'useful' (nyttig) knowledge, the success of which was considered a precondition for the creation of a modern polity based on reason.[2] Trailing the creation of scientific societies or academies in Paris (1634 and 1666), London (1645), Berlin (1700) and Petersburg (1724), this utilitarian discourse on society was institutionalized through the meetings and publications of the Royal Swedish Academy of Sciences. Instituted in 1739, the Academy was a learned society that gathered scientists and laymen who confessed to a seemingly boundless belief in the capacity of the arts and sciences to promote economic and moral progress.[3]

According to a brief and flattering history of the Academy published by one of its members in 1771, the genesis of learned societies was located in ancient Greece, the cradle of Western civilization. Since the early seventeenth century, they had been established throughout Europe, even in America, and were described as the institutional insignia of civilized nations (Sandels 1771: 9). According to the philosopher and sociologist Torgny Segerstedt, the Academy followed a general European trend and was created as a reaction to the inability (or unwillingness) of the universities – still largely under the sway of organized religion – to foster an emerging rationalist or critical spirit of learning. 'The new scientific societies,' writes Segerstedt, 'sought the support of the monarchy; those in power considered in their turn that the new sciences could be of significance for the commercial policies they adopted' (Segerstedt 1971: 12).[4]

On a theoretical level, the belief in the ability to improve the moral fabric of society was distinctly anti-Rousseauan. In 'A Discourse on the Arts and Sciences' (1750), Rousseau had famously argued that, contrary to the conventional belief that advances in the arts and sciences made people better, they contributed to moral decline (Rousseau 1993: 7). Commenting on the essay five years after its publication, Baron Carl Fredric Scheffer, one of Sweden's most prominent cultural and political figures at the time, dismissed it as a mélange of misconceptions. Its popular appeal, he claimed, derived solely from the author's stylistic verve. The thesis, he concluded without any felt need to produce arguments, had been falsified: 'nowadays, as in times past, no doubts may be entertained about the certain benefits that individuals and realms can derive from the application of reason' (Scheffer 1755: 12). In Count Scheffer's circles, the pursuit of enlightenment was justified by an increased economic and social need for practical social knowledge. The slow but steady development of larger social units – from households and private estates to towns and nations – created demands and challenges never before encountered (Ehrenpreus 1748: 5).

The patriotic rhetoric surrounding the Academy's goals and activities did not preclude a cosmopolitan outlook among its members, albeit often with a comparative focus that placed the Swedish nation in very good light, either in terms of actual achievement or in terms of potential. The views of one of its most illustrious members, the writer and then royal librarian Olof Dalin, are illustrative in this regard. On the one hand, he spoke with national fervour when he claimed that the diffusion of enlightenment in Northern Europe enticed foreigners to 'gaze at the Nordic countries with greater curiosity than ever Italy inspired'. On the other hand, he conceived of learned discourse in cosmopolitan terms. 'The entire learned world,' he proclaimed, 'now resembles a single Republic in which all People are Compatriots.' The idea of a transnational Republic of Letters was related to the unification of Europe, a process that Dalin claimed had been initiated in the mid-fifteenth century. A new spirit of governance, he noted, had converted the continent's sovereign nations into 'one Body in which all Powers are members, either to assist or obstruct each other, so that none can reign supreme' (Dalin 1749: 1–4).[5] According to Dalin, the great challenge to citizens in all nations was to advance the tenets of a still young European civilization. Other academicians praised reason and predicted that future generations would marvel at the achievements of 'our enlightened age' or 'this enlightened era' (Elvius 1746: 14; Mennander 1756: 24; Scheffer 1755: 2; see also Tessin 1746: 3–4 and Ehrenpreus 1748: 8–9, 5–7).

Some members explicitly associated the creation and subsequent successes of the Royal Swedish Academy of Sciences with the country's unique political system after the fall of absolutism in 1718. Relieved of the hardships under absolutism, the 1719/20 Constitution had been described as the work of 'angels' and the Church even changed the wording of prayer so that it read 'To the Honour of Thy Holy Name, and the safeguarding of each and all of us in our blessed Liberty' (cited in Roberts 1986: 59). In 1739, Dalin still spoke amiably about 'our Age of Liberty'; a fellow academician referred to 'our blessed government of Liberty' (Dalin 1749: 22; Mennander 1756: 14).[6] The historian Anders af Botin in 1757 wrote that he projected to write a comprehensive work 'which includes the history of the Swedish people after their liberty had been regained' (Botin 1757–64: vol. 1, preface). The Councillor of the

Realm Count Carl Gustaf Tessin discussed the mutual benefits of 'civil Associations' and the 'deliberations of Men of Letters' (Tessin 1746: 4). In 1771, when the political system of the Age of Liberty was in turmoil, another member identified the year 1720 as a time when 'a new Era for Sweden began to win sway ... The Citizens of the Realm were able, after a tedious and violent storm, to breathe fresher air. Peace and liberty were restored' (Sandels 1771: 11). An important reason why earlier attempts to establish a learned society on Swedish soil had failed, he argued, was the sense of bewilderment or lack of purpose that dominated domestic politics under late absolutism (Sandels 1771: 11).

The spirit of the new post-Absolutist era was accordingly complemented by a political system that gave impetus to the institutionalization of reason and progress. This political system was animated by the pronounced articulation of central themes in what theorists of 'multiple modernities' refer to as 'the cultural programme of modernity', not least the increased sense of historicity as a precondition for self-reflexive modes of social and political organization (Eisenstadt 1998; Wittrock 2000). Investigations into the state and dynamics of commerce had been encouraged during the meetings of the 1738 Diet (Sandels 1771: 11). This particular Diet has become associated with the ascent of parties in Swedish politics in general and the rise of the Hat party in particular, which wielded power until 1765 when the Cap party gained control over the government.[7] The economic policies of the Hats, which stressed import duties, state support to entrepreneurs and other measures to boost the economy, contributed to a political climate conducive to the establishment of an Academy of Sciences. Sten Lindroth's conclusion that it 'was sustained by the spirit of the age which it in turn sustained, soon to become a national institution for the benefit of the Swedish people, cherished by its citizens and those in office' (Lindroth 1978–81: vol. 3, 49–50) is clearly discernible in the speeches quoted above; as is Tore Frängsmyr's conclusion that the 1720s were crucial to the cultural regeneration, specifically the growth of science, that has become associated with a Swedish enlightenment (Lindroth 1978–81: vol. 3, 49–50; Frängsmyr 1998: 6–7).[8] In the eighteenth century, the connection appears to have been obvious, or at least seen as a necessary compliment to a government whose financial support was considered crucial to its own and the country's prosperity. A modern and civil society, it was believed, could not be created without the ordered application of the arts and sciences, and these could not fully prosper under unfree government. Thus, the state and science went hand in hand to create a new political order.

The Concept of Civil Society

In Swedish usage in the 1740s, the English term 'civil society' was translated as *borgerlig sammanlefnad, borgerligt samqväm* or *borgerligt samhälle* (*Kongl. maj:ts nådigste stadfästelse* 1741: 2; Ehrenpreus 1748: 23; Tessin 1746: 4; Wrede 1743). These terms were used interchangeably to denote what John Locke meant in the *Second Treatise of Government* (1690) when he discussed civil or political society: a form of social organization under a government bound by law, the opposite of a state of nature.[9] An explanation of key terms in the preface to a government-commissioned Swedish translation of the *Second Treatise* stated directly that the Swedish term borgerlig sammanlefnad was used as an equivalent to the Latin *Societas Civilis*. In the original English text, Locke used three English terms interchangeably to denote *Societas Civilis*: civil society, political society and commonwealth. In the Swedish title of the work, the adjective 'civil' (as in Locke's 'civil government') was translated as 'worldly' (*werdslig*), denoting a realm of politics that was the realm of the spiritual. 'Political power' (Lat. *Potestas Politica*) was accordingly translated as 'worldly power' (*werdslig makt*) (Locke 1726: preface).[10]

A Lockean understanding of civil society was put forth in a 1743 speech at the Royal Swedish Academy of Sciences delivered by Hindric Johan Wrede. Addressing the means to realize civil society, Wrede maintained that individuals lost their 'innate and natural liberty, or equality' when they became subjected to 'the control and governance of one or many'. The loss of natural liberty in the state of nature was compensated with the acquisition of something even greater, namely, 'the security, felicity, and benefits that are contingent on civil Society' (Wrede 1743: 6). Five years later, Carl Ehrenpreus made an analogy that singled out the rule of law as the mark of a civil society: 'The Commonwealth is not unlike a ship,' he suggested, 'its rig and canvas are the Law and Justice' (Ehrenpreus 1748: 23).

The concept of civil society played a central role in natural law education in Swedish universities in the seventeenth century, which relied heavily on the works of Hugo Grotius and Samuel Pufendorf. Especially Pufendorf, who had served as professor at Lund since 1667 and historiographer of the realm under Charles XI, was influential. His textbook in natural law, *De officio hominis et civis* (1673) was the key work in instruction in natural law during the Age of Liberty and was translated into Swedish in 1747, now accompanied by references to positive Swedish law (Nilsén 2000: 38). As had been the case of the 1726 translation of Locke's *Second Treatise*, the translation of Pufendorf's textbook widened the audience for these discussions, thus increasing their potential impact on public discourse.

According to Per Nilsén, the translation of Locke's work constituted 'a step towards the popularization of debates on the legal and philosophical nature of the state. Only now ... did the Swedish language acquire the first elements of a terminology of its own in this field' (Nilsén 2000: 102; Saastamoinen 1999: 16). In the case of Pufendorf's work, however, the addition of Swedish positive law, which in a sense nationalized a general work of jurisprudence, may at the same time have limited the potential reading public to students of constitutional law.

Pufendorf's theory maintained that the condition of fundamental insecurity that reigned in the state of nature, combined with the human disposition of sociability, or socialitas, gave rise to the formation of social groups and eventually to states. An initial social contract between individuals renouncing life in a state of nature was followed by a contract between rulers and ruled, whereby the former guaranteed the latter protection and the latter promised the ruler loyalty and obedience. Mutually constrained by a contract, rulers and ruled were thus united in a pursuit of societal perfection. Guided by a collective goal to advance the common good, individuals fulfilled their oath of loyalty by contributing to the best of the whole, while the ruler fulfilled his by protecting the safety and rights of individuals (Nilsén 2000: 40–42).[11]

As we shall see, there was also a much more practically oriented discourse on civil society that discussed the means to achieve a civil society here and now. This discourse, which was institutionalized in the proceedings of the Royal Swedish Academy of Sciences, did not come about as a reaction to theoretical accounts, but as a more or less pronounced corollary to them. Although economic growth was the primary concern both of the representatives of the state and of science, growth was not merely a question of invention and rationalization through varieties of engineering, or even of the spread of modern technology and knowledge among peasants, but also (and perhaps most fundamentally) a question of nourishing patriotic dispositions. In this way, civic education – processes of learning that addressed society at large rather than being confined to a particular institution like the school or university – became an important tool for creating an enlightened modern polity.

The Formation of Civic Morality

Although the concept of 'citizen' experienced a breakthrough in Swedish public discourse in the 1790s, questions pertaining to patriotism and civic virtues date back to the 1730s, when they were debated in the nascent periodical press (Christensson 1996: 105–69; Nordin 2000: 328–37). In the magazine *Then swänska Argus* (1732–34) – the appearance of which one historian of the press has characterized as 'the birth of the Swedish public sphere' – a more personal style of writing was applied as a means to 'nurture, guide and edify the public' (Vegesack 2001: 44).[12] The paper's didactic task was attuned to the brand of enlightenment espoused by the Royal Academy of Sciences in the 1740s and 1750s. Stressing qualities like virtue, industry and frugality, the magazine's editor Olof Dalin maintained: '[W]hen a Realm is virtuous and Wise, then it is strong, but when it is vicious and Foolish it is weak. What is the noblest element of which a Realm consists? Its inhabitants? Indeed. And therefore I conclude that no Realm may be strong and secure that does not have virtuous and wise Inhabitants' (*Then swänska Argus 1732–34*: no. 2, 7). The focus on morality and wisdom entailed a critical task. Of particular concern was the relationship between the individual and society. The normative approach was studiously dichotomous, pitting Stoic qualities like authenticity, simplicity and honesty against artificiality, vanity and foreign impulses. Dalin's satires tended to ridicule the vainglory of the nobility, the most obvious opposite of his own Stoic ideals (Oscarsson 2000: 101–4).[13]

In order to better understand eighteenth-century conceptions of the relationship between virtue and civil society we may consider Carl Henric Armfeldt's 1765 dissertation on the means to prevent the degeneration of civil customs. This particular work combined theoretical reflection with practical advice on how to ensure and develop order and liberty, and offers a detailed account of a rather typical view that appears in a more fragmented form in many other contributions that are treated in this chapter.[14]

Armfeldt's starting point was the structural social challenges posed by the birth of civil society. In a narrative familiar to readers of Grotius and Pufendorf, individuals at some point in history concluded that living in an organized society was more conducive to their well-being than remaining in a state of anarchy, even if it entailed a loss of freedom. Ever since human beings shed their God-given liberties in order to obtain 'individual comfort and public welfare', Armfeldt argued, they had incessantly sought the 'means of securing their felicity and laying the cornerstones of the welfare and continuance of Realms and Societies' (Armfeldt 1765: 1). The first step consisted of forming a 'civil commonwealth' (*borgerlig sammanlefnad*), a form of life and social organization regulated by more or less formalized rules of conduct. In order to transform these loosely configured commonwealths into organized polities, the means to preserve and boost a spirit of civility had to be identified. A number of possible means were ruled out: the exercise of brute force, protection by other states, and the accumulation of wealth, all of which would in the end prove counterproductive. As testified by what was known about the great empires of Western civilization, handed down to contemporaries by classical authors like Sallust, Livy and Polybius, the flourishing of order and liberty depended on the intensity and diffusion of civic virtues. In Armfeldt's words:

> The inhabitants' love of virtue and unsullied customs form the bedrock on which all former dominions have constructed their true felicity, strength and growth. When a noble spirit enlivens a State, when a love of mankind and obedience to the Laws of Nature are revealed in the acts and deportment of its inhabitants; when a zeal for the common weal unites all hearts to love their country, Laws are always revered and cogent; there will exist an enduring serenity and welfare in its Society and a general unconstrained respect beyond its borders. (Armfeldt 1765: 2, 4)

Armfeldt avoided subscribing to either an idealistic or a fatalistic view of human nature. Human beings were never simply good or evil. Virtues and vices were rather in constant conflict, within individuals and within societies; depending on context and situation. According to Armfeldt, humanity's lowest instincts had always existed among the lower segments of the population. A closer look at the history of humankind, however, showed that the level of civilization had always shifted with a government's relative ability to 'prevent and counter the general dissolution of customs in this country' (Armfeldt 1765: 5).[15] Morality was clearly understood by Armfeldt as a matter of state policy based on a practical, or Polybian or Machiavellian,[16] reading of the history of politics.

Armfeldt defined morality or virtue (*seder* or *dygd*) as a 'desire and ability to fulfill one's obligations in full compliance with the Law'. The corruption of morals was logically defined as 'the indifference, apathy and failure to fulfill the obligations prescribed by law' (Armfeldt 1765: 8–9).[17] He further distinguished between three kinds of morality/virtues: (1) Christian, (2) philosophical/natural and (3) civic, each corresponding to their basic source – the Bible, natural law and civic law respectively. The author's emphasis on the responsibilities of individuals towards society should not lead us to disregard the fact that his ideas at the same time placed a significant burden on the state. For although even the best of governments had to realize that complete perfection could never be produced from such materials as the human mind and spirit, the state was ultimately responsible for the prevention of moral corruption. Armfeldt was certainly clear on this, insisting that nothing was more important for 'Civil Societies' (*Borgerliga Samhällen*) than the maintenance of civic morality. Virtues had to be encouraged, vices discouraged, the cardinal question being how it should be done (Armfeldt

1765: 6–7). Not only the national wealth, but liberty itself, depended on finding an answer to it.

Because humans are prone to habit and prejudice, and since it is easier to prevent vices from developing at all than to expel existing ones, Armfeldt argued, governments should prioritize moral education at the early stages of individual development:

> Young people are the greenhouse of the state and he who desires to prevent the country from the impairment of vices and dissolute habits should consider this with ardor ... In the hearts of children many images may be imprinted; they provide a fertile soil in which the seeds of love of their Country, God and Neighbor may flourish and bear abundant fruit. (Armfeldt 1765: 12–13)[18]

Since the ability of parents to finance and oversee their children's education in most cases was limited, Armfeldt argued that public funds had to be channelled to support a number of educational institutions: schools and universities, libraries, laboratories, observatories and botanical gardens. He furthermore maintained that teachers had to be paid better, their status boosted and pedagogical methods modernized. Relying heavily on the French pedagogue François de Salinas de la Mothe-Fénelon, Armfeldt moreover discussed the necessity of educating women, since they reared children, thus performing within the private sphere an essential task that also belonged to the public sphere. To this end, the government should also create schools for impoverished women in the cities. As Armfeldt argued, governments of 'enlightened nations' that hoped to 'maintain their good civil customs' would also realize that they ought to institute charity schools to educate impoverished children in order to make use of a dormant human capital (Armfeldt 1765: 14–24, 32–33). The government's key role in the realm of civic morality had been phrased by an academician in 1743, who in a speech on the strengths of civil society argued for the government's duty to 'aptly exercise its tutelage over an irresolute Society, to foster virtue and extirpate vices' (Wrede 1743: 17, 26–30, 3). It is tempting to see in these views from the 1740s, 1750s and 1760s the beginnings of the modern interventionist or welfare state. History's particular role in the creation of civil society is the subject of the section below.

History, Virtue and the Study of 'Great Men'

According to Armfeldt, ancient Greek history writing, specifically the brand that Polybius (200–120 BC) called 'pragmatic history', was directly relevant to eighteenth-century concerns. Drawing on Plato's famous advice that sensible statesmen should study philosophy, Polybius had argued that both history and politics would mutually benefit from a close relationship. '[I]t will be well with history,' he concluded, 'either when men of action undertake to write history ... or again when would-be authors regard a training in actual affairs as necessary for writing history' (Polybius 1925: bk.12, 28, 405). And as Armfeldt concluded: 'Polybius is thus more than apt in commending the reading of history to young people, not merely to learn thereby of past events but with the assistance of Moral doctrines to observe their causes and be able to conclude from this what is beneficial for themselves and for the public weal' (Armfeldt 1765: 37). Since one could not ensure that historical findings and arguments would always be explained and embellished by an intermediary, that is, a teacher, questions of narrative assumed great importance in history writing. According to the historian, teacher and political writer Johan Hartman Eberhardt, historians who aspired to be of any social use should avoid two extreme ways of representing the past: the more fictional kind that invoked fabulous stories to tell 'historical truths' and the documentary kind, or the chronicle, which presented facts and events 'completely naked'. Instead of adopting either of these two narrative strategies, the enlightened historian should contextualize and moralize. The past should be told 'entirely in its context, with causes and consequences, and foster useful contemplation. It is in this last respect that history is called Pragmatic' (Eberhardt 1766–81: vol. 1, 2–3). Another writer identified the ability to explain causes and reflect on the meaning of events as the cornerstones of a modern pragmatic history, concluding that such a history 'is one of the most useful sciences that can be pursued and promoted in a society' (*Stockholms historiska bibliotek* 1755: 61).

The moral function of history was also discussed in more bureaucratic documents pertaining to teaching. The connection between history and ethics had been institutionalized in Sweden in the School Ordinance of 1693 (Ahnlund 1956: 161). According to the plan of study outlined in the 1724 Ordinance, which replaced the 1693 Ordinance and was in effect until 1772, the relationship remained much the same. According to the Ordinance, history and ethics should be taught, at the gymnasium level, by the same instructor. The historical part contained two tiers, universal history and what was referred to as 'historiæ patriæ', whereas ethics exclusively concerned civic morality. Aided by a few primers in ethics, the Ordinance stressed the teacher's responsibility to teach history as a guide to judicious and public-spirited action. Thus, teachers of history and ethics were expected to make sure that 'appetite and love of virtue and honorable conduct would be impressed in the hearts of the young, and conversely aversion and abomination for all that is evil [and] destroys peace and fellowship in public life' (Hernlund 1892: 47). A 1734 instruction to history tutors concluded that since the capacity to memorize peaks somewhere between a person's tenth and twentieth year, history should be taught most vigorously within this period (Bliberg 1734: 1). History could be taught through play and during meals; lessons could be improved by visual aids – chiefly maps – and by reading out loud. Proper historical pedagogy also involved group exercises, where students were invited to interact and test each other's knowledge. An additional and perhaps obvious suggestion to instructors who wished to hold their listeners' attention was to embellish or amplify the stories they told with vivid language and exciting commentary (Bliberg 1734: 3–6).

The idea of using the past as a means to teach morality was not limited to history proper. According to the clergy in Stockholm, for example, Cicero's *De Officii* was much more than a reservoir of Latin eloquence. This seminal work in classical rhetoric, they claimed, could 'yield much fruit and benefit in young people through their pleasing morals and the splendid examples from the history of Greece and Rome which formed the contents of this book and which should be diligently recounted to young people to inspire in their minds desire and inclination to all forms of civil virtues' (cited in Hernlund 1892: 30–31, n.1).[19] In contemporary discussions of the 1724 Ordinance, the importance of studying national history was also noted. As the clergy in Lund accentuated: 'our Swedish history must not be disregarded, at least not since 1520, so that the students learn as much, if not more, about the feats of Gustavus I [or Gustavus Vasa] and his successors as about Darius, Alexander the Great and several of the kind' (cited in Hernlund 1892: 45, n.4). History and ethics were fused from 1724 to 1807, at which time a new ordinance formally made history a separate subject. The need to teach morality through history did not, however, abate with the separation of the two realms of knowledge. History teachers remained obliged to 'arouse and inspire love of the fatherland and its felicitous form of government', even after 1807 (Ahnlund 1956: 165).

Of special importance in educational history was the branch of political history that went under the name of 'universal political history'. According to a contemporary definition, the works in this genre chronicled 'the most noteworthy events recounted in individual or Particular Political Histories [about peoples and their governments] and provide a context for them' (Salvius 1771b: 4). There was a specific chronology and narrative, which proceeded from biblical chronology and accounted for the four successive monarchies ending with Rome.

Textbooks in universal political history were described as a form of time travel where the guide and his travellers stopped whenever instructive events in history unfolded. The journey was an image of personal growth and experience that was central to pedagogy. In an allegorical textbook that saw three editions during the eighteenth century, young readers were taken along with the book's protagonist on the road of life in search of the temple of virtue. Inside the temple, Aristotelian virtues were displayed in a kind of museum of morality. A similar idea of the path to virtue was discussed by the influential French orator A-L Thomas, who in a notable speech on princely education described the prince's study of previous rulers as a walk through an imaginary mausoleum where their virtues and vices were inscribed on the tombs of his predecessors.[20] Similar notions were expressed in other educational texts. In an abridged history for beginners the writer and publisher Lars Salvius told his readers that he would accompany them 'as on a journey to demonstrate the paramount encampments and places to rest along this road. So much the easier will it then be for you to fix in your memory all the remarkable events that have occurred at each and every place' (Salvius 1771a: preface).

Although the aforementioned historian Eberhardt did not dispute the benefits of textual teaching techniques, he maintained that the best way to communicate historical knowledge was by means of oral transmission. However, since the spoken word was easily forgotten, authors should limit their ambitions to relaying only those events that were likely to trigger the listener's imagination and use them as starting points of more comprehensive or more detailed discussions of meaning and morality (Eberhardt 1766–81: vol. 1, preface). Works on individual kings and prominent statesmen were published recurrently, as were both comprehensive and abridged histories of Sweden, some of which were written specifically for educational purposes (see for example Salvius 1771a). The following poem, found in a preface touting history as a means to forge national identity, is illustrative of the idea of moralizing history:

> Come Cherished Youth, and learn with zeal
> What Sweden's annals can reveal:
> And briefly here I can rehearse
> Their many pages in my verse. [...]
> Accept this gift from cordial hand
> Which tells you of your Fatherland
> And welcomes you to join with those
> Whose company you should espouse.
> And if you cherish what I tend
> More for your profit would I lend:
> To help you thrive and prosper too,
> And make a worthy Swede of you.

So zealously seek virtue here,
In studying wisdom persevere;
Be Wise and Virtuous by renown
Though others Enviously should frown. (Berghult 1764: preface)[21]

In the kind of educational or moralizing history under review, works on classical rhetoric, universal history and Swedish history – in full-length or in abridged form – were of central importance. One particular genre, however, took on paramount importance: the glorification of 'Great Men', a moralizing biographical historical genre that can be traced back to the historiography of ancient Greece. By bringing to life examples to follow and to avoid, history could assist individuals in moral navigation. In an important sense, accounts of the past provided a public supplement to the teaching of virtue in the private sphere, where parents and relatives acted as role models for their children. In the social sphere, the exemplary function was performed by the nation's 'forefathers'. According to Carl Henric Armfeldt in his 1765 dissertation on civil society: 'Their shortcomings can serve to warn us; but their mores as encouragement to seek assiduously fame as worthy as theirs and felicity as well deserved' (Armfeldt 1765: 36–37). Equipped with the kind of virtual experience that could be derived from getting to know the social worlds of previous generations, present and future ones were better prepared to face up to the difficult choices in life. That history could provide moral guidance was considered a basic truth of life, and it applied to everyone, from statesmen to private individuals. As Eberhardt wrote: 'History, if duly honored, offers eminent benefits. She demonstrates the Providence of GOD in the fates of entire States and individuals, encourages virtue, through the judgments of posterity, arouses ready abhorrence of vice, provides instruction for Potentates and inspires all to reflection and prudence' (Eberhardt 1766–81: vol. 1, 3). According to this approach, writes the historian Hugo Valentin (1888–1963), '[h]istory became for the educated public a picture gallery which brought the great men of the past to life' (Valentin 1957: 147. See also Delblanc 1965: 89). Familiarity with the qualities personified by significant individuals from previous ages assumedly inspired the present generation to behave in ways that would honour the memory of the ancients. Moreover, successful imitation could in turn secure contemporaries a place in the expanding pantheon of 'Great Men'. Eager to gain the respect of present and future generations, individuals would seek out a behaviour that reproduced civility, the consequences of which were beneficial to the entire citizenry of a modern enlightened community (Delblanc 1965: 11).[22]

The uses of historical *exempla* in moral education were of course a central part of courtly and aristocratic instruction. Members of prominent families, clans and dynasties contemplated the examples of their forefathers as a form of guidance in the present. In the case of courtly education, the idea was that the virtuous behaviour of rulers would be imitated by subjects, thus strengthening both the institution of kingship and the moral fibre of the people (Delblanc 1965: 86).[23] As Delblanc concludes in his study of the honour motif in eighteenth-century literature:

> History was the source of edifying examples, and it was convenient to link, as Sallust did, history writing with the presentation of moral examples. The same idea can be found in the 'praefatio' to Livy's massive history. The study of history, it claims, offers citizens examples of what to imitate and what to shun. (Delblanc 1965: 86–7, 9)

Speakers in the Royal Academy of Sciences engaged in the practice of canonizing 'Great Men' by institutionalizing eulogies over deceased fellows, thereby contributing to the breakthrough in the mid-eighteenth century of the biographical genre in Sweden (Sylwan 1935: 90; Lindroth 1978–81: vol. 3, 52).[24] Inspired by Fontanelle's oratory in the Académie de Sciences in Paris, the Academy at Stockholm followed a general European literary trend that resulted in a 'golden age' for biographical writing (Sylwan 1935: 90–91). By eulogizing academicians of various social backgrounds, the Academy also contributed to what Delblanc terms a 'democratization of honor'. The tendency to eulogize public men – kings, princes and other prominent men of state – was complemented by praising common men whose deeds and character traits were worthy of emulation (Delblanc 1965: 91).

Taking into account that the principles and procedures of the Royal Academy of Sciences were egalitarian and that its members conceived of their own work as contributions to the common good, it is not surprising that members claimed that honouring individuals from their own group was beneficial to society at large (Karlsson 1999a: 5–28). Eulogies of great but common men served a dual purpose: they honoured academicians for their contributions to the work of the Academy as well as to society at large and presented them as examples for contemporaries and future generations to follow (see for example Ehrenpreus 1748: 3). Even as influential eighteenth-century historians and social thinkers turned to the study of laws and institutions to explain historical processes, the cult of 'Great Men' remained central at least up until the mid-nineteenth century (Valentin 1957: 147–49).[25] In the section below, two different media that were used to honour 'Great Men' will be analysed in terms of how contemporaries viewed the ways in which they contributed to the formation of civic morality: statues (visual representation) and biographies (textual representation).

Statues and Biographies

In a 1755 speech on the state of contemporary Swedish science, literature and the arts, the aforementioned Carl Fredric Scheffer argued that the degree of perfection differed from area to area. His general conclusion was that the country at present had no reason to feel inferior. The paralysis of envy had been broken by steady improvement, resulting in a firmly rooted culture of knowledge. Sweden's advances in the natural sciences were beyond dispute and recognized throughout Europe. With regard to *belles-lettres*, however, he substituted confidence with a question mark. As opposed to the international standing of the natural sciences, the development of literature was uneven and far from perfected. Commendable improvements had taken place in subjects like poetry, eloquence, medals and history – especially Scandinavian antiquities – but in a comparative European perspective the nation lagged behind in key areas, such as epic poetry, tragedy, comedy, iconography and Roman antiquities. Scheffer praised the country's historians for their diligent efforts to immortalize the individuals and events of the past. Future generations could hence rest assured that they: 'are likely never to lack Memorials of times past, nor lack in these Memorials the order and clarity, the gift of discernment, the truth and the pleasant mode of writing with which in other countries those who have described such fates have made their own names and those of whom they wrote immortal' (Scheffer 1755: 5–6). This view was supported by one of the century's most prolific collectors of historical documents, Samuel Loenbom. Introducing a collection of documents in journal form, *Svenska archivum* (1766–72), he argued that all 'enlightened and civilized Peoples' made sure that the history writing of the past and the present was handed down to posterity and that Sweden was second to no other nation in this regard (*Svenska archivum* 1766: vol. 1, preface). Although Swedish historical writing was judged to be in good standing, Loenbom argued that work remained to be done. His own specialty, the collection and publication of written documents, was an effort to secure the past for the benefit of posterity. Carl Christoffer Gjörwell, who considered himself a servant to posterity as well, surveyed the historical field on a general level in one of his historical journals and concluded that, besides the first two parts of Olof Dalin's political history, the nation still lacked major works in a number of areas, specifically church history and intellectual history (Stockholms *historiska bibliotek* 1755: vol. 2, 154).

Scheffer's main purpose was to inquire about a specific medium of historical representation. The nation had failed, he claimed, to recognize not only the beauty of but also the public utility of statues. Rhetorically pondering possible explanations, Scheffer asked:

> Have we not too possessed Heroes, that a Michelangelo would have deemed worth portraying by his life-endowing hand? Indeed, Gentlemen! You know that in this world there are to be found few Countries able to list Regents as great as ours; Few where there have lived such courageous, renowned and honored Men, both in Peace and War, as here amongst us. (Scheffer 1755: 10)

The patriotic rhetoric amplified the image of an unfortunate and possibly unintended lapse in Swedish cultural policy. That it nonetheless was a serious gap followed from the idea that statues had a practical social function, namely, to impress on the spectator a will to undertake patriotic or virtuous deeds. '[T]he Imposing Figures in Marble and Bronze,' said Scheffer, 'which adorn the Cities and Palaces of other countries arouse in strangers great approbation of their respect for virtue and heroism, and impress on all who see them an innermost yearning for the exploits and honor memorialized by such rewards' (Scheffer 1755: 10).

The same idea about the power of representation was formulated by one of the century's most prominent Swedish public architects, Carl Fredric Adelcrantz, who asked: 'what greater inspiration can there be to virtue, courage, perseverance than to see the images of great Heroes, wise Men and valuable Citizens adorning these prominent localities dedicated to their well-deserved honor by a grateful posterity' (Adelcrantz 1757: 23–24).

To illustrate the utility of art in the social realm, Adelcrantz interjected an analogy to the role of representation in religious sermons. With the exception of the Bible, Adelcrantz argued that the techniques of speech and writing could not nearly induce the same effect as could visual forms of representation. Religious visual representation, he argued, was able to touch the hearts and minds of citizens if: 'an enlightened and skilful Painter selects and portrays the most particular and moving circumstances for the subject he intends to depict, composes them duly in the order which can most easily be grasped by the imagination, and devotes to each item the choicest reverence and emphasis' (Adelcrantz 1757: 10). Even though the exclusion in ancient Greece of 'slaves or inferiors' from the production of art had grown untenable in an enlightened and meritocratic-egalitarian era like the eighteenth century, Adelcrantz maintained that the standing of Greek civilization was partly the result of having paid careful attention to the art of representation. If the men and women of the eighteenth century hoped to reinvent themselves in the image of the ancients, they had to recognize the pivotal role of the arts in fostering civil morality. The true value of the arts rested not with their immediate visual appeal, but the ideas that they expressed – or represented – and the sensations and actions they incited in the onlooker. In a modern society founded on secular values of civility, art became not merely a concern for courtly and aristocratic education, but a truly societal concern, a category of public works (Adelcrantz 1757: 5, 8).

Referring to Scheffer's 1755 speech, Adelcrantz offered an explanation why Stockholm was one of the few European capitals that lacked statues of great kings: long periods of training and the expensive materials. He also pleaded that 'a wise Government should take time in hand and anticipate the hopes of the Public'. The best example of a ruler that had improved the arts was, according to Adelcrantz, Louis XIV (1643–1715), who in just twenty years had raised the quality of the arts to a level that a country like Sweden could only hope to reach in a matter of a hundred years (Adelcrantz 1757: 24–27). The Sun King's care of the arts earned him the name of 'enlightened Statesman' and Sweden's then ruler, Adolph Frederick (1751–1771), was complemented as 'a King no less worthy the name of Father of the Arts than of his Country' (Adelcrantz 1757: 27, 42). Pehr Wargentin, the Royal Academy of Sciences' secretary, in his response to Adelcrantz's speech reinforced this point by promising that the kind of honour bestowed upon Louis XIV would fall on Adolph Frederick if he emulated the French monarch. Such an undertaking would make his 'Name great and His Reign over the Realm of Sweden unforgettable throughout posterity!' (Wargentin 1757: 45).

The moral to be drawn from the example is clear. If a state hopes to inculcate civic virtues it will need to replicate the strategies of representation practiced by the Church, the ancient Greeks or the court of Louis XIV. Erecting statues of history's 'Great Men' held a central place in such a strategy. The fine arts in general – including medals, engraving, tapestry weaving and mosaics – were considered important as regards 'the utility and the benefits their industrious pursuit affords the Civil Society' (Adelcrantz 1757: 4).

According to Scheffer, the fact that statues were 'visual media' made them particularly appropriate as catalysts of patriotism. In cultures where large segments of the population were still unable to read about morality from books, he argued, the shape of marble could speak more than printed letters on a piece of paper. As Scheffer wrote, in a nation bereft of statues 'that section of the Nation's population that lacks the ability to peruse the annals [may] remain ignorant of who has governed, defended, served or enlightened their Country' (Scheffer 1755: 10–11). Statues could spark the onlooker's patriotic spirit; the prospect of remembrance, perhaps even immortality, would inspire citizens to do great things for their nation. Statues were hence useful to a civic education that ventured to disseminate patriotic emotions to ever-wider circles of society.

Adelcrantz went further in specifying the relative impact of visual versus written media. Like orators and poets, painters and sculptors had one chief objective: 'to render true to life, move and persuade'. In pursuing this essentially rhetorical task, the visual artists had the upper hand, since their representations targeted not the ears and the intellect, but the eyes and the imagination. 'While the impression of the first endures for one day,' the state architect claimed, 'the latter lasts a lifetime.' Moreover, the works of the visual artist transgressed boundaries of language, age and social status:

> A Chinaman or wild American has as great an understanding as a Swede or an Italian. Orators and Poets are only understood by a handful, Artists by everyone. Infants reach out their hands for their works before they can speak: and they move unlettered Peasants as mightily as any King. In one word, the speech of artists is understood by all countries, by all ages and by all estates. (Adelcrantz 1757: 13)

Scheffer and Adelcrantz would probably have contended that contributing to the common good enhances individual happiness, but his speech about the utility of statues, measured in a civilized and patriotic citizenry, was occasioned by social or political considerations: order, progress and honour. Having praised Adolph Frederick and his Queen Lovisa Ulrica for paying attention to the fine arts, Adelcrantz towards the end of his speech turned to the Diet to deliver a promise of the utility of the arts that also illustrates the state's interest in representation. The recent creation of an Academy of Painting and the delivery of pensions and other forms of economic compensation to artists, he assured the Diet, 'are likely to become yet another reason for the Public to praise the concern of their Government for the true welfare of their Nation' (Adelcrantz 1757: 42). If the state to an extent had become dependent for its functioning on the morality of the people, attending to the fine arts, the argument went, would guarantee the government the support of the citizenry and make it respected.

The belief in the didactic potential of the past was also expressed by the authors of three major attempts to introduce historical biography to Sweden in the 1750s: Anders af Botin, Carl Christoffer Gjörwell and Anders Schönberg. According to Botin, history undoubtedly served an educational purpose. A good memory, access to primary sources and the ability to write prose were not sufficient to carry out this task. When executed truthfully, judiciously and written in a suitable style, accounts of the past

> prevail pleasantly on the Reader's fancy and attention, and similarly implant in his heart love of virtue, detestation of vice, reverence for GOD's Providence: may his understanding be enlightened by examples of the sagacity of some, admonished by the precepts of the ignorance of others ... Without reverence

for GOD, without respect for virtue, and without love of the human race, a Historian has failed his purpose, and produced what is worse than nothing, unless his Work furnish our minds with reflection and enlightenment, our hearts with improvement and comfort, our fancy with invigorating respite and profitable diversion. (Botin 1771: 3–5)[26]

Botin's basic idea here is that the capacity of history to influence people's behaviour made it tempting for all kinds of projects, both good and bad. Thus, every history book that was published entailed a certain risk, a fact that made criticism a matter of utmost importance. A historical account that failed to separate the important from the unimportant risked becoming a winding tale without purpose, and thus incapacitated to 'move and persuade' (Botin 1771: 5). Botin's own work in political history, *Utkast till Svenska Folkets Historia* (1757–64), was novel in the sense that he abandoned chronology and instead created time periods which he in turn systematically analysed in sub-sections dedicated to a discussion of the availability and quality of sources; an overview of the most important actions of rulers; intellectual developments; religious practices; economic and legal systems; popular mentalities; and accounts of the 'Great Men' that lived during the respective time period. As Nils Eriksson points out, eighteenth-century observers concluded that Botin had been influenced by Voltaire's path-breaking *Siècle de Louis XIV* (1751) in this respect (Eriksson 1973: 31–33). Moreover, the work was clearly written and used typography as an aid to reading comprehension. Each page was accompanied by a heading telling the reader which period the author discussed, a technique that was refined by also including the chapter numbers, when Botin's account of the sixth period (covering the years 1389–1520) came out in 1764.

Now, history's contribution to the formation of a civic morality applied to all genres, but it was most pronounced in the biographical genre. In his introductory remarks to a projected series in the genre, Botin commented on the deficit of biographical literature in Sweden. A cultivated people that held science in high esteem, he proposed, deserved better and accordingly requested two transformations: political history had to be made more readable and historical biographies that 'lend us wisdom by example' had to be published. Like other historical genres, Botin continued, biographies 'instruct us that they who are happy are those who follow the principles of virtue and abstain from intentions that lead neither to the glory of God nor to the honor of their Fatherland' (Botin 1750: 3–4).

Relaying the mechanisms and consequences of the virtuous and the villainous, the historical biography promised individual and common happiness. The struggle between good and evil was likened to a theatre where protagonists of the past embodied particular character traits, such as hauteur, rowdiness, vindictiveness, greatness, vanity, melancholy and staunchness. Perhaps more than any other of the human sciences, Botin concluded, history was unique in that it 'apart from its usefulness also has the power to entrance and, as it were, bewitch its readers with a multitude of events and dire fates: a Spectacle in which we see vice and virtue compete in the guise of ever-changing Characters, Destinies and Transformations' (Botin 1750: 6). Botin's own work in the genre was well received by the scholarly community. Commenting on Botin's efforts when his second biography of great Swedish men appeared, one of the country's scholarly reviews wrote: 'Other cultivated Peoples, even among our closest Neighbors, have cherished the Memories of their great Men and to pay them due reverence and encourage Imitation of their conduct have caused Histories of their Lives to be written and published' (*Lärda Tidningar* 1754: 201).[27]

The past was understood to possess a unique way of stirring the imagination of readers; and the focus on great individuals provided the essential elements of this idea of history as theatre or drama. Unlike the drama proper, however, the historical biography contained no fictional elements. As Henrik Julius Woltemat, one of the most prolific writers of history textbooks of the century, suggested in a definition of the term 'history', the events of the past had to be written in a language that could engage the reader, but this in no way suggested that the line between history and literature was blurred. He wrote: 'What is history? History is a true Account of numerous remarkable past events. [It] is therefore very different from Romances, Fables and Sagas, which have been invented. The more vivid the account given by history of what has occurred or happened, the more pleasant it is' (Woltemat 1770: 3). According to Botin, fictional sources such as the old sagas were not really sources at all; and where fully reliable sources were unavailable, the historian had to keep silent. For this reason, many of the great men of ancient times could never be the subjects of a truthful historical biography. As for the question of the intentions behind a protagonist's actions, Botin warned the historian against speculating too wildly into the psychology of their historical actors but conceded that a history devoid of intentionality would rob it of 'the adornment, value and utility that such considerations afford' (Botin 1750: 9–10).

'Great' individuals were not necessarily good individuals. Botin thus followed the classical conception of history as a genre that concerned itself with both the admirable and the lamentable, presenting life as an incessant demand to choose rightly. This is precisely why truth was so central to the genre. As Botin wrote: 'In sooth, I take my heroes as I find them. I delineate good and ill impartially, and each and every one as the accounts in our oldest and most excellent annals give me motive, reason and cause' (Botin 1750: 14). A similar attitude to biography was voiced in the historical journal *Stockholms historiska bibliotek* where an honest approach to one's subject was described as the hallmark of a worthy biography (*Stockholms historiska bibliotek* 1755: vol. 2, 254–70).

Botin clearly perceived the potential conflict between norms and facts in historical writing. On the one hand, he concluded, history was a 'science, which is to edify us with its examples'. On the other hand, the 'life and soul' of historical writing was 'truth'. Botin identified a straightforward solution to this dilemma of morality versus truth. The normative demand that followed from history's pedagogical task in practice meant that the historian 'offers us handsome deeds to follow'; truthfulness required of the historian to bring to the surface a protagonist's blemishes and lapses of judgment, thus relaying 'what is odious as a warning' (Botin 1750: 15). In this way, the potential conflict between morality and truth could be bridged: an educational history that included both the good and the bad could be truthfully written, since both were of pedagogical use. In fact, balancing positive and negative traits was, according to Botin, a reflection of human nature. History could not provide a single example of either pure virtue or pure vice, for the simple reason that such beings existed neither among the dead nor among the living. The most perfected human being imaginable was an individual that could be said to possess the least number of weaknesses. The most praiseworthy were, by the same token, those who knew their faults and had the courage to correct them (Botin 1750: 15).

This view of the plasticity of human nature and the contingency of virtue further explains the centrality of distinguishing between 'Great Men', on the one hand, and good men, on the other, a distinction that was analysed in more detail in Anders Schönberg's contribution to the biographical genre. As for the utility of writing about the past, Schönberg, who in 1762 would be appointed *historiographus regni*, considered it so obvious that arguments to that effect were superfluous. 'To deal at length with the benefits and uses of history would be to recount what everyone knows and nobody contests,' he told his readers (Schönberg 1756: vol. 1, preface). Schönberg too observed a problem related to the anachronistic or moralistic view of history that was central to the biography. Between the events and personalities of history and the text meant to instruct contemporary readers stood the writer and the context within which he or she approached the subject. A people characterized by a pacifist mentality would thus value peaceful rulers while a more belligerent nation would honour warrior kings. To rid biography from the idiosyncratic value systems of present generations, Schönberg offered a rather conventional theory of just government, according to which a good ruler wielded power for one purpose only: the well-being of his subjects. If historians followed these maxims, their accounts would yield the expected benefits (Schönberg 1756: vol. 1, preface).

The purpose of this excursion was to emphasize the ambiguity of character. Since rulers are human beings, they display positive and negative traits. Here appears again the notion that a ruler 'whose virtues outweigh his vices' could rightly be considered a good ruler (Schönberg 1756: vol. 1, preface). Greatness in itself could not, however, guarantee a king or emperor a place in the pantheon of virtue and it was the biographer's task to tease out the relationship between two phenomena: greatness, which was typically understood as related to military feats, and goodness, which by contrast was related to domestic affairs, in areas such as agriculture, education and the arts (Schönberg 1756: vol. 1, preface; see also *Lärda Tidningar* 1750: 201). According to Schönberg, only good rulers were suitable to the project of educating for virtue. The definition of what constituted goodness in this context was up to the biographer to decide; Schönberg did so by listing thirty-two maxims of state (Schönberg 1756: vol. 2, preface). The actions of kings and emperors were crucial elements in a pedagogy of virtue that relied heavily on the power of representation and imitation (Schönberg 1756: vol. 2, preface). Biographies could not do without them.

With regard to the subjects that were suitable for historical biography, Schönberg's inspiration, the Norwegian-born playwright, historian and moralist Ludvig Holberg's popular biographies, had included individuals that, according to him, contributed to moral education as personifications of vice, the most striking one being perhaps the biography of Mohammed.[28] Translated into Swedish by the prolific writer and publisher of historical works Carl Christoffer Gjörwell, it was included in the second volume of a biography of his from 1756. The life of the prophet from Mecca could prove instructive to Swedish readers. Although European writers in their treatment of Mohammed were said to have been blinded (occasionally) by their own hostility towards and/or ignorance of Islam, Holberg's biography adhered to an ethnocentric narrative that modern scholarship labels 'Orientalism' (Gjörwell 1755–56: vol. 2, 3).[29] Mohammed personified a corrupt individual whose vices could in principle be found everywhere. At the same time, the biography in question closely related his vices to a religious moral system, Islam. Thus, the two cardinal vices that the prophet was said to suffer from – ambition and lechery – were furthermore said to be sanctioned in the Quran and form the backbone of the Islamic faith (Gjörwell 1755–56: vol. 2, 34–36). With a few exceptions – for example the practice of giving donations to the needy, caring for the poor, tolerance of religion, seriousness – the Islamic religion was devoid of lessons in virtue (Gjörwell 1755–56: vol. 2, 39). A man of trade from his early years, Mohammed in his late twenties married into a family fortune, an aquisition that his biographer said developed in him 'pride and ambition' (Gjörwell 1755–56: vol. 2, 5). The life of Mohammed was predictably contrasted with that of Christ, with the explicit intention to demonstrate Mohammed's 'false vocation, mission and religion' (Gjörwell 1755–56: vol. 2, 39–40). Finally, readers were told the moral of the story, namely, that Mohammed 'after every consideration is and remains the greatest deceiver of man that has ever lived' (Gjörwell 1755–56: vol. 2, 39–40).

Concluding Remarks

As I have tried to show in this chapter, social utility for an emerging enlightened modern nation was believed to be the ultimate end of inquiries into the past in the eighteenth century. In that sense, historical research was no different from any other branch of knowledge. History did, however, have a particular social task. It was conceived within an emerging language of civil society, which outlined humankind's ascent from a lawless state of nature to a form of social organization where laws governed the relations between individuals and groups. A constitutive aspect of the idea of a civil society was the citizenry's ability and willingness to freely respect laws and contribute to the good of the whole. A predominately negative appreciation of humankind's natural inclinations as selfish but malleable meant that moral education became integral to the creation and maintenance of a civil society. History writing, a seemingly unanimous chorus of eighteenth-century intellectuals concluded, provided one of the most effective means to foment a civic and secular morality.

History's unique ability to bring to life examples of virtue and vice were believed to instil in people a concern for the common good, thus mobilizing them in the civilizing project of the state. Once imparted, patriotic dispositions and a shared sense of purpose would aid the nation to fulfil its promise of perpetual progress. This brand of 'pragmatic' history was not clearly demarcated from ethics: the two subjects were taught side by side throughout the eighteenth century. Statues and biographies of 'Great Men' as well as moralizing narratives were conceived of as important instruments to create and maintain a civil society based on values like liberty and labour. At a time when enlightenment critiques of superstition cohabited with a nearly obsessive preoccupation with industry, patriotism emerged as a supreme social virtue and it became one of the historian's tasks to advance it through his or her writings.

The analysis also reveals the intensity with which politicians, academicians, publicists and artists believed that art, ritual and symbolic representation harboured the potential to influence minds and direct action. To the writers of historical biographies, whose approach to the past has been discussed in this chapter, the book of history may not have been more revered than the Bible, but the force with which they argued that the history of the nation and humankind could create bonds that enable civil society nonetheless suggests that secular narratives and examples became indispensable tools to instil in the population a sense of civility and patriotism. The state architect Carl Fredric Adelcrantz's reflections on the power of symbolic representation are particularly illustrative in this regard. Discussing the social benefits of erecting statues of 'Great Men', contrasting this function with purely aesthetic factors, Adelcrantz argued that such statues connected the population with their past and encouraged them to do great things for their nation. Moreover, a clearly visible heroic past also contributed to raising Sweden's standing in the eyes of other nations. Although this view was arguably in part a public justification for individual interests, such as securing appointments to public office and pensions, it nonetheless relays how historical writings were legitimated in public discourse, and thus provides information about the normative parameters of historical discourse in eighteenth-century Sweden.

Notions of history's social task, as well as a sincere belief in the power of representation, were not new to the middle of the eighteenth century. Indeed, politically motivated artistic and intellectual production is as old as organized politics itself. The novelty rather appears to be the projects to which history was put to use. Although generations of scholars had written histories to aid statesmen in performing the duties of their office and conceived ceremonies to impress foreign courts and delight social elites, the mid-eighteenth-century works analysed above targeted a much wider audience for their histories. The great benefit that contemporaries associated with visual representations of history, such as statues, was that they could be 'read' even by illiterate people.

Visual historical imagery was, however, a marginal medium compared to written texts. Writers and printers were acutely aware of the issues raised by the advocates of visual representation, specifically the need to adapt the media to the competence of the audience. For history to fulfil its promise as an instrument of a secular morality believed to lend support to a modern nation, accounts of the past had to be disseminated throughout society, a stylistic and technological challenge that eighteenth-century writers and printers took very seriously.

Notes

1. This article was written with financial support from Riksbankens Jubileumsfond and the Swedish Collegium for Advanced Study.
2. The concept of 'utility' in eighteenth-century Swedish discourse is studied by Patoluoto 1979: 1–21.
3. The standard works on the Royal Swedish Academy of Sciences are Hildebrand 1939 and Lindroth 1967, vol. 1–2. The most recent work is Kärnfelt 2000, which specifically deals with the popularization of knowledge.
4. See also Lindroth 1978–81: vol. 3, 48.
5. For a discussion of cosmopolitanism and eighteenth-century historiography in Europe, see O'Brien 1997.
6. The standard Swedish dictionary, *Svenska akademiens ordbok*, does not list 1749, the year of Dalin's speech, but 1751 and 1755 as the first instances of this usage of the term 'Age of Liberty'.
7. The parties of Hats and Caps ran across estate lines, although members of the upper nobility and commercial groups tended to belong to the former party while members of the lower nobility, clergymen and peasants tended to belong to the latter. The Hats tended to national prestige and defence and were supported by France. The Caps were in favour of less aggressive foreign policy and were supported by Russia. See Carlsson 1981; Metcalf 1977; Roberts 1973; Valentin 1915; Lagerroth 1915.
8. Although the initiative to create an academy of science came from an amateur physicist, Mårten Triewald, its actual institution is credited to a politician: the Hat and nobleman Anders Johan von Höpken. See Lindroth 1978–81: vol. 3, 489, 56. On the Hat regime and its policies, see Roberts 1986: 111ff.
9. 'Where-ever therefore any number of Men are so united into one Society, as to quit every one his Executive Power of the Law of Nature, and to resign it to the public, there and there only is a *Political*, or *Civil Society*. And this is done wherever any number of Men, in the state of Nature, enter into Society to make one People, one Body Politick under one Supreme Government, or else when any one joyns himself to, and incorporates with any Government already Made' (Locke 1969 [1690]: 343).
10. The original English title of the *Second Treatise* was *An Essay Concerning the True Original, Extent, and End of Civil Government*. On the details of the English editions of Locke's *Treatise*, see Peter Laslett's seminal introduction in Locke 1969 [1690]. The Swedish translation was a highly official affair. In addition to being commissioned by the Chancery College, it carried the stamp of royal privilege, was published in the royal printing house and was translated by the royal translator. For a more detailed analysis of the concept of civil society in the Swedish context, see Hallberg 2006. For an analysis of the transformations of the sources and transformations of the concept in European discourse, with particular emphasis on the Aristotelian and renaissance political vocabularies, see Hallberg and Wittrock 2006.

11. As Frängsmyr (1972) has shown, these ideas on the origins and constitution of states and societies reached a wide European readership through the works of Christian Wolff, published between 1740 and 1750. Wolffianism became influential in constitutional law education in Sweden as well, especially at Uppsala. Wolff's major works in natural law were *Jus Naturæ methodo scientifica pertractatum* (1740–48) and *Institutiones Juris Naturæ & Gentium* (1750).
12. Dalin's magazine had around five hundred subscribers and was also sold as single copies. It was also distributed in the provinces. See Oscarsson 2000: 98–104. After 1734, when *Then swänska Argus* was discontinued, thirty journals that more or less reproduced its content and form were started, including *Den Philosophiske Mercurius* and *Den Swenske Patrioten* (1734–35); *Skuggan af den döda Argus* (1735); *Thet Swenska Nitet* (1738); and *Then Swenska Sanningen* (1739–40). See Oscarsson 2000: 108. According to a notice in *Stockholms historiska bibliotek* 1755, vol. 2, 150–51, the magazine was still talked about and in high demand in 1755. According to the same source, it was also translated into Danish. Popular demand at home reportedly resulted in a second revised edition in 1754.
13. On the whole, Dalin did not rebuke noble status, but his critique of status attributes was appropriated in the more systematic campaigns against the first estate that would erupt after his death in 1763. See also Carlsson 1962: 56 and esp. Hessler 1943.
14. Professor Pehr Adrian Gadd, an influential eighteenth-century academic inquiring into the relationship between patriotism and prosperity, chaired the defence of this dissertation. It is not unlikely that the dissertation was written by the senior academic, which was not unusual in seventeenth- and eighteenth-century academia (Lindberg 1976: 2). For the sake of convenience, Armfeldt will be treated as the author of the dissertation.
15. The author in this context uses corporeal metaphors, speaking of the decline of morals as 'a wound ... in the body politic' and 'harmful fluids ... in the body of the State' (Armfeldt 1765: 5–6).
16. Understood as a modern approach to political thinking. See Wootton 1996: 1–4. See also Skinner 1981.
17. He also made a vague distinction between virtues that emanated from the intellect, the will and religion (Armfeldt 1765: 9–11).
18. On the relationship between age and moral education, see also Wrede 1743: 26 and Polhem 1745: 9.
19. According to Delblanc (1965: 86–87), Plutarch's biography of Pericles was for the same reason an influential collection of moral examples in Western discourse, from the renaissance to the romantic era.
20. The allegorical textbook, *Ett nätt och kort Begrep af hela Sedo-läran uti en mycket nyttig och nöjsam Historia om Aretophilo* (1735) and Thomas are discussed in Delblanc 1965: 21, 106.

21. See also Bliberg 1734: 10, who also uses poetry to entice his young readers.
22. Or as David Lowenthal (1997: 47) puts it: 'Like pilgrimages to the relics of antiquity, the study of history improved the character and inspired patriotism'.
23. For an example of this view, see Pufendorf 1688: preface.
24. Funeral oratory had been practised in the higher echelons of Swedish society in the seventeenth century. It had also been a minor concern of the learned society that the Academy superseded the Society of Science (*Vetenskapssocieteten*) at Uppsala.
25. See e.g. the discussion of Botin's work in the next section of the present chapter.
26. Botin argued that the country still lacked a rigorous work in political history. The closest approximation to such a work was Olof Dalin's history of the realm (1747–62), which he found wanting in several respects (Botin 1771: 7ff.).
27. For a review of Botin's biography from 1750, see *Lärda Tidningar* 1750.
28. For Holberg as a historian, see Westergaard 1952: 168–70; Østergard 1992: 7–9.
29. For the tradition of 'Orientalism' and its pejorative uses to describe non-Western culture, see Said 1978 and Rendall 1982.

References

Adelcrantz, Carl Fredric (1757) *Tal om de fria konsters värde och nytta; hållit för kongl. vetenskaps academien vid praesidii nedläggande, den 23 julii, år 1757.* Stockholm: Salvius.
Ahnlund, Nils (1956) *Tradition och historia.* Stockholm: Norstedt.
Armfeldt, Carl Henric (1765) *Afhandling, om Medel, At Förekomma Borgerliga Seders Almenna Fördärf.* Åbo: Frenckell.
Berghult, Anders (1764) *Kort inledning til den gamla och nya swenska historien, uti frågor och swar, til ungdomens tjenst författad.* Stockholm: Nyström/Stolpe.
Bliberg, Petrus Andrae (1734) *Christian Weisens Kloke Hofmästare, Det är: Kort doch tydelig Anledning huruledes en Sorgfällig Informator skal uti historien underrätta De sig anförtrodde Läro-Piltar; Samt så handleda dem i Unga Åhren, at de sedan, utan särdeles beswärlighet och hinder, sjelfwe må kunna läsa historien och anwända den sig til nytta.* Stockholm: Horrn.
Botin, Anders af (1771) *Anmärkningar vid herr hof-cancellerens och riddarens Olof v. Dalins Svea rikes historia.* Stockholm: Salvius.
—— (1757–64) *Utkast till svenska folkets historia.* 4 vols. Stockholm: Salvius.
—— (1750) *Af stora och namnkunniga svänska mäns lefverne första stycket. Om then kongl. prinsen Styrbjörn,* vol. 1. Stockholm: Salvius.
Carlsson, Ingemar (1981) *Parti – partiväsen – partipolitiker 1731–43: kring uppkomsten av våra första politiska partier.* Stockholm: Almqvist & Wiksell.
Carlsson, Sten (1962) *Bonde – präst – ämbetsman: svensk ståndscirkulation från 1680 till våra dagar.* Stockholm: Prisma.
Christensson, Jakob (1996) *Lyckoriket: studier i svensk upplysning.* Stockholm: Atlantis.
Dalin, Olof (1749) *Tal vid praesidii afläggande om Sverige i sit ämne och Sverige i sin upodling, hållit i kongl. svenska vetenskaps academien, den 29. apr. 1749.* Stockholm: Salvius.

Delblanc, Sven (1965) *Ära och minne: studier kring ett motivkomplex i 1700-talets litteratur*. Stockholm: Bonnier.
Eberhardt, Johan Hartman (1766–81) *Utkast til allmänna historien i äldre och nyare tider*. 4 vols. Stockholm: Hesselberg/Pfeiffer/Ordens-Tryckeriet.
Ehrenpreus, Carl Didrik (1748) *Tal om den förmån och nytta som fria konster och handaslögder tilskyndas af historien, hållit för kongl. vetensk. academien af Carl Ehrenpreus, då han lade af sit praesidium den 23 april 1748*. Stockholm: Salvius.
Eisenstadt, S.N. (2000) 'Multiple Modernities', *Daedalus* 129(1): 1–30.
Elvius, Pehr (1746) 'Svar', in Carl Gustaf Tessin, *Kårt tal om svenska språkets rykt och upodlande, hållit för kongl. svenska vetenskaps academien, af Carl Gustaf Tessin, då han afträdde sit praesidium d. 10. januarii 1746*. Stockholm: Salvius.
Eriksson, Nils (1973) *Dalin – Botin – Lagerbring: historieforskning och historieskrivning i Sverige 1747–1787*. Göteborg: Göteborgs universitet.
Frängsmyr, Tore (1972) *Wolffianismens genombrott i Uppsala: frihetstida universitetsfilosofi till 1700-talets mitt*. Uppsala: Uppsala universitet/Almqvist & Wiksell.
―――― (1998) 'Fanns det en svensk upplysning?', in Ronny Ambjörnsson, Pär Eliasson and Björn Olsson (eds), *Upplysningen i periferin*. Umeå: Umeå Universitet.
Gjörwell, Carl Christoffer (1755–56). *Stora och namnkunniga menniskjors lefwernesbeskrifningar och caracterer*, vol. 1–2. Stockholm: Nyström/Salvius.
Hallberg, Peter (2006) 'The Nationalization and Popularization of Political Language: The Concept of "Civil Society" in Swedish' in Peter Wagner (ed.), *The Languages of Civil Society*. New York and Oxford: Berghahn Books, 55–82.
Hallberg, Peter and Björn Wittrock (2006) 'From Koinonìa Politikè to Societas Civilis: Birth, Disappearance and First Renaissance of the Concept' in Peter Wagner (ed.), *The Languages of Civil Society*. New York and Oxford: Berghahn Books, 28–51.
Hernlund, Hugo (1892) *Bidrag till den svenska skollagstiftningens historia under partitidehvarfvet 1718–1809, I:B. Öfversigter och öfriga bilagor, Bilaga IV*. Stockholm: Isaac Marcus' boktryckeri.
Hessler, Carl Arvid (1943) "Aristokratifördömandet". En riktning i svensk historieskrivning', *Scandia* 15: 209–66.
Hildebrand, Bengt (1939) *Kungl. Svenska vetenskapsakademien: förhistoria, grundläggning och första organisation*. 2 vols. Stockholm/Uppsala: Kungliga vetenskapsakademien & Almqvist & Wiksell.
Karlsson, Christer (1999) 'Åminnelsetal i Kungl. Vetenskaps-akademien'. Working paper, Centrum för vetenskapshistoria, Kungl. Vetenskapsakademien, Stockholm, Sweden.
Kärnfelt, Johan (2000) *Mellan nytta och nöje: ett bidrag till populärvetenskapens historia i Sverige*. Göteborg: Göteborgs universitet.
Kongl. Maj:ts nådigste stadfästelse på svenska vetenskaps academiens grund-reglor. Gifven Stockholm i råd-cammaren den 31. martii. 1741. Stockholm: Kongliga tryckeriet/Momma.
Lagerroth, Fredrik (1915) *Frihetstidens författning: en studie i den svenska konstitutionalismens historia*. Stockholm: Bonnier.

Lärda Tidningar (1750), no. 51. Stockholm: Salvius.
—— (1754), no. 50. Stockholm: Salvius.
Lindberg, Bo (1976) *Naturrätten i Uppsala 1655–1720*. Uppsala/Stockholm: Uppsala Universitet/Liber.
Lindroth, Sten (1967) *Kungl. Svenska vetenskapsakademiens historia 1739–1818*. 2 vols. Uppsala: Kungliga vetenskapsakademien & Almqvist & Wiksell.
—— (1978–81) *Svensk lärdomshistoria*. Stockholm: Norstedt.
Locke, John (1726) *Johan Lockes Oförgripelige tankar om werldslig regerings rätta ursprung, gräntsor och ändamål*. Stockholm: Kongliga tryckeriet.
—— (1969) *Two Treaties of Government*. Cambridge: Cambridge University Press.
Lowenthal, David (1997) *The Past is a Foreign Country*. Cambridge: Cambridge University Press.
Mennander, Carl Fredric (1756) *Tal om bok-handelen i Sverige, hållit för kongl. vetenskaps academien vid praesidii afläggande, den 8 maji, 1756*. Stockholm: Salvius.
Metcalf, Michael F. (1977) 'The First "Modern" Party System? Political Parties, Sweden's Age of Liberty and the Historians', *Scandinavian Journal of History* 2: 265–87.
Nilsén, Per (2000) *Att stoppa munnen till på bespottare och underrätta andra: den akademiska undervisningen i svensk statsrätt under frihetstiden*. Lund: Juridiska fakulteten.
Nordin, Jonas (2000) *Ett fattigt men fritt folk: nationell och politisk självbild i Sverige från sen stormaktstid till slutet av frihetstiden*. Eslöv: Symposion.
O'Brien, Karen (1997) *Narratives of Enlightenment: Cosmopolitan History from Voltaire to Gibbon*. Cambridge: Cambridge University Press.
Oscarsson, Ingemar (2000) 'Med tryckfrihet som tidig tradition (1732–1809)' in Karl Erik Gustafsson and Per Rydén (eds), *Den svenska pressens historia: I begynnelsen (tiden före 1830)*, vol. 1. Stockholm: Ekerlid, 98–215.
Patoluoto, Ilkka (1979) 'Nyttobegreppet i 1700-talets Sverige', *Historisk tidskrift för Finland* 64: 1–21.
Polybius (1925) *The Histories*, vol. 4. London: Heinemann.
Pufendorf, Samuel (1688) *Samuel Pufendorfs Innledning till swänska historien, med där till fogad ökning ställt emot en fransos, Antoine Varillas benämd*. Stockholm: Eberdt.
Rendall, Jane (1982) 'Scottish Orientalism: From Robertson to James Mill', *The Historical Journal* 25(1): 43–69.
Roberts, Michael (1973) *Swedish and English Parliamentarism in the Eighteenth Century*. Belfast: The Queen's University.
—— (1986) *The Age of Liberty: Sweden, 1719–1772*. Cambridge: Cambridge University Press.
Rousseau, Jean-Jacques (1993) *The Social Contract and Discourses*. London: Dent.
Saastamoinen, Kari (1999) 'Political Vocabularies in Early Modern Sweden'. Paper presented at the *History of Concepts – The Finnish Project in European Context Conference*, 15–18 September, at Tampere, Finland.
Said, Edward W. (1978) *Orientalism*. New York: Vintage.

Salvius, Lars (1771a) *Svenska historien, til yngsta begynnares tjenst sammandragen*. Stockholm: Salvius.

—— (1771b) *Den universala politiska historien, yngsta begynnare til tjenst sammandragen och fortsatt til närvarande tid*. Stockholm: Salvius.

Sandels, Samuel (1771) *Tal, om kongl. svenska vetenskaps academiens inrättning och dess fortgång til närvarande tid, hållit för kongl. vetensk. academien, vid praesidii nedläggande, den 6 november 1771*. Stockholm: Salvius.

Scheffer, Carl Fredric (1755) *Tal, hållit för kongl. vetenskaps academien vid praesidii afläggande, den 2 augusti, år 1755*. Stockholm: Salvius.

Schönberg, Anders (1756) *Hjältars sammanliknade historier; på baron Holbergs sätt*. 2 vols. Stockholm: Salvius.

Segerstedt, Torgny (1971) *Den akademiska friheten under frihetstiden: en sammanställning*. Uppsala: Uppsala universitet/Almqvist & Wiksell.

Skinner, Quentin (1981) *Machiavelli*. Oxford: Oxford University Press.

Stockholms historiska bibliotek (1755), vol. 1–2 Stockholm: Nyström/Gjörwell.

Svenska archivum (1766), vol. 1. Stockholm: Kongliga tryckeriet.

Sylwan, Otto (1935) 'Till svensk biografis historiografi', *Samlaren* 35(1): 90–112.

Tessin, Carl Gustaf (1746) *Kårt tal om svenska språkets rykt och upodlande, hållit för kongl. svenska vetenskaps academien, af Carl Gustaf Tessin, då han afträdde sit praesidium d. 10. januarii 1746*. Stockholm: Salvius.

Then swänska Argus (1732–34), no. 1–16. Stockholm: Schneider.

Valentin, Hugo (1915) *Frihetstidens riddarhus: några bidrag till dess karakteristik*. Stockholm: Geber.

—— (1957) *Den fjättrade Clio: sju essäer till belysning av historikerns tidsbundenhet*. Stockholm: Natur och kultur.

Vegesack, Thomas von (2001) *Iakttagelser vid gränsen: när skönlitteraturen möter sina vedersakare*. Stockholm: Natur och kultur.

Wargentin, Pehr (1757) 'Svar, Gifvit på Kongl. Vetensk. Academiens Vägnar, Af Des Secreterare' in Carl Fredric Adelcrantz, *Tal om de fria konsters värde och nytta; hållit för kongl. vetenskaps academien vid praesidii nedläggande, den 23 julii, år 1757*. Stockholm: Salvius, 27–29.

Westergaard, Waldemar (1952) 'Danish History and Danish Historians', *The Journal of Modern History* 24(2): 167–80.

Wittrock, Björn (1998) 'Early Modernities: Varieties and Transitions', *Daedalus* 127(3): 19–44.

Woltemat, Henrik Julius (1770) *Anwisning til hela stats-historien: Det är en kort beskrifning af de märkvärdigaste ifrån äldre til närwarande tid uti Europa, Asien, Africa och America florerande staters största förändringar, och förnämsta öden. De första begynnare til tjänst, uti wissa frågor och swar*. Stockholm: Wennberg & Nordström.

Wootton, David (1996) 'Machiavelli and the Renaissance' in David Wootton (ed.), *Modern Political Thought: Readings from Machiavelli to Nietzsche*. Indianapolis and Cambridge: Hackett, 1–4.

Wrede, Hindric Jacob (1743) *Tal om et borgerligit samhälles eller et land ock rikes rätta styrka, samt sätt ock utvägar at komma där til, hållit för kongl. svenska vetenskaps academien den 26 januarii år 1743.* Stockholm: Salvius.

Østergard, Uffe (1992) 'Peasants and Danes: The Danish National Identity and Political Culture', *Comparative Studies in Society and History* 34(1): 3–27.

CHAPTER 6
The Metamorphoses of Norwegian Reformism

Rune Slagstad

The Norwegian modernization project has a centre in the political. So have the historical accounts of the project. The most influential historian since 1945, Jens Arup Seip, describes the shifting political regimes – the 'civil servants' state' (1814–1884), the 'Liberal Party state' (1884–1940), the 'Labour Party state' (1945 to ca. 1980) – in terms of which elite groups had control of resources of power and thus were able to operate from strategic positions in the central political machine (Seip 1974, 1981). The shifting regimes are determined by the political struggle for power, by gaining it and exercising it. This Machiavellian perspective on politics as a strategic power struggle was challenged in the 1970s by Francis Sejersted, the first Conservative historian of any weight in the Norwegian system for generations. The study of politics also requires a concept of negative power, the binding of the ongoing exercise of power with legal and constitutional ties, and a concept of communicative power, the ability to agree on the common good through free discussion. The Conservative historian challenged Seip's radical interpretive hegemony by calling on two theoreticians with roots in the Marxist tradition, Jon Elster and Jürgen Habermas (Sejersted 1984, 1988).[1]

Sejersted shed a clear light on the tension between politics and law, between democracy and constitutionalism, and between the political and the legal institutions in modern Norwegian history. My reconstruction adds a third institution, the intellectual-academic one. To encapsulate the systematic place of different forms of scientific knowledge in this modernization project, the 'knowledge regime' is my preferred central concept. The term refers to a constellation of political power, legal normativity and scientific knowledge. The latter gives such a regime supplementary institutional characteristics beyond the political and the legal: its identity is also determined by which forms of knowledge are predominant in the political institution. In the Norwegian system, the shifting political regimes have to a remarkable extent been accompanied by a shifting knowledge discourse. The shifting knowledge regimes are dependent on the interplay between intellectual reform and political reform that has been a characteristic element of the Norwegian system for nearly two hundred years. This serves to make clear one feature of Norwegian reformism since the early nineteenth century. Regardless of whether its ideological dress has been liberalism or socialism, one consistent characteristic has been its basis in science: it has been a scientific reformism.

The present interpretation of the modernization project in the Norwegian system is not intended as hermeneutic history of ideas from above, nor as documentation of the history of mentality from below. I am seeking my foothold at an intermediate level, in the 'ideologists of action'. They can be seen as a version of 'knowledgeable agents' as used by Anthony Giddens. Giddens distinguishes between 'tacit stocks of knowledge which actors draw upon in the constitution of social activity', and 'discursive consciousness, involving knowledge which actors are able to express on the level of discourse' (Giddens 1979: 5). Ideologists of action are 'knowledgeable agents' in a stronger sense: creative producers of society who are bearers of a politically active ideology. In response to Mary Douglas's thinking institutions they might be called institutional thinkers, often with reforming force (Douglas 1986).[2] Institutional thinkers both shape and are themselves shaped by the regime's institutions.

My reconstruction of the shifting knowledge regimes is mediated via institutional thinkers and their social imaginaries. The project relates to three knowledge regimes. The 'civil servants' state' was established through the revolution of 1814 and its dual transformation of both political and academic institutions. It was the *Sattelzeit* of the Norwegian system,[3] with the establishment of the so-called 'professor-politicians' and their legal knowledge regime. They were replaced towards the end of the nineteenth century by a democratic-pedagogical knowledge regime. Its context was the breakthrough of parliamentary democracy in 1884 and the emergence of a new profession of schoolteachers, bearers of a popular democratic educational tradition with politically formative force (the Liberal Party state). When the Labour Party gained control of the political centre in 1945, it did so in coalition with the new economists. The Norwegian modernization project culminated in the Labour Party state, its knowledge regime that of the social sciences. Following the demise of the social democratic regime in the 1980s, some features of a new knowledge regime have become visible.[4]

I

Modernization commenced in Norway as a political and constitutional phenomenon: following a national and constitutional revolution in 1814, Norway broke out of the Dano-Norwegian dual monarchy, created a new constitution, and entered a union with Sweden (dissolved in 1905). The Norwegian nation acquired a new centre in the constitutional system for the formulation of political will, for legislation and for judicial practice. Power assumed a new form, a legal and communicative form. In 1811 Norway had acquired her own university, founded in Humboldt's spirit. University and constitution alike sprang from liberal ideals of intellectual and political freedom. The university, it was thought, must be in the capital, geographically close to the central institutional machinery which was under construction, a ship of state, as a centre for the nation's academic culture and for the training of civil servants.

The avant-garde of the new state were the lawyers, including some who were to be leading figures of the Norwegian system throughout the nineteenth century. The rapid rise of the lawyers entailed control of key state positions, in the government, in the civil service, at the university and – for many years – in the Storting (the legislative assembly). It was by means of the law that the system was established, it was managed according to the law, and it was under the law that it would be reformed.

A reform-bureaucratic knowledge regime was given its basic design in the 1830s by two young lawyers, Frederik Stang and Anton Martin Schweigaard, who were to become the regime's principal strategists. They were both young men in their twenties when they worked out their ideological platform. They represented a student revolution that succeeded. Laden with ideological knowledge, they captured the central positions in the corridors of power. In 1840, Schweigaard was appointed to the new university chair in 'Law, Economics and Statistics'. The chair soon became the ideological centre of the modernization project. The merger with economics and statistics underlined that law was a governing science. Schweigaard's powerful position derived from his double role as both a professor and a member of the Storting, in which he was the dominant figure for nearly three decades from 1842. The university professoriate gave him cultural capital, his position in the Storting access to the political apparatus. The university was the nation's ideological transformer, where ideas transmitted through professors and students were converted into an institutionally effective ideology of action. Stang entered the Government in 1845 in the newly established Ministry of Home Affairs, and became the Government's strong man in the ensuing decades. The ministry became the principal instrument of modernization in two directions: modernization of the bureaucracy through the new governing ideology, and modernization of social life through a strong central government. The two strategists won control of the two newly established key institutions of the legal knowledge regime: the academic-intellectual and the political-bureaucratic institution.

The ideology which linked the modernization chair to the modernization ministry was 'scientific reformism'. It provided the platform for the reforming governing elite, and gave legitimacy and direction to an actively intervening state. For the country to be lifted forward – modernized – the bureaucracy, too, would have to be reformed and become a dynamic instrument for central government initiatives and activity, based on modern expertise. The reformist bureaucracy meant the drawing of a new front line in the conflict with the traditional bureaucracy, its professions and their monopolies on positions of authority: theologians in ecclesiastical, officers in military, and lawyers in administrative affairs. New professions were lining up, and being advanced – by the reformist lawyers. Newly won expertise enabled scientific progress to be channelled into government. Applied natural sciences produced new technical know-how for the development of the communicative infrastructure; medicine gained new insights into the connections between disease and hygiene; and pedagogics delivered a new understanding of learning mechanisms. The strategists of modernization saw that the knowledge of the new professions amounted to specialized expertise that was ideally suited to their policies of reform. This was an early example of the type of reform coalition or discourse coalition between science and politics which was to be a constituent element of the Norwegian system.

The ideology of economic modernization preached by Schweigaard and Stang was economic liberalism, but in a specific version. The freedom of the market was combined with a notion of state initiatives and 'strong central government'. The result was liberalism filtered through the state, a capitalist market economy in which the state played a prominent intervening part. This was in clear opposition to 'the English school', with its doctrine of a passive, non-intervening state. The idea 'that forces left to themselves find their most advantageous application' cannot be allowed to direct 'actual state practice': 'So if the principle of non-intervention is rejected as the paramount maxim of the political economy, a space is created for the influence of society's will also in economic affairs' (Schweigaard 1847). For these liberal strategists of modernization, one key word was 'plan'. State-purified liberalism was planning liberalism. The civil service elite became public entrepreneurs, national strategists. In the modernization carried out under the civil servants' state for decades from 1840, state intervention was a defining characteristic: state intervention as the new society's midwife, but also as an enduring feature of this new Norwegian system. Capitalism was established, on the initiative of senior officials, as capitalism staged by the state.

According to Schweigaard 'actual state practice' was also subject to other norms than those which followed from the calculation of private utility. 'Awakening productive forces' and 'increasing national wealth' were of course important to the national economy, but, as Schweigaard taught his students, the most important thing was that it promoted 'moral progress', 'standards of conduct', 'the perfection of political and legal institutions' (Schweigaard 1847). Towards the end of his life, after more than a generation in his country's leadership, Stang commented that a people's level of cultural development appears in its ability to 'co-operate for public purposes' – 'noble communism' (Stang 1880–84).[5]

Stang and Schweigaard came to power with a modernization programme which saw capitalism as also a civilizing force. Society as the good community could not be brought about along liberal lines through market competition alone, but required control by the visible hand of politics – and by the moral standards of social institutions. As a governing project, the knowledge regime of the civil servants' state was anchored in law, while as a cultivating *Bildung*-project it was bound to philosophy (and theology). The regime combined ideological elements of utilitarianism and German idealism and thus demonstrates a characteristic feature of Norwegian intellectual life: the parallel breakthrough of both enlightened rationalism and romanticism in the decades from 1830 on, which left both movements in mutual tension as expressions of the modern. It points forward to an expressive-institutional identity as a third ethical motivation for the modernization of society, beyond 'individual autonomy' and 'instrumental mastery', designated by Peter Wagner (following Castoriadis) 'the double imaginary signification of modernity' (Wagner 1994: 18). Reconstruction of the Norwegian modernity project calls for a triple imaginary signification.

II

Towards the end of the nineteenth century, new popular groups challenged the cultivated bourgeoisie's hegemony in the Norwegian system both politically and ideologically. The political conflict culminated in 1884 with the change of regime and the defeat of the civil service state elite with the introduction of parliamentary democracy based on the competing political parties. The regime of the professor-politicians was replaced by a democratic-pedagogical knowledge regime. Its context was of course the breakthrough of parliamentary democracy and the emergence of a new profession of schoolteachers.

Typical of the Norwegian project was the nationwide integration of the elites in a 'reform compromise'. In the Norwegian system, the cultivation project of the public servants emerged as a compromise between 'civilization' and 'culture', between Franco-English rationalism and German idealism. The compromise on reform reached by the elite also had a formative effect on the Liberal Party state's nation-building, which became much more firmly rooted in democracy. One of the reasons why the new regime's cultural reform project carried so much weight was that it depended on a compromise between the competing educational elites. The reformist wing of the *Bildung*-bourgeoisie, with a liberal attitude to planning, merged with the elites of popular culture, the common ground being their closeness to political democracy. What emerged was a coalition of the centre and the left, with intellectuals in a defining role. It was this compromise which gave the new era one of its characteristic features: the hegemonic integration of the broadly-based popular movement in the governing system, i.e. a democratic government.

The democratic development of Norwegian society can partly be explained by the integrative nature of the school institution. If Norway's history over the past two centuries were to be summed up in one term, that would have to be 'the educational revolution'. School reforms anticipated and accompanied political reforms. The very core of the Norwegian school system, a unified curriculum based on public primary school for all, reflected the integration of the popular with the official. The radical school reforms after 1884 combined ideals found both among the democratic grass roots and in modern science. They plotted the unique future course of the Norwegian educational system, which took a quite different direction from those found elsewhere on the continent. School was not just an agency for the reproduction of the ideology of the centre, but also a modernizing institution which raised new elite groups with roots in the populace. The new educational project brought together the rational and instrumental drive to acquire useful knowledge and the expressive romantic belief in moulding one's identity in its historical context, to form a third overriding objective: the democratic training of competent citizens for participation in the country's public affairs.

The educational tradition which produced the teachers was one of folk culture. Its most important mediators were the *folk* high schools, which came to Norway in the 1860s, inspired by Grundtvig's Danish *folk* high schools. These schools institutionalized the romantic-expressive educational ideal. Underlying them was Herder's idea of finding oneself, as an individual and as a people. The *folk* high schools became the home of national authenticity. The 'teacher seminars', later the 'teacher training schools', were deeply influenced by the same tradition. As the transmitters of democracy to ordinary people, they were institutionally independent of the nation's single university and geographically scattered all over the country, often located in rural districts.

The guiding principle for these schoolmen was their pedagogical perspective on society: society as a pedagogical space. Their theme was the consolidation of popular government by means of popular education. The teachers and their institutions became a pillar of the new pedagogical and democratic knowledge regime. Teachers tended to identify themselves with the communities they came from and to which they often returned. The authority from a distance which had been exercised by the civil service elite was challenged by an authority of solidarity which teachers could obtain because they were of the people. Teachers were 'organic intellectuals' in Gramsci's sense of the term.

Members of this teaching profession found their identities in democracy's ethical dimension, democracy as enlightenment for the people. Taken in this sense, popular enlightenment is not merely 'enlightenment', but also a question of training to assume authority. '*Folk* life' must be elevated to 'social life'. It was this social ethos that gave the teaching profession its mobilizing force in the struggle for public opinion in the 1940–45 war years. To the Germans' surprise, it was the teachers who took the lead in the cultural opposition to the occupying power.

The Norwegian term *folkelighet* was coined from the German *Volkstum*, but in their substance the two concepts are opposed. In Norway's case, the social rank and file were not mobilized for the consolidation of dictatorship, but for the extension of democracy. Their focus on the state was a feature the German and Norwegian systems had in common, distinguishing them from the Anglo-American system with its much weaker state. In this orientation towards the state lay a democratic ambiguity. The tendency in the Norwegian system to favour a strong state was radicalized by leading social democrats into state reformism. This state reformism transcended the instrumental, the realization of the just society through expanding state intervention, to approach 'identity-forming': the state as the expression of the social community. What was new about this ideology, compared to state-purified liberalism, was the radicalization of central government. The state and society finally became identical in the sense that the state expressed society's collective rationality, elevated beyond divisive special interests.

Like the German, the Norwegian *Bildung*-bourgeoisie was formed by a common educational culture, rooted in the state norms of the university and the authority it conferred. In the Norwegian as in the German context, a tradition was thus established of 'reform from above'. But the German and Norwegian traditions differed in two important respects. For one thing, there was in the Norwegian system no sharp distinction between the *Bildung*-bourgeoisie and the commercial bourgeoisie; the *Bildung*-bourgeoisie was also economically entrepreneurial. Secondly, it was characteristic of the Norwegian system for 'reform from above' to be combined with 'reform from below', with the reforming elite of the *Bildung*-bourgeoisie forming coalitions with the elite representing popular education.

According to this account, popular movements can be seen as something more than cultural bulwarks raised in outlying districts to resist the modern. They were distinctive educational projects involved in modern nation-building. They formed part of the struggle for political and cultural hegemony. There was a social-ethical dimension to that struggle that went beyond winning power and realizing interests. Taking their experience of social disrespect as a point of departure, the popular movements sought recognition in the public space. Acknowledgement of norms, values and experience originating among ordinary people enriched the system's identity. Right from the earliest period of the civil servants' state, the cultural and political struggle was fought out in full view of a liberal public that was joined in the ensuing phases by new groups and movements springing from popular culture. The sustaining values of these popular movements were modern and democratic in nature: equality, self-government and self-determination. The strength of this popular transformation of the bourgeois public sphere in its turn made possible the formative integration of the labour movement in the system.

III

At the end of the 1800s, at the same time as the major democratizing school reforms, a new legal discourse also came into being, with the abandonment of the old morally-based theory of criminality in favour of a criminal law founded in the social sciences. The new criminology sought its grounds in a modern science which analysed the causes of criminality and asked which form of penalty might be helpful. In 1896, with the adoption of the Act relating to the Treatment of Neglected Children, Norway became one of the first countries to establish a public child welfare institution. The reform was in keeping with the pedagogical reform ideology of the time. The age of criminal responsibility was raised from ten to sixteen. The youngest offenders were thus moved beyond the reach of the penal code: they were no longer to be punished, but treated, and raised to be law-abiding. The public sector was given broader powers to intervene in private life: moral decline in the home and private circumstances that might induce a youngster to embark on a life of crime could give grounds for intervention.

Neither trends in criminality nor social problems in general were so urgent in Norway in the 1890s as to demand new solutions. Decisive for the adoption of the child welfare reform were impulses from a completely different sector of social life – the need for segregation in the school system: 'The school politicians of the 1890s wanted to establish a more democratic educational system. They needed to segregate pupils who socially and behaviourally impeded this work' (Dahl 1985: 113). This need for segregation, which followed the introduction of compulsory school attendance, was brought out into the open in the big primary school reform of 1889. For primary school to become a facility common to all the nation's children, a unified school irrespective of social standing or geographical location, 'the firm and indispensable condition' was the freedom to segregate certain pupils: the educationally handicapped, the disabled, the contagious (also in the moral sense) and the difficult children (Dahl 1985: 120).

The idea of establishing reform schools put forward by criminologists won the support of the teaching profession; they would be 'of the greatest importance also for normal schools'. The bill of 1896, originally presented in the guise of a social penal code, came increasingly to be regarded as an education act. The act of 1896 was a historical compromise between law and pedagogic, adopted in the light of the pedagogical thinking underlying the reformist ideology (Dahl 1985: 130).

The child welfare act of 1896 led immediately to the establishment of state reform schools, where different groups of children with different problems were gathered under the same roof for treatment according to the same method: discipline and education. Problems soon arose at the institutions, and with them the need to separate client groups, to keep the less from the more difficult. This called for further selection procedures, in which the new scientific profession of psychiatry was given wide discretion to determine who was to remain in the final category of the 'most difficult'. The interwar years brought a new advanced fine-grading instrument, test psychology, regarded as a very promising instrument in the service of popular hygiene. With the assistance of science, it would be possible to search through the last category of deviants to distinguish those who might improve from the degenerate variants from which a healthy social body must be protected.

A whole range of reform projects sprang from this pedagogical-democratic knowledge regime, from reform institutions to sterilization programmes. The new knowledge regime was not formed in defence against revolutionary forces that might threaten the system, but in response to an important aspect of the popular enlightenment project: a unifying normality. The breakthrough of the unified school project in 1889 paved the way for a new normality discourse. The further primary school was developed into a real unified school, 'the greater the duty of society to ensure that the parents shall feel safe against having their schoolchildren exposed to harmful influences' (Dahl 1985: 131). The reforms of the day were 'normality' reforms involving segregation of the deviants. It was a question of protecting normality, which gave society as a whole a right to intervene against deviant individuals or those who might become deviant. The example illustrates a conjunction that was to become increasingly common: between the scientifically based interest of the professions in reform, and the state.

IV

The avant-garde of the new Norwegian state after 1814 were the lawyers. As the key discipline in the modernization project, law became two-sided: a law of rights rooted in legal-liberal conceptions of individual autonomy versus a governing law tied to utilitarianism, the legitimizing protection of the private on the hand of the individual versus the governing instrument of reform on the hand of bureaucracy. This duality was reflected in modernization's breakthrough phase in the decades after 1850.

Modernization policy created dividing lines between various elites also within the civil servants' state, sometimes as clashes between the highest state bodies, the Storting, the Government and the Supreme Court. These conflicts found extreme institutional expression in connection with the question of judicial review: the competence of the Supreme Court to review legislation in relation to provisions in the constitution. Some senior officials opposed the policy of modernization and succeeded in certain cases in invoking the Supreme Court's powers of review in defence of their rights. The dispute over judicial review followed a dividing line within the bureaucratic elite between the advocates of governing law and the advocates of a law of rights. One party supported 'the power of the administration' in the interests of 'the good of the whole', while the other argued for 'the rights of the individual' out of regard for 'the protection of the individual'. The dispute over the constitutional legitimacy of judicial review grew even sharper around 1884 with the introduction of parliamentary democracy. The reigning bureaucratic elite were dethroned by the emerging farmers' movement, organized in the Liberal Party (*Venstre*). The liberals rejected judicial review as simply an antidemocratic delaying tactic in the debate on the constitution. As the leader of the Liberal Party, Johan Sverdrup, put it in 1887, 'It is in the last instance only the majority that can protect the minority' (Slagstad 2001: 267).

The liberals sought to eliminate judicial review and to redefine the constitutional law, despite the fact that the Supreme Court and the law professors had as long ago as the 1860s established that it was indisputable constitutional law 'that the judiciary authority is the protector of the constitutional rights of the individual vis-à-vis the other two state bodies' (Aubert 1865: 77). There would be disagreement, sometimes very sharp disagreement, over its legitimate position in the system, but judicial review itself is no longer disputed. It is also beyond dispute that Norway obtained this liberal legal institution very early, probably as the first country after the United States (Slagstad 1995: 81ff.).

The reformism in the Norwegian system has been a legal reformism. The change of political regime in 1884, when the civil service elite surrendered political power to the new Left movement, is a case in point. Ministers from that elite were impeached, before a tribunal comprising the Supreme Court and members of the Storting. The Supreme Court Justices attended the impeachment hearings, where they were in the minority and knew that they would be voted down. They allowed themselves to be voted down, thereby legitimizing the parliamentary constitutional revolution to which they themselves were opposed (Sejersted 1988a: 143). Here the Supreme Court played its part as guardian of the constitution in an ironic sense: the Justices were so bound by constitutional law that they gave legitimacy to its transformation.

The democratization of the state legitimized expanding state intervention in social life, culturally as well as economically. The capitalist expansion from the end of the 1800s on, which marked a breakthrough in the Norwegian system for industry based on hydropower, gave rise to a new discourse on the relation between private ownership rights and public regulation. Control over water power resources became the chief bone of political contention, culminating in the Supreme Court's 'great concession ruling' of 1918. The case concerned the Concession Act of 1909 and its provision concerning the 'right of reversion', according to which concessions to acquire waterfalls were granted for a limited period (sixty to eighty years), and that the waterfall and the accompanying facilities would become state property free of charge on the expiry of the concession period. The question tried before the Supreme Court was whether or not the landowner who wished to sell the waterfall rights could demand compensation for the lower price resulting from the right of reversion. The claim for compensation was rejected by the Supreme Court majority. In this ruling of 1918, the Supreme Court confirmed the new view of rights of ownership which the Conservative leader, law professor Fredrik Stang the younger, had described a few years earlier as a modern right of ownership 'with an ever stronger social colouring' (Stang 1935: 15). Speaking first for the majority, Justice Backer – like Stang, a Conservative – put the matter as follows: 'It is clear that the legislature has and must have extensive powers to restrict rights of ownership, in order that property can be disposed of in accordance with the various considerations which social conditions and social developments at any given time make it necessary to take into account' (*Norsk Retstidende* [Norwegian law gazette] 1918: 405).

The year 1918 is comparable for the Norwegian Supreme Court to the year 1937 for the American Supreme Court, which marked a turning point for Roosevelt's 'New Deal' policy. The conflict which grew very bitter in the United States and lasted for more than a generation was in Norway's case over after only a few years, and resulted in more of a compromise. As a result of the 1937 ruling, the American Supreme Court withdrew from questions concerning economic rights, gradually virtually specializing in democratic and liberal rights. In Norway, the Supreme Court's ruling of 1918 paved the way for stronger political limitation of property rights, a definitive signal from the Supreme Court that the era of economic liberalism was at an end. The new capitalism operated as a social economy which presupposed the arrangement of the intervening government.

The radical regulation policy adopted after 1945 led to sharp ideological confrontations. The opposition regarded the proposed legislation governing prices and rationalization as a kind of underhand socialization of business and industry. In 1952–53 the dispute culminated in a constitutional compromise. The Labour Party met the Conservatives halfway by definitively abandoning its socialization project, in return for support for a 'functional-corporative democracy' in addition to a 'territorial-parliamentary democracy' (Sejersted 1988b). The outcome was a corporative-parliamentary mixture, to which Stein Rokkan applied the formula 'Votes count, resources decide' (Rokkan 1987: 206ff.).

The Labour Party's reform technocrats waged a campaign against the lawyers aimed at displacing law as the hegemonic ideology (Slagstad 1991: 215ff.). Law lost its predominance, but was far from disappearing from governing discourse. The technocratic reforms, too, were usually of the nature of legal reforms, as had also been the case in the course of the big dispute on regulation policy, in which the economists had been in the front line. At the heart of the battle was what became known as 'Lex Brofoss'. And it all boiled down to a price law, a deradicalized prices act. The quarrel also gave rise to a number of liberal law reforms aimed at protecting individuals, among other things against the reform technocracy and its spread of enabling legislation (including the Storting's ombudsman for public administration, 1962). The ability of law to 'stabilize change' (Luhmann 1981: 113ff.) has made it a significant integrative force in the gradual system reform that has marked Norwegian society and the other Scandinavian societies. Social democratic reformism has also been a legal reformism.

V

The professor-politicians of the civil servants' state were capitalist entrepreneurs as well as cultural ideologues. In the new capitalist market economy, pursuit of one's own interests gained a legitimate place, but in the view of the ideologues of the civil servants' state it presupposed the controlling hand of the state if it was to work for 'the good of the whole'. The Liberal Party state was a response also to the expansion of industrial capitalism; it originated in the wish to limit the domain of market logic in an expansive phase. The capitalist system under the Liberal Party state reflected a ruling compromise between two logics, one of democratic justice and one of market economy efficiency. The dispute over the first factory acts around 1900 confronted the value of capital with the value of work, the value of capitalists with the value of workers. The Liberal Party state, too, was an educational project. There were, for instance, two sides to the demand for a ten-hour normal working day: it would promote better ordered production and thereby improved products, but it would also leave the worker time to improve his skills and elevate his 'moral standpoint'. The Liberal Party state also led to a unique compromise between two influential political elites. On one side stood a financial elite of big shipowners belonging to the Liberal Party who acted as national political strategists with the prime minister at their head; on the other stood the representatives of the popular education elites, who won central positions in the political system. After the liberal phase, the financial elite would cease to play a formative part in political life, and while popular education became an integral part of the social democratic project, its ability to shape policy gradually diminished. The hegemony passed to a technocratic governing elite. Its origins, too, can be sought in the reformist bureaucratic circles that had been so important to the civil servants' state as a modernizing regime. This governing elite of reforming bureaucrats continued to grow independently of the change of regime in

1884, and expanded explosively in the Labour Party state.

The Labour Party came to power in 1935, but it was not until 1945 that the social democrats, with a majority in the Storting, also won control of the bureaucratic machinery. The new regime proved to be a political regime in social science garb. A new form of state arose with drastically extended governing powers, drawing on new experts and their knowledge. To this social science knowledge regime, the time from the end of the nineteenth century seemed a period of intellectual transformation. A disintegrating society brought forth a new discourse with a new cognitive representation of society. The knowledge situation was open, with an ongoing search for new concepts, new solutions and new arrangements. Themes, problems and areas of dispute were formulated by representatives of the new expertise. Specialists took their reforming ideas with them into the thick of the social struggle, where they were seized and annexed by the movements of the day. Social debate was formed by the new social sciences. The answers science gave tended to entail state intervention on the basis of scientific knowledge. They presupposed the establishment of a new machinery that would have to be manned by the new experts to ensure that what was done was in accordance with scientific knowledge. Expert power and state power mutually reinforced each other. The work of the professor-politicians was brought to completion by the labour movement and its scientific reformists.

Peter Wagner describes the new 'knowledge-policy-connection' of the interwar years as 'outright discourse coalitions for modernization between social scientists and reform-oriented policy-makers'. It 'propagated a profound transformation of the role of the intellectual, from distant and critical observer to activist policy designer and technician. This transformation is based on a conceptualization of the planning of societal development by a scientific informed elite' (Wagner 1994: 113). If this is an adequate general description of the political-intellectual landscape in the Western world from the 1930s on, Norway is an exception. For it was precisely this 'profound transformation of the role of the intellectual' that had characterized the Norwegian system ever since the time of the professor-politicians one hundred years earlier. It was an enduring feature, extending from what Wagner calls 'liberal modernity' to 'organized modernity', though in the Norwegian context it was ratcheted up in the 1930s.

The Labour Party state marked the breakthrough of the social sciences in the Norwegian system, with a new scientific vocabulary, new ways of thinking and new ways of putting knowledge into practice. It was a two-sided breakthrough, comprising both a governing science, headed by economists, and an opposition science founded in sociology. This was a divided social science: on the one hand there was the discourse of government of the reform technocrats, addressed primarily to the regulating and intervening government administration, and on the other there was the educational discourse of the reform democrats, in which the social sciences primarily addressed the debating and acting public. Science and politics were mediated in one case through the administration and in the other through public communication.[6]

The leading figure in Norwegian economics was Ragnar Frisch, who on his accession to a chair at the University of Oslo in 1931 presented economics as a science of social engineering on natural science lines. Frisch had previously worked on utilitarian theory, on questions relating to the measurement of utility. He introduced the term econometrics and became one of that discipline's founders. The new doctrine turned customary economic ideas upside down. It was revolutionary in theory and applicable in practice. The Institute of Economics was established in 1932, with funds from the Rockefeller Foundation among others, and with Frisch at its head.

Frisch won through in economic circles in the 1930s – and in political circles after 1945.[7] But even in the early 1930s he played a scientific part which had a political impact. The national route he proposed out of the major economic crisis around 1930 was taken up by the Labour Party's ideological strategists. Frisch's ideas made a significant contribution to the party's crisis programme of 1934. That programme was admittedly of negligible importance in overcoming Norway's economic crisis. Nevertheless, it helped a great deal in overcoming the party's ideological crisis; revolutionary, anti-parliamentary Marxism was abandoned in favour of national democratic planned reform.

Erik Brofoss, a disciple of Frisch's, became Minister of Finance in 1945. Through Brofoss, Frisch's brand of economics became the principal governing instrument for the social democrats, a reform coalition, with the national budget as the big strategic innovation, prepared by Frisch and his circle of young economists from the end of the 1930s. Economists won positions in the administration, and influenced the administrators with their science. They moved up onto the bridge of the ship of state, setting the course with a way of thinking that became hegemonic. It is difficult to say whether the economic elite were the instruments of the political elite or vice versa. Einar Gerhardsen, who was the Labour Party Prime Minister for much of the 1945 to 1965 period, and indeed gave it its name (the 'Gerhardsen era'), was in no doubt about who was in the lead: 'in the Government, too, we had a feeling that he (Brofoss) saw it as his task to "educate" us. And so he did, very thoroughly' (Gerhardsen 1971: 125). Brofoss was eager to train the people's representatives in the ways of thinking called for by the new economics; his marathon-length financial speeches served the same purpose. Brofoss regarded the Storting as virtually a *folk* high school – and everyone knew who was laying down the syllabus. The economic knowledge regime was linked to three institutions, the 'iron triangle', which were densely populated by the new economists: the University's Institute of Economics, the Central Bureau of Statistics, and the Ministry of Finance.

As the economists saw it, their science was an expression of a higher rationality, exclusive knowledge that conferred control over the guiding mechanisms of social life. This made them spokesmen for the radical notion that politics can be turned into a science – that it is possible to exercise rational control over the development of society by means of modern science. The political system of government should build 'on rational reflection' and not be a 'result of the play of chance'. For Brofoss, himself a politician, but also of the Frisch school, 'the play of chance' meant the uncontrolled market – and the uncontrolled politicians. With economists in charge, so Professor Frisch had proclaimed, three-quarters of all political dispute would become superfluous. But in 1966, the year after the Labour Party lost power, Petter Jacob Bjerve, an important intermediary between Frisch and Brofoss and director of the Central Bureau of Statistics from 1949 to 1980, was obliged to concede that things had not gone as quickly as Frisch had foretold. It had to be admitted 'that we still have no body of "economic engineers"' (Bjerve 1966: 1f.). But Frisch had developed the necessary theory, and electronic computers could provide the technological apparatus with which to realize the dream of 'a science of economic engineering' (Bjerve 1966: 17f.). Leif Johansen, too, who next to Trygve Haavelmo was Frisch's most outstanding student, pinned his faith on computers, but was not quite as optimistic with regard to the possibility of realizing the dream under social democratic welfare capitalism: it was only under a socialist planning system that economics would be able to do itself justice and 'play the role as a "social engineer"' (Johansen 1963: 514).

After 1945 American scholarship was opened up to Norwegian social research. Young social scientists and philosophers got scholarships to the United States, and American guest professors were invited to Oslo. One of the latter was Paul Lazarsfeld, who spent the fall of 1948 in Oslo. In his opening lecture, 'What is sociology?', Lazarsfeld described economics and demography as model sciences. After a hundred-year history, they were 'fully developed sciences': 'They attempt to explain the regularities and to predict future developments.' (Lazarsfeld 1948). That was the perspective in which Lazarsfeld wanted to establish sociology as a statistically-based instrument of government, along the same lines as economics. 'But sociology is not yet in the stage where it can provide a safe basis for social engineering. This is not surprising if one considers how young sociology is. It took the natural sciences about 250 years between Galileo and the beginning of the industrial revolution before they had a major effect upon the history of the world.' One must not expect social research to save the world overnight, but one must equally not lose sight of the long-term objective: 'the hard tasks of developing in the end an integrated social science, which can help us to understand and control social affairs'. In a farewell interview, Lazarsfeld proclaimed that empirical social research had made such progress in recent years that he regarded the forthcoming American presidential election as 'unnecessary': 'We can read from curves and tables that the Republicans will win' (Mjøset 1991: 144). A few days later, the Democrat Harry Truman was re-elected.

'Indefatigable, Lazarsfeld worked for the propagation of his conception of sociology all over Europe. In 1948, he convinced the Norwegian government to establish an Institute of Social Research where he became the first visiting professor' (Pollak 1980: 173). This account is by Michael Pollak, one of Pierre Bourdieu's close associates. It shows the danger of conspiration-sociology analysis. The facts were virtually the opposite of the picture Pollak presents. The initiative to set up the Institute of Social Research did not come from Lazarsfeld, but from the circle around the philosopher Arne Næss. In an important strategic move aimed at persuading the authorities, including the university leadership, to go in for the new social sciences, a decision was taken to invite an American star. For that purpose, Vilhelm Aubert was dispatched to Columbia University in New York. The invitation went first to C. Wright Mills, who declined, and then to Paul Lazarsfeld, who accepted. There is some historical irony here: Vilhelm Aubert became the leading spokesman for a sociology that rejected the programme of governing sociology which Lazarsfeld presented during his stay in Oslo, and felt himself much more attracted to C. Wright Mills, who would not come but who made Lazarsfeld's Oslo lecture a prime target in his own key work of social criticism (Mills 1959). Historical dialectics of this order are not easy to pin down in simple one-dimensional models that seamlessly merge the functional with the conspirative. The same can be said of the interpretation of Norwegian social research as we move further into the 1950s.

Research capital flowing from the Americans' intellectual Marshall Plan also reached the Institute of Social Research (though not as a main source). What is remarkable from the Bourdieu point of view is that it did not generate social research that conformed with the system. On the contrary, the American capital with other sources funded what became a main stem of radical intellectual opposition within the Labour Party state (including Vilhelm Aubert in the sociology of law, Nils Christie in criminology, and Johan Galtung in peace research). This opposition sociology often sought to adopt a perspective on society from the viewpoint of the governed, the deviants, the under-privileged, the losers in relation to the modernizing mainstream. Generally speaking, even opposition sociology became a governing science. Outsiders would be integrated by means of social reforms. It wanted more of what was already plentiful, a welfare state under public administration. From the late 1960s on, several new social research institutes sprang up attached to various segments of the government system. The institutions of the welfare state expanded, partly on the basis of social scientific knowledge. New arrangements for putting the knowledge into practice were established at the intersection between politics and bureaucracy (Engelstad 1996).

The final chapter so far of the history of scientific reformism in the Norwegian system concerns research into the position of women, with the new feminism of the 1970s as its point of departure. The expressive formation of identity was a dominant concept within the movement's criticism of society. This expressive feminism had a utopian vision of a society sustained by other values than those that were attached to instrumental utility. The feminist revolution in daily life opened the way to society as a normative community of experience – not merely a market arena or a field of governing. Its criticism of the Labour Party state's instrumentalism pointed the way to an expressive social collectivity within which individuals could achieve a sense of recognition and belonging. But the vision of what Charles Taylor has referred to as 'a post-industrial *Sittlichkeit*' disappeared (Taylor 1979: 125ff.).

Women's studies, an offspring of opposition sociology, was transformed like it into a governing science. Just as the civil servants' state was conquered by a liberal coalition based on the agrarian movement, and the Liberal Party state by the advancing labour movement, so the Labour Party state was conquered by the feminist movement. The state which grew so large in its Labour Party phase, and which was regarded by the new feminist movement as a patriarchal guardian state, became the chief instrument of reform in the struggle for women's liberation. The increase in women's power has since the 1970s been a function of increased central government power. And in its Norwegian context the ideology underlying the reform has characteristically been that of scientific reformism. With its proximity to social research, the Norwegian women's movement has been more pro-state than in other countries, accordingly regarding law as a suitable instrument for reforming the system. The integration of women, what Helga Hernes has labelled 'state feminism', confirms a characteristic feature of the Norwegian system (Hernes 1987: 136): the ability to integrate by means of reform compromise. Fundamental to the process has been the interplay between innovative popular movements and the regulating powers of the state, mediated by way of social scientific reformism: a combination of 'feminising from below' and 'state feminism from above'.

VI

The Labour Party state was a knowledge regime in the sense that modern Norway was to be created through the mobilization of positivist science, with the new social science professions as the avant-garde in social democratic policies of reform. There were a number of motives underlying this positivism. One was the possibility on the basis of the new social sciences of creating a new society – and, as the boldest added, a new man. The rationalist turn that European thought had taken with Descartes was refined and concentrated in twentieth-century scientism in the dream of constructing a new world virtually from scratch. In Norway, as in Sweden, this scientific dream merged with a second dream, socialism. Scientific socialism in its Scandinavian form was not a revolutionary tyranny, but a reformist dream of government.

The most important intellectual debate in the Labour Party state concerned positivism. It went on from the mid-1950s right through the 1960s. It formed a parallel to the German *Positivismusstreit* of the 1960s (Adorno vs. Popper, Habermas vs. Albert), but whereas the German dispute was principally a controversy between schools of philosophy of science, the Norwegian one also concerned regimes, and the question of the Labour Party state as a positivistic knowledge regime. For the claim that the Labour Party introduced socialism in Norway is more than doubtful. It would be truer to say that what was introduced under the Labour Party state was positivism.[8] Positivism became the hegemonic ideology, frozen as it were into the body of society. (The same can be said of Sweden, but there positivism was so strongly placed that there was no corresponding dispute over it.) Habermas's study of 'Technology and Science as "Ideology"' was written in 1968 in the immediate context of the German dispute over positivism. One of Habermas's points concerned the function of positivism as a compensatory programme: 'The substitute program prevailing today ... is aimed exclusively at the functioning of a manipulated system. ... Therefore the new politics of state interventionism requires a depoliticization of the mass of the population' (Habermas 1971: 103f.). This view would convey no meaning within the Norwegian system, in which positivism, far from being a compensatory depoliticization ideology, rather had a mobilizing effect on the politics of reform. Positivism legitimized the regime's scientific reformism. This reform project was driven by an ethical search for justice, which could not be theorized as a normative institutional project within the horizon of governing positivism.

The leading anti-positivist critic of the regime was Hans Skjervheim. His first study, *Objectivism and the Study of Man*,[9] was a counter to Arne Næss's *Erkenntnis und wissenschaftliches Verhalten*, written under the influence of the Vienna circle's logical empiricism.[10] Næss was for many years the only professor of philosophy in Norway and had considerable intellectual influence. What began as a disagreement between Skjervheim and Næss over the theory of knowledge grew into a controversy over the social sciences, over their foundations and their self-understanding. In his critique of the regime, Skjervheim mobilized the very philosophical tradition against which Schweigaard, one of the system's founding fathers, had warned. The social democrats had put brackets round Kant and Hegel in favour of positivism. The positivist direction taken by the social sciences derived from 'the instrumental mistake': the reduction of practical-communicative acts to technical acts. There is a difference between 'counting on others and counting others' (Skjervheim 1959: 143). The critique of instrumentalism was a theoretical criticism with moral and political implications: treating instrumental reason as an absolute undermines social liberality, the mutual recognition of each individual's autonomy. Thus the critique of instrumentalism also applies to Schweigaard, the founder of governing science in a Norwegian context. Kant's *Praxis*-concept points to morality as constituting social reality, the foundation which also makes the liberating instrumental act possible. A radical critique of instrumental governing rationality was also formulated by Jon Elster: 'If one regards planned change as a process in which one seeks the best means for realising a given aim, it is highly likely that one will fail. ... Not instrumental rationality, but normative ideas, should direct the processes of change' (Elster 1984).

The critique of instrumentalism was concerned with the whole of the reflexive aspect of society's production of knowledge. The self-knowledge of members of society is changed by new knowledge; the changed self-knowledge in its turn becomes the object of scientific analysis. Reflexive sociology becomes 'society's reflection about itself', it 'expresses society's increasing self-understanding, its increasing self-reflexivity' (Østerberg [1963] 1993: 56). This was the reflexive sociology that Giddens identified in the 1970s when he brought together 'the double hermeneutic' and 'institutional reflexivity' as constituent features of modern society and its conceptualization (Giddens [1976] 1993: 6ff.). In the modern system there is no superior judge in a position to determine with definitive authority what the nature of the social reality is. Various authorities can be and are invoked. But their competence, too, may sooner or later be redefined. No tradition, not even the scientific, can lay claim to an undisputed position from which to define the necessary action. Sociology is a reflexive interpretative science rooted in the social *Lebenswelt*. The identity of sociology is precarious, just as the reflexive identity of modern society is precarious. The present interpretation of Norwegian modernity is accordingly concerned not only with the establishment of new institutions, such as the constitutional state or the market, or new moral principles, such as utility and rights, but also more generally with new ways of imagining society.

The critique of positivism is a pointer towards a new knowledge regime in the Norwegian system, a change of regime that can also be considered a change of era. The Norwegian modernization project unfolded among shifting regimes in a system with a centre, a political centre. That premise has become less certain with the latest change of regime. The new global era has been accompanied by the expansion of the ideology of market liberalism in the Norwegian context as well. This ideology has attacked a main pillar of the Norwegian system, that is to say the State as the governing centre. This attack has collected ideological ammunition from the anti-positivist critique of governing science. The time has come for a depoliticized market economic knowledge regime. The new regime may well prove to be both post-industrial and post-national, but not post-democratic if it is to remain true to another fundamental feature of Norwegian modernity. For the conception that guided his thinking, Skjervheim used the term antinomies, the interminable contradictions in social life: 'the fact that society seen from one angle is a plurality of individuals, where the relation between unity and multiplicity is a problem, with no unambiguous solution' (Skjervheim 1976: 446). This view highlights democracy as a system in which each and every one is obliged to recognize the equivalent position of everyone else. The other is recognized as an opponent to be persuaded, not as an enemy to be crushed. Movements critical of the system have repeatedly had to learn from the same experience: in order to win through in this democratic system, you have to be socialized to it. Over the past two centuries, our system has established an arrangement for the full play of even the keenest conflicts over the goals and direction of society. That is where the success of the Norwegian system has lain. No particular group or class has been able to occupy democracy. The constitutional state and democracy have been the medium of social change. Even the sharpest disputes have been resolved through integration and transformation.

Notes

1. Elster/Slagstad 1988 was an attempt to place this Norwegian debate in an international context. For Sejersted the motif of Odysseus tied to the mast illustrated the notion of the suspension of politics in liberal constitutionalism. Elster introduced the Odysseus motif in the 1970s in seminars also concerned with the development and formation of the Norwegian state (Elster 1979). See also Sejersted's comparative study of Norwegian and Swedish social democracy in Sejersted 2011. The work by Habermas which chiefly attracted Sejersted's attention was Habermas 1962. It was available in a Norwegian version in 1972. An American edition only appeared nearly twenty years later. This paper draws on my more extensive studies in Slagstad 1998 and 2001; see also Rudeng 1999.
2. Michael Walzer's internal social critics present a certain parallel to the 'ideologists of action' or the 'institutional thinkers' (Walzer 1988).
3. "Sattelzeit" is Reinhart Koselleck's term for the transforming period in European political history 1750–1850, see Koselleck 2004.
4. Peter Wagner's works on the sociology of modernity have been important sources of inspiration in my work: Wagner 1990, 1994, 2001a, 2001b.
5. Stang resigned as Prime Minister in 1880 and died in 1884.
6. The coincidence in time of governing science and opposition science distinguishes the Norwegian system from the general picture Peter Wagner draws of social science and reform coalitions: 'the demise of the modernisation-oriented reform coalitions led to the emergence of the critical action research approach' (Wagner 2001b: 71).
7. Frisch won the first Nobel Prize in Economics in 1969 (jointly with Jan Tinbergen). His most prominent student, Trygve Haavelmo, was awarded the Nobel Prize in 1989.
8. For a discussion of Norwegian socialist social philosophy focusing on the positivism debate (Jon Elster, Dag Østerberg, Audun Øfsti), see Slagstad 1979.
9. Skjervheim's study (presented 1957, published 1959) challenges the positivist concept of 'unity of science'. Referring to Husserl among others, Skjervheim seeks to show the relevance of a critical extension of Dilthey's *Verstehen*-related problems to the social sciences as a third form of science beyond the traditional humanities/natural sciences dichotomy. On the significance of Skjervheim's contribution, see Habermas 1967: 3f. and Habermas 1981: 163 f.
10. In his early Vienna dissertation (Næss 1936), Arne Næss had defended a more open philosophical position than for instance Rudolf Carnap or Otto von Neurath. Under the influence of his critics Næss gradually abandoned positivist standpoints in favour of a Spinozian deep ecology (Næss 1989). In 1965, when Næss in his study drew together Carnap, Heidegger, Sartre and Wittgenstein, he provoked an outcry in *Dagens Nyheter*, Sweden's leading cultural newspaper. Carnap never forgave Næss for putting him and Heidegger together in one and the same book (Næss 1965).

References

Aubert, L.M.B. (1865) 'Om den dømmende Magts Virksomhed' (On the work of the judiciary), in *Ugeblad for Lovkyndighed, Statistik og Statsøkonomi,* V.
Bjerve, P.J. (1966) 'Teknisk revolusjon i økonomisk analyse og politikk' (The technical revolution in economic analysis and politics), *Statsøkonomisk Tidsskrift* (Economics review) 1.
Dahl, T.S. (1985) *Child Welfare and Social Defence.* Oslo: Norwegian University Press.
Elster, J. (1979) *Ulysses and the Sirens.* Cambridge: Cambridge University Press.
—— (1984) 'Skeptiske tanker om samfunnsplanlegging' (Sceptical thoughts on social planning), *Forskning og fremtid* (Research and the future) 1.
Elster, J. and R. Slagstad (eds) (1988) *Constitutionalism and Democracy.* Cambridge: Cambridge University Press.
Engelstad, F. (1996) 'Norsk sosiologi siden 1969: problemer og utfordringer' (Norwegian sociology since 1969: problems and challenges), *Tidsskrift for samfunnsforskning* 2.
Gerhardsen, E. (1971) *Samarbeid og strid. Erindringer 1945–55* (Cooperation and conflict, memoirs 1945–55). Oslo: Tiden.
Giddens, A. (1979) *Central Problems in Social Theory.* London: The MacMillan Press.
—— (1993) *New Rules of Sociological Method* (1976), 2nd edn. Cambridge: Polity Press.
Habermas, J. (1962) *Strukturwandel der Öffentlichkeit.* Neuwied: Luchterhand.
—— (1971) *Toward a Rational Society.* London: Heinemann.
Hernes, H. (1987) *Welfare State and Women Power. Essays in State Feminism.* Oslo: Scandinavian University Press.
Johansen, L. (1963) 'Marxism and Mathematical Economics', *Monthly Review* 1.
Koselleck, R. (2004) *Futures Past. On the Semantic of Historical Time.* Transl. and with an introduction by Keith Tribe. New York: Columbia University Press.
Lazarsfeld, P. (1990) 'What is sociology?' (1948), reprinted in *Sosiologi i dag* (Sociology today) 4.
Luhmann, N. (1981) *Ausdifferenzierung des Rechts.* Frankfurt: Suhrkamp.
Mills, C.W. (1959) *The Sociological Imagination.* New York: Oxford University Press.
Mjøset, L. (1991) *Kontroverser i norsk sosiologi* (Controversies in Norwegian sociology). Oslo: Universitetsforlaget.
Næss, A. (1936), *Erkenntnis und wissenschaftliches Verhalten.* Oslo: Dybwad.
—— (1965) *Fire moderne filosoffer* (Four modern philosophers). København: Gyldendal.
—— (1989) *Ecology, Community, Lifestyle.* Cambridge: Cambridge University Press.
Pollak, M. (1980) 'Paul F. Lazarsfeld: A Sociointellectual Biography', *Knowledge: Creation, Diffusion, Utilization* 2(2).
Rokkan, S. (1987) *Stat, nasjon, klasse* (State, nation, class). Oslo: Norwegian University Press.
Rudeng, E. (ed.) (1999) *Kunnskapsregimer. Debatten om 'De nasjonale strateger'* (Knowledge regimes – the debate on 'De nasjonale strateger'). Oslo: Pax.
Schweigaard, A.M. (1904) 'Forelæsninger over den politiske Økonomi' (1847), in Schweigaard, *Ungdomsarbeider* (Early works). Kristiania: Aschehoug.

Seip, J.A. (1974 & 1981) *Utsikt over Norges historie* (View of Norwegian history), vols. 1 & 2. Oslo: Gyldendal.

Sejersted, F. (1984) *Demokrati og rettsstat*. Oslo: Universitetsforlaget.

—— (1988a) 'Democracy and the Rule of Law: Some Historical Experiences of the Contradictions in the Striving for Good Government' in J. Elster and R. Slagstad (eds), *Constitutionalism and Democracy*. Cambridge: Cambridge University Press. 1988.

—— (1988b) 'From Liberal Constitutionalism to Corporate Pluralism: The Conflict over the Enabling Acts in Norway after the Second World War and the Subsequent Constitutional Development', in J. Elster and R. Slagstad (eds), *Constitutionalism and Democracy*. Cambridge: Cambridge University Press. 1988.

—— (2011) *The Age of Social Democracy*. Princeton: Princeton University Press.

Skjervheim, H. (1964) 'Sosiologien som vitskap: positiv eller kritisk disiplin?' (Sociology as science: A positive or critical discipline?) (1962), in *Skjervheim, Vitskapen om mennesket og den filosofiske refleksjon* (The science of man and philosophical reflection). Oslo: Johan Grundt Tanum.

—— (1976) *Deltakar og tilskodar og andre essays* (Participant and spectator and other essays). Oslo: Johan Grundt Tanum.

—— (1992) 'Tillit til vitskapen og tillit til mennesket' (Trust in science and trust in man) (1959), in H. Skjervheim, *Filosofi og dømmekraft* (Philosophy and judgement). Oslo: Universitetsforlaget.

Slagstad, R. (1979) 'On Norwegian Marxism', *Marxist Perspectives* 1.

—— (1991) 'Norwegian Legal Realism since 1945', *Scandinavian Studies in Law*, 35.

—— (1995) 'The Breakthrough of Judicial Review in the Norwegian System', in Eivind Smith (ed.), *Constitutional Justice under Old Constitutions*, 81ff.

—— (1998) *De nasjonale strateger* (The national strategists). Oslo: Pax.

—— (2001) *Rettens ironi* (The irony of law). Oslo: Pax.

Stang, F. (1880–84) *Statsøconomie* (Political economy), Håndskriftsamlingen (The manuscript collection of the National Library), Oslo.

—— (1935) *Indledning til formueretten* (Introduction to the law of property) (1911). Oslo: Dybwad.

Taylor, C. (1979) *Hegel and Modern Society*. Cambridge: Cambridge University Press.

Wagner, P. (1990) *Sozialwissenschaften und Staat. Frankreich, Italien, Deutschland 1870–1980*. Frankfurt: Campus.

—— (1994) *A Sociology of Modernity*. London: Routledge.

—— (2001a) *Theorizing Modernity*. London: Sage.

—— (2001b) *A History and Theory of the Social Sciences*. London: Sage.

Walzer, M. (1988) *The Company of Critics. Social Criticism and Political Commitment in the Twentieth Century*. New York.

Østerberg, D. (1993) 'Metasosiologisk essay' (Metasociological essay) (1963), in *Østerberg, Fortolkende sosiologi* (Interpretative sociology). Oslo: Universitetsforlaget 1993.

CHAPTER 7
Alternative Processes of Modernization?

Gunnar Skirbekk

What does it mean to be 'modern'? To be Chinese and modern? Muslim and modern? Norwegian and modern? Is there, basically, just one way of being modern? Or are there 'multiple modernities' (cf. Eisenstadt 2000; Arnason et al. 2005) – different ways of becoming modern and of being modern? In short, is the process of modernization one and unilinear? Or, are there alternative processes of modernization?

Before we proceed to address these questions, it is important to note the political urgency of the underlying context. Today we are confronted with challenges that could be cast in these terms: is there a conflict between the West and the Muslim world due to pre-modern aspects in the institutional development and social imaginary of the latter? Is Western modernity, with its consumerism and demography, a sustainable society? And what about China in this respect? Moreover, to what extent is the West, for instance the United States, really modern according to the main criteria, such as the requirement of a 'modernization of religious consciousness', including an open and enlightened 'criticism of religion'? These are timely questions, demanding critical and nuanced analyses of various aspects of modernization, of how they manifest at different stages and in different regions and countries. This paper aims to address some of the theoretical issues that have arisen in attempts to understand this underlying context, specifically, whether the processes of modernity are singular or multiple.

Two Theories of Modernization

There are probably as many different views on these questions as there are theories of modernity and modernization. One kind of theory of modernity and modernization is conceived in the terms of a predictive social science in search of causal explanations. This kind of theory often operates with the hypothesis that there is only one process of modernization which, by internal necessity, leads to some ultimate stage. From this perspective the process of modernization is 'deterministic, endogenous, and unilinear'.[1] Theories of this kind flourished in North American sociology after each of the two world wars. Modernization was conceived as an unavoidable development in terms of industrialization and individualization, extensive deregulation and market economy, privatization of religion and the death of ideology, and multiparty democracy. In short, this view holds that we are all moving towards a situation that resembles the Anglo-American world as it was seen at that time.

Another kind of theory of modernity and modernization – the one that is embraced here – is conceived in terms of a 'reconstruction' of intellectual learning-processes and institutional differentiations. Those in favour of a reconstructive approach have different views on how the processes of modernization should be conceived. There are, for instance, different opinions as to whether there is basically one line of development or various paths. We can divide these theorists into 'universalists', reconstructing what they conceive to be the unavoidable steps in the intellectual and moral learning-processes leading up to the present stage of modernity, and 'pluralists' who conceive these processes as rather 'contingent and multifarious', just as they conceive modern societies as an open-ended multitude.

Processes of Modernization: One or Many?

We shall look into these questions, discussing whether (or to what extent) there are alternative processes of modernization. We begin by asking: what could rightly be seen as 'unavoidable characteristics' of modern societies, and thus as arguments against the pluralist reconstruction? (cf. G. Skirbekk 1993, 2007).

(1) When we in a serious discussion seek to ascertain what is true and right in a given case we cannot, for self-referential reasons, exclude relevant arguments, nor can we decide to exclude persons who might contribute to the discussion. I cannot assume that I am right without taking the counter-arguments into account. In this sense we are unavoidably bound and obliged by what Habermas called the 'forceless force of the better argument' and by a mutual recognition of other persons as both reasonable and fallible (like oneself).

This kind of reflective discussion requires a particular attitude: flexible and open for change, according to the better arguments, and firm against the temptation to give in to social pressures to comply with popular but dubious opinions.[2] This is a particularly modern conception of how to handle basic validity questions, that is to say questions of truth and of justice. It is a conception of 'discursive rationality' that for self-referential reasons is unavoidable in any culturally modern society. Hence, in this very important sense, there is only one modernity.

(2) Moreover, modern societies are inherently connected to scientific and scholarly research. And all scientific and scholarly disciplines rely on discursive rationality (manifested for example by the fact that all disciplines have their doctoral disputations). Hence the principles mentioned above are also ideal presuppositions for scientific and scholarly research. (They are presupposed ideally, although they are not always fulfilled.)

Simultaneously, modern scientific and scholarly research is characterized by a plurality of different disciplines, each with its specific concepts and methods. There is not one all-embracing scientific and scholarly truth, but a plurality of perspectives that cannot be overcome by any all-embracing meta-theory. But we can do our best in reflecting on these various perspectives and discursively try to sort out their comparative strengths and weaknesses in various cases.

This is not easy, but nor is it impossible, and it is an urgent task since there is always a danger that some perspective might obtain an excessively dominant position and thus lead to biased understandings – consider the danger of ignoring the long-term ecological affects of industrial projects that are predominantly understood in economic and technological terms. Furthermore, scientific and scholarly research is not merely perspectivistic, it is also fallible and uncertain in various ways. Hence, scientific and scholarly research is basically a self-critical procedure, an 'organized skepticism' (Merton 1968). All in all this means that modern societies, to the extent that they are based on scientific and scholarly research, have to incorporate the attitudes and institutional arrangements that are required for this kind of discursive rationality and organized scepticism.

One of the necessary institutional implications is that basic research (and hence universities) should be governed neither by religious or ideological agents or institutions, nor by special political interests or market forces. Some institutional autonomy is required.[3] The same is true as an institutional condition for an enlightened public sphere and for enlightened political deliberations and decisions. Hence, in modern societies there is a need for 'institutional differentiations', such as the one between religion and the judiciary system – not least because there is an irreducible (reasonable) plurality of religious and non-religious world views, in the modern world.[4] At the same time there is also a need for institutional interaction, for instance between the judiciary and the political system, as well as between politics as power and politics as open and public discussion and will formation.

Basically there has to be some differentiation between the main institutions, such as state, market and culture (life-world). On the one hand, political opinions differ as to the best way of differentiating these institutions. On the other hand there are extreme versions of imbalance that are clearly detrimental for any modern society, as when the state fatally overrides both economy and culture (cf. the Soviet Union), or when the market (in all-embracing capitalism) overrides both the state (including the judiciary system) and the life-world (including interpersonal relations), or when a traditionalist clan system takes the place of the state and its sub-institutions as well as of market transactions (as in Somalia today). Hence there are clearly some extreme versions of institutional imbalance that should be avoided in any modern society. All in all, this means that there are some institutional differentiations that are required and some institutional arrangements that are not predetermined. In this respect our reconstructive approach to the question of modernization indicates both some degree of necessity and some degree of contingency.[5]

At the outset we focused on self-referential requirements in processes of modernization and thus on arguments in favour of what can be seen as necessary for all modern societies, and against the pluralist view. But at the same time we have also emphasized (i) the plurality inherent in scientific and scholarly research, as well as pointing to (ii) a possible variety of institutional arrangements, and referring to (iii) the irreducible plurality of reasonable world-views, both religious and non-religious (cf. G. Skirbekk 2006). The plurality of world-views has an affinity with the question of 'value plurality'. Even though some basic normative principles of justice might be discursively justified (as procedural context-transcending norms for the regulation of conflicts), many value questions are clearly contextual, culturally dependent, or simply a matter of taste, and are thus beyond any universal justification. In this sense we may operate with a distinction between universal norms and contingent values. In the realm of value questions, of different cultural codes and traditions, there is thus ample space for legitimate variety and creativity. Hence the pluralist conceptions of modernization processes find strong support when we focus on these questions.

Thus, to the question 'are the processes of modernization one or many?' we can briefly summarize our reconstructive deliberation in these terms: there is an unavoidability (and 'oneness') related to discursive rationality and its requirement for special mental abilities and institutional arrangements. Within these restraints there is space for some plurality in institutional arrangements. And finally there is reasonable disagreement on various value questions and world interpretations – both religious and non-religious – and hence there is an unavoidable plurality in these cases.

Special Experiences

A further step: in the processes of modernization, we must cope with both unavoidable principles and discursive claims on the one hand and with contingent values and opinions on the other. In addition we have deeply entrenched special experiences and learning-processes: different societies have gone through different historical crises and events. Topography, material conditions, catastrophes, wars and inherent sociocultural tensions, these are among the (more or less) contingent factors that make a difference to the collective identity, institutional arrangements and political culture of a society.

In order to illustrate this point, we may look at some striking differences among Western nations, like France and the United States. In both countries political modernity was manifested via universalist declarations of human rights at the end of the eighteenth century. But their conceptions of the state–market relationship and of the role of religion in modern societies are strikingly different. In France (like Germany and the Nordic countries) the state was given a more dominant role in the processes of modernization than in the U.S. (or U.K.). In France, 'freedom of religion' predominantly meant (and means) a freedom to criticize religion whereas in the U.S. it primarily meant (and means) a freedom for various Protestant sects and other religious convictions to be left alone. Voltaire and the French philosophers of the Enlightenment operated in a different sociocultural setting than the first European settlers of North America, and they promoted another intellectual culture that still prevails.

To the extent that these countries (France and the U.S.) are modern countries in the sense of the general requirements outlined above, we can (in these two cases) talk about different processes of modernization in terms of different learning processes and institutional differentiations.

Interplay between Lutheran State Officials and Popular Movements

In this section we shall take a look at some of the special processes of modernization that occurred in the Scandinavian countries, especially Norway, with the aim of elucidating alternative processes of modernization.

Characteristic of the processes of modernization in the Scandinavian countries is, broadly speaking, an interesting interplay (mainly in the nineteenth century) between Lutheran state officials and popular movements and elites. The Scandinavian countries were among the very few Lutheran states with almost no other confessions for a long period of time.[6] These countries were also characterized by historically quite unique popular movements.[7] On this background they had, by the middle of the twentieth century, combined a comprehensive welfare state, including widespread material redistribution, with a high degree of tolerance within the rule of law, and a high degree of political cohesion – more so than in most other countries. It is worth noting that the state played a much more significant role here than in the Anglo-American world. At the same time, early popular movements and their elites obtained political positions quite distinct to those of their counterparts in France.

Some thinkers (like Habermas) have conceived of tolerance as a fruit of the learning processes among citizens who are confronted with different (religious) confessions within the same political community (starting with the Westphalian peace, after the wars of religion in the seventeenth century). How then could mono-confessional countries, like the Scandinavian states, finally be among the most tolerant communities? This question indicates that a focus on the processes of modernization of the Scandinavian countries might be of some interest for the overall conception of alternative modernization processes. However, I shall here restrict myself to discussing some of the main characteristics of the Norwegian processes of modernization.

Norway in Nineteenth Century: A *'Beamtenstaat'* (par excellence)

At the outset, a few facts about Norwegian history should be mentioned, as an introductory remark. In the eighteenth century the monarchy of Denmark-Norway was a state under the rule of law, to a large extent governed by enlightened state officials. A common school system was established in the 1730s, one motivation being the promotion of literacy so that everybody could read the Bible, required for the confirmation of Christian youth in Lutheranism. At the end of the eighteenth century a large percentage of Norwegian farmers (peasants) were landowners. Literacy was widespread and the writings of a cultural modernizer like Ludvig Holberg (1684–1754) got a broad audience, including among the farmers. As a result of the Napoleonic Wars, Norway entered a union with Sweden in 1814, but with a newly written and progressive constitution and hence as a politically independent state (except for foreign affairs). At an early stage, due to the Black Death,[8] and later, due to the power-related politics of the Danish kings (Rian 2007), the national nobility was fatally weakened – around 1814 there was practically no nobility in Norway.

Broadly speaking there were three classes at that time: (i) State officials (around 0.2 per cent of the population) – mainly university-educated lawyers and Lutheran theologians, plus higher military officers – who became particularly influential for two reasons: there was no nobility, and these state officials were allowed to perform the double role of state servants and active politicians; (ii) Citizenry, with their living related to fishery, mines, mills, forestry, shipping and trade – in other words, they were not dependent on a landowning nobility; (iii) Farmers (peasants) represented the majority of the population (about 90 per cent in 1814). To a large extent they were literate; many were landowners (around 1814, approximately 57 per cent). An exceptionally high percentage of the members of the Constitutional Assembly of 1814 were farmers or representatives of the rural communities (approximately one third). And for historical reasons the farmers (peasants) represented the national heritage, since there was practically no national nobility, and state officials had for the most part a Danish background.

In short, at the beginning of the nineteenth-century Norway was predominantly run by state officials (a Weberian *Beamtenstaat*, par excellence), but with a progressive Constitution, and with a strong peasantry. Gradually, through the National Assembly (*Stortinget*), a democratic opposition supported by the popular movements gained force. In 1884 Parliamentarianism was introduced by the opposition, an event that represented a decisive weakening of the political role of the state officials and the coming-to-power of the Left, supported by popular forces and by the radical intelligentsia. Democracy was adopted in terms of multiparty parliamentarianism with extended franchise for men in 1898. In 1913 the franchise was extended to women.

Now let us briefly look at some major aspects of the popular movements and their elites in Norway during this period.

Popular Movements and Elites

Haugianism was the first popular movement, initiated by Hans Nielsen Hauge (1771–1824), a young peasant who had a religious vision while working in the field in 1796, at the age of twenty-five. Haugianism was at the same time a religious movement (within Lutheranism, against official Lutheranism), and a class movement against Lutheran state officials (Gilje 1997).

Max Weber identified Puritan ethics (Calvinism) as a precondition for capitalism. The Haugians played a similar role in Norway. For religious reasons they favoured hard work and modest consumption. The result was capital accumulation and reinvestment – in paper mills, saw mills, salt production, fishery, ship building, farming and trade. Haugianism combined charismatic leadership and a national network of solidarity (between 'brethren and sisters' – not individualistically). The Haugians promoted modernizing activities and learning processes on a broad scale: economic activities, socio-political organization, training in speaking in assemblies (women were welcome both as speakers and leaders), promoting literacy and thereby creating an alternative public sphere. For instance, approximately one-in-four Norwegian citizens, inclusive of new-born infants and the elderly, bought a copy of Hauge's writings in a time of hunger and hardship.

Haugianism soon became a breeding ground for political actors. They were members of the Constitution Assembly in 1814; they were elected to the National Assembly (*Stortinget*) and to political positions in local communities. By 1840 their main aims had been reached: wider religious and economic liberties. Gradually Haugianism became integrated in Norwegian society, with some regional differences, recognizable even today. However, they remained within the Lutheran State-Church; they did not redefine themselves as an independent religious community.

With the Haugians (but also, for example, through the influence of the Danish theologian Grundtvig), and due to an alternative school system (*folkehøjskole*) and an alternative public sphere, a version of the typically Scandinavian phenomenon of 'popular education' (*folkeopplysning* and *folkelighed*) gained recognition and became a decisive factor in the formation of a more egalitarian society – roughly speaking, education and cultural formation of the people, for the people, by the people. This was in opposition to the traditional educational system and ideology, but definitely had the aim of 'raising the people', and raising oneself, culturally and educationally.

Hauge was harshly treated by the authorities – jailed in 1804 and finally released in 1811,[9] physically weakened and with health problems. However, Haugianism as a movement prevailed and became quite influential. In many ways it changed Norwegian society permanently, from below. Hence, there was a struggle for recognition and tolerance, not between (religious) confessions, but between opposing socio-cultural groups and their elites: the typically Scandinavian dialectics between Lutheran state officials and popular movements.

The Thrane Movement, initiated by Marcus Thrane (1817–1890) in 1849 and inspired by the uprising in France in 1848, was at the outset a spontaneous protest against food shortages. The movement was supported by unprivileged people in the cities, but even more so in the countryside.

Thrane was a utopian socialist (like Proudhon) and mildly Christian. He soon became a successful organizer. He and his followers organized workers' associations (*Arbeiderforeninger*). After one year there were around 414 associations with thirty thousand members, probably around 2 per cent of the total population at that time, organized on both the local and national levels. They effectively established an alternative public sphere with their own newspaper (*Arbeiderforeningernes Blad*).

The political programme was initially rather moderate: for reduced customs tariffs in pursuit of cheaper food, against alcohol abuse, for better schools for average people, for universal military service (a popular requirement already in 1814), and for a general right to vote for all men. The programme was turned down and the movement became more clearly class-oriented: redistribution of land, support for peasants who wanted to cultivate new land, establishing a state bank for people with few resources, social security for the elderly and disabled.

In 1851 the Thrane movement was suppressed by force by the authorities (the state officials). Thrane was jailed. When released he did not take part in political activities, and after some time he left for the U.S. where he lived out the rest of his life. In a sense, then, the Thrane movement was but an episode – however, an important lesson was learnt: popular movements need to organize and they need an alternative public sphere. And there was more to come.

The Farmers' Friends (or 'people's friends': *bondevenn* or *folkevenn*), led by Søren Jaabæk (1814–1894) from around 1865, represents the third wave of popular movements, starting spontaneously and gradually gaining power by self-organization and self-education and by the use of an alternative public sphere. The farmers' friends organized themselves on all levels: locally, at the county level, and nationally. They got approximately thirty thousand members in three hundred associations. They published a newspaper, *Folketidende*, printing approximately fifteen to twenty thousand copies per issue.

Jaabæk was elected mayor (*ordfører*) in his local community in 1841 and was elected to a seat in the National Assembly in 1845, where he became the leader of the opposition (*bondeopposisjonen*). The farmers' friends acted against city privileges,[10] and thus for liberalism, and were against high public spending, especially for the state officials.[11] In short, they defended their class interests and used the National Assembly to fight against the dominant political position of the state officials, especially in the government – hence, the political fight for Parliamentarianism was an important one.

Briefly, their programme included: support of reading associations (*leseselskap*), opposition to alcohol abuse, support for social security, for savings banks, and for joint associations of producers and consumers (*samvirke*). Around 1870 the movement was radicalized: for the separation of state and church, against Lutheran confirmation,[12] in favour of civil marriage, and against monarchy. In short, Jaabæk's basic ideal was a society with egalitarian harmony.

In addition to these three waves of popular movements (Hauge, Thrane, Jaabæk) I would like to mention two other movements with a more specific agenda: the 'language movement' (*målrørsla*) and the 'Women's movement' (*kvinnerørsla*).

The Language Movement: When Norway got its political independence in 1814 the written language was Danish. It was immediately understood by all Norwegians but spoken (more or less correctly) only by the upper classes, especially by the state officials who had been educated in Copenhagen. The people, especially the peasantry, spoke different dialects, originating from the old Norwegian language of the Viking period, the language of Norse literature.

Hence, the new nation of 1814 was confronted with a strategic question: should one continue with Danish, or try to reformulate a Norwegian language? As it turned out, Danish as a written language prevailed for approximately a century – Norwegian authors like Ibsen wrote in Danish and published their books in Denmark. But for national and pedagogical reasons steps were taken to change the written language into a Norwegian language. Two main strategies were available: reformulate a modern Norwegian language from the Norwegian dialects, or change the traditional Danish language stepwise in accordance with spoken Norwegian in the upper classes. Both strategies were followed, and thus two official Norwegian languages gradually developed.

Simultaneously there was a conflict between these two strategies and these two languages, a conflict that continues still. This conflict has both national and social elements; at the end of the nineteenth century it was intertwined with the general conflict between state officials (who traditionally wrote Danish) and popular movements (supported by the Left party, established in 1884). This dual situation continues today, resulting in what might be described as blending 'a fight for cultural dominance' (in the sense of Gramsci and Bourdieu) and 'a recognition of others' (as per Derrida) – the latter being an unintended result of a learning process that led to some degree of cultural tolerance.[13]

The Women's Movement: Comparatively speaking, women in Norway traditionally had a strong position, legally and socially. But with professionalization and urbanization new challenges emerged, and the role of women in modern societies became a political question for popular movements as well as a major concern for poets and artists (cf. *Nora* in Ibsen).

The Norwegian Feminist Association (*Norsk Kvindesags-Forening*) was established in 1884, the year of the introduction of Parliamentarianism – one of its leaders, Gina Krog (1847–1916), belonged to the left wing of the Left party (*Venstre*). The following year, 1885, the Association for the Franchise for Women was established (*Kvindestemmeretsforeningen*), with Gina Krog as chairperson until 1897. (In 1898 it changed its name to *Landskvindestemmeretsforeningen*.) They fought for universal rights: the right to vote, the right to higher education, and legal rights for married women.

Also the women's movement represented a blend of spontaneous movement and organization abilities – one achievement was the founding of the journal *Nylænde* (1887), as an alternative public sphere. And its organizational ability was clearly demonstrated in 1905, when Norway unilaterally broke the union with Sweden: only male citizens were allowed to vote for or against the union (368,208 voted 'no', 184 'yes'). Women citizens were not allowed to vote, hence they organized their own 'private' vote for women, and in a two-week period 244,765 women had voted – two-thirds of the male votes, an amazingly high number.[14] One of the leaders was Betzy Kjelsberg, a supporter of the *Venstre*.

A Local Case (1880–1920): The Interplay of Persons and Institutions

To get a sense of what was going on at a local level, in the lead up to the introduction of Parliamentarianism and into the early twentieth century, roughly the period between 1880 and 1920, I shall discuss a particular community – a county in East Norway, not far from the Swedish border (in the middle of the Scandinavian peninsula, as it were) – focusing on the interplay of persons and institutions. Its economy was based on agriculture, forestry and related industries. Forestry was its primary source of wealth. Farms were often middle-size, based on paid labourers. The preceding discussion of popular movements, their elites, and Lutheran state officials provides general background for this local community, as we shall see, focusing on the interplay between some influential persons and some special institutions (H. Skirbekk 1946–1947; Overrein 2001).

The country's notable institutions include: (i) political institutions in a broad sense, beginning with spontaneous discussion groups, establishment of trade unions and widespread participation in new political parties; (ii) the establishment of a newspaper as a local public sphere; (iii) the establishment of a local *folkemuseum* to promote historical awareness of the local and national heritage, carried by the traditional agrarian community; and (iv) the establishment of a *folkehøgskule* (people's high school) and a teachers' college to promote education and cultural self-esteem for future generations – inspired by the educational ideals of the various popular movements.

The influential persons under consideration here include: (i) the forest owner (1836–1917) – a rich idealist supporting cultural and educational initiatives; (ii) the politician (1859–1934) – a leftist farmer supporting the workers and the unprivileged, promoting a discursive and organized political culture; (iii) the scholar (1873–1932) – a teacher, ethnologist and (at the end of his life) state official of the regional school system, and a supporter of the democratic-national movement; and (iv) the editor (1877–1951) – the son of Swedish immigrants, supporting the social and democratic-national movement by his pen and his position as a newspaper editor.

Political Institutions in a Broad Sense

'In the beginning was the Word': In 1881, a local 'conversation association' (*samtaleforening*) was founded by three young farmers (among them our politician, 22 years old at the time), who had been together in a local school for young people, established in 1873. According to the founders:[15] 'By coming together in order to discuss topics of common interest and to have lectures, the aim of this association is to be enlightening and educating' (*opplysende og dannende*).

An important point concerning procedure: each meeting began by having two persons presenting opposite positions on a chosen topic, on the understanding that serious discussion requires pro and con, arguments and counter-arguments. Some of the topics discussed (according to written reports) included:

- 'Should women have greater juridical autonomy and should one open access for her to most positions?' (The speaker for the affirmative was Eivind Torp [1844–1890], director and teacher of the school just mentioned.)
- 'Is the present way of paying priests satisfactory?' (In short, questioning the economic conditions for state officials. After a lively discussion of various aspects of the remuneration system, there was general agreement for a resolution recommending the abolition of special payments for each service rendered by a clergyman.)
- 'Will the associations of the armament of the people function conveniently and should one join them actively or passively?' (This kind of ar-

mament was meant to support the army, but it became a leftist case, not favoured by the authorities, since in reality it was an armament of the people. In the lead up to the Norwegian withdrawal from the union with Sweden in 1905 questions of defence were of great importance. There was a lively discussion, overwhelmingly in favour of people's armament.)

- 'Does the constitution allow for a royal veto in constitutional matters and if so of what kind?' (This was a crucial question in the conflict between Swedish and Norwegian politicians – the king was Swedish – and in the fight for parliamentary democracy.)
- 'Are there major deficiencies in social life in our county and what could be done to improve the situation?' (During the discussion our politician and another person made the proposal that one should establish workers' associations [*arbeidersamfunn*].)
- 'What is the relationship of the literary and political Left to Christianity?'
- 'Is a republic to be preferred to monarchy?' (Our politician presented pro-republic arguments.)
- 'How could agriculture most conveniently be made useful?'
- 'Is our welfare system for poor people on the right track?' (Arguments in favour of improvements were presented by our politician, who (i) made an appeal to Christian altruism [while warning against moralizing], (ii) expressed belief in the sciences [*Wissenschaften*] to improve the standard of living, and (iii) spoke out against abuse of alcohol; he also proposed (iv) to transfer the farms of state officials into institutions for work and education for young people.)
- 'Who should have the right to vote in our country?'
- 'How should school and home most conveniently collaborate?'
- 'Advantages and deficiencies of private schools compared with public schools.'
- 'About the property rights for men and women in marriage.'
- 'What are the special causes for the deep gap between workers and the well-to-do, and how could this relationship be improved?'
- 'Should the jury system be introduced in our country?' (This was an important question concerning the status of the supreme court [and the role of state officials]. Jury and parliamentarianism were twin questions in the power struggle between the state officials and the Left.)
- 'Is war a crime and could it possibly be abandoned?'
- 'What are appropriate means against alcoholism (*drukkenskap*).'
- 'Popular enlightenment' (*folkets opplysning*) (Eivind Torp criticized liberalist capitalism for making living conditions worse for the workers and for creating contempt for the workers. He defended a decent Christian life [*sunt kristenliv*], better schools, and extended juridical rights.)

The transition to parliamentarianism in 1884 represented a decisive weakening of the political role of the state officials and the coming to power of the Left, supported largely by popular forces and movements and by the radical city intelligentsia. An important and recurring topic in this discussion association around 1884 was the question of how the working class could be organized and how it could organize itself (for and by the people). Politically empowering the working class demands organizational solidarity among various progressive groups, but in the end it should be achieved by the workers themselves. According to the association's reports, 'The purpose (of workers' organizations) is to promote the well-being of the workers. The case must be promoted by those who gain (and seek) their living by the use of their hands.'

Other topics discussed after 1884 included rules for the police and questions of school reform. There was a heated discussion on the language question at its final meeting in 1885, the year in which the parliament decided that New Norwegian[16] should have equal legal status with Danish-Norwegian.[17] At that final meeting our politician asked all the members to join the local workers' association (*Arbeidersamlag*).[18]

This story is interesting as an example of accumulating learning-processes: first, enlightened discussions (pro and con); then organize trade unions to improve working conditions and promote public education; then join political parties to take part in party politics. This local story thus conforms to a Habermasian ideal: the importance of a discursive public sphere and of learning-processes, bottom up (as it were).

Newspaper

A local newspaper was established early in 1901 as an alternative public space. It was a newspaper for the Left, aimed at raising social questions and reporting on the workers' movement at home and abroad. It advocated an association of 'farmers of the left and workers of the left' (*venstrebønder og venstrearbeidere*) – that is, the newspaper was to the left in the Left (in the political party *Venstre*). It was initially an organ of *De forenede norske arbeidersamfunn* (the united Norwegian workers' association) which in 1911 adopted the name *Arbeiderdemokratene* (workers' democrats). Our editor was appointed to this newspaper already in 1901 (at the age of twenty-four), and remained there until 1921, when the newspaper was taken over by *Bondepartiet* (Farmers' party). As the party newspaper for *Bondepartiet*, it maintained a leftist and radical profile; for instance, its editor from 1968 till 1994 had voted for the Norwegian Communist Party (*NKP*) in his early youth and was later active in the social-democrat youth movement *AUF*. This is the heartland of the 'red county' (*det raude fylket*) in Norway.

Folkemuseum

The new *folkemuseum* was the symbol of pride in the local and national heritage that had been transmitted through a long tradition of the agrarian society. This local community was basically progressive and forward-looking, but it was also proud of its local and national heritage. Political identity-building therefore had a historical component: in 1911 this local *folkemuseum* was established, a museum for and by the people. It soon became the third largest folk's museum in Norway (after *Folkemuseum* in Oslo and *Sandvikske samlinger* in Lillehammer), despite the fact that it was located only 30 km (on flat land) from the county capital, which had a similar museum. To understand how this came about we must consider the interplay between persons and institutions. The four persons we have mentioned were all involved in the establishment of this museum. They collaborated and supplemented each other: the editor with media and public space, the scholar with historical expertise, the politician with political capital, and the forest owner with economic resources. They were all animated by a social and cultural pride for *folkekulturen*, the culture of the people. Together they represented a powerful agency, in collaboration with many other people in the community.

Schools

Schools were established to promote education, with an idealist (ideological) agenda. With the economic support of the forest owner a local *folkehøgskule* (people's high school) was established in 1928, influenced by the ideals of the Danish theologian and writer Nikolai Fredrik Severin Grundtvig, which means that it was 'open-minded' (*frilyndt*), not pietist or orthodox in religious and cultural matters. A teachers' college (*lærarskule*) was also established – again, only 30 km away from the county capital, which was home to another teachers' college. This school, too, was conceived as *frilyndt*, in a contrast to other teachers' colleges. Both types of school were important for the kind of alternative education and identity-formation that was supported by *Venstre* and the popular movements in Norway. A significant proportion of the young people who were educated in these kinds of schools became major agents for the *Venstre* regime and for the promotion of attitudes in favour of the democratic-national ideas of the popular movements in the nineteenth century.

So far we have looked at some special institutions established in this local community in the late nineteenth and early twentieth centuries. Other institutions were certainly important too, such as the new political parties, various public institutions, such as schools and health insurance, as well as institutional and technological developments in agriculture, forestry, infrastructure and communication. Taking a look at the four persons that we have selected may help indirectly to elucidate the important roles of these other institutions by highlighting the interplay between persons and institutions.

The politician: His father (1817–1870) was a farmer and a Haugian, but a moderate one, favouring education, socio-cultural formation, enlightenment ideals, and the 'protestant (work) ethics' – his handwritten diary from 1841–1848 bears witness to his self-discipline through the rational use of time.[19] His list of books and publications from 1860 (at the age of forty-three) contains 148 titles, including writings by Hans Nielsen Hauge and Ludvig Holberg as well as religious literature and various practical and useful books. When he died he urged his son, then eleven years of age, to seek education and knowledge ('that rust and rot cannot destroy'). Some of the activities of that son, our politician who was also a farmer, include:

- 1881–1885 Co-founder and active member of the local 'conversation association' (*samtaleforening*).
- 1887–1919 Member of the community government (heradstyret) for thirty-two years, beginning at the age of twenty-eight.[20]
- 1893–1895 Mayor (*ordførar*).
- 1893–1903 Member of the national board of De forenede norske arbeidersamfunn (the United Norwegian Workers' Association).
- 1893–1929 Director (forretningsførar) of local trygdekasse (public health insurance service).
- 1901–1907 Vice Mayor (*viseordførar*).
- 1901 First candidate on the election list for Arbeidardemokratane (Worker Democrats), the party that won the election.
- 1918–1930 Director of the local branch of the (public) Bank of Norway.
- First chairman of local branch of *Venstre*.
- Member of the board of local workers' association (*Arbeidersamfunn*), for approximately fifteen years.

In addition to his day-to-day efforts to achieve improvements in farming, forestry and infrastructure, and so on, he is also noteworthy for several specific political issues:

- 1893: Efforts to reduce working hours for farm workers, and an extra meal a day.
- 1894: May Day demonstration (the first in Norway outside the cities).
- 1895: Organizing trade unions and building a trade union house (a *folkets hus*).
- Efforts for social security in the form of public disability insurance (whether by disease or accident) and old age and retirement pension schemes.
- Efforts for better education for everyone: free school material and free education after compulsory public school.
- Campaign for the republic, against monarchy.
- Campaign for the armament of the people (before 1905).
- Campaign for New Norwegian language.
- Campaign against alcohol abuse.

The editor is first generation Norwegian. Both of his parents had moved to Norway from Sweden. He was significantly influenced by the socio-cultural ideals and attitudes of popular movements in Norway (but without religious pietism), and he was an influential cultural personality with an excellent pen and a social consciousness. In addition to his many activities in the local community, as an editor and a cultural figure, he was also a member of the board of the national association of the press (*Norsk presseforbund*).

The scholar was a teacher and an ethnologist and became the school director for the region (a state official).[21]

The forest owner was a genuine idealist with strong beliefs in the democratic-national ideals and aims of the popular movement. He was rich in terms both of money and social connections. For instance, he supported the new museum, provided funding for the local *folkehøgskule*, and donated around forty-six thousand books to the public library.

Special Modernization Processes: Some General Points

We began with a discussion of general questions concerning alternative processes of modernization. In order to make our discussion more specific, we looked at special learning-processes and institutional differentiations in Scandinavia, characterized by the interplay between Lutheran state officials and popular movements, focusing more specifically on modernization processes in Norway, especially in the nineteenth century. Finally we looked at a local case in Norway in the late nineteenth and early twentieth centuries.

Summarizing what I have said above about popular movements and their elites, nationally and locally, I would like to emphasize a few points of general interest:

- They had an ability to organize themselves, to transfer spontaneous popular movements into economic, political and educational institutions.
- The main movements came in three waves (as it were), each time as a process in which spontaneous movements or actions became organized and institutionalized[22] – what could not easily be realized in a singular simultaneous event could thus be obtained by repeating processes, from spontaneity to organization.[23]
- These popular movements operated on a broad scale: in the economic field, on the political level, and in matters of education and formation.
- Deliberation and organizational work were combined.
- They discussed and organized on all levels, locally, regionally and nationally.
- They used the media of their time as an alternative public sphere.
- Education was conceived as self-education, an educational project that includes practical and theoretical training as well as consciousness raising on behalf of one's identity and cultural background.[24]
- The leaders of the popular movements behaved as civilized and reasonable persons. Thus the interaction between politically active state officials and the leaders of the popular movements resulted in some basic mutual trust. Hence, when the state officials 'abdicated' in 1884, they knew that nothing drastic would happen to them or to the country. This kind of basic trust is certainly a cultural precondition for a well-functioning democracy, requiring a peaceful change of power.
- All agents operated within the same Constitution and the same Confession. The learning processes of tolerance for 'the others' did not result from the experience of confessional plurality – practically everybody was a Lutheran – but from special experiences of socio-cultural and linguistic differences.[25]

The latter point deserves a special comment. Whereas many of the points referred to above may have equivalents in the other Nordic countries, there are some peculiar factors in the case of Norway, due to the absence of a national nobility and the 'foreignness' of the state officials. The Norwegian farmer was seen as the representative of the national heritage. Hence the popular fight for democracy merged with the fight for recognition of the national heritage. We got a democratic nationalism, from below – probably a unique constellation. Whereas Norway developed a homogeneous political culture (how to do things), it remained somewhat heterogeneous in terms of cultural codes and identity formation.[26] Furthermore, the popular movements tended to be pro-modern. That is, they were pro-enlightenment in the sense that they favoured science and new technology as well as education and a progressive public sphere, and they were to a large degree progressive in social politics, in favour of improved working conditions and social security.

The question, then, is: can these processes, roughly similar across the Nordic countries, explain the fact that these countries, in the mid-twentieth century, before late capitalist affluence, were able to combine a universal welfare system and economic redistribution with a high degree of tolerance?[27] At least we can say this: there are some deep-rooted processes in the modernization of the Nordic countries that are peculiar – to the extent that Scandinavian words like *folkelighed*, *folkhem* and *folkedanning* remain almost untranslatable. But they are crucial, and they do allude to what could probably be seen as *le charme discret des pays Nordiques* (the gentle charm of the Nordic countries).

Conclusion: It is Time to Conclude

Processes of modernization – one or multiple? And what about the claim that processes of modernization are deterministic, endogenous, unilinear?

Taking the latter question first: we have looked at cases of modernization processes, especially in Norway. In these cases various exogenous and contingent factors evidently played an important role: the Black Death weakened the nobility and radically reduced the population, which eventuated in better access to land for farmers who survived; partly due to topography, there was no room for serfdom and thus better conditions for farmers; and a war that was lost (in 1814) provided an occasion for writing a new constitution. Nor does this case support the unilinear view, which implies that there is only one road towards modernity. In this case the processes of modernization differ on essential points from those of the Anglo-American world as well as those of France and Germany. The role of Lutheran state officials in interplay with progressive popular movements and elites makes a difference. So, evidently the argument that modernization processes are deterministic, endogenous and unilinear appears to be refuted by the Norwegian (and Scandinavian) case.

As to the former question ('one or many?'), from a reconstructive perspective: in discussing the question of alternative processes of modernization we initially focused on unavoidable characteristics of the modern condition, partly connected to the need for discursive and reflective rationality and for an understanding of the sciences and the humanities as 'organized scepticism', and partly connected to the need for some basic institutional differentiations. In this respect there is *one* modernity. At the same time however, there is apparently a certain margin for alternative institutional arrangements and for different values and world-views – *plurality* in this respect is itself a characteristic of modernity. In this sense, debates regarding the possible and desirable arrangements and forms of life continue.

The realm of what is possible includes some room for choice, but not everything that is possible can be freely chosen: we cannot choose to have experiences and learning-processes that we have not gone through ourselves. We cannot experience other people's experiences, and we cannot ourselves 're-make' such experiences when they are so tightly connected to particular events and conditions. Consequently, even though there are different ways of being modern and alternative processes of modernization, it remains to be seen what this means in terms of what we possibly can learn from each other. Similarly it remains to be seen what we today can learn from earlier experiences in our own society.

Hence, when the question 'Are the processes of modernization one or many?' is addressed from a reconstructive perspective, there are some fairly strong arguments in favour of the view that any successful process of modernization must accept and appropriate some basic ideas and establish some basic institutional arrangements. In this sense there are some learning processes and institutional differentiations that are necessary preconditions for any modern society. It follows, then, that the processes of modernization are singular ('one'). Our examination of Norway's modernization processes lends support to this conclusion. At the same time, though, this case also reveals how various special factors influence processes. In short, there are in fact alternative processes of modernization. In this sense, processes of modernization are plural ('many'). To conclude, we must recognize, on the whole, a blend of necessity and contingency in the processes of modernization.

This general conclusion has two major implications. On the one hand it allows for a criticism of societies that deviate from essential characteristics of modernization, such as a modernization of consciousness and a certain institutional differentiation. On the other hand it opens for intercultural curiosity and dialogue, for mutual understanding and learning.

So, what does it mean to be modern and Chinese, modern and Muslim, modern and Norwegian, or modern and American? It necessarily entails a basic 'modernization of consciousness' and basic institutional differentiations. But how this could and should be done is the kind of question we need to discuss with each other, and hence it is useful to look into various cases of such processes of modernization, in order to understand each other better and possibly to improve unsatisfactory and unsustainable constellations.

Faced with the challenges of modernity in a precarious world situation there is evidently a need for such inter-cultural dialogues, for possible changes and improvements. Then there is also a need for serious discussion, whereby the participants recognize each other as autonomous persons and thereby take arguments seriously, which unavoidably implies that we, as reasonable and fallible persons, are open for mutual criticism, for giving and taking good reasons.

So, are the processes of modernization one or many? Yes, both – correctly understood. As a next step we should ask: what kind of modernity is likely to be a sustainable one? At least we know that a readjustment of the interrelationship between the main institutions and sub-institutions should be reconsidered, starting with the relationship between market economy, politics and civil society – for evidently, unrestrained capitalism and sustainable modernity entail conflicting perspectives and demands (G. Skirbekk et al. 1992), and unrestricted consumption and reproduction are incompatible with a sustainable future.

Notes

1. Cf. the comprehensive discussion in Knöbl (2001).
2. It also requires special institutional arrangements to help neutralize the influence of factors that are irrelevant to validity questions.
3. I do not share the view that autonomous basic research is historically outdated (cf. the discussion on 'mode 2' in science studies).
4. Superstitious and irrational beliefs do not belong to this field of reasonable disagreement (cf. John Rawls 1993, pp. 54ff.).
5. If we change our approach, and raise questions of 'sustainability', we are faced with other challenges. For instance, to what extent is modern capitalist consumerism ecologically sustainable in the long run? These are certainly complex questions, involving not only problems of scarce resources and of pollution and climate change, but also problems of demographic unsustainability and global epidemics. These questions point at urgent challenges, given that we want to avoid the worst scenarios and take the precautionary principle seriously. Consequently, there are some important constraints on possible versions of modernity, constraints that are revealed by such functionalist considerations, rather than by reconstructive analyses of the past.
6. Say, throughout the seventeenth, eighteenth and nineteenth centuries. Other Lutheran states were Estonia and Prussia.
7. From the early nineteenth century (see later).
8. Fourteenth century.
9. During the Napoleonic War, in 1809, he had been temporarily released in order to help the state promote salt production, which was desperately needed due to British blockades and food shortages.
10. E.g., privileges concerning saw mills and trade (from the mid-seventeenth century).
11. Especially their income and retirement pension.

12. Lutheran confirmation promoted literacy. On the other hand, it included a public examination in the church that (in a Foucauldian perspective) may be seen as a system of class-based control and disciplining.
13. But the tension still prevails, and not only between *nynorsk* and *bokmål*. There is also a tension concerning the balance between a more Danish and a more Norwegian profile within *bokmål*, for instance in newspapers. E.g., well-formulated articles written in official *bokmål* with traditional Norwegian words and expressions (like *fram* and *boka*) are systematically changed in the main newspapers into words and expressions closer to Danish (like *frem* and *boken*).
14. This was before e-mail and mobile phones, in a topographically difficult country with a widely scattered population.
15. GS translation (word-by-word), here and later.
16. At first called *landsmål*, later *nynorsk*.
17. Our politician started using New Norwegian soon after that decision. From his collection of books we also know that he could read Old Norwegian (the Norse language).
18. In the last of the handwritten reports we find announcements for Blue Band (*Blå Bånd*), an association against alcohol abuse, and for the Oslo newspaper *Verdens Gang*, distributed by the Left party.
19. Interestingly, he (a farmer) wrote small epigrams in Latin whereas leading state officials (like Schweigaard) worked actively to reduce the role of Latin in Norwegian education, in order to promote skills that were seen as more practically useful.
20. Norway got local governance by a law of 1837.
21. His older brother, a forest owner who in early years had studied in Leipzig, was a member of the national assembly (*Stortinget*) and held central positions in the national forestry and timber industry organizations, including the board of industrial company Borregaard. (Their grandfather had been a member of the farmers' opposition in the national assembly of 1821.)
22. Both spontaneity and organization are necessary – but it is very difficult to achieve both at the same time. Spontaneity without organization leads in the end to political weakness. Organization without spontaneity leads to bureaucratization.
23. Such learning-processes might lead to a mind-set that is open for future mobilization (as seen in the women's vote in 1905). Cf. also the Norwegian votes against EU membership.
24. Cast in the untranslatable terms of *folkeopplysning* and *folkelighed*.
25. Compared with a politically centralized and culturally and linguistically homogenized country like France, Norway may look like an early 'post-modernist' society with an inherent 'multi-culturalism' – with cultural heterogeneity and political homogeneity.
26. The topography of the country might have contributed to this heterogeneity.
27. Here we do not raise the critical question as to whether it will last, under the conditions of globalized capitalism, with ecological and demographic challenges (cf. G. Skirbekk 1996).

References

Arnason, J.P., S.N. Eisenstadt and B. Wittrock. (2005) *Axial Civilizations and World History*. Leiden/Boston: Brill.

Eisenstadt, S. (2000) *Comparative Civilizations and Multiple Modernities*, v. 1–2 (especially v. 2). Leiden/Boston: Brill.

Gilje, N. (1997) 'Hans Nielsen Hauge and the Spirit of Capitalism', in Fjelland et al. (eds), *Philosophy Beyond Borders*. Bergen: SVT Press, 255–69.

Knöbl, W. (2001) *Spielräume der Modernisierung*. Weilerswist: Velbrück Wissenschaft.

Merton, R.K. (1968) *Social Theory and Social Science*. New York: The Free Press.

Overrein, P. (2001) *'Hvor ånden bærer bud' – Østlendingen fra Arbeiderdemokratene til Orkla*. Elverum: Østlendingen.

Rawls, J. (1993) *Political Liberalism*. New York: Columbia University Press.

Rian, Ø. (2007) *For Norge, kjempers fødeland*. Oslo: Det norske samlaget.

Skirbekk, G. (1993) *Rationality and Modernity*. Oslo/Oxford: Scandinavian University Press/Oxford University Press.

———. (1996) 'The Idea of a Welfare State in a Future Scenario of Great Scarcity', in Eriksen and Loftager (eds), *The Rationality of the Welfare State*. Oslo: Scandinavian University Press.

———. (2006) 'Religion and Modernity', in G. Skirbekk *Religion, Modernity, and Rationality*. Bergen: SVT Press.

———. (2007) *Timely Thoughts*. Lanham: University Press of America.

——— et al. (eds). (1992) *The Commercial Ark. A Book on Evolution, Ecology, and Ethics*. Oslo: Scandinavian University Press.

Skirbekk, H. (ed.) (1941–1982) *Årbok frå Glåmdalen*. Elverum: Austmannalaget.

CHAPTER 8
Nordic and Finnish Modernity: A Comparison

Risto Alapuro

Bo Stråth's essay 'Nordic Modernity: Origins, Trajectories and Prospects' (2004) covers Finland, along with Sweden, Denmark and Norway. In his view a largely similar model of progressive politics 'broke through [in these countries] in the 1930s as a response to the Great Depression. Everywhere in Norden red-green Social Democratic-Farmers' Party reform coalitions emerged in attempts to cope with the economic crisis, and extreme political alternatives were marginalized' (2004: 5; see also Stråth in this volume: 27). From this vantage point Stråth discusses the historical preconditions of the model, emphasizing above all two factors underpinning 'a more progressive and egalitarian development in the North', namely 'the strength of the peasant freeholders and [the strength] of the urban middle classes' (2004: 5). It was these forces that finally broke through in the 1930s, even though, as Stråth repeatedly remarks, there was nothing predetermined in this path.

Stråth's conception provides a useful starting point for reflecting on the place of Finland in the Nordic constellation and to relate it to the Nordic master narrative.

1. A Model of Progressive Politics

A major point in Stråth's interpretation is the way he portrays the role of social democracy, which he sees as 'a continuation/transformation of Lutheranism and parish political culture and of social liberalism' (2004: 9; cf. Stråth in this volume: 30). For him a necessary precondition of the red-green coalition lay in the Social Democrats' transformation into people's parties, which attracted not only worker but also (urban) middle class support. Stråth concurs with George Mosse's view that in the interwar period socialists generally made efforts 'to combine *völkisch* and socialist thought' (2004: 7; cf. Stråth in this volume: 27). This was true especially in Sweden, which 'could be seen, in ideal typical terms, as representative of a broader Nordic pattern of development' (2004: 8; also Stråth in this volume: 28). The combination was crystallized in the idea of *folkhem*, originally cherished among conservatives. In Stråth's interpretation the point is not only the outcome of the 1930s, however, but the long period of conflict and contention that shaped the development before the final breakthrough (2004: 8).

During that preceding period, peasant freeholders played a prominent role, both as economic and political actors and as a central collective figure in the Nordic foundation myths. That figure, constructed by intellectuals and the clergy, has been instrumental in reconciling the tension between freedom and equality in Nordic political culture. There is a linkage to the nineteenth-century popular movements that developed people's communicative capacity and that were characterized by ideas of responsibility and self-realization and by other elements of individualism. For peasants, participation in parish meetings provided a useful training ground to develop communicative capacity, which later manifested itself in the creation of a link between social democracy and (social) liberalism.

The '(numerically small) urban middle classes' (2004: 7; cf. Stråth in this volume: 27) and liberalism enter Stråth's picture notably through their connection with social democracy. Mainstream liberalism in Norden was, from the late nineteenth century onwards, a social liberalism that relied on the state. In the interwar period social liberal parties based on middle classes and peasants and/or agrarian parties were able to cooperate with the Social Democrats. 'In the North, liberalism merged with the state into an ideology of modernity, and later on, petty bourgeoisie and the small farmers, guided by a socially-oriented liberalism, merged with the workers against dominant economic interests' (2004: 13), thereby creating the Nordic model of progressive politics.

2. Finland's Place

In Stråth's picture Finland displays certain particularities that differentiate it from the Nordic mainstream and especially from its ideal-typical case, Sweden. True, he maintains that historically the peasant freeholders' economic, political and cultural role, for example, was as central in Finland as it was in the other Nordic countries. It is perfectly legitimate to stress the role of Finnish peasants as carriers of freedom, equality and education, their place in the national 'foundation myth', and their contribution to the individualism that was developed and reshaped in popular movements and parish meetings. But in the 1930s, Stråth reminds us, conditions in Finland were much more conflict-ridden than elsewhere. The Social Democrats apparently did not transform themselves into a 'people's party' (2004: 7; also Stråth in this volume: 27) to the extent Stråth says they did in Sweden, owing to the Communists on their left flank. Also, the middle classes as well as the peasants encountered tough barriers in approaching the Social Democrats. Notably, these differences go back to the Civil War, Stråth points out, even though there were other factors as well: in Finland liberalism was closer to classical economic liberalism than to the social liberalism prevailing elsewhere. In the other Nordic countries '[d]emarcation lines – essential to the discursive construction of community – were drawn *within* the so-called bourgeoisie and *within* the farmer class, between high and low bourgeoisie, large and small farmers or crofters' (2004: 16; cf. Stråth in this volume: 40). But such demarcation was less often the case in Finland than elsewhere: Finland 'deviated from this Nordic pattern of community construction from the Civil War of 1918 to the 1950s' (2004: 16; see also Stråth in this volume: 40). The class divisions were reinforced by the non-socialists' monopolization of the national rhetoric after the Civil War to an extent unknown in the other Scandinavian countries. In short, Finland 'gave a polarizing twist to the [Nordic] pattern' (2004: 14; see also Stråth in this volume: 36).

3. Internal and External Processes: Structures and Events

Stråth's overall characterization of the Finnish particularities in a Nordic perspective is certainly a valid one. Yet some of the implications that follow from his view seem questionable. To clarify the matter, I will reframe the Nordic context with Finland in it.

The conflict-ridden Finnish conditions in the interwar period caused Stråth to raise the question of whether Finland, which 'had gone through a civil war and been on the brink of a Fascist coup in the 1930s' (2004: 10), shares the Nordic pattern of social democracy as a continuation or a transformation of Lutheranism and parish political culture, and of social liberalism, and of the concomitant model of containing tensions between freedom and equality. Stråth suggests no answer to this question, although he considers the Finnish specificity as a useful indication of contingencies in the development of the Nordic model, whose adoption was not historically predetermined in any Nordic country. Other outcomes were possible: 'the Finnish case shows precisely how open the Scandinavian path was to other possibilities, and how close the authoritarian alternative was after all [in the 1930s]. ... The only path dependency is the one which can be laid out ex post – in the sense that dependency on the past for future developments always comes with a degree of indeterminacy.' (2004: 10; cf. Stråth in this volume: 31).

There is a connection between Stråth's unanswered question about the applicability of the Nordic pattern to Finland and the much more general issue of 'the degree of indeterminacy' in the Nordic development, an issue that Björn Wittrock (2004: 57–58) and Johann Arnason (2004: 104–5) also raised in analysing Sweden's and Iceland's paths to modernity, respectively. I would like to take a closer look at this issue and to qualify it in certain respects. In particular, if one can argue, as I will, that even in Finland – the allegedly deficient Nordic case – the development was to a significant degree 'predetermined', then one can relativize Stråth's view of a high degree of indeterminacy in the Nordic path.

Two distinctions, implicit in Stråth's account, seem appropriate here. One is the distinction between internal and external processes. Arnason (2004: 104) evokes this distinction when he points out that 'a different relationship between internal and external determinants of change' separates Iceland from the mainstream of Nordic modernity. The second, and related, distinction differentiates 'structures and institutions' from 'events'. In view of these distinctions, the role of the freeholding peasantry and the urban middle classes, with their many ramifications, are structural factors, whereas the Finnish Civil War in 1918 was an event. Both distinctions are heuristic devices rather than strict analytical distinctions. Yet both appear helpful in reflecting on the role of indeterminacy in the Nordic development and especially in the Finnish case.

I will first suggest that internal structures and institutions were (even) more determinant than Stråth is ready to admit, by pointing out how similar were the results in all the Nordic cases, despite a wide variety in the nature of external pressures to which each was subject in the emergence of modern politics. The most salient case is Finland: although, owing to an external impetus, Finland moved in one leap from a quite narrow system of representation to universal suffrage for men and women, nevertheless a very similar party system and initial configuration of political forces emerged there as in the Scandinavian countries. Second, I will consider the specific role of that spectacular event, the Civil War, in Finland's subsequent development. I will endeavour to show on the one hand, the war's limits in differentiating Finland from its Nordic neighbours, both in the short run and in the long run, and on the other hand, its place as an extreme expression of a broader pattern, the impact of the Russian connection on Finnish political culture.

4. Exogenous Processes and Indeterminacy in the Establishment of Mass Politics

The larger European constellation has shaped the experience of every Nordic country. In the cases of Finland, Norway and Iceland, it can be argued that even their emergence as modern states is contingent, if not accidental. The creation of Finland was determined purely by external factors. As Edward C. Thaden (1984: 82) put it, 'Finnish autonomy, and even the existence of a Finnish nation, can be considered an incidental by-product of wars between Sweden and Russia during the eighteenth and the beginning of the nineteenth centuries.' David Kirby (1986: 294) compared the linguistic balance in Finland in the early nineteenth century with that in contemporaneous Wales and concluded that the Finnish language could have been marginalized in Finland as the Welsh language was in Wales had Finland remained a part of Sweden. The establishment of Norway was also far from predetermined. As Øyvind Østerud (1996: 36) observes: 'Has national consciousness and quest for sovereignty been weaker in Scotland or in Kurdistan or in many other potential and unsuccessful nation-states than it was in Norway before 1814? Very unlikely. Norway got the opportunity for emancipated status as a gift from dynastic European politics – that is the closest we can get.' (On Iceland, see Arnason 2004.)

This degree of contingency distinguishes the latecomers from the two Nordic states established earlier, Sweden and Denmark. It is a useful reminder of the indeterminacy in the formation of the European state system (see Tilly 1993), and it undoubtedly left an imprint on the state identities of Finland and Norway in the nineteenth and the early twentieth centuries. In that period wars and other interstate crises in Europe shaped the rhythm of the internal political reforms, both in Sweden and Denmark as well as in Finland and Norway, all of which existed then as separate political units. It is striking how similar were the alliances and other aspects of modern politics in all four countries, despite major differences in the timing and the modes of extension of political rights (for more detail, see Alapuro 1985).

The country least affected by international crises was Sweden, where the constitution of 1809 resulted from the Napoleonic wars, that is, from Sweden's loss of Finland to Russia in 1808–1809. During the rest of the nineteenth century and the beginning of the twentieth, popular organization, mobilization, and collective action were to evolve purely in opposition to the domestic upper class, which was firmly entrenched within the political structures and not exposed to blows from the outside. Within its shrunken borders this established European national state and former great power had an exceptionally secure geographical location. It also had the slowest and most difficult time achieving political democracy, both as regards universal suffrage and in adopting the principle of parliamentarism, 'a slow, step-by-step democratization' (Knudsen and Rothstein 1994: 211). Here the working class had to struggle for political rights against domestic power-holders who were safeguarded from international pressures. In this 'representative of a broader Nordic pattern of development' (Stråth 2004: 8) the Social Democratic Party, founded in 1889, was anchored in a strong trade union movement, and liberal support was needed in the fight for universal suffrage and other reforms.

In the two other Scandinavian countries popular efforts to extend political rights were facilitated by the fact that the political systems in the era preceding the period of mass organization and mobilization were far more democratic than in Sweden, a result of international crises. Absolutist rule came to an end after Denmark was defeated in the war with Prussia in 1849, and the new constitution provided for nearly general (but not secret) adult male suffrage in what was at the time one of the most liberal electoral systems in Europe. It was in these conditions that the Labour Party (founded as early as 1878) was able to fight for final suffrage reforms and parliamentarism and to form an alliance with the *Venstre*, Denmark's Liberal Party. As for Norway, which was lost by Denmark in the Napoleonic wars, the Norwegians were in a position to institute very radical suffrage reforms. The new electoral system remained in force during Norway's union with Sweden under a shared king and was considered the most democratic in Europe at the time. Later, in the 1880s, the principle of parliamentarism was forced through rather easily by the Norwegians, who opposed the King of Sweden. The Norwegian Labour Party was founded in 1887 and, as in Sweden, was based on the trade unions, which at first were dominated by the Norwegian Liberal Party, *Venstre*. The two parties cooperated in the struggle for suffrage reform (1898) and continued to work together thereafter until the dissolution of the union with Sweden in 1905. The Danish labour movement resembled the other Scandinavian movements in that it too originated from and was based on the trade unions.

In sum, in Denmark and Norway the achievement of universal suffrage and the adoption of the principle of parliamentarism were facilitated by comparatively democratic political systems, which had been introduced earlier as a result of international crises. These crises affected the timing of the extension of political rights and the emergence and consolidation of social democracy, but the nature of the movement reflected domestic structural conditions in both countries. As in Sweden, the Social Democratic movement developed through alliances with the liberals.

In Finland the external impact was much more radical than in Scandinavia. There an international crisis – the first Russian Revolution in

1905 – not only provided an initial impetus for democratization, that is, it furnished the initial framework in which the Socialist mobilization was later to take place, as happened in Denmark and Norway, but it was also largely responsible for the process of the political mobilization itself. The crisis in Russia led to the replacement of the extremely narrow corporate system of representation by a unicameral assembly based on universal and equal suffrage for both men and women in 1906, only a few years after the Labour Party had been founded (1899) and even before a nationwide trade union organization had been created. The number of qualified voters was multiplied tenfold. The scale of change was unique in Europe. Yet, significantly enough, the results were very similar to the other Nordic countries, with a preponderance of peasants and workers showing up in the emerging pattern of mass politics. The party system that emerged resembled those in Sweden, Denmark and Norway (Mylly 1980: 277–89). The resemblance testifies to the weight of social structural and institutional similarities in all cases and of the ensuing similarities in the early stages of popular organization. In Finland the nineteenth-century popular movements were especially important in paving the way for a strikingly smooth transition to universal suffrage (see Alapuro 2006). Even though the transformation was far more rapid and thorough than in the Scandinavian countries, the resulting pattern paralleled the Scandinavian one. Whereas the Russian crisis in 1905 provoked jacqueries in the Baltic provinces of Russia – nobles killed, manors burned, records destroyed, churches sacked – in Finland the same power vacuum resulted in a large-scale organization of a Scandinavian type.

In effect, outside encroachments affected the timing and the rhythm in the extension of political rights and thereby shaped the timetable in the rise of social democracy and the peasant-worker alliances, but these encroachments did not prevent a fundamental similarity from evolving in the political pattern. Even Finland, where the external dependence was most obvious and the change most spectacular, fits the Scandinavian picture. But this is not to deny that within this overall framework specifically Finnish aspects appeared. For example, the linkage of social democracy with liberals remained more modest than was the case elsewhere in *Norden*, as Stråth (2004: 13) points out. In Finland the worker movement never needed liberal allies from the polity to enter it, as the Nordic sister parties did.

5. Events and Indeterminacy

In this portrayal of Finland as basically similar to its three Scandinavian neighbours, the Finnish Civil War and its bloody aftermath, the so-called

White Terror, constitute a real deviation. The sudden and thorough democratization of the political system and the accompanying large-scale mobilization in the beginning of the twentieth century was, in all its spectacularity, in line with the long-term structural and institutional factors, and could be integrated into the national narrative. The Civil War in the winter and early spring of 1918 could not. The event was a clash between Finns, but it broke out because Finland was closely dependent on Russia in the tumultuous year of 1917, especially in the maintenance of order (see, for example, Alapuro 2004). The Civil War was a crisis that practically no one could have foreseen, not even during the first half of 1917.

In describing an 'eventful sociology', William Sewell defines events as 'that relatively rare subclass of happenings that significantly transform structures' (1996: 262). '[E]vents bring about historical changes in part by transforming the very cultural categories that shape and constrain human action' (Sewell 1996: 263). This view is implicit in Stråth's hesitation to consider Finland as another Nordic case: in reflecting on her peculiarity, he specifically refers to the Civil War and the ensuing risk of a Fascist coup in Finland. Stråth is certainly right. The war indeed transformed or at least seriously undermined existing 'cultural categories', if by these we understand those features of political culture that he outlines in his overview. But to what extent did the war transform those categories? Even though no precise answer exists to this kind of question, it is possible to make a rough assessment in relating postwar Finland on the one hand to the Scandinavian neighbours, who shared internal structures with Finland, and on the other hand to Eastern European countries, which shared with Finland a comparable dependence and an exposure to political crises in the wake of the First World War.

In comparing Finland with the Scandinavian states, a perspective opposite Stråth's can be adopted. Instead of emphasizing the closeness of the authoritarian alternative, it can be pointed out that even such a spectacular event as the Civil War could not tip the balance of social forces to the point of plunging Finland into Fascism in the 1930s. It is significant that no takeover occurred, despite the events of the Civil War a little more than a decade earlier. A crucial factor in placing constraints on the escalation of fascist-type repression (after the ban on Communists) in the early 1930s was the solid position of the independent peasantry and their party in the state and society. The exclusion of the Social Democrats would have unbalanced the political system to the advantage of the Right, a development that was unacceptable to the Agrarians and the other centrists. That the fall of the semi-Fascist movement was to a very large extent determined by the peasantry is clearly indicated by the failure of the movement's leadership to mobilize the peasant rank and file behind an attempted coup d'état in 1932. Rather than revealing a high degree of indeterminacy, it seems to me that the crisis showed the strength of Nordic structural and institutional factors and, conspicuously in the culminating phase, the strength of the peasant class, or, more precisely, of the farmers and their party.

Well organized and mobilized and with a well-established position in the political system, the Finnish peasantry was totally unlike the Eastern European peasantries, which were frequently exploited by the political elites. The difference is clear if we relate the Finnish crisis to a comparable crisis in Romania or the Baltic countries. In Romania the peasant party provided no counterforce to Fascism. A closer example is the Baltic states, which also lived in the shadow of the USSR and which, like Finland, had faced an attempt at revolution at the end of the First World War and banned the Communists. There, strong landed elites and labour-repressive agrarian systems had predominated and the peasant parties were less autonomous than the Agrarian Union in Finland. While Finland in the 1930s arrived at a peasant-worker coalition formed by the Agrarians and the Social Democrats (in 1937), these countries fell under authoritarian systems.

Thus, despite the trauma of 1918, Fascist intrusions remained limited in Finland.

6. The Scandinavian Class Compromise and Finland

Another perspective on the crisis of 1918 is to consider it as the most extreme manifestation of the long-term dependence on Russia that marked the Finnish political culture in the nineteenth and twentieth centuries. To evaluate its significance in the Nordic context we should first remember that the Nordic model of progressive politics, described by Stråth, was also affected by external constraints, at least if we believe analysts like Peter J. Katzenstein (1985). He sees the Nordic cross-class collaboration as an aspect of 'democratic corporatism', which emerged in the 1930s and the 1940s as an adjustment strategy of vulnerable small European countries in 'a hostile world' (1985: 35). The cornerstones of Katzenstein's thesis are Denmark, Norway and Sweden. There, political alliances were formed between farmers and workers, and agreements were concluded between the central organizations of business and the labour movements. Factors underlying these compromises included a freeholding peasantry and the rise of distinct agrarian parties, as well as the reformist social democracy (Katzenstein 1985: 136–43, 159–81).[1] Democratic corporatism appears mainly in an economic adjustment perspective (1985: 24): 'For the small European states economic change is a fact of life. They have not chosen it; it is thrust upon them.'

As stated above, Finland in the 1930s did not fit into the picture of the corporatist compromise. A telling fact is that, unlike Scandinavia, in Finland employers refused to conclude collective agreements, and the rate of unionization was low. If in the Scandinavian states the main theme was a high degree of political inclusiveness as an element of mainly economic adjustment strategy, in interwar Finland the main theme was a low degree of political inclusiveness as the central element of political adjustment strategy to a perceived external political threat. If understood as a Liberation War from Communist Russia with which the Finnish revolutionaries had joined forces, the Civil War led to emphasis on patriotic unity and to exclusion of the 'Marxist' working classes from the nation: non-socialists monopolized the national rhetoric, as Bo Stråth remarks. But at the same time the war was only the extreme manifestation of the Eastern dependence that consisted of Finland's consolidation as a political unit in the Russian empire and then of its existence as an independent state in the shadow of the Soviet Union. In the nineteenth and early twentieth centuries the Russian connection created a peculiar sensitivity to questions of national vulnerability and success, and led the Finnish elite to adopt a kind of internally structured self-control in coping with the Russians. The national margin of manoeuvre was largely considered to be best maintained or even enhanced through a reconciliatory 'realism' – by anticipating the situations the Russians were likely to consider critical or unacceptable in their relations with the Finns and thereby avoiding problems in advance.

This sensitivity to questions of fragility was accentuated in the post-Civil War period. The war forcefully modified perceptions of loyalty and disloyalty and the linkage between conflict and a quest for consensus. After 1918 there existed an extremely close connection between what was 'outside' and what was 'inside' – between the insecurity over national survival vis-à-vis the Soviet Union and the perceived necessity of internal integration to face the threat from outside. The connection was epitomized by the Communists, a part of the Finnish population, who were seen as a kind of fifth column controlled by the Soviets. In other words, the internal conflict was enormously heightened by its perceived external linkages.

All this being said, the structurally based, Scandinavian-type readiness to cross-class collaboration made itself felt as well in the way that a need for conformity was coupled with a tolerance for plurality. Importantly, it involved a perceived necessity for reconciliation of some sort: both a quest for integrity and an awareness that in order to attain internal cohesion, a degree of plurality had to be allowed. The tolerance, as forced as it may have been in many cases, in fact materialized in the role of the Agrarians, as pointed out above, and in the position of the Social Democrats. The latter were not only allowed to participate in politics after 1918, but in 1937 they formed a coalition government with the Agrarians, thus following the example of the Scandinavian neighbours, even though the Social Democrats' role was definitely more limited than the role of comparable parties in Scandinavia (Kettunen 2001: 230). The coalition was no minor achievement given that the two parties had stood on opposite sides in the Civil War.

Essential here is a kind of combination of conflict and consensus. Finnish historian Pauli Kettunen (2004) remarks that two opposite views of the conflict regulation in Finland have been put forth. According to one line of argument, which has been invoked above, the tradition in Finland is more conflict-ridden than elsewhere. But there is another line of argument that emphasizes consensus instead of conflict and reminds us that a conception of a common national interest has been unusually strong in Finland, often based on 'external necessity' both politically and economically. In this view general interest does not manifest itself through a compromise between group interests, but through a pre-existing consensus that appears as a necessity for protecting the common good rather than as a negotiated outcome of different alternatives.

In Kettunen's interpretation these two views are not contradictory but two sides of the same coin. Both a high level of conflict and a high level of consensus capture, in combination, the character of the Finnish conflict regulation. They exclude compromise that 'is based on the mutual recognition of the particular rather than universal nature' of interests. They imply that the protagonists, each of them, have a view of the common interest (the consensual aspect), but these views may differ in a way that makes negotiation between them difficult (the conflict aspect): 'The conflicts in which both parties strongly appeal to a universal interest may grow bitter and fatal, as the means of regulating them hardly exists' (Kettunen 2004: 292–93). An example is the appeal to the 'people' as a legitimating argument on both sides of the Civil War. It has been suggested that the struggle over who had the correct conception of the people and who had the right to represent them added to its bitterness (Liikanen 1995: 332).

Parallel to this suggestion is Henrik Stenius's view of differences between Swedish and Finnish mass organizations in the late nineteenth century. In Sweden mass organizations manifested particularistic interests, but in Finland they were more often harnessed to support a national cause (Stenius 1983 and in this volume). Stenius traces this difference to the different state-making histories of the two countries. Sweden was an established state and nation, whereas Finland was a latecomer.

A related topic is the just-evoked theme of the 'people' (*kansa*). The dependence on Russia apparently contributed to the tone and intensity this concept acquired in Finnish political culture. In the nineteenth-century process of popular organization the right to represent the 'will of the people' became the central legitimation basis for political activity (see Liikanen 1995). Bo Stråth says that in Sweden 'the national identity was based on the concept of *folk*, people, rather than nation' (1994: 57). But indicative of the high intensity of the concept of *kansa* in the Finnish language is that the word appears not only in the notion of people (*kansa*) but also in the notion of nation (*kansakunta*) and the notion of citizen (*kansalainen*) (see Liikanen 2003; Stenius 2003). It is a telling fact that later, in the twentieth century, appealing to the 'people' was shared by political groups of all persuasions, from the Left to the Right.

In the post-1918 White imagery, however, the role of the 'true' people was granted to the free peasants. Therefore, one might conclude that, as a consequence of the bourgeois monopolization of the concept, the *völkisch* theme, which according to Stråth served to build a bridge between Social Democrats and Farmers' and middle class parties, may have penetrated the Finnish Social Democrats less than the Scandinavian Social Democratic parties. Yet another fact is that because the notion of the people had been permeating the whole Finnish political culture since the nineteenth century, it was available to the Finnish worker movement well before the interwar period. It can be hypothesized that in fact the pervasive presence of the notion of the people helped in finding a common ground between the Social Democrats and the Agrarian Union without the need for a 'discursive struggle over the definition of the [people]' (to paraphrase Stråth 2004: 8; cf. Stråth in this volume: 28).

7. On the Ethos of Finnish Corporatism after the Second World War

One more war – the Second World War and a narrow preservation of national independence – was needed before the corporatist compromise was reached in Finland, first in the mid-1940s in the form of national-level collective agreements between labour market organizations, and later through tripartite incomes policy agreements among labour market organizations and the state. The corporatist compromise left its mark in the long-term political tendency to believe that Finland had no choice but to adjust to the externally determined constraints. After the Second World

War this attitude re-emerged and pervaded the art of dealing with the Soviet Union, a mode of adjustment that was later coined 'Finlandization'. Its corollary in internal politics said that democracy is not a free choice between different alternatives but the adoption of a necessity.

> The common interest does not materialize itself [in Finland] through a compromise between different groups but is a pre-given task that must be made clear to everybody. As much as the circumstances after [the war] changed, it appears that this view has endured and often determined the line of action in ... less fateful situations as well. The compromises have been willingly portrayed as the only possibility. They have been presented rather as a necessary evil to save the common good than as a result of the existence of different alternatives. (Kettunen 1998: 292)

After the war the perceived narrowness of the margin for manoeuvre was accentuated by the emergence of the Communist party from underground. The Communists became one of the big parties, comparable in size to the postwar French and Italian Communist parties.

The shadow of the Soviet Union fell across the introduction of collective agreements in the middle of the 1940s. Later on, at the end of the 1960s, a system of wide incomes policy agreements began to be established. Agreements were regularly concluded between the central interest organizations of blue- and white-collar workers, private- and public-sector employees, agricultural producers, and the government (Kettunen 2001: 245). The concern in Finland about the unity of the nation in the form of internal integration has forcefully enhanced the perceived need for corporatism, more than in Scandinavia. To cite economist Juhana Vartiainen (2007):

> The core of the postwar economic success consists of efforts to make compromises in a way that fortifies the preconditions of economic activity and restricts the full use of the numerical strength of the trade unions. ... The Soviet Union was a threat externally, but the external threat forced the Finns to adopt such compromises [internally] that were acceptable to all parties. Finland could not afford an economic failure, and there was no other choice but to develop the society in such a way that also the workers and the political Left could come to feel that it was just towards them.

The necessity of a certain tolerance was built into the conception of pluralism, which gained ground in the cultural emancipation and modernization from the 1960s on. That is, the importance of national cohesion seems to underlie even the tolerance of differences and disagreements. Liberalization was furthered to a large extent with the ultimate objective of national consensus in mind. This argument was used especially in the political sphere. It has even been argued that in the 1960s, pluralism became a kind of norm: then everybody had to be tolerant and liberal (Heiskanen 1983: 321).

8. The End of Exceptionalism?

Seen in the double perspective of Scandinavian structures and institutions and Eastern dependence, a way to summarize Finland's place today, after the end of the Bolshevik century, is to stress her growing similarity to the other Nordic countries. Finland is 'no longer the Nordic exception' (cited in Kettunen 2004: 300). Within the country the conflict dimension opposing the Communists and others progressively eroded during the 1970s, the decade when 'consensus' was coined as the keyword in Finnish politics. The return to the Scandinavian political course was completed through the dissolution of the Communist movement at the end of the 1980s. Apparently, the blow to the radical left discourse has been exceptionally hard in Finland. This intellectual tradition was less firmly established there than in France or Italy, two other Western countries with large Communist movements in the post-Second World War decades, and popular support for Communists was more difficult to reproduce after the exhaustion of the legacy of the Civil War.

Also, many labour market features in the corporatist Nordic model have become established in recent decades. A high degree of employee and employer organization and organizational unity, the priority of collective agreements, and the tripartite cooperation among trade unions, employer organizations and the government (Kettunen 2004: 299) endured in Finland to an even greater degree than in the other Nordic countries.

Another, partly related perspective for comparing Finland with the other Nordic countries stems from Pauli Kettunen's characterization of Finland as a combination of conflicts and consensus, or, in his words, of 'too much conflicts' and 'too much consensus' (2004: 292). In this perspective the former aspect has now disappeared and consensus has taken over. Politics is still, to a considerable degree, seen 'as fulfilling national necessities', but now the tendency is strengthened by the European integration. There is a specific Finnish version of the 'competition state', forced to wage a continuous struggle in the world market. It appears in the conception of a national community that must survive under the constraints of economic globalization and that is even constructed through economic competitiveness. The earlier prevalence of a necessity-based consensus is helpful here. 'Globalization has been dealt with [in Finland] as a *national* challenge in a way characterized by discursive and institutional continuities' (Kettunen 2004: 306).

The view of consensus as necessity dictated by (external) constraints implies that an 'ethos of defence' is still instrumental in defining Finland and the Finnish identity. It seems that the Finns' comparatively very positive attitude towards the European Union results, in part, from their defensive attitude arising from Finland's past. In Finland the EU membership has not become a divisive factor: the parties have made EU politics in the spirit of consensus (Tuomioja 1997: 34–37, 40).

Finland shares with other Nordic countries the need to adapt to the exigencies of globalization and to benefit from it. As Bo Stråth states (2004: 19–20; also Stråth in this volume: 43–44), this pressure is undermining the Nordic model. But curiously enough, the same pressure may maintain the discourse about the models, including the Nordic one(s). Pauli Kettunen remarks that the notion of a 'Nordic model' was hardly used before the 1980s. The discussion of models is an indication of 'increasing reflexivity as an aspect of globalization. Reflexivity is nourished by the imperatives of competitiveness, which include the need for continuous comparisons' (Kettunen 2004: 303).

Notes

1. He adds to these factors the specialization in exports and proportional representation (Katzenstein 1985: 150–54, 157–81), which characterize all Nordic countries, including Finland.

References

Alapuro, Risto (1985) 'Interstate Relationships and Political Mobilization in the Nordic Countries: A Perspective' in Risto Alapuro et al. (eds), *Small States in Comparative Perspective: Essays for Erik Allardt*. Oslo: Norwegian University Press, 93–107.

────── (2004) 'The Finnish Civil War, Politics, and Microhistory' in Anna-Maija Castrén, Markku Lonkila and Matti Peltonen (eds), *Between Sociology and History: Essays on Microhistory, Collective Action, and Nation-Building*. Helsinki: SKS, 130–47.

────── (2006) 'The Construction of the Voter in Finland, c. 1860–1907', *Redescriptions. Yearbook of Political Thought and Conceptual History* 10: 41–64.

Arnason, Johann P. (2004) 'Icelandic Anomalies', *Thesis Eleven* 77: 103–20.

Heiskanen, Ilkka (1983) 'Epilogi: yhteiskuntatieteet, käytännön yhteiskuntateoria ja maamme älyllinen ilmasto' in Jaakko Nousiainen and Dag Anckar (eds), *Valtio ja yhteiskunta. Tutkielmia suomalaisen valtiollisen ajattelun ja valtio-opin historiasta*. Porvoo, Helsinki and Juva: WSOY, 297–335.

Katzenstein, Peter J. (1985) *Small States in World Markets: Industrial Policy in Europe*. Ithaca: Cornell University Press.

Kettunen, Pauli (1998) 'Suojeluskunnat ja suomalainen kansanvalta' in Risto Alapuro (ed.), *Raja railona. Näkökulmia suojeluskuntiin*. Porvoo, Helsinki and Juva: WSOY, 273–92.

—— (2001) 'The Nordic Welfare State in Finland', *Scandinavian Journal of History* 26: 225–47.

—— (2004) 'The Nordic Model and Consensual Competitiveness in Finland' in Anna-Maija Castrén, Markku Lonkila and Matti Peltonen (eds), *Between Sociology and History: Essays on Microhistory, Collective Action, and Nation-Building*. Helsinki: SKS, 289–309.

Kirby, David (1986) 'Finlands nationella identitet. Komparativa synpunkter', *Finsk Tidskrift* T. 219–20, 6, 289–300.

Knudsen, Tim, and Bo Rothstein (1994) 'State Building in Scandinavia'. *Comparative Politics* 26: 203–20.

Liikanen, Ilkka (1995) *Fennomania ja kansa. Joukkojärjestäytymisen läpimurto ja Suomalaisen puolueen synty* [with a summary in English: 'Fennomania and the People: The Breakthrough of Mass Organization and the Birth of the Finnish Party']. Helsinki: Suomen Historiallinen Seura.

Liikanen, Ilkka (2003) 'Kansa' in Matti Hyvärinen et al. (eds), *Käsitteet liikkeessä. Suomen poliittisen kulttuurin käsitehistoria*. Tampere: Vastapaino, 257–307.

Sewell, William H., Jr. (1996) 'Three Temporalities: Toward an Eventful Sociology' in Terrence J. McDonald (ed.), *The Historic Turn in the Human Sciences*. Ann Arbor: University of Michigan Press, 245–80.

Stenius, Henrik (1983) 'Massorganisation och nationell sammanhållning', *Sosiologia* 20: 112–24.

—— (2003) 'Kansalainen' in Matti Hyvärinen et al. (eds), *Käsitteet liikkeessä. Suomen poliittisen kulttuurin käsitehistoria*. Tampere: Vastapaino, 309–62.

Stråth, Bo (1994) 'The Swedish Path to National Identity in the Nineteenth Century' in Øystein Sørensen (ed.), *Nordic Paths to National Identity in the Nineteenth Century*. Oslo: KULTs skriftserie no. 22, 55–63.

—— (2004) 'Nordic Modernity: Origins, Trajectories and Prospects', *Thesis Eleven* 77: 5–23.

Thaden, Edward C. (1984) *Russia's Western Borderlands, 1710–1870*. With the collaboration of Marianna Forster Thaden. Princeton, NJ: Princeton University Press.

Tilly, Charles (1993) *Coercion, Capital, and European States, AD 990–1990*. Oxford: Basil Blackwell.

Tuomioja, Erkki (1997) 'Suomi matkalla Euroopan ytimeen', *Ulkopolitiikka* 34(3): 34–42.

Vartiainen, Juhana (2007) 'Sovinnontekijä pohjusti Suomen menestyksen' (a book review). *Helsingin Sanomat*, 14 February.

Wittrock, Björn (2004) 'The Making of Sweden', *Thesis Eleven* 77: 45–63.

Østerud, Øyvind (1996) 'Norwegian Nationalism in a European Context' in Øystein Sørensen (ed.), *Nationalism in Small European Nations*. Oslo: KULTs skriftserie no. 47, 29–39.

CHAPTER 9
Paradoxes of the Finnish Political Culture

Henrik Stenius

Asking what type of Nordic political culture Finland lived in during the Grand Duchy period (1809–1917), I distinguish between two kinds of Finnish specificities. One type consists of specificities, or 'determinants', that help us to understand why actors in Finland ended up on tracks that differed from the roadmaps of their contemporaries in the other Nordic countries. What distinguishes the Finnish political culture from the other Nordic countries? To identify the most important differences one has to focus on the Grand Duchy period of Finnish history. In the first part of the article I deal with these specificities. In the second part I start with defining what I regard as the crucial Nordic specificities compared to the rest of Europe in order to discuss the Finnish way of being Nordic. This argumentation requires a longer historical perspective, beginning in the post-Reformation period.

I. What Distinguishes the Finnish Political Culture from the Other Nordic Countries?

Post-Napoleonic Europe was a formative period when the political public was stirred to reflect and re-think the fundamentals of the power structures of the contemporary societies. In order to be part of that public, they had to take a stand on how the polities of the new geopolitical map of Europe should be legitimized (alternatively, argue why they were not legitimate political entities), for instance, the new polities of Finland (1809) and Norway (1814) and the reshaped geographies of the old kingdoms of Denmark and Sweden. The challenges included the question of what sort of political regimes – for their own countries, as well as for European countries in general – should be regarded as legitimate. The point of departure was that powerful political rhetoric could no longer base the legitimacy only on dynastic principles. It is this period we have to go back to if we want to have a deeper understanding of why the Nordic countries, despite fundamental similarities, generated different political cultures in the nineteenth as well as the twentieth century. After all, there were, in this formative period, decisive differences between the institutional-administrative points of departure that the political actors in the Nordic countries had as their empirical material when they thematized their country-specific 'historical experiences', and, accordingly, framed the 'horizon of expectation' for their respective countries, re-conceptualizing notions like patriotism, freedom of association, church, opinion, state, officials, citizen, democracy and local governance.

Old and New States

Compared to the regimes in the old countries, Sweden and Denmark, the political mobilization in Finland and Norway had a different relation to the power centres in their respective countries. On a constitutional level Denmark and Sweden were two old monarchies, whereas Norway and Finland were regions where the pretence of having home rule or constitutions of their own only emerged through the European turbulence created by the French Revolution and the Napoleonic wars. The citizens in the new polities/states worked out their own ways of relating themselves to decision-making in the central kernel of their polity, ways that differed radically from those of the two old states.

Trust in the central governmental institutions of Denmark and Sweden in the period before the French Revolution was based on different kinds of mechanisms.[1] However, the crucial argument here is that the central governmental bodies in both cases had an unquestioned legitimacy that made it difficult for an opposition to harbour any serious ambitions to jeopardize the status of these institutions. These institutions stood out as something elevated, nature given, divinely gifted, or 'fabulous' (in the sense of fable): in short, inaccessible and unapproachable for the mobilized middle class and the land-owning peasantry looking for more political prestige and standing. In these two countries one can therefore find two parallel set of norms: on the one hand, values and norms connected to the regimes of the old officialdom, and on the other hand, alternative models for participation among and collaboration between the mobilized groups. The emancipated civil society, in other words the new middle-class political public, had a clear distance from everything that was connected to the regimes of the old officialdom. In

Denmark, this distance became part of an enduring dual public space with the old elite continuing to live their lives within one (detached) side and the broad mobilization anchored in the popular movements in the other. In Sweden, on the other hand, a corresponding split was gradually dissolved by the introduction of a series of new corporative arrangements. This transition was backed by the fact that the old elite, the aristocracy, accommodated themselves to new constitutional, political and economic realities, thus preserving a strong position in society.

In Norway, Finland and Iceland, countries that were conceptualized as newborn nation-states (or reborn nation-states, which was the way most national politicians in Norway and Iceland interpreted their own history), the mobilization process became a part of the consolidation of the state/nation. The aim was to transform the whole nation, the top as well as the bottom, the government as well as its citizenry. The distance between the state apparatus, the world of the officials and the civil society was short. The project of transition in Finland was borne more by the state, while in Norway the burden was shouldered more by the civil society. In the minds of many Norwegians was a suspicion that the officials were turning away from serving Danish interests to running errands for the Swedes. In Finland, in contrast, one can only to a very limited degree detect a corresponding mistrust of the officials – except during the very first years and the last decades of the Grand Duchy.[2] However, in both Norway and Finland, all national politicians – indeed, all politicians – lived within one and the same political culture. In these countries there were no noticeable double standards, one for officials and one for the citizenry.

As a new polity, Finland emerged first as a 'state'. Only gradually during the decades after 1809 did Finland start to be targeted and conceptualized as a 'nation' (Alapuro 1988). The ideological reorientation was slow, because becoming a part of the Russian Empire meant that political life in Finland during the first part of the nineteenth century became restricted. The mobilization in Finland, as in Iceland, was delayed in comparison with the other Nordic countries. The public debate, as in Iceland, had for a long period to get along without the kind of revitalizing injection that only a regularly assembling diet could provide. Such practices were not introduced in Finland until 1863 (and in Iceland, 1845). Another reason for the delay was that the independent entrepreneurial class grew at a slower pace of development than the growth of the wage-earning class.

The first generation of political leaders of the Grand Duchy, figures like Bishop Jacob Tengström (1755–1832) and Count Gustaf Mauritz Armfelt (1757–1814), were not progressive and were not imbued by the new European ideas about the nation as the guiding light of legitimate polities. These leaders set the tone for Finnish political conduct. Loyalty to the Grand Duke was seen as a cornerstone of Finnish patriotism. This realpolitik paradigm was taken over by the next generation of political leaders. This group of the Finnish Literary Society (founded in 1831) mobilized a patriotism that combined Finnish nationalism with a profound loyalty to the Grand Duke (the Tsar). Here it is illuminating to contrast the civic and political attitudes in Finland with the corresponding conduct in Poland, another nationalistic region within the Russian Empire. Such social voluntary activities as choir singing and fencing were means by which Finland demonstrated its loyalty to the Grand Duke in the 1820s and 1830s, whereas the same instruments were used in Poland to show opposition to Russian rule and were therefore criminalized (Stenius 1987).

The leading political figure of this generation, Johan Vilhelm Snellman, articulated a Hegelian state philosophy for Finland. He adopted the Hegelian thinking, modifying it towards a voluntaristic position that emphasized the important moral responsibility of each citizen. Everybody had a duty to take part in the state project through the educational process congenially expressed in German as *Sittlichkeit* and *Bildung*.

The Finnicization of all sections of society, including higher education and the state apparatus, seemed in this early period of the Fennomanian history to be a definite utopia for most parts of the political public. Although 88 per cent of the population spoke Finnish as their mother tongue (the rest were mainly Swedish-speaking), the language was still only the language of the peasantry, not in use and not being developed for use by the upper sections of society. Nevertheless, the extraordinary historical fact is that, already during the last few decades of the century, the Snellmanian language programme had almost completely been carried out in that the state apparatus had been Finnicized, with both Finnish and Swedish as official languages, while Finnish became the language of higher education, academia and art.

In the 1860s, in a period when the Diet started to assemble on a more regular basis, giving an early impetus to the formation of political parties, a group of liberal politicians challenged the Snellmanian interpretation of the most efficient strategy for consolidation of the Finnish nation. The Fennomanian party, with Snellman as its spiritual father, anchored its strategy to, on the one hand, loyalty to the Russian regime and, on the other, to a proactive cultural and educational programme that gave Finnish-speaking culture prestige and dominance in every section of society. The liberal grouping, for their part, recruiting their supporters primarily from the Swedish-speaking educated class, thought that the best guarantee for a Finnish nation to survive and thrive was to emphasize the importance of giving the Finnish society at all levels – the central and local official level as well as in the voluntary associations of the civil society –

constitutional practices and constitutional legitimacy. The liberals did not challenge the culture of loyalty, but thought that even more important was to connect Finnish political culture to the liberal middle-class culture of Western Europe in general, and of Scandinavia in particular.

The tension between these two competing strategies became a lasting theme that in different variations has popped up from time to time in Finnish political life. There were, however, political features common to both parties. For instance, nobody believed in the possibility of rapid political change, or that Finns themselves could have any influence on the timetable for any substantial political change. In this atmosphere of standing by, the Fennomanians bided their time by taking part in their own *Sittlichkeit* project, strengthening the Finnishness of officialdom as well as among the citizenry with their flourishing voluntary associations. The belief that Finns could not themselves speed up the pace of political change was one side of the coin. The other consisted an awareness that Finns could, to be sure, delay progress if it inadvertently provoked the Russian regime to impose repressive measures. Activism, or military mobilization as in the form of the Garibaldian rifle club,[3] thus did not occur in Finland – at least not until the turn of the century, when one part of the liberal-constitutional party felt that the only realistic way to fight against the new Russified order was through active armed resistance.

The tension between loyalist Fennomanian nationalism and liberal constitutionalism hardened into antagonistic positions, especially during the period of intensified Russification policies towards the end of the Grand Duchy period. In a longer perspective, the arguments of these groupings eventually lost the ability to mobilize segments of the population as the public came to consider the arguments of both sides to be valid. Comprehension of Fennomania as a movement thus becomes puzzling. The Fennomanian movement had never, as a matter of fact, had a congruent mass organization or a formalized organizational core to lead it. This became even more the case after Finland became independent and Finnishness was broadly taken on board as a fundamental feature of the independent state. When the Finnish right-wing movement in the 1920s and 1930s launched radical Finnicization as a political programme, they failed to achieve recognition as the sole custodians of the Fennomanian legacy.

Neither did the liberal constitutional doctrines become lasting mobilizing principles. One important feature of Finnish liberalism was the fact that the liberals, from the 1860s on, failed to position themselves as the democratic movers of the society, leaving this initiative to the Fennomanians. They also failed to be the first and foremost movers of liberal economic reforms. These reforms were driven by J.V. Snellman as well as progressive

Russian politicians (Björkqvist 1986). Liberalism never became an efficient rallying cry able to push through a congruent mass organization.

Important for the argumentation in this article is, firstly, the fact that the constituent doctrines of the Finnish political culture did not lead to congruent parties. Secondly, that the political parties did not live their lives exclusively in the civil society. On the contrary, the public administration was politicized, adjusting the hierarchical structures of the society. The parties were integrated into the hierarchical structures, which undermined their role as watchdogs over officialdom. Finnish officialdom thus did not stand out as the 'other'. On the contrary, the officials were important collaborators in consolidating the state and the nation. The officials and the citizenry had the same agenda.

Strong versus Weak Local Government

Looking at decision-making at the local level, one notices important differences between the West-Nordic (Denmark and Norway) and the East-Nordic (Sweden and Finland) traditions regarding the relations between the subjects and the officials designated to guide, guard and govern them. The officials had, in the early modern period before the French Revolution, a strong position in the Danish realm (including Norway), whereas an unbroken tradition of local government within the frame of the parish was strong in the Swedish realm (including Finland). Here one has to realize that, when Finland became part of the Russian Empire in 1809 as an autonomous Grand Duchy, Swedish laws continued to be in force. After 1809, instead of converging with the Russian judiciary, the legal system of Finland continued to be formed according to Nordic standards.

Although the patterns of local-level decision-making in the different Nordic countries converged during the nineteenth century, especially after the 1870s (Jansson 1987), the historical lessons from pre-modern times continued to have an impact on the minds of the people. In West Norden, suspicion of local community officials continued to thrive in Denmark and Norway, although they were no longer appointed from above. The new reform movements in these two countries preferred to organize the new society outside of the sphere controlled by the officials. 'Society' became a concept connected to a sphere that, for the officials, was inaccessible – or at least not easily accessible. The aim of the social movements was to launch their projects, such as voluntary associations, schools, co-ops and savings banks, in the emancipated, civil society out of the reach of officialdom. The ideal of universalism had to be balanced against an equally strong counter principle: scepticism against standardized and centralized solutions. Such solutions raised suspicion.[4]

In Sweden and Finland, local government was not considered to be a clear-cut outgrowth of the central administration, nor was it unambiguously considered by the reform movements to be an enemy. Despite the strong position of the officials and the correspondingly limited possibilities to freely set up projects in civil society, the political public in Finland avoided displaying resistance against the class of officials. There were the historical memories from the eighteenth century, including the habitus of the parish priests, who represented the central government in the local community and the local community in its relation to the central government (Aronsson 1997). Even more important was the fact that the Finnish officials were recognized as Finns. They were not Russians.[5] They were regarded as an important part of the common nation-building project. Such a responsibility was formally a part of the office, especially for clergy and teachers. In Sweden as well as in Finland the voluntary associations collaborated closely with local government. There was no demand – except for a short transition period in Sweden at the turn of the century – to keep the voluntary associations at a distance from official decision-making at the local community level. Especially in Finland, one can find a great variety of examples of how the elected assembly of the municipality collaborated with the popular movements. The result, however, was always the same: a shift to a new kind of corporative rule where the voluntary associations shouldered their own part of the common responsibility for governing the local community. The precondition for such governance was the fact that the peasantry were accustomed to regarding their political duties, partaking in common decisions, as binding.

In Sweden and Finland the concept of 'society' comes close to the notion of 'what we have in common'. According to a frequently used rhetorical phrase, 'society takes responsibility for' different sorts of issues, which communicates first of all that the issue in question is in good hands and, secondly, that the government, church, municipality and NGOs will agree on a rational division of labour. There is room for divergent, local solutions, but at the same time, a preparedness to accept statutory, standardized norms.

The Swedish and Finnish civil societies were not, in the same sense as the Danish and Norwegian, a space for free projects in the local community outside the immediate control of the officials. Interestingly enough, there were also corresponding differences on a central level, which can help us to understand why Danes and Norwegians are more prepared to take initiatives without first asking permission from the authorities.

Sweden and Finland belong to a small group of European nations that never became injected by the special kind of civic self-righteousness that can come with having a constitutional national assembly. Denmark and Norway did have such experiences in their historical memories, from their constitutional national assemblies of 1849 and 1814, respectively. In their historical memories, they did have a moment when the 'representatives of the people' assembled to discuss and approve rules for how their countries should be governed.

The Fennomanian movement succeeded in giving shape and new qualities to the political landscape of the Grand Duchy. Their starting point was a society with a Swedish-speaking officialdom whose lives were remote from those of the broad masses, the large majority of which were Finnish-speaking. Making the educated class nationalist and making the nation educated (the programme of Snellman) meant radically narrowing the distance between, on the one hand, the citizenry, and on the other hand, the officials in the governmental centre of the Grand Duchy and in the local municipalities. The political culture revolved around an axis between the citizenry and the officialdom, leaving the political parties in the background.

II. The Finnish Way of Being Nordic

Turning now to the second part of the discussion, the perspective on Finnish specificities changes. Having examined the historical experiences that help us to understand why the political actors in Finland were inclined to approve of social values and political orientations that generated a different political culture compared to other Nordic countries, we turn now to a particular interpretation of what is specifically Nordic compared to the rest of Europe. The question to be discussed here is what the Finnish actors did out of a common Nordic heritage. Analysing the Finnish way of being Nordic, I do not claim that the actors consciously recognized such a notion as specifically Nordic. The argument is rather that the characteristics that I interpret as specifically Nordic were part of their historical knowledge or mindset without necessarily being acknowledged as Nordic characteristics by the historical actors themselves.

The point of departure here is not the formative period of nation-building after the French Revolution, but the post-Reformation centuries, when the Nordic societies opted for distinctively and definitely different tracks compared to the rest of Europe, and thus constituted a 'historical region' of their own, with their own historical experiences but without constituting a polity. The Nordic societies were 'Islamicized' in the sense that the European mediaeval separation of spiritual power (of the Pope) and secular power (of the Emperor) faded to the background amidst the reunification of religious and worldly power. In Nordic societies, the Reformation was a state-driven project, not a protest from below. It was a successful project in the sense that it prevented society from being split into subcultures, which was the case in neighbouring Germany and the Netherlands. Of decisive importance for their future development was the fact that the laws and the norms of the state were the same as those of the church. The moral and legal codes were identical, not giving much space for alternative religious or political conduct.

In the following, I will discuss in more detail particular features of the Nordic political culture of convergence, consensus and conformity, and, according to the objective of this article, comment on how the Finnish political culture dealt with these features. The three features, which I thus regard as having had a decisive influence on Nordic political culture and which can be analysed as paths staked out in the post-Reformation period, are: 1) the relation between a strong state and the use of universalistic principle, 2) the effective instruments of inclusion, especially taking into account the importance of cultural socialization, and 3) how a weak notion of opposition paved the way for a smooth transition into modernity.

Strong State and Universalism

It is a commonplace among scholars analysing the Nordic welfare state to refer to the importance of universalistic principles. There is a rather broad consensus regarding the character of the Nordic societies, as welfare states rooted in a conformist Lutheran culture of a Nordic type, preconditioned by a strong state that is ready to intervene in every section of society, and with a system of universal social policies accompanied by a high degree of wealth distribution – as a special type of welfare state in contrast to income transfer states of Central Europe (Esping-Andersen 1990; Kangas 1994; Kosonen 1993; Kautto et al. 1999). Although there is much consensus, analysts still put the emphasis differently when looking for the historical roots: the strength of the rural class in societies of a highly agrarian type (Baldwin 1990); the strong bureaucratic apparatus (Stein Kuhnle in unpublished papers from 1996, referred to in Kautto et al. 1999); the strong, centralized state where the secular and ecclesiastical bureaucracy are mixed (Flora 1986; Knudsen 2000; Makkola 2001; Stenius 1996), which in the Danish case was underpinned by a combination of pietism and absolutism (Knudsen 2000); the reciprocal relation between the centralized state apparatus and the strong local community with a particular tradition of 'ruling by assemblies' (Trägård 1999; Aronsson 1997); the participatory culture of the peasant society based on a free peasantry (Sørensen and Stråth 1996).

Two aspects of this extensive discourse about the historical roots of the Nordic welfare state are worth mentioning here. Firstly, they are all variations on a theme: a marked interdependency between the strong state and the support for egalitarian traditions due to a systematic application of universalistic solutions. Secondly, in discussing these questions, the discourse is always Nordic. The historical roots of democracy in the Nordic countries are not considered national; they are comprehended as Nordic practices and doctrines; practices and doctrines that have been enriched by European practices and doctrines.

The argument I would like to elaborate here is this: if one regards universalism in combination with a strong state as *the* characteristic that makes political culture in the Nordic countries different from political cultures in other historical regions, then, one could argue, Finland appears more Nordic than any other Nordic country.

The constitutional moment in Europe after the French Revolution was marked by the competition and balance between reform and reaction, between a political system without a class of privileged aristocrats and a system where the old aristocracy succeeded in preserving its position as guardians of the common interest. People like Tocqueville stood for the first way of thinking. According to him, civil society and especially voluntary associations could shoulder the responsibility of guarding the common interest (Tocqueville 1997). One way of describing the political culture of the young Grand Duchy is to say that such thinking did not exist in Finland for a long time. The first generations of state philosophers, including Johan Jacob Tengström (1787–1858) and Johan Vilhelm Snellman (1806–1881), could only think in the abstract, Hegelian concept of the state as the only institution that could take responsibility for the common good. Again showing their dependence on Hegelian thinking, Tengström and Snellman stressed the importance of disassociating the Finnish educated circles from the individualistic thinking of Romanticism. Tengström thus actively warned the Finnish public not to let themselves be affected by the strong spirit of Romanticism in Sweden (Jalava 2006).

The same kinds of arguments were repeated by political thinkers of later generations. For example, Thiodolf Rein (1838–1919), who succeeded Snellman as professor of philosophy, stated at the end of the century, in a situation where particular interests were materializing in political parties and NGOs of different kinds, that Finns could not afford to follow the Swedish models or political doctrines of an 'individualistic political science'. They should instead swear fidelity to the national interest.

Such doctrines were not confined within the walls of academia. They were particularly important for people working in the civil society of voluntary associations and popular movements. The voluntary associations of Finland were at least as strong as those in other Nordic countries. The way they consolidated their position was, however, different. In Finland the popular movements consolidated themselves under one and the same central organization. In some respects this umbrella organization provided much free ideological space, in other aspects, limited space. According to a maxim 'it is better to smooth things over and let them coalesce, than take a hard stand and push them away', all of the local branches of the movement were persuaded to subordinate their local associations to the central organization, even when their local association might have very different views on ideological and strategic matters. One could borrow the term 'centerism' from Karl Kautsky, who coined the term to describe such a strategy for the international labour movement. The core message of this '-ism' was to avoid breakaway from the central organization, and thus hinder the splitting into isolated sects. In the case of the Finnish popular movements, there was a clear limit regarding free ideological space: all of the popular movements were subjected to a strong nation-building imperative. The mobilization into voluntary associations was an essential part of the consolidation of the young nation. In discussing local government above, I pointed out that the citizenry in the voluntary associations collaborated with teachers, clergy and other representatives of the local officialdom in the important projects of local community. Here I can add that strong contradiction between the popular movements and officialdom never arose, and that the participation of officialdom in building the national edifice gave the national project a trademark of political impartiality.

During the first decades of the twentieth century, monitoring the legal status of the voluntary associations was on the political agenda in all of the Nordic countries. Whereas the parliaments in the other Nordic countries decided to protect the citizens' freedom of association by refusing to pass any particular laws to monitor and thereby possibly limit this freedom, the diet in Finland decided to protect the same freedom by passing a particular law. According to this law, which came into force 1919,[6] any voluntary association wishing to become a juridical person had to have their rules approved by the authorities and at the same time be enrolled in an official register. It is worth mentioning that this law is not hollow or ineffectual. It still impacts on Finnish civil society.

The church, including the revivalist movements, has been an essential partner of the nation-building project in all of the Nordic countries. However, the church and the revivalist movements played different roles in the nation-building processes in each. According to the centrist logic of the political culture in Finland, the high church in Finland was not so high and, correspondingly, the low church not so low, enabling all of the denominations and doctrinal lines to stay within the official state church and to take part in the nation-building project. Here we can add that Laestadianism, the special revivalist movement of the northern parts of Finland, Sweden and Norway, was a genuine transnational movement, that is, until the Finnish branch broke out and established a national association of its own. In the agonizing years of the 1918 Finnish Civil War, some parts of the revivalist movement even claimed that they represented the 'genuine' Finnish people more than anyone else. I will return to this discourse of authenticity at the end of this chapter.

In an atmosphere of apprehension and a political culture where politicians were just waiting for a more opportune time, the focus on 'statist projects' and on the importance of trust between the citizenry and the officialdom that were regarded as a part of national project generated a mentality of obedience to the law according to which 'obedience' was more important than 'taking part in creating' new laws. This is why we can talk about a reverse constitutionalism, and, only with a few semantic tricks, use 'constitutionalism' (*con* + *statuare* = making rules together) to describe the political culture in Finland. This became especially accentuated during the period of Russian repression in the last decades of the Grand Duchy, when the more aggressive liberal front against repression labelled themselves 'constitutionalist', meaning exactly not making new rules but defending existing laws.

It may be that the Finns are more obedient than their neighbours in the other Nordic countries.[7] More important than a discussion of who is more obedient, perhaps, is to analyse what sort of obedience we are talking about in the Finnish context. Usually Finnish obedience is claimed to be a legacy of the rigid Russian rule. There was in the Grand Duchy period, to be sure, a predisposition for a strong centralized government, self-restraint and limitations of political/civil rights. The culture of obedience may, however, be only indirectly linked to the Russian rule in Finland. It was not, in the first place, a tsarist agency that imposed this obedience. The mentality was, on the contrary, strongly promoted by Finnish actors themselves at all levels of society. This accounts for the strength of this tradition.

In this article I have purposely chosen the terms 'state' and 'statist activity', knowing that a vocabulary of 'government' is much more common in the English language, at least in the U.K. I have consciously avoided the term government, which in the English-speaking world is not only more common but a vocabulary that fits the political culture in many English-speaking countries, England in particular. The notion of a strong central government is not the main point of this chapter, which refers, rather, to a more comprehensive state concept, an entity that signifies an attitude more than a type of formal apparatus, an entity that thus penetrates all the levels of society. It is significant that, in the political language of the period when party politics and more parliamentary practices were being introduced, the Finnish word for 'politics' was *valtiollinen toiminta*, which in a word-by-word translation is 'state-oriented activity'.

I have here argued for the thesis that Finland can be regarded as the most statist of the Nordic countries, a country with a political culture of realpolitik. It acknowledges and approves of political power relations in a national perspective: bide your time, and meanwhile be obedient, work hard, become educated and be nationalistic. But it is a realpolitik that does not give much guidance or many instruments for how to change the political structures.

Instruments of Inclusion, and the Question of Broad-based Education in Particular

The universalistic figure of thought in modern Nordic societies is rooted in the conformist ideals of their pre-modern Lutheran societies. In these, one can detect several rigid, but nonetheless effective, practices of inclusion underpinning the conformist culture: the social cleavages in the old peasant societies were, first of all, less drastic than in feudal Europe;[8] especially in East Norden, the peasantry took an active part in the decision-making of the local community; the social margins were kept small by forcing people to work and not giving philanthropy any important place; unusually broad literacy was introduced to promote ideological conformity; and the early production and diffusion of practical knowledge lulled the citizenry into believing that knowledge can substitute opinion.

The endeavour to make the ideological climate as homogenous as possible had consequences for the Nordic concept of 'citizen'. In more southern parts of Europe, the concept of citizen meant that each individual had the same relation to the state *despite* the diversity in their ethnicity and social standing.[9] In the Nordic countries, individuals were citizens *because* people were similar to each other socially, ethnically and religiously. Moreover, the concept of tolerance was defined in pedagogical terms of patience: tension between reason and irrationality rather than conflicts between subcultures (the attitude of 'little by little you will understand that this is the best for you').

The historical experiences of conformism, control and inclusion were such that the issues of education and cultural socialization were already strongly emphasized in the pre-modern societal thinking in the Nordic countries. In the horizon of expectations of the early generation of Nordic society modernizers, these issues became even more important. All the central nation-building figures of the Nordic countries – people like N.F.S. Grundvig in Denmark, Johan Vilhelm Snellman in Finland, Jón Sigurðsson in Iceland, Henrik Wergeland in Norway, and Carl Adolf Agardh and Erik Gustav Geijer in Sweden – conceptualized education in a utopian and emancipatory manner as a key element of the concept of citizen. The Greek notion of *paideia*, or the German notion of *Bildung*, was regarded as relevant not only for the elite, but for the whole community. It is illuminating to compare this conceptualization with the situation in the Anglo-Saxon world, where this dimension of education was not accentuated. One can choose Thomas Paine as a typical exponent of a British or American way of conceptualizing citizenship. When he – in a spirit of antimonarchism and anti-aristocracy – talked about representation and political rights, what he had in mind was freedom of speech, the right of individuals to have their own views and to be able to express them. Education was not part of this discourse.

One obvious way to understand why the Nordic countries stressed the importance of education is to refer to their standard diagnosis of the Northern periphery as being backward and therefore in urgent need of educational investments.[10] But the question of moral and cultural education in the Nordic countries is not as simple as that. It is not only a question of modernity (for example, 'how does my country rank in the march of modernity?').

Unfortunately, there is no academic discourse on Nordic moral education (the Nordic model of *Bildung*) comparable to the huge discourse available on the Nordic welfare-state model. This means that my conclusions on Nordic specificities are at this point not anchored in any consensus among scholars in the field on Nordic specificities. However, if one wants to give prominence to the importance of the broad and proactive cultural and moral educational element in the Nordic universal concept of citizen, then, I would argue that Finland must be regarded as the most Nordic of countries.

It is difficult to assess how deeply the national ideology articulated by the elite permeated the consciousness of the citizenry and their organizations. All of the big popular movements and their local branches in Finland, including the labour movement, had ambitious cultural objectives: to establish their own libraries and reading rooms, to organize lectures, write and distribute pamphlets and newspapers (papers published for the whole movement as well as local newspapers, often handwritten), to arrange public festivals and sports events, and to perform in their own choirs, orchestras and theatre ensembles. The book market and the public libraries expanded rapidly during the second half of the nineteenth century. A diverse array of daily papers for different political audiences and different geographic regions turned Finland into one of the leading countries of newspaper readers. The figures concerning cultural activities were, in a European comparative perspective, high, as were the figures for other Nordic countries.

What made the Finnish cultural programme different can perhaps best be shown by compiling figures on cultural activities. However, more important is to try to explain the more zealous objectives of the cultural programme, which was approved by a large number of the public. The ordinary schools should have 'statist' and patriotic objectives, different from the liberal goals of competition, competency and control. The voluntary associations should correspondingly have the same elevated, patriotic ambitions, avoiding superficial entertainment.

When Snellman targeted the education issue, he addressed the people (who should have more *Bildung*) as well as the educated class (who should be more conscious of the national issue). The ordinary citizen thus had an obligation and the right to participate in promoting *Sittlichkeit* and to take part in the building of the nation-state. The concept was thus, to an extreme degree, an anti-masculine citizenship, in contrast to the Central European type according to which a man became a *Statsbürger* only after first serving in the army. This does not, however, allow us to think of the Finnish concept of citizenship as a feminine concept. Culture was, to be sure, approved, but culture was hierarchical and dominated by males with statist insights.

The thinking of the elite coincided with the objectives of the popular movements. However, the tension between the elite and the citizenry remained. The vertical dimension of *Bildung* was never denied. The goal was not a levelling or horizontalization of culture. The elite, their knowledge and their cultural accomplishments should be recognized, approved and esteemed. But the elite should be inclusive. They should not only address their equals among the upper classes, they should also address the people – which is what Jean Sibelius, Arvid Järnefelt and their artist friends did.

The anti-particularistic and anti-individualistic figures of thought influenced the cultural programme. Romanticism and symbolism were marginalized tendencies. Here, again, the vertical relation of production and distribution between experts and laymen was given prominence. In this sense, the public sphere preserved the pro-active vertical direction, keeping an eye on those in power who had knowledge and patriotic insights to offer. The problem was that they were not critical.

Out of this came a paradox. The cultural citizen was a person with strong self-esteem and a natural immunity against manipulation of his or her political and civil rights. But the republican citizen, trained in dealing with a citizenry of different sorts of opinions, was weak, which had fatal consequences (Stenius 2004).

Smooth Transition

The Nordic *Sonderweg* to modernity was smooth. The notion of 'opposition' was weak, not causing dramatic ruptures. To start with, the Reformation failed to generate a notion of opposition in the ideological mindset of the Nordic Lutherans. The project was driven from above by the king and his men, not as a protest from below. Protestantism did not (until the late eighteenth century, when there was a split between the low and high church) conceptualize church practices in terms of 'top down' and 'bottom up'. Neither did the second reformation, the pietism of the eighteenth century, generate a notion of opposition in the Nordic countries (until, as mentioned above, the very late eighteenth century).

If we turn our eyes to voluntary associations in pre-modern Europe, we notice similar patterns. The religious-philanthropic societies in late-medieval Italian towns, the learned academies in Italy from the end of the sixteenth century, and the Masonic secret societies in Britain from the end of the following century were, in the eighteenth century, imitated, transplanted and re-conceptualized all over Europe, having a great variety of goals, and, with the exception of the Nordic societies, expressing ideological and religious diversity and political rivalries. These associations harboured the oppositional potential, but not in the Nordic countries. The crucial feature of the Nordic associations of that period was, on the one hand, their ambitious ideological objectives, and on the other hand, their deliberate efforts to express loyalty to the regime and thus avoid a polarization of society.[11]

The transition from a corporative pre-modern society, regulated and controlled by a system of privileges, into a modern class society with a broad net of popular movements started in the Nordic countries in the mid-nineteenth century and matured (or was stabilized in a comparatively fixed pattern of voluntary organizations including political parties) during the first decades of the twentieth century. The most striking feature of the Nordic transition process was the linear, comparatively rapid and undramatic changeover from the old corporative society (mercantilism) to a new kind of corporative society (a trade union society). In the rest of Europe, there was an interregnum of 50–150 years between the dissolving of the old guilds and their privileges, and the setting up of a society with legitimate trade unions. This interim period was marked by hard, often violent confrontations. The Nordic societies, in contrast, did not experience these tensions to any significant extent. Strikes were not criminalized as such, although other forms of legal and policy measures limited the influence that labourers could have on working conditions and wages.

If this picture of the Nordic *Sonderweg* to modernity as smooth and linear, without any upheavals, is accurate, then Finland cannot be regarded as part of the common Nordic political culture, the reason being that something went terribly wrong in this country. The cruel and merciless civil war in 1918 stands out as quite a conundrum.

The nation-building imperative was so strong that everybody became more or less Fennomanian nationalists. The label Fennomanian lost, at least to some extent, the capacity to single out any particular group in society.[12] There had been heated political conflicts in Finland in the period from the 1850s to the civil war. In the late 1850s, the old Fennomans and liberals began an agonizing political debate. For several decades around the turn of the century Finnish-language nationalists and Swedish-language nationalists had carried on a heated exchange over the relation between language and nation. During the period of hardening Russian repression at the turn of the century, the liberal constitutional party thought that the strategy of their conservative counterparts, of attempting to maintain a relation of trust with the Duke/Tsar, was fatally flawed and in fact the worst strategy possible. The conservatives had similar thoughts about the constitutionals. In the end, the debate between socialists and non-socialists in Finland was as heated as in any other country. There were severe political disagreements, but at the same time both the political right and the political left competed over who was the true representative of the old Fennomanian tradition, or, more precisely, who had the correct interpretation of what would be in the best interest of the nation and its people.

How was it possible that a civil war could break out (1918) in a country where all political camps lined up behind Finnish national values, where the citizens' appreciation of the state and its servants was comparatively high, where the citizens regarded law abiding as an important virtue, where the freedom of association, including the right to strike, never became a major or contested political issue, where all the important actors wanted to show that the fight for a common national cause mattered, and where the labour movement did not sign up to a strategy of radical activism aiming at a violent revolution? History research has pointed out the relevance of the huge cleavages between the social classes and the widespread social misery. The sudden abolishment of a police and military force in the aftermath of the Russian February Revolution has also been referred to as an explanation for the war. Analysts have also explained that the way the Russian government rejected the reforms that the democratically elected diet (during the period 1907–1917) had approved had a demoralizing effect. It became almost impossible for the political decision-makers to practise and to internalize parliamentarian thinking. One can still add that, in all the crucial strikes before the First World War, the employers imported strike-breakers from abroad. Through this behaviour the employers in Finland expressed what they thought was in accordance with the national common good. All of these factors have been offered as explanations for why the civil war broke out.

Contingency looms very large in the background of the Finnish Civil War. But the fact that the war turned out to be such a brutal and barbarous conflict can only be explained by the fact that the citizenry had no effective tools for dealing with these contingencies. One cannot exaggerate the momentousness of the poorly developed capacity to conduct republican, horizontal communication. All of the eagerness to bridge particularistic interests ended in a situation where the voluntary associations failed to conduct organized discussions that acknowledged the different particularistic interests. What counted instead was an adjustment to what should be regarded as being in the national, common interest. What was missing was the positioning, the articulation of one's own stand, and, from such a point of departure, efforts to reach acceptable compromises. In short, formalized, legitimate decision-making. The rivalry concerned who could claim that she or he was in possession of *the* correct interpretation of what the nation and its people wanted and needed. Both sides of the front were convinced that there could be only one correct interpretation: truth is not a matter for negotiation, voting or making compromises. The more or less unavoidable correlate of this kind of logic is that the correct interpretation must be one's own position. Another correlate is that those who can claim to represent the 'authentic people' have precedence when it comes to the right to interpret the state and the future of the nation project. At this point the Finnish consensual mentality revealed its reverse side. There was a contemptible but nonetheless widespread consensus that 'authenticity' could be used as a key political concept.

All civil wars are cruel; but the Finnish was more irreconcilable than (most) other civil wars. One conceptual history expression of this irreconcilability is found in the naming policies for the '1918 events'. No consensus has ever been reached, although the debate today is no longer as heated as in some previous periods of Finnish history, over whether the war was a war for independence, a class war, a war of brothers, a war of citizens, a revolution, civil war or just 'the events of 1918'. Here one could compare with the aftermath of the Irish Civil War of 1922–23. In that political culture an agreement was reached soon after the war that the Irish War was a civil war. In Ireland with its history of political violence, this war was not regarded as the greatest tragedy and therefore the naming of it was not a particularly major issue (Kissane 2005).

Reconciliation was the main theme of the political culture in Finland during the decades following the tragedy of 1918. Reconciliation had its strategic target in a convergence in one hegemonic public sphere of the 'true interest of the nation', again putting the particularistic interests aside. The political margins should be eliminated as efficiently as possible. The radical right was criminalized and marginalized already in the 1930s. The radical left was likewise criminalized by specific laws in the early 1920s and early 1930s. But these laws did not succeed in marginalizing the radical labour movement. The communists and their allies played an important role as a badly integrated part of the civil society up until the 1970s. One can talk about a reconciliation that included all of the different parts of the left only from the 1960s onward, a reconciliation that denied that there is only one historical truth, and likewise, denied that there are multiple historical truths, the number of truths being just two.

* * *

Analysing the two questions on Finnish peculiarities from a Nordic perspective, we end up with two major paradoxes. Firstly, the Finnish historical experiences, that is to say the Russian century, sets Finland far and noticeably apart from the other Nordic countries, but, on the other hand, also made, or contributed to making, Finland a particularly paradigmatic case of basic pan-Nordic tendencies, such us a statist culture with universalist solutions to societal challenges. Secondly, this statist Finland, recognized and acknowledged as loyalist, law abiding and with a remarkable capacity to mobilize into movements and projects of civil and cultural activities, did not prevent the nation from splitting into two antagonistic camps and brutally and efficiently killing each other.

Notes

1. In Sweden a regime with strong estates had a profound legitimacy. In Denmark an absolutistic feudal state was bolstered by an alliance between the king and a new mercantile class of prosperous entrepreneurs. The regime remained stable with the

help of a class of high-ranking officials and the emerging, remarkably uncorrupted, features of a modern *Rechtstaat*. The aristocracy remained strong in Sweden despite the fact that the system of estate representation was abolished in 1809.

2. In the second part of the nineteenth century, Finnish liberals accused conservative Fennomans of 'stepping the St Petersburg line', which did not mean that they were accused of being errand-boys for the Russian government but for using unconstitutional means to achieve their own political goals in Finland.

3. The rifle club movement in Sweden in the 1860s, which was the first large-scale popular movement in Sweden, was one variant of this type of mobilization. The Turn movement in Germany was another variant. The corresponding movement in Finland was the voluntary fire brigades, but to the extent that this movement had militaristic features they were very well hidden (Stenius 1987).

4. Studying the history of protest movements one can ask whether one should conclude that a tradition of anti-stately mobilization in West Nordic countries still asserts itself. In the Norwegian as well as the Danish populist movements one can still identify a strong anti-state dimension, although populism in West Norden has successively turned against ethnic minorities. They mobilize people who do not want to pay taxes to the state. Interestingly enough corresponding populist movements in Sweden and Finland differ in this regard. Sweden did have such a party in the 1990s, but that party remained ephemeral. In the Populist Party in Finland you cannot find such an agenda.

5. It was a well-acknowledged, obvious fact that the governor general, who was not of Finnish descent, recruited among the high aristocracy in the immediate environs of the Emperor, represented Russia. The Finnish identity of the governors, each reigning over one of the eight provinces of the Grand Duchy, was generally evident, despite the Russian government trying to integrate the Finnish Grand Duchy more closely to the Russian Empire during the so-called years of Russian repression at the turn of the nineteenth century.

6. The one-chamber diet passed such a law in 1909, but the Grand Duke did not approve it. The law instead became one of the first reforms passed by the parliament of the newly independent Finland.

7. One can object to this common view by arguing that there is a kind of carnivalistic craziness in Finland that is lacking in other Nordic countries. Still, today we can identify different sorts of ostentatious behaviour performed in a border region that, nevertheless, carefully avoids transgressing into the sphere of criminal behaviour.

8. The Danish case is special with distinct feudal features, although Danish feudalism was never of an Eastern type. The peasants could not be sold apart from the land. A law from 1682 prohibited the landowners from throwing their peasants off the farms. The Danish peasants were never deprived of their rights of inheritance. This position of the peasants can be explained by the fact that it was from the peasants and not from the landowners that the king collected his taxes and recruited his soldiers. From the end of the eighteenth century, the landowning aristocracy recognized the advantages of a free peasantry. A great number of

peasants bought the copyholds of the landowners, which was in accordance to many landowners' interests in their efforts to modernize the manors using free labour instead of the relatively ineffective villainies (Knudsen 1991).
9. Thomas Paine stated in the *Rights of Man* I (1791: 124) that 'law-religions, or religions established by law' make a modern citizenship impossible.
10. The populations of Denmark, Norway and Finland in the 1860s were roughly the same size, about 1.7 million inhabitants each. In this period, Finland had 20 book publishers and 13 bookshops, while in Norway the corresponding figures were 60 and 124, and in Denmark 119 and 263. In Sweden, with a population of 4.2 million, the numbers were 114 and 164. These figures, known in Finland at the time (cited from the newspaper *Hämäläinen*, 4 November 1867), show that Finland was a backward country at least compared to other Nordic countries.
11. However, history writing has focused on important events of party politics that only with some difficulty fit the timid image of Nordic history suggested above. Firstly, the Swedish history writing on the period, when the power of the Swedish king was limited (1721–1772), usually called the 'Age of Liberty', describes a struggle between two parties in the diet (*hattar*/the Hats and *mössor*/the Caps or Nightcaps) taking governmental position in turn, and, accordingly, relegating the party not in power to the opposition. Secondly, it has been a commonplace, especially in the history writing in the nineteenth century, to picture the Swedish turn of events during the period from the late seventeenth to the early nineteenth century, as an uninterrupted series of revolutions (Kurunmäki 2000). However, the constellations these statements are referring to were not apt to generate an opposition in the sense of 1) mobilizing broad layers of the public, or 2) generating a repertoire of symbols, institutions (clubs or societies) and traditions that would be attractive additions to the rhetorical arsenal of future political actors.
12. After the First World War and the Finnish Civil War, the radical Finnish-speaking right used old Fennomanian rhetoric, but had to cast themselves as something other than Fennomanian. They chose to label themselves as a movement fighting for 'an *authentic* Finnishness' (*aitosuomalaisuus*), thus introducing the empty and dreary discourse of who is and who is not the most authentic!

References

Alapuro, Risto (1988) *State and Revolution in Finland*. Berkeley: University of California Press.
Aronsson, Peter (1997) 'Local Politics – The Invisible Political Culture' in Østen Sørensen and Bo Stråth (eds), *The Cultural Construction of Norden*. Oslo: Scandinavian University Press.
Baldwin, Peter (1990) *The Politics of Social Solidarity. Class Bases of the European Welfare State 1875–1975*. Cambridge: Cambridge University Press.
Björkqvist, Heimer (1986) *Den nationalekonomiska vetenskapens utveckling I Finland intill år 1918*. Åbo: Publications of the Research Institute of the Åbo Akademi Foundation.

Esping-Andersen, Gøsta (1990) *The Three Worlds of Welfare Capitalism.* Cambridge: Polity Press.

Flora, Peter (ed.) (1986) *Growth to Limits. The Western European Welfare States since World War II*, vol. 1: Sweden, Norway, Finland, Denmark. Berlin and New York: Walter de Gruyter.

Jalava, Marja (2006) *J.V. Snellman – mies ja suurmies.* Helsinmi: Tammi.

Jansson, Torkel (1987) *Agrarsamhällets förändring och landskommunal organisation. En konturteckning av 1800-talets Norden.* Uppsala: Almqvist & Wiksell International.

Kangas, Olli (1994) 'The Merging of Welfare State Models? Past and Present Trends in Finnish and Swedish Social Policy', *Journal of European Social Policy*, 4(2).

Kautto, Mikko, Matti Heikkilä, Bjørn Hvinden, Staffan Marklund and Niels Ploug (1999) *Nordic Social Policy. Changing Welfare States.* London and New York: Routledge.

Kissane, Bill (2005) *Politics of the Irish Civil War.* Oxford: Oxford University Press New York.

Knudsen, Tim (ed.) (2000) *Den nordiska protestantisme og velfærdsstaten.* Aarhus: Aarhus Universitetsforlag.

Kosonen, Pekka (1993) 'The Finnish Model and the Welfare State in Crisis' in Pekka Kosonen (ed.), *The Nordic Welfare State as an Idea and as Reality.* Helsinki: The Renvall Institute, University of Helsinki.

Kuhnle, Stein (1996) 'International Modelling, State and Statistics - Scandinavian Social Security Solutions in the 1890s' in Dietrich Rueschemeyer and Theda Skocpol (eds), *States, Social Knowledge and the Origins of Modern Social Policies.* Princeton: Princeton University Press.

Kurunmäki, Jussi (2000) *Representation, Nation and Time. The Political Rhetoric of the 1866 Parliamentary Reform in Sweden.* Jyväskylä: Jyväskylä Studies in Education, Psychology and Social Research.

Stenius, Henrik (1987) *Frivilligt – jämlikt – samfällt. Föreningsväsendets utveckling i Finland fram till 1900-talets början med speciell hänsyn till massorganisationsprincipens genombrott.* Ekenäs: Svenska litteratursällskapet i Finland 545.

―――― (1996) 'The Good Life is a Life of Conformity: The Impact of Lutheran Tradition on Nordic Political Culture' in Østen Sørensen and Bo Stråth (eds), *The Cultural Construction of Norden.* Oslo: Scandinavian University Press.

―――― (2004) 'The Finnish Citizen. How a Translation Emasculated the Concept', *Redescriptions. Yearbook of Political Thought and Conceptual Change*, Vol 8.

Sørensen, Østen, and Bo Stråth (eds) (1997) *The Cultural Construction of Norden.* Oslo: Scandinavian University Press.

Tocqueville, Alexis de (1997) *Om demokration i America*, Lund Atlantis (original French two volume edition *De la démocratie en Amérique* 1836 and 1840).

Trägårdh, Lars (1999) 'Det civila samhället som analytiskt begrepp och politisk slogan' in Erik Amnå (ed.), *Civilsamhället.* Stockholm: Statens offentliga utredningar.

CHAPTER 10
Icelandic Anomalies
Jóhann Páll Árnason

> Islands are places apart where Europe is absent.
> W.H. Auden (1969)

According to one of the most widely read contemporary historians, 'Iceland is anomalous in almost every way' (Fernandez-Armesto 2000: 368); and although this particular author is so far out of touch with the record that he thinks there were cities in medieval Iceland and Greenland, his *aperçu* is not a bad starting point for reflection on a very atypical offshoot of the European tradition. An inventory of anomalies might begin with Iceland's ambiguous status within the region discussed by other contributors to this volume. On the one hand, the idea of a Nordic world would be incomplete without reference to the only country that produced a distinctive literary tradition during the formative medieval phase of Nordic history and maintained linguistic continuity throughout later transformations. For those who want to add a civilizational dimension to the historical identity of the region, the Icelandic legacy has always been a key piece of evidence. Toynbee's idea of an 'abortive Scandinavian civilization', most adequately documented in thirteenth-century Icelandic literature, is perhaps the best-known variation on this theme. On a more practical level, modern developments elsewhere in the region – and the concomitant reconstruction of traditions – led to growing interest in the Icelandic past and its present traces, beginning with seventeenth-century antiquarian pursuits sponsored by the Danish and Swedish monarchies, but taking a much more broadly public turn with the nineteenth-century ascendancy of Romanticism. Strategic use of this cultural capital was crucial to the success of modern Icelandic nationalism.

On the other hand, the Icelandic historical experience is – as even a cursory glance will show – in many ways quite unlike developmental paths more or less common to the core Nordic countries. Bo Stråth's essay in this issue notes some exceptional features that set Iceland apart from the mainstream of Nordic modernity. But the most basic contrast is perhaps to be found in a different relationship between internal and external determinants of change. Abrupt technological and geopolitical shifts, due to external influences, played a decisive role in the modernization of Iceland. The landmarks include an 'industrial revolution in fishing' (Karlsson 2000: 287) at the beginning of the twentieth century; British and American occupation during the Second World War, accompanied by windfall profits on foreign markets (put to good use by a developmentalist coalition of conservatives and the radical Left at the end of the war); and a radical change in the political environment with the onset of the Cold War. Compared to the other Nordic countries, the encounter with advanced modernity came later and had more spectacular effects. It seems more difficult to reconstruct the story in terms of an internal logic. No narrative of the kind outlined in other case studies in this issue – tracing an intelligible but not predetermined path from early modernity to the late twentieth century – has so far been written about Iceland, and the present writer certainly does not feel qualified to try; and as suggested above, the main obstacle is the structurally less self-contained character of the modernizing trajectory (Finland is, in this negative sense, closer to Iceland than the three core countries). The spectacular self-destruction of Icelandic neo-liberalism (at the time of writing, the consequences of the 2008 financial collapse are still unfolding, and the only possible prediction is that they will shape the course of events for a long time to come) adds a new chapter to this story. In view of what is now known about the record of the Icelandic banks and the behaviour of their leading representatives, there can be no doubt that the disaster had to happen. The international financial crisis aggravated the problem, but the whole regime was on a suicidal track well before the final phase. In that sense, the driving forces were internal. More importantly, however, the neo-liberal episode that lasted from 1991 to 2008 has no parallels elsewhere in the Nordic world, and cannot be presented as a logical continuation of earlier developments. The Icelandic version of casino capitalism, put on the rails during the 1990s and in full flight after the turn of the century, was a response to mutations of the global capitalist order and an extreme version of trends operating on a much larger scale; the break with the structures and self-images of the preceding period was very explicit, even if often expressed in terms that seem wide of the mark. Advocates of neo-liberal policies found a surprisingly large audience for their claim that Iceland had, for much of the twentieth century, been some kind of Soviet-style economy; the ambition to leave Nordic models behind and adopt American ones (forcefully expressed in a semi-official document from 2006), was central to the neo-liberal project. The extreme silliness of the rhetoric that accompanied these efforts, not least at the highest levels of political self-representation (see the discussion in Guðmundur Hálfdanarson's paper in this collection), is becoming a source of amazement in a changed world, and its erstwhile appeal seems hard to understand.

There is, however, another side to this deviation from the main pattern. The crucial impulses to modernization came from outside, and they transformed a peasant – or, more precisely, sedentary pastoral – society whose nineteenth-century problems mostly seem to have been due to disruption of a fragile balance between population and environment, rather than to any innovative trends from within (Hálfdanarson 1993); but the responses to changing conditions crystallized into a national movement, and neither the rapid formation nor the resilience of the national identity essential to the success of this movement can be understood without taking account of much older preconditions. Although the medieval heritage alone did not – as many Icelandic nationalists liked to think – make the Icelanders a nation, its exceptional importance for the long-term process of nation formation can hardly be doubted. A very distinctive historical experience, accompanied by vigorous cultural articulation, left a legacy bound to affect all later interaction with the broader Nordic world and its European civilizational background. In that sense, it seems justified to describe Iceland as an unusually clear-cut case of cultural path dependence, but also a reminder that path dependence should not be mistaken for pre-programming. Icelandic history might – at several successive junctures – have taken other roads than those which in the end led to the building of a nation-state; the enduring significance of the medieval sources consisted in pointing to possibilities that would otherwise have been much less easy to envisage. Whether the medieval background or the modern context was 'more important' (Hermannsson 2005 – a critical comment on an earlier version of this paper) is hardly a meaningful question. It is not at all clear what the criterion for measuring the relative weight of these two very different factors should be. What matters is their interaction in a certain historical setting, not a putative order of precedence. Nation formation is a complex process, often involving multiple historical layers, and the task of historical analysis is to trace the combinations of these layers, rather than to rank them in terms of importance.

New Societies and their Trajectories

As the above considerations suggest, the Icelandic experience does not lend itself to the same approach as the other cases discussed in this book. A more recent modernizing turn, with less structured results, should be set against the background of a more formative, easily mythologizable but also inevitably controversial medieval past. The following discussion will try to locate this problematic within a broader comparative perspective.

One of the most provocative and original interpretations of Iceland as distinct from the other Nordic countries was put forward by the American sociologist Richard Tomasson (1982). Drawing on the work of Louis Hartz and his associates (1964), who had coined the concept of 'new societies' to describe the overseas offshoots of European civilization, Tomasson defined Iceland as the 'first new society', created by an early wave of migration but structurally similar to later products of European expansion and settlement. His main interest was a 'thick description' of contemporary Icelandic society, and in that context, the reference to new societies served to underline a common aspect: the long-term effect of overseas migration on social relations and attitudes. He did not discuss Iceland's specific place within a historical typology of new societies. Seymour Martin Lipset, who wrote a foreword to the book, obviously had that unanswered question in mind when he suggested that Iceland might be seen as 'truly a fragment culture of medieval Europe' (Tomasson 1982: V). Although this is not to be taken as a description of unchanging conditions, it is – as will be seen – a pertinent reminder of background connections to be explored. But before going further in that direction, a closer look at the ambiguities and loose ends of Hartz's analytical model of new societies may be useful.

For Hartz, the new societies were transplanted 'fragments of the larger whole of Europe', and separation made them lapse 'into a kind of immobility' (1964: 3). Inherent trends of each fragment could still unfold, but the whole argument stresses a structural loss of transformative potential and momentum – all the more so since Hartz also stresses the intellectual unoriginality of the new societies. The fragments are, more specifically, defined in terms of a developmental sequence that comes surprisingly close to Marxist views and with a strong emphasis on ideological categories: feudal-clerical in Latin America and French Canada, bourgeois-liberal in the United States, labour-radical in Australia. But in the long run, that is to say in the twentieth century, the fragments are bound to collide with a more radical and global version of the European revolution. This was Hartz's reading of the Cold War constellation, and he clearly saw the confrontation as a more serious challenge to the most powerful new society than it proved to be. For present purposes, however, it is more important to note another doubtful claim: Hartz's account of separation, self-contained history and subsequent conflict seems to rule out the possibility that new societies might – in and through the very act of separation – transform their European legacies in original ways, and that this could lead to further development through self-demarcation from the old world. In other words: ongoing, formative and differentiating interaction of the 'fragment universe' (Hartz 1964: 20) with the former whole might be a more significant part of the story than the model would have it. Hartz admits that the new nationalism – the conversion of a fragmentary identity into a more complete national one – enhances the contrast to Europe, and he briefly alludes to imperial rule as a factor that may affect developments on both sides. But these marginal considerations do not weaken his main thesis. It was left to later scholars to introduce themes and perspectives which changed the whole problematic of new societies. Recent work on the two Americas and their respective modernities has underlined the mutations that accompanied the transfer of European models, the more programmatic deviations from European precedents after the breakdown of transatlantic imperial structures, and the long-term development of distinctive twists to the cultural and institutional patterns of modernity. With this revised frame of reference in mind, we should now return to the analysis of Iceland as a new society.

Medieval Foundations

Hartz's original theory of new societies situated them in the context of a global but pre-eminently European modernizing transformation, with a strong emphasis on its revolutionary character, and later reformulations are linked to unfolding debates on early and multiple modernities. The Icelandic experience belongs to another historical world: here we are dealing with a new society that took shape in connection with 'the first European revolution' (Moore 1999), with the crystallization of Western Christendom as a separate civilization with distinctive cultural and political traits. It is the only case of its kind (the other Norse settlements in the North Atlantic area were either too short-lived or too dependent to fall into the same category), and this would seem to be the most decisive of the anomalies mentioned above. Some specific aspects should be noted.

Following R.I. Moore, the crucial phase of the 'first European revolution' can be dated from the late tenth to the late twelfth century CE, but this period saw the maturation and institutional consolidation of forces that had been at work in post-Carolingian Western Europe. In particular, advances in state formation within the institutional framework of monarchy are now increasingly recognized as a defining feature of the early second millennium. Different European regions were characterized by variants of this pattern. The settlement of Iceland and the creation of some core institutions preceded the epochal turn of the continental transformation, but a deviation from dominant trends was already apparent, and the maintenance of anomalous political forms in a world of ascendant monarchies set the Icelanders more and more clearly apart from the European mainstream. The fact that they had no king was a wonder – and sometimes a scandal – to foreign observers. Given the lack of written sources prior to the early twelfth century, we can only speculate about the level of conscious nonconformity at the time when the Icelandic Free State was established.[1] Thirteenth-century sources claim that the settlers left Norway because of forcible unification under a king, but this had obviously become an ideological theme, and its historical truth-content is hard to assess. Setbacks to Viking settlements in the British Isles may have been as important as developments in Norway; but it is also true that migrants from there did not import their model of colonization (for example, the Orkneys became a mini-monarchy with a much more hierarchical social order than Iceland).

Be that is it may, the settlers went on to create a unified but non-monarchic polity in a large and very sparsely populated island. The foundations were laid in the first half of the tenth century (the traditional date of 930 is imprecise) and endured until the Icelanders swore allegiance to the Norwegian king in 1262. No political order of the same type emerged anywhere else in Europe, but as an exception to the main pattern of the High Middle Ages, it can be compared to other cases. Michael Borgolte (2002: 211–20) refers to Iceland and the Italian communes as 'free-states in a world of monarchies'. Some basic contrasts are obvious: Iceland 'knew neither the formation of urban communities, nor elective authority' (ibid.: 211). But if the idea of a republican order, revived in medieval thought on the basis of the Italian experience, is (as Borgolte suggests) taken to imply the two key principles of authority bound by law and power vested in a plurality without a supreme centre, the Icelandic Free State may be described as a republican regime sui generis (not as an early democracy – claims of that kind, popular among an earlier generation of Icelandic scholars, seem anachronistic, and so is the description of the *Alþing* as 'the first parliament'). A comprehensive and extremely elaborate legal system, valid for the whole country, was the cornerstone of the Free State, and the sources testify to an all-pervasive legalistic spirit: 'the cultural focus was on law' (Byock 1988: 7) There is no reason to doubt the traditional view that Icelandic law was established after extensive study of regional laws in Norway, but there was no detailed imitation of any older model, and no precedent for the imposition of a complete legal framework on a comparably large area (it was not until much later that Scandinavian monarchs started trying to unify the disparate legal traditions of their domains).

As for the power structure that lent force and stability to the legal order, the details are more controversial. It centred on a large number of chieftains (this is an awkward translation of the Icelandic term *goði*, but no better one seems to have been suggested); they made up the legislative body (the core of the annual countrywide assembly) and nominated juries to settle all kinds of disputes. It is less clear to what extent they wielded other kinds of power. They had some religious or cultic functions, but very little is known about this part of the picture, and tenth-century paganism seems to have been in an advanced stage of decomposition (although still capable of interesting variations in response to the advance of Christianity). Since there was no central executive, they had no delegated power, and there was – in contrast to the general Western European pattern – no fusion of territorial lordship and landed property. The chieftaincies were not defined as territorial units. Chieftains were not elected by their followers (the status was in principle hereditary, but could be transferred or even sold, and on some occasions, newcomers seem to have acquired it in a less procedural way); but a farmer could in principle renounce his chieftain and opt for another one, and although this was in practice rare, the contractual relationship implicit in this rule does not seem to have been a mere fiction. Chieftains were wealthier than the average farmer, but this was a difference in degree rather than in kind; the first steps towards regular taxation were taken in the last stage of the Free State, and before that, chieftains had to rely on less regular sources of income.

In view of the evidence, the claim that 'each chieftain led a miniature state' (Sigurðsson 1999: 204) seems vastly overstated. It makes more sense to describe the whole system as a 'self-limiting pattern of state formation' (Byock 2001: 76). The familiar mechanisms analysed by Norbert Elias – culminating in the twin monopolies of taxation and violence – could not operate in the Icelandic context. A state-building logic is nevertheless evident in the effort to limit conflict and contain the pursuit of coercive power; there was no thoroughgoing pacification of society (feuds were a part of the system, although their forms and functions are matters of debate among scholars), but the whole institutional framework was designed to limit the scope and impact of violence. The Icelandic sagas are not, as an eminent English authority on legal history would have it, 'about men whose chief occupation was to kill one another' (Bryce

1901: 312); nor can their subject matter be described as 'the hopelessness of universal murder in a narrow space' (Borkenau 1981: 286). Closer reading has focused attention on the procedures of conflict management and dispute resolution in an acephalous but post-tribal society.

The distinctive political institutions of the new society were thus conceived and constructed as a deviation from the continental mainstream; although we cannot assume that the ideological contrast evident in twelfth- and thirteenth-century sources was operative from the outset, the invention of an alternative order must have involved some conscious drawing apart. This was, however, only the first phase of a complex interactive process. The next landmark was Christianization, beginning with official conversion in 1000 CE. As Jesse Byock argues (2001: 297–301), the events of that year illustrate both the strength and the adaptability of the institutional framework: an established procedure of conflict resolution was applied to the conflict between pagan and Christian, with the result that Iceland became a part of Western Christendom but retained significant links to a pre-Christian heritage. The conversion was also a foreign policy decision: a move to deflect the threat from an aggressively proselytizing Norwegian monarch. 'Christ was let in but the king was not' (Karlsson 2000: 37). But even Christ had to settle for a more modest position than on the continent. Most historians now seem to agree that a pre-existing combination of religious and political authority made change easier. The chieftains 'went' Christian and maintained some of their traditional power over the organization and economy of religious life. In the struggle for wealth and power, the Church faced structural disadvantages everywhere in the Nordic world, but far more so in Iceland than in Scandinavia; it could not mount a successful offensive until after the incorporation of Iceland into the Norwegian kingdom.

It is a matter of open debate whether this pattern of conversion – quite unlike any other in medieval Europe – had permanent effects of the kind that would mean a more limited in-depth Christianization than elsewhere in the Nordic world (the present writer inclines to that view, but the case will not be argued here). The direct impact on cultural growth is indisputable. The literary tradition that crystallized in the twelfth and thirteenth centuries was an intricate mixture of pagan and Christian elements; its pre-Christian aspects have always seemed obvious enough to be singled out by those who look for evidence of a distinctive Nordic civilization in the making, but cut short by absorption into Western Christendom. The historiography that developed as an integral part of this tradition – from the first history of the Icelanders, written in the 1120s, to Snorri Sturluson's thirteenth-century history of the Norwegian kingdom – was more secular in spirit than any other medieval works in that field.

The flowering of literary culture constitutes the third step – after the constitution of a polity and the conversion to Christianity – in the formation of Iceland as a new society, and the most decisive one for the later course of history. The Icelanders – as Bryce put it, 'a handful of people scattered around the edge of a vast and dreary wilderness' (1901: 358) – developed their own variant of the 'twelfth-century renaissance' in Western Europe. But for comparative purposes, a more long-term perspective may be useful. The process of vernacularization – the replacement of cosmopolitan languages by local ones which first become media of literacy and then vehicles of literary culture – has recently been noted as an important but strikingly understudied aspect of cultural history (see especially Pollock 1998, 2006; the key cases to be compared are Europe and India, where Latin and Sanskrit yielded to vernaculars, but in different ways and with different consequences). European vernacularization reached a turning point in late medieval and early modern times, but the process can be traced back to much earlier beginnings, especially in North Western Europe; significant developments in Anglo-Saxon England preceded the first steps towards literacy in the Nordic world (the idea of English as a *lingua quarta*, alongside Hebrew, Greek and Latin, goes back to the eighth century), but the rapid and complete vernacularization that took place in Iceland in the twelfth century has no parallel. A text known as the 'first grammatical treatise', written around 1150 and sometimes credited with pioneering the idea of phonemic distinctions (Haugen 1972) shows that there was a reflexive side to this abrupt shift: the author discusses the adaptation of the Latin alphabet to the Icelandic language and refers to earlier English solutions to similar problems.

It is not easy to explain the vernacular turn. Sheldon Pollock lists 'assertions of religious individuality on the part of European rulers' (1998: 62) among the factors likely to have been of long-term importance. This does not apply to Iceland: there were no rulers, and the acephalous political elite that had engineered the conversion to Christianity could – for the time being – take an advantageous *modus vivendi* with the Church for granted. The specific situation of a new society in the context of the Middle Ages must have counted for something, and a loose analogy with Hartz's analysis of the precocious and peculiar nationalism of later new societies may be useful. It would be anachronistic to speak of nationalism in twelfth-century Iceland, and the society created there was not so much a fragment as a niche where a mixture of deviation and compromise could survive for some time. But in a more general sense, the construction of collective identity in a new territory, with strong emphasis on a collective memory of taking possession and charting a distinctive path, may be seen as a comparable case. The grammatical treatise mentioned above begins with a statement on the need for every 'nation' to write down its laws in its own language, and to record events that have happened in its own country, as well as memorable tidings from elsewhere (the term used, *þjóð*, is still the Icelandic word for 'nation'). This view was obviously in line with a broader trend: the most striking and durable result of the vernacular turn was a phenomenal output of narrative writing. The later Free State was surely the story-telling society par excellence. One of the first books in the vernacular (apart from legal codes) was a history of the Icelanders; a later 'Book of Settlements' recorded the colonizing process in detail; a large body of work, culminating in Snorri Sturluson's *Heimskringla*, dealt with the history of the Norwegian kingdom (notwithstanding the political separation, a special relationship to Norway seems to have been a part of Icelandic identity from the outset). But the most widely known and culturally significant narratives are the 'Sagas of the Icelanders', mostly written in the thirteenth century, but situated in tenth- and early-eleventh-century Iceland. In their case, the relationship between historical content and literary creation has been a subject of unending controversy: the most recent round of debate – with a significant input from anthropologists – has drawn attention to the portrayal of social patterns and conflicts (often in imaginary settings), rather than of remembered events.

Although there is every reason to assume that identity-building was a key factor, the volume and diversity of narrative writing went far beyond needs or motives of that sort. This was the medieval Icelandic type of cultural surplus, and it remains a puzzling phenomenon. An early view from within the Nordic world is summed up in a statement about the Icelanders by a late-twelfth-century Danish chronicler: '*inopiam ingenio pensant*' (they compensate for poverty by ingeniousness). The ingeniousness he had in mind was obviously not of the technical kind, and the comment has often been taken to mean that the invention of stories and the interest in older times (at home and abroad) served to compensate for an austere life-world. There is further evidence that the Icelanders had – in the other Nordic countries – built up a reputation as poets, antiquarians and historians. But other perspectives have prevailed in modern scholarship. The details of the discussion are beyond the scope of this paper, but with regard to the 'Sagas of the Icelanders', an idea by the most influential (but certainly not uncontested) Icelandic scholar in the field is worth noting (Nordal 1993: 149–59). This genre of sagas reflects a mood of pessimism and disillusion that is all too easy to relate to a historical background. It seems likely that living conditions had deteriorated due to a worsening climate as well as ecological damage (the settlers had come from a different environment and shown little understanding of the new one); closer contacts with the outside world and growing dependence on foreign trade had made the precarious character and position of the Icelandic polity more obvious; most importantly, internal power struggles were tearing the Free State apart (as noted above, the original chieftaincies cannot be described as miniature states, but the term may be applicable to the domains of powerful families that rose to prominence in the late twelfth and early thirteenth centuries). In short, the new society had good reasons to take a very disenchanted look at itself.

As the above analysis suggests, medieval Iceland – more precisely: the social, political and cultural order that prevailed from the tenth to the thirteenth century – is best seen as a very distinctive variant within the civilizational domain of Western Christendom, rather than a pre-Christian culture surviving into the High Middle Ages and capable of more articulate resistance to Christianization than were the pagan societies on the continent. The latter interpretation has often seemed attractive to those who wanted to emphasize the unique features of Iceland's medieval legacy (apart from Arnold Toynbee, mentioned above, it is worth noting that Halldór Laxness – the most significant figure of twentieth-century Icelandic culture – was at one stage a forceful advocate of this view, although he later changed his mind). But the link to Scandinavian paganism is too tenuous, the transformations during the historical lifespan of the Free State too visible, and the Christian background to the cultural flowering of the twelfth and thirteenth centuries too fundamental for the 'paganist' thesis to be tenable (for further discussion see Arnason 2009). If we want a shorthand label for this Icelandic version of Western Christendom, the title of Gunnar Karlsson's recent work, *Goðamenning* (Karlsson 2004) seems the most appropriate answer. *Menning* is the Icelandic word for culture; *goði* is, as noted above, the term used to describe the power elite of the Free State. Karlsson's analysis stresses the social profile and the ethos of this group as keys to the understanding of three successive transformations: the tenth-century construction of a political order, the particular mode of Christianization, and the emergence of a literary culture in the twelfth century.

Memory, Decline and Survival

Because of its singular importance for later Icelandic history, I have discussed the medieval legacy at some length. The historical experience of the Free State and the corresponding cultural memory – embodied in a literary tradition – were central to the formation of collective identity. The sagas were read throughout later centuries, perhaps not as widely as romantic nationalists liked to imagine, but they certainly remained a part of popular culture (more generally speaking, there was no clear dividing line between elite and popular culture in pre-modern Iceland). This enduring link to a formative past gave modern Icelandic nationalism a historical basis without which it could hardly have taken off. I see no reason to disagree with Gunnar Karlsson when he writes: 'not all peoples feel the need to find a golden age in their past, and whether they do or not may depend to some degree on what really happened in the past. Iceland felt the need for a revival at least partly because it had unusually good material in its past on which to base it' (Karlsson 2000: 365; this book is by far the best comprehensive survey of Icelandic history, and the present paper is heavily indebted to it). Moreover, the historical experience of the Free State – although not democratic in any accepted sense of the word – lent itself to interpretations that helped to align nationalism with democratic trends. Leaders of the nineteenth-century national movement took the view that since Norwegian sovereignty (later inherited by the Danish composite monarchy) was accepted by an assembly on behalf of the community, a redefinition of sovereignty (brought about by the conversion of an absolute monarchy into a constitutional one) should entail a renegotiation of Iceland's relationship with the larger state which it had joined; this line of argument involved some streamlining of legal history, but it was politically sound. It linked the aspirations of Icelandic nationalism to the broader struggle for popular sovereignty within the mutating Danish state.

The nineteenth-century mobilization of cultural memory came after a long period of a very different character, and a brief look at that background is needed to put the sequel in perspective. Late-medieval changes to the Nordic scene had a lasting effect on Iceland's geopolitical and geocultural position. The grand strategy of the thirteenth-century Norwegian monarchy had aimed at the creation of a North Atlantic empire, including repossession of older Norse settlements on the margins of the British Isles; this project came close to complete success, but it was very short-lived. At the end of the century, Norwegian rulers reoriented their strategy towards dynastic manoeuvring and expansion within the Scandinavian–Baltic world; after the fourteenth-century near collapse of the Norwegian state (largely due to the Black Death, which seems to have hit the country – or at least the ruling elite – harder than any other part of Europe), the interstate balance of power shifted, and the upshot of further developments was the formation of a Denmark-centred pan-Nordic monarchy in 1397. This re-centring of the Nordic world was arguably a more decisive turning point in Icelandic history than the annexation by Norway; the country became a very minor, remote and marginal dependency of a state which was for a while the largest but proved to be the most fragile of Europe's composite monarchies. The following four centuries were not the least anomalous chapter in Icelandic history. Early modern trends and transformations had a significant impact, but in ways markedly out of tune with the West European mainstream.

The Reformation, imposed by Danish authorities (the last Catholic bishop was executed after armed struggle in 1550) was not only – as in some other countries – a revolution from above, but also from outside. On the other hand, its cultural effects were counterbalanced by the staying-power of the local language: in contrast to other domains of the composite monarchy, the Lutheran wave of vernacularization did not entrench Danish. Isolation reinforced the general tendency of absolutism to translate into 'an oligarchy of officials' (Karlsson 2000: 154). A centralizing shift thus prompted local steps towards state formation.

Efforts to improve popular education, inspired by Danish pietism and preparatory to the Enlightenment, took the distinctive form of an 'educational revolution without schools' (ibid.: 169): households were successfully entrusted with the task of raising literacy levels. In all these respects, early modern innovations gave rise to peripheral variants, without any major changes to the core structures of Icelandic society. But for Icelandic nationalistic historiography, the period in question was not simply marked by dependence and peripheralization. It came to be seen as a time of all-round decline, and as such, it provided a suitable backdrop to the nineteenth-century national revival. The merits and demerits of this interpretation are now widely debated by Icelandic historians; revisionist accounts have even gone to the other extreme and constructed an early modern 'golden age' of peasant society, but that view has found very few supporters.

Although there is no scholarly consensus on the balance sheet of the centuries between 1400 and 1800, it can be safely said that the 'degeneration theory' is not easily dismissed. On the most material level, evidence of deteriorating conditions is now beyond dispute. The climate changed for the worse, and this led – among other things – to the abandonment of grain cultivation, which had never been more than a subordinate part of the economy, but came to an end around 1500. Natural disasters struck again and again, beginning with the Black Death, which seems to have killed about half of the population between 1402 and 1404, and ending with a late-eighteenth-century famine (after a volcanic explosion) which brought the population down to about forty thousand. More complex issues arise when it comes to the socio-cultural dimensions of decline. The Danish anthropologist Kirsten Hastrup (1990a, b) interprets the whole period as a phase of 'cultural deconstruction'; her argument is highly controversial, but to my mind sound on some crucial points, and it has some bearing on the question of nation formation as a long-term process. Hastrup does not propose a one-sidedly culturalist explanation of decline: there is no denying the momentous impact of natural catastrophes and political marginalization, but especially with regard to the latter factor, cultural perceptions of and responses to the changing situation must also be taken into account. As Hastrup puts it (1990b: 300), 'Europe produced a kind of history to which Iceland could not accommodate because the Icelanders had a timeless vision of history'. More precisely, the timeless vision was a defensive but in the upshot aggravating reaction to changes imposed from elsewhere. It was anchored in an idealized past but went beyond the mythicizing turn that had already been taken in thirteenth-century literature. Hastrup describes it as an 'uchronia', a transfiguration of the past into a parallel universe. But the most provocative part of her argument is the claim that this 'uchronic' mentality affected social life at the most basic level: 'during the four centuries of cultural deconstruction in Iceland, the very vitality of tradition was detrimental to social reproduction – not on its own, of course, but in conjunction with a whole set of other factors' (Hastrup 1990a: 199). She traces the ramifications of this deconstructive logic in various domains. It enhanced the symbolic and institutional primacy of household farming in a society more dependent on fishing than its self-image would admit; the cultural canonization of an atomized rural society was not only an obstacle to progress in the devalued fields of activity, but seems also to have led to stagnation and retreat at the very core of the farming economy (so much so that Hastrup speaks of 'a decreasing area of domesticated nature' (1990b: 291)) and a shrinking of the social realm in relation to its territorial basis. Contemporary sources suggest that Icelandic forms of social life were in many ways out of tune with the civilizing processes that unfolded in Western Europe. The self-inventive relationship of the new society to the old world had, as it were, gone into reverse.

The Nationalist Turn

Around 1800, the threats to the survival of Icelandic culture and identity were more visible than the background strength gathered during the eighteenth century. The early-nineteenth-century Danish linguist R.C. Rask, who did most to accredit the idea of Icelandic as the original language of the whole Nordic world, thought that it was doomed to extinction; this was his main reason for insisting on more organized study and preservation of the Icelandic literary heritage. Efforts with that end in view were soon to feed into a rising tide of nationalism. But the political potential was not evident from the outset. Historians seem to agree on this: in early-nineteenth-century Iceland, an indisputably distinctive linguistic and cultural identity did not *ipso facto* translate into political nationalism. The situation changed rapidly in the 1830s and 1840s, and in a sense, a turning point was reached in 1851, when the Danish authorities in Iceland dispersed an assembly which had put forward demands amounting to 'a constitution for a practically independent Iceland'(Karlsson 2000: 212). This move – clearly made with broad popular support – foreshadowed the sustained push that led to the establishment of a sovereign state (in personal union with Denmark) in 1918. The final separation in 1944 was perhaps less obviously implicit in this early challenge.

In retrospect, nationalist politicians and historians saw the rapid change after 1830 as an exemplary case of 'national awakening', all the more so since the new political activism coincided with a spectacular revival of Icelandic as a literary language. But from the more critical perspective of recent scholarship, this standard figure of nationalist rhetoric is no more valid than elsewhere. On the other hand, a social-structural explanation – the most familiar and straightforward antithesis to nationalist self-affirmation – would seem particularly unconvincing: during the period in question, there were no changes to Icelandic society that could account for the massive political and ideological reorientation. The search for more adequate understanding must begin with the point that the transformation was not a self-contained process. The nationalist turn in Iceland must be analysed in the broader context of the Danish composite monarchy shifting from one political regime to another (see Uffe Østergård's paper in this issue; as he shows, the Danish state was – although very much a part of the Nordic world – in some ways similar to political formations in Central and East Central Europe). Compared to the composite state par excellence, the Habsburg Empire, developments within the Danish monarchy took a straighter path: a more constructive response to the July revolution of 1830 was followed by a successful transition from absolutism to constitutionalism in 1848. But in a constitutional (and in the long run increasingly democratic) regime, the multinational character of the state was bound to pose political problems which had not arisen under absolutist rule. The local issue around which the new problematic crystallized most quickly – the Schleswig-Holstein question – had repercussions which affected a much larger part of Europe, from Vienna in the south to Iceland in the north. In more general terms, the Danish case exemplifies an important point about modern nationalism. The politicization of cultural identities is of crucial importance, but it is not (as Ernest Gellner's seminal but one-sided analysis suggested) simply a result of trends inherent in industrial society as such; it occurs in multiple contents and takes multiple directions. Political transformations of composite states were not the least important sources of such effects. In that regard, the Icelandic experience fits into a recurrent pattern. More distinctive features of the ensuing process should be briefly noted.

The importance of the Danish background is evident in the fact that the idea of a separate representative assembly for Iceland was first floated by a reformist Danish nobleman (Karlsson 2000: 201). But it was very quickly taken up by people closer to practical concerns: in the following year (1832), an Icelandic law student in Copenhagen published an essay arguing for a separate Icelandic assembly. This was the first sign of active involvement on the part of a community that came to play a leading role. A small group of Icelandic intellectuals in Copenhagen gave the nationalist movement a cultural and ideological charge that could not have come from anywhere else. For a comparative perspective on their achievement, we may turn to Charles Taylor's essay on nationalism and modernity (1998). Taylor stresses the refusal of 'metropolitan incorporation' (205) as a crucial (albeit unequally developed) component of nationalist ideas and movements. This refusal expresses the attitude and defines the outlook of indigenous elites at the receiving end of modernizing processes initiated by the West; it is most articulate when combined with direct experience of metropolitan culture, and it responds to a challenge that is 'lived … in a certain register, that of dignity' (ibid.: 206). It develops into what Taylor terms 'a call to difference' and a creative adaptation of traditional resources. Key parts of this description fit the case in question. In particular, those who articulated the refusal were located in the very centre of the metropolis, involved in its cultural life, and receptive to cultural currents of the broader European environment. But in contrast to the cases most clearly in Taylor's sights (non-Western elites coping with a conquering West), this redefinition of the relationship between core and periphery took place in the context of a Western state moving from the absolutist to the constitutional democratic form of political modernity. As for the tradition invoked to sustain the 'call to difference' its medieval sources were all the more relevant and valuable since they also carried meaning for the metropolis and gained in prestige through the shared culture of national romanticism. But it is tempting to suggest that in addition to the medieval foundations, the ability to refuse also owed something to the 'uchronic' detachment that had (according to Hastrup) prevailed during the centuries of decline.

The impeccably constitutional and non-violent character of the push for sovereignty sets the Icelandic case apart from most other national movements in conflict with composite states (the contrast to Ireland is striking, but was sometimes disregarded by Icelandic nationalists who found the idea of parallels appealing). Jón Sigurðsson (1811–79), the most able and authoritative spokesman of the independence movement, was probably the only nationalist leader who spent much of his adult life working on research projects funded by the very state whose authority he was contesting. But the constitutionalist strategy did not diminish the need for a broad basis. The movement could never have succeeded without strong and lasting support throughout Icelandic society. This is not to say that there was any pre-established harmony or principled agreement between the intellectuals in Copenhagen and the political leaders of the peasantry in Iceland. Recent research, undertaken in explicit opposition to the previously dominant school of thought, has highlighted the tensions and divergences that troubled relations between the two sides (see especially Hálfdanarson 2001). The liberal modernism of Jón Sigurðsson and his closest associates was uncongenial to those who strove to preserve the controls and conventions of a very tightly knit peasant society. Defenders of the domestic status quo could even invoke nationalism against reforms initiated by the Danish state. But it would seem vastly oversimplified to posit a uniform and principled contrast between modernizing intellectuals and conservative farmers. Although nineteenth-century Icelandic society was, for obvious reasons, not characterized by high levels of self-transformative capacity, its responses to new problems and openings (due, among other things, to the abolition of the Danish trade monopoly) were too varied to fit into that scheme. To sum up, the critics of nationalist historiography (including its left-wing variants) have shown that nationalism did not merge or harmonize with any general logic of progress or liberation. The points at issue can be linked to theoretical controversies. Modernist interpretations of nationalism have, broadly speaking, taken two different lines. An influential and internally diverse school of thought has tried to explain nationalist ideas and movements as logical or causal consequences of more fundamental trends inherent in modern societies (Ernest Gellner's work is the best-known example). More recently, and in critical response to the first claim, others (most forcefully Liah Greenfeld) have portrayed nationalism, more than anything else, as the driving and directive force of modern transformations, and argued that it has played this role from the very outset of modernity. Both approaches are open to basic objections, but more obviously so in some contexts than others; Iceland appears to be a clear-cut case of nationalism transcending both versions of the modernist view. The nationalist imaginary crystallized as a way to make sense of encounters with a modernizing world (most directly in the political sphere), and to articulate a changing but always important relationship between tradition and modernity; it gave rise to a discursive community within which multiple ideological and political currents (some of them more modernist than others, or representing different version of modernism) could dispute the field. This legacy had a lasting impact on Iceland's most recent history.

Twentieth-century Trends

As will be clear from other contributions to this issue, nationalism has not been irrelevant to twentieth-century Scandinavian history. But because of the long-drawn-out struggle for independence and the persistence of a political culture rooted in this experience, the nationalist tradition was stronger in Iceland. To take an obvious example, it has left its mark on the party system. Some analysts have seen this as a matter of divisions between isolationists and integrationists, intertwined with the more conventional dichotomy of left and right (cf. Karlsson 2000: 329). But it can also be argued that a shared nationalist background lent itself to different uses and interpretations that set the whole constellation apart from the Scandinavian pattern. Social democratic hegemony is one of the most familiar features of the latter; although there are, as the case studies in this issue show, major differences between the countries in question, the history of the Icelandic Social Democratic party – marked by splits and setbacks – stands out as an exception. It is too early to assess the consequences of its recent merger with a large part of its former rival on the Left, and the economic collapse has in any case derailed the strategy on which this realignment was predicated. During the twentieth century, it was overshadowed by three other political formations, all of them atypical in the Scandinavian context; they have all made more successful use of nationalist themes, and although this is certainly not the only reason, it has clearly been a significant advantage over the Social Democrats (who seem to have been hampered, during a decisive phase, by close links with the Danish Social Democratic Party). A conservative party with a strong populist streak has dominated Icelandic politics for most of the sixty years since the foundation of the republic; it drifted in a more neo-liberal direction after 1980 and underwent a near-total conversion during the last decade of the century, but this has not obliterated the nationalist connection symbolized by its official name (Independence Party). The Icelandic equivalent of the interwar 'red-green' coalitions in Scandinavia was dominated by a farmers' party which also controlled the cooperative movement; its leader – Jónas Jónsson (1885–1968), arguably the most pivotal figure in twentieth-century

Icelandic politics – had also been involved in the foundation of the Social Democratic Party and done more than anybody else to formulate a nationalist-reformist agenda that defined the parameters of political debate well beyond the phase of his personal ascendancy. Finally, the 1938 merger of the Communist with the left wing of the Social Democratic Party created the first Eurocommunist party (Gilberg 1980: 220), and the only one to pursue that course over a relatively long period; in contrast to the West European Communist parties (with the late exception of the French one in the 1980s), it participated in two coalition governments during the Cold War.

The different configuration of party politics is one of the reasons for another (and perhaps more lasting) contrast between Iceland and Scandinavia. The Icelandic welfare state has often – at home and abroad – been presented as a version of the Scandinavian model; recent work by Stefán Ólafsson (1999, 2006) has clarified the issue and shown that the deviation goes much further than commonly assumed. 'The Icelandic system remains smaller, less costly, less generous and less redistributive', and it has 'significantly shifted its character towards the American/Anglo-Saxon liberal welfare regime, especially in the area of social security benefits' (Ólafsson 2006: 214; the author also underlines some similarities with the liberal-labour welfare regimes in Australia and New Zealand, and is not averse to the idea that such features might have something to do with the heritage of settler societies). This mixed version of the welfare state is obviously not a product of politics alone. But the fact that significant reforms (and borrowings from Scandinavian models) have been initiated by coalitions including the Left suggests that the political factor is anything but negligible. Conversely, a less solidly reformist political culture, together with a more unsettled overall pattern of modernity, has made Iceland more receptive to neo-liberal currents than the other Nordic countries.

Further discussion of twentieth-century developments is beyond the scope of this paper (they are analysed at greater length in Guðmundur Hálfdanarson's contribution to this book), and so are the current prospects. Suffice it to say, with reference to the questions raised at the beginning of the paper, that as the consequences of the crisis unfold, they are bound to affect our views on the longer-term background. As the neo-liberal mirage evaporated, associated visions of history also lost their credibility. The official picture of the 'Icelandic economic miracle' obscured the fact that the most genuine economic progress was achieved during a period when economic policies and priorities were much closer to Nordic models (Ólafsson 2008). On a more serious level, reinterpretations of twentieth-century Icelandic history must face problems arising from changes to their contemporary frame of orientation. From the 1980s onwards, the tide seemed to be turning in favour of a narrative model centred on conflicts between modernizing and traditionalist forces, rather than on the established image of left-right polarization reflecting social struggles. The new scheme stressed the pervasive influence of conservative nationalism, not least on political and cultural movements commonly seen as belonging on the left side of the main divide, and doubts were thus cast on their modernizing pretensions. This line of argument was never easy to reconcile with the complex and changing alignments of socio-political forces in twentieth-century Iceland (in particular, the catch-all notion of conservative nationalism tended to disintegrate when confronted with the historical record). Now the idea of a modernizing mainstream gradually triumphing over traditionalist resistance has become a good deal more obviously suspect than before: can the ideal-typical axis of the modernist narrative escape identification with the all-too-real modernizing project that went off the rails in 2008? Further reflection on that issue is bound to raise a whole set of questions that cannot be pursued here. But they will definitely not translate into reasons for returning to a more self-contained conception of national history. On that level, the critique of nationalist historiography remains as valid as ever. The neo-liberal episode would not even have been imaginable without the global ascendancy of financial capital at the end of the twentieth century. The most recent experience is therefore another reminder of the need to situate Iceland's modern transformations in a global setting. However, this does not eliminate the question of internal preconditions for specific responses to global situations. And in that context, it seems legitimate to signal a return to the issues outlined in the first section of the paper. If Iceland's historical identity is to some extent marked by a combination of Nordic regional characteristics with features more reminiscent of anglophone settler societies, it is at least conceivable that this mixed background has something to do with the reckless and ill-fated attempt to leave the Nordic world behind. This is not the least interesting of the problems that will be on the agenda of historians trying to make sense of 2008 and all that.

Notes

1. It is not easy to find an adequate term for the Icelandic polity between the tenth and thirteenth centuries. I follow Byock, Hastrup and Borgolte in using 'Free State' rather than 'Commonwealth'.

References

Árnason, J.P. (2009) 'A Mutating Periphery: Medieval Encounters in the Far North', *Gripla*, 14–47.
Auden, W.H., and L. McNeice (1969) *Letters from Iceland*. New York: Random House.
Borkenau, F. (1981) *End and Beginning*. New York: Columbia University Press.
Borgolte, M. (2002) *Europa entdeckt seine Vielfalt*. Stuttgart: Ulmer.
Bryce, J. (1901) 'Primitive Iceland', in J. Bryce, *Studies in History and Jurisprudence*, vol. I. Oxford: Clarendon Press, 312–58.
Byock, J. (1982) *Medieval Iceland. Society, Sagas and Power*. Berkeley: University of California Press.
—— (2001) *Viking Age Iceland*. London: Penguin Books.
Fernandez-Armesto, F. (2000) *Civilizations*. London: Macmillan.
Gilberg, T. (1980) 'Communism in the Nordic countries: Denmark, Norway, Sweden and Iceland' in D. Childs (ed.), *The Changing Face of Western Communism*. London: Croom Helm, 205–59.
Hálfdanarson, G. (1993) 'Íslensk þjóðfélagsþróun á 19. öld' (The development of Icelandic society in the nineteenth century), in G. Hálfdanarson. and S. Kristjánsson (eds), *Íslensk þjóðfélagsþróun 1880–1990*. Reykjavík: Háskólaútgáfan, 9–58.
—— (2001) *Íslenska þjóðríkið: uppruni og endimörk* (The Icelandic nation-state: its origins and its limits). Reykjavík: Reykjavíkurakademían.
Hartz, L. (1964) *The Founding of New Societies* (with contributions by K.D. McRae, R.M. Morse, R.N. Rosecrance and L.M. Thompson). New York: Harcourt, Brace & World.
Hastrup, K. (1990a) 'Literacy and Morality: Cultural Deconstruction in Iceland 1400–1800', in K. Hastrup, *Island of Anthropology*. Odense: Odense University Press, 184–200.
—— (1990b) *Nature and Policy in Iceland, 1400–1800*. Oxford: Clarendon Press.
Haugen, E. (1972) *First Grammatical Treatise. The Earliest Germanic Phonology*. Edition, translation and commentary. London: Longman.
Hermannsson, B. (2005) *Understanding Nationalism. Studies in Icelandic Nationalism, 1800–2000*. Ph.D. thesis, Stockholm University, Department of Political Science.
Karlsson, G. (2000) *The History of Iceland*. Minneapolis: University of Minnesota Press.
—— (2004) *Goðamenning*. Reykjavík: Heimskringla.
Moore, R.I. (1999) *The First European Revolution, ca. 975–1215 AD*. Oxford: Blackwell.
Nordal, S. (1993) *Fornar menntir* (Ancient culture), vol. 2. Reykjavík: Almenna bókafélagið.
Ólafsson, S. (1999) *Íslenska leiðin* (The Icelandic road). Reykjavík: Háskólaútgáfan.
—— (2006) 'Normative Foundations of the Icelandic Welfare State' in S. Kuhnle and N. Kildal (eds), *Normative Foundations of the Welfare State: The Nordic Experience*. London: Routledge, 214–36.
—— (2008) 'Íslenska efnahagsundrið' (The Icelandic economic miracle). *Stjórnmál og stjórnsýsla* (Politics and Governance), web journal, 4(2).

Pollock, S. (1998) 'India in the Vernacular Millennium: Literary Culture and Polity, 1000–1500', *Daedalus* 127(3): 41–74.

────── (2006) *The Language of Gods in the World of Men. Sanskrit, Culture and Power in Premodern India.* Berkeley: University of California Press.

Sigurðsson, J.V. (1999) *Chieftains and Power in the Icelandic Commonwealth.* Odense: Odense University Press.

Taylor, C. (1998) 'Nationalism and Modernity' in J.A. Hall (ed.), *The State of the Nation: Ernest Gellner and the Theory of Nationalism.* Cambridge: Cambridge University Press, 191–218.

Tomasson, R. (1982) *Iceland: The First New Society.* Minneapolis: University of. Minnesota Press.

CHAPTER 11
Icelandic Modernity and the Role of Nationalism

Guðmundur Hálfdanarson

Sú kemur tíð, er upp úr alda hvarfi
upp rís þú, Frón, og gengur frjálst að arfi.
Öflin þín huldu geysast sterk að starfi,
steinurðir skreytir aptur gróðrarfarfi.
...
Þá mun sá Guð, er veitti frægð til forna,
fósturjörð vora reisa endurborna,
þá munu bætast harmasár þess horfna,
hugsjónir rætast. Þá mun aptur morgna.

The time will come, after the century's turn
you will rise, Iceland, and walk free to claim your inheritance.
Your concealed forces will rush with vigour to work
again, the colour of vegetation will adorn gravel slopes.
...
At that time, the God who gave us fame in the past,
will raise our reborn native land,
then will the tragic wounds of the vanished time be healed,
ideals come true. Then there will be a new dawn.
(Hafstein 1901)

At the turn of the twentieth century, the future looked bright to most Europeans. This was, in Stefan Zweig's words, 'the Golden Age of Security' (*die Zeitalter der Sicherheit*), and the world appeared – at least to those who belonged to the privileged sectors of European society – stable and politically secure (Zweig 1944: 16–17). To them, the first years of the new century were also 'the age of reason' (*das Zeitalter der Vernunft*), as Europeans enjoyed more freedom of action and expression at this time than they had ever before; scientific discoveries had paved the way for technical and industrial revolutions, fuelling hopes for a century of progress, liberty and peace. Optimism of this kind also coloured much of the Icelandic public discourses in the years before the First World War. Poets, pundits and politicians welcomed the twentieth century as an era of freedom and prosperity for Iceland, or a time when the nation would finally live up to its potential. The fact that Iceland was one of the poorest countries in Western Europe at the beginning of the twentieth century did not dampen people's enthusiasm.[1] Thus, although most of the scientific inventions, which symbolized modernity among the neighbouring nations, were still totally absent in Iceland, newspaper editors and their intellectual confrères never doubted that soon Iceland would enter the track of the modern age.

The apparent discrepancy between what people desired and what they had was the topic of one of the many articles in the Icelandic press celebrating the coming of the twentieth century. 'The main distinctive feature of our national life during the century that has passed is, in fact, that we have missed out on so many of the things that have exemplified the civilized nations in the nineteenth century,' the politician and newspaper editor Björn Jónsson commented in his paper, *Ísafold*.

> We never acquired the machines of the nineteenth century ... and even if we would have acquired them, we would not have known how to use them. The tremendous impact of science on the economy in other parts of the world during the past century has left us more or less unaffected. After this nineteenth century, the century of production, the great century of prosperity, we are just as ignorant as we were one century ago in everything relating to obtaining the wealth we know that exists all around us.

Therefore, the great project of the new century, for 'all good Icelanders', Jónsson concluded, was to pull the nation 'into the flood of progress' (B. Jónsson 1901).

The primary reason for people's optimism in Iceland, in spite of the country's apparent poverty and slow pace of change, was the unfaltering belief in the positive effects of national self-determination on the economic and social progress of the nation. In 1874, the Danish king had 'given' his Icelandic subjects their first constitution, formally ending his absolute rule in the province. With the constitution, the parliament, 'Alþingi', had received legislative authority in Iceland's domestic affairs, in addition to the right to manage the Icelandic national – or regional – budget. After that, during the last quarter of the nineteenth century, the editor of the newspaper *Þjóðólfur* maintained in his turn-of-the-century editorial, there had been more progress in Iceland than the nation had experienced during 'all the other three quarters of the century combined' ('Aldarhvörf' 1901). The same nationalist euphoria was evident in Einar Benediktsson's *Aldamótaljóð* ('Turn-of-the-Century Poem'), for which the author won the first prize in a poetry contest organized to mark the beginning of the twentieth century. Benediktsson relates the dawn of progress, piercing the darkness of the past, to the first steps of the struggle for independence in the mid nineteenth century:

Vér munum aldamyrkrið fyrst,	First we remember the centuries of gloom
svo morgun framfaranna,	then the morning of progress,
er bókarmennt og lærdómslist	when literature and science
brá ljósi' á hugi manna;	cast a ray of light into people's minds;
og 'Fjölni', reisn vors feðramáls,	and *Fjölnir*, the renaissance of our fathers' tongue,
og fundinn þjóðarinnar;	and the nation's assembly;
og löggjöf vora og fjármál frjáls	and our legislation and budget free
einn fjórðung aldarinnar.	one quarter of the century.

(Benediktsson 1901)[2]

The tone was similar in Hannes Hafstein's *Íslandsljóð* ('Iceland's Poem'), also composed to mark the beginning of the new century (Hafstein 1901). 'The time will come,' the rising star of Icelandic politics predicted, 'when you will rise, Iceland, and walk free to claim your inheritance.' Only then was God prepared to resurrect the nation and lead it to its earlier fame – and then 'there will be a new dawn' for Iceland.

Three years later, on 1 February 1904, Hannes Hafstein was granted the opportunity to put his nationalist rhetoric into action, as he became the first minister of the one-man home-rule government for Iceland. Even the archconservative governor of Iceland, Magnús Stephensen, whose post was abolished with the institution of the new regime, saw this change as a beginning of a new era; 'what I have sorely lacked is initiative, creative ideals and other abilities to clear the route for progress,' he proclaimed at a banquet held to honour the new minister on the day he was sworn into office ('Ágrip' 1904). Implicit in Stephensen's self-criticism was his faith in Hafstein, who allegedly possessed all the qualities that the governor lacked. Thus, Stephensen thought, the new minister was exactly the man that Iceland needed at this juncture in its history.

The history of the Home Rule Period in Iceland (1904–18) seems to confirm this opinion, as the first two decades of the twentieth century were a time of social and economic transformation in Iceland. The Gross National Product fluctuated wildly in these years, as it has through much of Iceland's recent history, but the average annual growth from

1904 to 1918 was considerably stronger than it had been at least until the 1890s (G. Jónsson 1999: 370–71; Jónsson and Magnússon 1997: 703; M.S. Magnússon 1993: 112–22). Moreover, at the end of the First World War, the basic foundations of modern society had been laid in Iceland, with extensive mechanization of the fishing industry, the completion of a telegraph cable connecting Iceland with Europe in 1906, the institution of free and obligatory schooling for Icelandic children between the ages of 10 and 14 in 1907, the foundation of the first Icelandic steamship company in 1914, and the formation of the first two modern political parties in 1916, to name just a few of the many important changes that took place in the period from 1904 to the end of the First World War (Kjartansson 2002: 11–77).

The admirers of Hannes Hafstein are in no doubt about his contribution to this transformation of Icelandic society. 'Hannes Hafstein [was] the leader who turned the ideals, which we younger members of the Home Rule Party had believed in, into reality,' wrote Jón Þorláksson, later the first chairman of the Conservative Party and prime minister of Iceland, in Hafstein's obituary (Þorláksson 1923: 9). The leaders on the political right in Iceland have perpetuated this idea of Hafstein's status as the founding father of Icelandic modernity. In the words of Davíð Oddsson, prime minister of Iceland from 1991 to 2004, the nation was blessed to have such an exceptionally gifted person at the helm during these fateful years. But, there were other reasons for this change, in Oddsson's opinion. Hafstein came to office at the right moment; 'freedom was the source of energy which the nation had lacked for so long. Faint hopes had certainly lain dormant in the nation, and it had its dreams and desires, but the right initiative and the duty to accomplish did not rest on the right shoulders until home rule was acquired' (Oddsson 2004).

Behind these accolades for the first minister of the Icelandic home rule and his role in promoting Icelandic modernity are two linked assertions about the relations between nationalism and modernization in Iceland. First is the belief that modernity in Iceland was instigated by the political elite and that the actual trajectory of the modernization process was designed and defined by the politicians. Second is the assumption that national self-determination was a necessary precondition for the transformation from 'traditional' to 'modern' society in Iceland. These are, to a certain extent, the founding ideas – or myths – of the Icelandic nation-state, and they still guide Icelandic political thought. But do they stand up to closer scrutiny, one might ask. Was Icelandic modernity simply the logical result of the nationalist struggle and national self-determination?

Nationalism and Modernity – Two Trajectories into the Promised Land

The call for political, intellectual and economic regeneration was a core element in Icelandic nationalism from the time it was first formulated in the 1830s throughout the nineteenth century. Superstition and apathy were a national curse, wrote the author of the first editorial of the journal *Fjölnir*, published in 1835, and they had to be exorcized from the Icelandic *Volksgeist*. The nation's lethargy had prevented it from living 'a prosperous and useful, pleasant and happy life' in the country, the editors commented, sentencing it to centuries of poverty and economic stagnation. This was not a 'natural' or necessary state of affairs in Iceland, they argued, because in the distant past the situation had been very different. During the first centuries of Icelandic history, the inhabitants of this remote island had been paragons for other Europeans, admired for their energy and artistic prowess. When this golden age came to an end, as Iceland became a part of the Norwegian monarchy in the late thirteenth century, it was as if the nation had been lulled to sleep. The soul could be awakened, however, 'when rational arguments direct it towards energy and happiness', the editors observed. For this to happen, they concluded, 'anyone, who wants to be called an Icelander, must have the desire to break a small crack in the dams and to open a passage for the stream of national life' ('Fjölnir' 1835: 1–4).

Fjölnir, which can be regarded as the harbinger of cultural nationalism in Iceland (Egilsson 1999: 31), appeared at a critical juncture in Icelandic history. Since the early nineteenth century, there were increasing doubts in Denmark about the viability of the composite and multi-ethnic monarchy, and this was bound to influence the attitudes of Icelanders towards their place in the world and their relations to Copenhagen. In 1840, five years after the publication of *Fjölnir's* first issue, King Christian VIII announced his intention to institute a regional diet in Iceland, calling it Alþingi after the general assembly for Iceland which had been founded in the first half of the tenth century and abolished in 1800. The king suggested that the assembly 'would meet at Þingvellir [the 'Assembly Plains', where Alþingi had convened in the past] and it should be, as far as possible, organized in the same manner as the assembly of old' ('Kongelig Resolution' 1863). To Tómas Sæmundsson, one of the four editors of *Fjölnir*, the royal declaration was clear proof of the king's intellect and liberality. 'Never has Iceland received a gift as great as this one from any of her kings,' he wrote in an article published posthumously in 1841. He was particularly heartened by the fact that the assembly was to be truly 'national', that is, it was to be based on Icelandic political norms and structures rather than 'foreign' conceptions of government. 'When we consider the Alþingi of old,' he wrote, it was 'on the one hand, a kind of a festival for the whole nation, arousing its spirit ... On the other hand, it was a convention of the most important men in Iceland for the purpose of passing laws and judgements in people's legal cases, a legislative assembly and the highest court of the land combined.' It was crucial to revive not only the institution itself, Sæmundsson argued, but also the procedural rules on which it had been based, because a parliament which was not modelled on the old Alþingi 'would be disconnected from and foreign to our nation'. A parliament of that sort served no purpose at all for the development of national life, and for that reason it was better to have no parliament in the country than to import a foreign institution (Sæmundsson 1841: 73–79).

The emerging nationalist leader in Iceland, the philologist Jón Sigurðsson, objected strongly to Sæmundsson's vision of the new parliament in an article he published in 1842. Alþingi was to be a 'modern' institution, he argued, based on similar ideals to other representative parliaments in nineteenth-century Europe. 'If the only purpose of our existence would be to demonstrate to other nations how people lived in the Nordic countries in ancient times,' he wrote in a sarcastic response to Sæmundsson's reflections on the new Alþingi, 'then it would be most appropriate to dress us up in old costumes and move us to Christiansborg Palace in order to exhibit us there every Thursday, as any other antiquities, to tourists and academics' (Sigurðsson 1842: 62).[3] For this reason, Sigurðsson rejected Þingvellir, located in lava fields about a day's ride to the north-east from Reykjavík, as the site for the new parliament. This was certainly the place where Alþingi had met every year for almost nine centuries, making it the *lieu de mémoire par excellence* in Iceland, but 'good sense and foresight' told him that the new Alþingi should be held in the burgeoning capital of Iceland, Reykjavík. The main argument for Reykjavík was, in his estimation, that if the country wanted to 'follow the times and other civilized nations' it needed a political and cultural centre, or a true capital city, and it was natural to place its parliament in the heart of this centre. The intellectual and administrative forces of Iceland were to be collected in this focal point of national life, while it was also to serve as a point of contact between Icelandic society and the outside world, from which ideas and goods would spread to other parts of the country. If Reykjavík was to become a centre of this sort, it needed institutions such as the new Alþingi, and if Alþingi was to become a modern institution, rather than a historical relic, it had to be placed in the new regional capital (Sigurðsson 1841: 126–27; Hálfdanarson 2001a).

It is tempting to interpret the political ideals of these two early spokesmen of Icelandic nationalism as examples of diametrically different political discourses, where Sæmundsson represents the 'romantic' or 'idealist' view of Iceland's future, while Sigurðsson promoted 'liberal modernity' and 'pragmatism'; the first saw Alþingi as a 'national assembly', but the latter as 'an assembly of representatives of the nation' (Finnbogason 1907: 106). One could even suggest that Sigurðsson was victorious in these political skirmishes, because when Alþingi was established with a royal decree in 1843, its organization seemed to follow his suggestions very closely ('Forordning' 1864; 'Kongelig Resolution' 1864). Moreover, it is clear that Iceland's trajectory into the promised land of national self-determination followed the paradigm of the 'times and civilized nations,' rather than seeking inspiration in the nation's past as Sæmundsson had suggested. If this line of argument is correct, Jón Sigurðsson could be termed the 'author' or 'intellectual father' of Icelandic modernity, as his position as the undisputed national hero seems to indicate.

The problem with this understanding of the causal relationship between modernity and nationalism in Iceland is twofold. First, it is based on the general assumption that the modernization process in Iceland was formed primarily through political discourse – or, to quote a recent study on Icelandic nationalism, that Iceland 'simply talked itself into modernity' (Hermannsson 2005: 350). Second, it assumes that there was a relatively straightforward and clear-cut connection between the political discourses of intellectuals like Jón Sigurðsson and the actual reception of their ideas.

Looking at Jón Sigurðsson's political legacy first, it is clear that it is both ambivalent and complex. Thus, although he can, undoubtedly, be classified as a classic 'liberal' in the nineteenth-century sense of the term, as he endorsed the usual programme of democratic representative government, freedom of expression and laissez-faire economics, it seems to be his historical nationalist arguments rather than his liberal programme which secured his place in the pantheon of the Icelandic nation-state (Hálfdanarson 2001b: 77–96; Hermannsson 2005: 173–210). In the 1860s and 1870s, his intransigent nationalism and relentless struggle with the Danish government, which often seemed to emphasize legal formalities more strongly than the substance of the debate, drove many of his liberal supporters into obstinate opposition to his politics. Sigurðsson's most vocal adversary in this era was an erstwhile admirer, Arnljótur Ólafsson, a country pastor and long-time member of Alþingi from northern Iceland. Ólafsson, who was one of the most liberal members of the Icelandic parliament in the latter half of the nineteenth century, turned against Sigurðsson in the early 1860s. In part, this was based on personal disagreements between the two men that had little to do with political principles, but Ólafsson also rejected what he once called

Sigurðsson's 'negative formalism and formal negation', in reference to what he regarded to be Sigurðsson's pointless and sterile debates with the Danish government on the historical and legal rights of Iceland in its relations with the Danish monarchy (Ólafsson 1871). When Alþingi was given control over the regional budget in 1874, Ólafsson saw this as a golden opportunity to fulfil the dreams of the early national-liberals, including Jón Sigurðsson himself, of using the new authority of the Icelandic parliament to improve the economic and intellectual state of the nation, and thus to make the country capable of standing on its own feet. This perspective is reflected in a humorous letter from Ólafsson to an Icelandic friend and fellow critic of Sigurðsson, Gísli Brynjúlfsson, professor of Icelandic studies at the University of Copenhagen, written in 1879. There he comments on the political situation in Iceland:

> We don't need to bicker and debate, nag, mourn and cry over our servitude and bondage, we only need to demonstrate sound reason and to keep our eyes open, and to *act, work, perform.* We are independent enough from these so-called Danish fetters, ropes, chains, shackles, and I don't remember what to call them; we could play like a calf let out of its stall or a lamb let out of its pen, if our cursed traditional weakness, helplessness, lack of imagination, lethargy and many other bad habits and customs had not become so stuck and incorporated in our minds, hearts, and spirit. (Ólafsson 1879)

Ólafsson's acerbic remark could be taken as a commentary on the heated debates which dominated Icelandic parliamentary politics during the last decades of the nineteenth century. On one side of the political spectrum was the majority in parliament, who slavishly followed Jón Sigurðsson's leadership and example in what Ólafsson deemed to be a quixotic struggle with the reactionary government in Copenhagen, demanding changes of the Icelandic constitution but reaping nothing but instant vetoes from the king. On the other side were those who wanted to set these debates aside, for a time being at least, and to lead 'Icelanders from the desert of stagnation and obsession, where they had roamed for much too long in cultural and social matters, towards modernity: to transform the national mentality', to quote a recent biography of one of the most important of these self-styled 'progressives' in the late-nineteenth-century Alþingi (Þór 2004: 103).

This debate was not resolved until a new liberal government in Denmark cut the Gordian knot in 1902, inviting Icelanders to set up their own home-rule government. With this change, the executive power was moved into the country, establishing an Icelandic nation-state in an embryonic form. Until then, the Icelandic parliament had spent most of its energy on the constitutional debates with Denmark, while it is difficult to detect any consistent economic policy in its actions and resolutions. In part, this can be explained by the fact that the government of Iceland was not responsible to Alþingi until 1904, with the institution of home rule, and therefore the parliament had only limited power over the machinery of the state or the country's economic policy. In part, this can also be seen as a logical continuation of Jón Sigurðsson's intransigent nationalist politics. In Sigurðsson's view, the main purpose of politics was to fight the Danish government, while he thought that the economy would improve more or less automatically with increased personal freedom of action in Iceland. 'I want to preserve our claims, even if we gain nothing,' he wrote in a letter to a friend in 1865; we have to 'make constant demands, but try at the same time to establish cooperation and association to improve our lot'. Iceland did not really need more autonomy than it already had, he wrote in another letter during the mid-1860s, because 'we have enough freedom to improve our situation and enough wealth to tax ourselves, without asking the Danes or the government' (*Minningarrit* 1911; 387 and 392–93). In short, his belief was that national self-determination was not a prerequisite for economic or social progress, but rather the opposite – that is, in order for the nation to govern itself, it had to be economically independent. But Jón Sigurðsson had not much to say about how this was to happen, beyond his belief in the invisible hand of the free market, and therefore he never developed a consistent and pervasive strategy for the modernization of Iceland. It is, therefore, difficult to trace the link between Sigurðsson's political discourse and the modernization of Icelandic society around the turn of the twentieth century – he certainly did not obstruct the transformation of Icelandic society, but neither did he lay out a clear roadmap towards Icelandic modernity.

Icelandic Modernity: Ideals and Realities

While the members of parliament bickered about the country's constitutional status, a social and economic revolution had already started in Iceland. In a few decades, beginning in the late nineteenth century, the country transformed from what the third president of the Icelandic republic, the archaeologist Kristján Eldjárn, once called an 'Iron Age society', firmly rooted in the material culture of prehistoric Scandinavia, to the 'mechanical age' of industrialized modernity. The nineteenth-century peasants utilized techniques brought to Iceland with its first settlers around one thousand years earlier, Eldjárn maintained, and they exploited their natural environment in the same manner as had been done since the beginning of human habitation in the country. Describing an inland valley in the northern part of Iceland, which was first settled in the tenth century but deserted at the end of the nineteenth century, Eldjárn envisaged the first and last inhabitants of the region. Although they were separated by an entire millennium, these two farmers belonged to the same mental and material universe, he wrote, and therefore they would have been able to enter each other's world with relative ease. With the advent of modernity, however, this mutual comprehension and continuity was broken for good. In his restless search for efficiency and comfort, the modern farmer abandoned the narrow peripheral valley, where machines cannot be applied and where spring arrives late. For the modern visitor, to quote Eldjárn again, 'it is as if nothing has happened [in this valley]. Numerous generations have disappeared without a trace, and their toil has amounted to nothing more than maintaining the tribe and bringing it with the slightest sign of life into the future' (Eldjárn 1961: 45–46).

'Modernity' in Iceland has many faces, but Kristján Eldjárn points to two of its most obvious characteristics – its insatiable desire for the new and its seeming rupture with the past. In this process, modernity transformed the Icelandic social mentality, because until the beginning of the twentieth century Icelanders were noted for their almost innate 'antipathy for all novelties [and an] unwavering devotion to the old', to quote the autobiography of one former governor of Iceland, Carl Emil Bardenfleth. For this childhood friend of King Frederik VII of Denmark and minister of justice in the Danish government at the end of the 1840s, Iceland's welfare and development depended entirely on its close relations with Denmark, because the isolated island could not, he thought, survive without Danish assistance. When 'the young generation's fantasies about the golden fruits of Icelandic autonomy would show themselves to be nothing but illusions', he argued, Iceland's self-government would only lead to 'long-lasting stagnation in Iceland's progress towards culture and civilization' (Bardenfleth 1890: 31–36). By the beginning of the twentieth century, this had all changed, however, as the once staunchly conservative Icelanders seemed prepared to rush into the new world without regret.

It was not only the pace of the transformation in Iceland that was unexpected, but also the form it took when it started. Agriculture had always been the foundation of the Icelandic economy and society, and most nineteenth- and early-twentieth-century commentators assumed that this would continue to be the case in the foreseeable future. These attitudes were, partly at least, a natural reaction to the radical nature of the Icelandic modernization – it was simply hard for anyone to imagine the future as drastically different from the past as it turned out to be. But they also reflected pervasive social attitudes in Iceland, where agriculture had always been seen as much more than economic activity. This belief appears in a nutshell in an article written in 1914 by Guðmundur Hannesson, professor of medicine at the newly established University of Iceland and a member of Alþingi for the nationalist Independence Party. There this social reformer discusses the future employment of the young generation in Iceland, at a time when the population was reaching the one hundred thousand mark for the first time in the country's history. As countless commentators before him, Hannesson was convinced of the countryside's superiority over the emerging fishing towns and villages by the coast, especially when it came to prepare children for their adult life. To support his argument, Hannesson pointed out that the fisheries were, by their nature, less dependable than agriculture, and the fishing banks around the Icelandic coast were far from inexhaustible. Moreover, 'the sea influences people in a different manner from the countryside', Hannesson contended; it 'breeds a different kind of people'.[4] Most farming households, with their stability and natural order, 'accustom people to orderliness, thrift and diligence, although often they will also be stingy and conservative', he observed. In contrast, the sea, which in good years provided huge profits for those depending on its bounty, encouraged 'lack of foresight and extravagant spending'. Therefore, the people of the countryside were, according to Hannesson, the 'most responsible and resolute part of the nation'. Finally, the fishermen spent long periods at sea, leaving their families on their own for weeks, and this had very adverse effects on their family life, and the children in particular. This unfortunate situation was clearly demonstrated in the language of the fishermen, 'with all of its ridiculous expressions', especially when it was compared to 'the pure language of the countryside'. His conclusion was, therefore, that farming in Iceland had to be boosted, enabling it to absorb the rapidly growing population of Iceland, and this would only happen through the 'vigorous support of parliament' (Hannesson 1914: 145–48).

The distrust of the sea was deep-seated in the Icelandic political and social mentality. Usually the arguments against the fisheries evolved around the themes mentioned above; according to the conventional wisdom in Iceland, the sea was too 'treacherous' (*svikull*) or 'fickle' (*hvikull*) to be depended on, and therefore people had to be encouraged – if not forced – to live in what was seen as the morally pure countryside.[5] To ensure the domination of the rural economy, the traditional Icelandic labour and social legislation raised various obstacles to discourage those who wanted to settle by the sea from seeking employment outside of the agricultural sector. These legal codes came under increasing criticism in the late nineteenth century, not least from the Danish government, as they were deemed to violate the modern ideals of personal freedom and economic liberty. To begin with, the majority in Alþingi jealously defended the Icelandic labour legislation, but gradually and grudgingly it had to give in. Thus, by the first decade of the twentieth century, the parliament had lifted most of the restrictions on the freedom of employment, establishing a comparatively open labour market for the first time in Icelandic history (Hálfdanarson 2001b: 62–76 and 99–109; G. Jónsson 1981).

We should not, however, interpret the support for agriculture in early-twentieth-century Iceland primarily as a reactionary response to modernity, as some historians have hinted (Ásgeirsson 1988). As noted before, there was general agreement in Iceland at the turn of the twentieth century that the economy needed to change, and that Icelanders had to enter the so-called 'flood of progress'. The future which the *fin-de-siècle* apostles of modernization expected, however, was rooted in the Icelandic experience, and therefore they were convinced that agriculture would continue to play a hegemonic role in the cultural and economic life of the nation. These ideas had strong resonance in the Icelandic nationalist discourses, because it was commonly believed that the Icelandic peasants had not only maintained the national culture through centuries of foreign rule, but that the Icelandic language and cultural traits could only be preserved and nurtured in the 'natural environment' of the countryside (Matthíasdóttir 2004). 'At the present, the same danger threatens most European nations,' wrote the influential intellectual, Professor Sigurður Nordal, in 1925; 'people flock from the countryside to the cities, where they degenerate in a short period of time and are disconnected from their natural ways of life.' This was an even greater threat in a country like Iceland than it was in the more populous states of Europe, because it had always been extremely sparsely populated and had no 'national city culture' of its own. Therefore it was of utmost importance for the country's future to improve the living conditions and educational opportunities in the rural areas, in order to bring prosperity and modernity into the peasants' homes – and thus to keep the rural population in their 'natural habitat'. But first and foremost, it was imperative 'to awaken the sense of duty among the young generations towards the land, the farms and, above all, towards the race, the culture'. Each generation is just a brief moment in the history of the nation, he concluded, and one generation 'has no right to destroy what innumerable generations have tried to preserve' (Nordal 1996 [1925]: 194–95).

One can sense a feeling of urgency and despair in these words, published in the organ of the nationalist Youth Association of Iceland, *Skinfaxi*. The problem was that people did not heed the advice of the well-meaning nationalist intellectuals, but continued to move from the countryside to the towns and villages by the sea, thus radically altering the settlement patterns of the country. In 1890, Iceland had truly been a 'peasant society', with only around 10 per cent of the population residing in fishing villages and towns with two hundred inhabitants or more, but thirty years later, at the end of the First World War, this ratio was up to almost half of the total population (Jónsson and Magnússon 1997: 90). For this reason, many politicians and political commentators feared that the countryside would simply be deserted in a few decades if the authorities did not intervene to shift the balance in favour of the rural areas. In 1934, the 'Red-Green' government of the Social Democrats and the farmers' Progressive Party addressed this issue, forming a so-called 'economic organization committee' to study what they regarded as a national predicament. In the spirit of the times, it presented a state-sponsored economic plan which was to reverse the rural exodus in Iceland. While small farms and cottages, especially those in remote inland valleys and in the mountains, were to be abolished, new farmland was to be broken in more fertile and populated parts of the country, and farms divided where natural conditions were favourable and agricultural products could be marketed with ease. The planned economy was to be based on scientific inquiry, the committee suggested, as the state would consult specialists before new farms were established. 'This is necessary,' the committee stated in its report, 'because most of the few new farms that have been established during the last decades are located in rather unfavourable places.' This unfortunate development had to be brought to an end, because it 'is so expensive to build new farms that it is utterly indefensible for the legislative authorities not to supervise where and how they are established' (*Álit og tillögur* 1936).

What makes these plans interesting is not how effective they were, because in the end they were not, but rather that they give us an idea of how the political elite of the first half of the twentieth century saw the social and economic development in Iceland. As far as there was a coherent 'nationalist' vision of the modern world in Iceland, it focused on the development of rural life, at the same time as the leading nationalist intellectuals and politicians were deeply suspicious of – if not outright hostile to – the urban economy and culture. But the people who laid the economic and social foundations of Icelandic modernity were not politicians or nationalist intellectuals, but rather the anonymous crowd who escaped destitution and unemployment in the countryside in search for work by the coast, in spite of the rules and regulations prohibiting their move and the hundreds of newspaper articles and political sermons chastizing the urban poor and praising the moral purity of the inhabitants of the countryside. Moreover, nationalism was hardly the primary motivation of the entrepreneurs who invested in the fishing industry at the beginning of the twentieth century, but rather the prospect of making a handsome profit in an expanding economic sector. The collapse of the traditional peasant society during the last decades of the nineteenth century created immense opportunities for those who were ready to seize them – and the interesting fact is that many of the entrepreneurs in the fishing industry came from the margins of Icelandic society rather than from the old landowning elite.[6]

The role of nationalism in Icelandic modernization is, therefore, more complex and difficult to determine than the nationalists themselves want us to believe. Some have argued that the strong belief in the nation and its future boosted the self-confidence of Icelanders during a crucial period of their history, and this, in turn, encouraged people to improve their lot and to break new economic grounds.[7] But if this was the case, one has to ask why Icelandic modernity turned out to be so different from the one the nationalists desired, and why their attempts to preserve the social and economic hegemony of agriculture failed so miserably. To answer these questions one has to remember that it is impossible to separate 'modernity' and 'nationalism' into two distinct categories where one influences the other. Thus, nationalism in Iceland was an integral part of the modernization process rather than its trigger, and therefore it neither started nor impeded it. 'In the last 500 years or so there has been an intensification and acceleration of technological, demographical and political processes,' writes Jonathan Hearn in a recent reassessment of nationalism. 'Nationalism appears to be a rather malleable artefact of this unstable environment' (Hearn 2006: 231). Seen in this manner, nationalism was not the reason why Iceland was pulled into the 'flood of progress', because it was part and parcel of the 'flood'. Therefore, the real contribution of nationalism to Icelandic modernization lies not in initiating the economic and social transformation of the late nineteenth and early twentieth centuries, but rather in shaping the nation's self-perception and determining how Icelanders positioned themselves in the world.

The Nationalist Grand Narrative: A Nation Comes of Age

The Icelandic struggle for independence came to a ceremonial end on 17 June 1944, as the members of Alþingi, thousands of Icelandic spectators, and a number of foreign guests assembled at Þingvellir to celebrate the foundation of an Icelandic republic. The most significant moment of this memorable day came when the first president of the republic, Sveinn Björnsson, signed the republican constitution into law, thus signifying the formal inauguration of the new regime. The symbolic value of the ceremony was obvious to everyone present, but its political meaning was open to interpretation. To the leader of the Socialist Union Party, Einar Olgeirsson, the foundation of the republic marked 'the elimination of the last remnants of foreign oppression' in Iceland, at the same time as it restructured the country's social and political order. From now on 'all authority came from the nation itself', he argued, and if 'we want to use the word "revolution" for an act where a nation seizes a right it has been denied for centuries, then a kind of revolution has taken place here in Iceland' (*Alþingistíðindi* 1944: 65). Brynjólfur Bjarnason, who had served with Olgeirsson in the leadership of the Communist Party of Iceland and followed him into the Socialist Union Party in 1938, saw the new regime in a totally different light. While he applauded the foundation of the republic as one of the most important moments in the history of Iceland (Bjarnason 1944), he doubted that this event in itself would lead to revolutionary changes in the country's social structure and politics. When German forces occupied Denmark in April 1940 and Britain seized control over Iceland in the following month, the two partners in the monarchical union were placed in opposite camps in the Second World War. From that moment, the former dependency had, for all practical purposes, freed itself from Danish control. Since then, the Icelandic government structure has 'been the same as it was in most other European republics', Bjarnason stated, and consequently the republican 'constitution only confirmed the existing conditions of the Icelandic government' (*Alþingistíðindi* 1944: 101–2).

Looking at the facts, Bjarnason seems to have had a strong case. The constitution of the new republic was, to a large degree, the same as the one the Danish king had 'given' Icelanders in 1874, and thus the republic formed no revolutionary break in Iceland's constitutional history. Moreover, the constitution closely resembled similar documents in other European democracies, promising the citizens of Iceland various rights which had never been mentioned in the ancient Icelandic legal codes. Olgeirsson's interpretation was, however, in line with the prevalent opinion in Iceland at the time, as in a number of patriotic speeches the foundation of the republic was compared to a new homecoming for the Icelandic nation: 'The long-awaited goal of this nation's struggle for political freedom has been attained,' Gísli Sveinsson, the conservative Speaker of Alþingi, declared to the crowd that had gathered at Þingvellir in 1944 to celebrate the foundation of the republic. 'At last, the nation has returned home with all of its belongings, sovereign and independent. The political severance from a foreign country is completed. The Icelandic republic has been established. Ancient liberty has been reclaimed' (Jóhannesson 1945: 165; see also Hálfdanarson 2006). Thus, in the eyes of its architects, the new republic was not a replication of a foreign model, but a fulfilment of aspirations Icelanders had had for centuries. 'We have come here today to raise again the banner which was lowered at this same place 682 years ago,' the Prime Minister of Iceland proclaimed at the same occasion, referring to the moment when the medieval Icelandic chieftains agreed, also at Þingvellir, to accept the rule of the Norwegian king in 1262. But, he continued, 'true to the ideal of liberty, which the nation has always nurtured, today, here at the Law Rock [*Lögberg*], we are going to revive the constitutional form which generations [of Icelanders] have desired' (Jóhannesson 1945: 152).[8] This sentiment was repeated time and again during the summer of 1944, and it has been reiterated often since (see for example, J. Jónsson 1949: XVIII): Icelanders did not found a new republic at Þingvellir in 1944, but resurrected a medieval state.

To the modern ear, these comments may seem a simple rhetorical device, meant to arouse the patriotic spirit of the nation at a critical juncture in its history. It is obvious to anyone who cares to examine the political history of Iceland that the twentieth-century democratic republic had little in common with the political regime of the so-called Commonwealth period in Iceland (ca. 930–1262), except for the fact that the territorial boundaries of the two polities coincide. But when viewed in their discursive context, these comments symbolize the historical vision of Icelandic nationalism. The most important elements of this historical understanding were, firstly, the idea that the Icelandic republic was an Icelandic institution rather than a foreign import. This notion underscored the belief in the primordial existence of the nation; it was the nation, existing since the country was first settled during the late ninth and tenth centuries, that constituted the state, but the state had not constructed the nation. This reflects the constitutional ideas of German idealists, such as the philosopher Johann Gottlieb Fichte, who regarded, to quote Pheng Cheah, 'the territorial state and its institutions [as] an external mechanism of national culture that should be subsumed by the nation, infused with its vital spirit, and made to serve its work' (Cheah 2003: 130). In this scheme of things, the cultural elements of the nation have always played the primary role, while the state only serves to mark the territorial framework for the national community. In order to gain any legitimacy, the state has to express the true 'spirit of the nation' – the *Volksgeist* – and to suit its particular needs. For this reason, the Icelandic nationalists emphasized the Icelandic essence of the republic, in spite of its very Western and modern character. Secondly, the emphasis on the struggle for freedom, which the nationalists saw as the core of Icelandic history (Olgeirsson 1945: 386), served as proof that love for the fatherland, or the desire for national self-determination, was a primordial sentiment in the nation. It had emerged in Iceland, or so people believed, with the birth of the nation in the Settlement Period, and it had survived in a subdued form with the nation through all its tribulations under foreign authority (Aðils 1903).

In this manner, the notion of the resurrection of an ancient republic in Iceland emphasized the unbroken continuity of Icelandic history at the same time as it drew a clear and unambiguous line between 'us', the Icelanders, and 'them', the rest of the world. It was as if with the creation of the republic, the nation had resumed a voyage it had abandoned when it became part of the Norwegian monarchy rather than entering the modern world as a democratic nation-state. In other words, the perception was that Iceland entered modernity through the country's past, but not by adopting the ideals of the 'civilized world' as Jón Sigurðsson had advocated in his early political statements. It is in this historical vision that we should seek the role of nationalism in shaping the Icelandic modernization process. Since the beginning of the twentieth century, all political acts in Iceland have been measured by patriotic standards, at the same time as they have been translated into the language of nationalism. This is clearly reflected in the Icelandic political system, which is still formed by the nationalist ideals of the early twentieth century. The right-of-centre Independence Party, which was traditionally the largest political party in Iceland, gained its dominance as the true inheritor of the independence struggle with Denmark. This legacy is still maintained by the party's staunch opposition to the European Union, which it regards as a threat to Iceland's sovereignty. Moreover, the parties to the far left of the political spectrum, from the Socialist Union Party in the 1940s and 50s to the present-day Left-Green Movement, have proudly touted their nationalist credentials (Kristjánsdóttir 2008: 312–24). The European programme of the Left-Greens is practically identical to the one of the Independence Party, as in its 2007 general assembly, the Left-Green Movement simply declared that 'entering the European Union, with the renunciation of the national sovereignty and independence it entails, is out of the question' ('Utanríkis- og alþjóðamál' 2007).[9]

In essence, nationalism has shaped the way in which Icelanders write their modern history, but their modern history, to a large degree, has been determined by developments and discourses that came from abroad. It is, to put it differently, globalization which has set the modernist agenda in Iceland, meaning that while the nationalists declared that Iceland's future lay in its past, the Icelandic economy and society was rapidly becoming very similar to the surrounding world. This apparent paradox has typified the political history of modern Iceland; that is, the distinctive features of the 'nation' became the central themes of

Icelandic politics, and the most important sources of people's identities, at the same time as these features were rapidly disappearing.

Icelandic Venture Capitalists as Latter-day Vikings

At the end of the twentieth century, Icelandic society took a new and unexpected turn, which was almost as drastic as its transformation in the first decades of the century. The most obvious signs of these changes were the rapid increase in the number of immigrants in Iceland, mostly from the eastern part of Europe, and the emergence of a new class of Icelandic venture capitalists who invested feverishly and recklessly on the European financial markets. The new character of the Icelandic society and economy did not undermine the Icelandic national identity however, as the economic sovereignty and homogeneity of the nation continued to be among the most important concerns of the Icelandic politicians at the same time as these same politicians willingly opened the country and its economy to global market forces.

Iceland took one of the most important steps towards this path of globalized modernity in 1994 when the so-called European Economic Area Agreement with the European Union came into effect. Although the agreement falls short of full membership of the union, it thoroughly integrates the country in its inner market. As the agreement was debated in Alþingi in 1992, many members of parliament warned against this opening of the country, fearing the influx of immigrants from the continent and the economic dependency which they believed would follow the opening of the Icelandic borders. 'I think, for example, that everyone can agree that the tiny Icelandic society is in infinitely greater danger from all kinds of takeovers than the very large societies in Europe', argued Steingrímur Hermannsson, former prime minister of Iceland, in 1992. 'Do people think ... that the large German banks will have any trouble taking over the Icelandic banks', he asked his fellow parliamentarians. 'People have to have their eyes open to this and to protect, as far as possible, the minuscule Icelandic society from this development' (Hermannsson 1992).

As it turned out, the economy developed in the opposite direction from what Hermannsson had predicted. Instead of a wave of foreign takeovers, a small group of Icelandic venture capitalists bought a number of European companies and financial institutions, constructing international corporations on a scale never experienced in Iceland before. The apparent wealth and power of these tycoons aroused ire in some observers, but was viewed with admiration by others. The president of Iceland and former chairman of the socialist People's Alliance, Ólafur Ragnar

Grímsson, provided one of the most interesting interpretations of the meteoric rise of these capitalist magnates. To him, they instigated a new age for Icelandic society, not only 'in commerce and finance but also in science and the arts'. The success of these financial adventurers was no coincidence, the president postulated in a speech he gave at a meeting of the Society of Icelandic Historians in 2006, but could be traced to 'elements in our culture and history'. Hence he asked the audience to consider 'how qualities we have inherited from our ancestors give us, perhaps, an advantage in the international arena and how perceptions and habits that for centuries set their stamp on our society have proved valuable assets for today's achievers on the international stage'. Thus in Grímsson's view, the postmodern era of global capitalism had its roots in the late ninth century, at the beginning of the Age of Settlement, as allegedly the Icelanders of the early twenty-first century had inherited the 'bold and adventurous spirit' of the first inhabitants of their country. In other words, the venture capitalists were genetically and intellectually linked with the medieval Vikings, who 'travelled throughout Europe, up the great rivers of Russia and all the way east to Constantinople, south to the Mediterranean and west to settle in Iceland and Greenland, and even, for a time, in America'. The businessmen should not forget, the president concluded, 'that their success has grown out of Icelandic history, culture and moral sense' (Grímsson 2006).

Needless to say, this imaginative interpretation of Icelandic history was treated with considerable scepticism by Icelandic historians, one of whom accused the president of harbouring what he called 'self-congratulatory conqueror principles' (S.G. Magnússon 2001, 2006). In the light of the sudden and painful crash of the 'new capitalism' in the autumn of 2008, when the economic empires of the Icelandic venture capitalists – which apparently were all built on sand – collapsed like houses of cards, Grímsson's statements sound strangely out of touch with reality. They are, however, a perfect example of how Icelandic nationalists have regarded social change. In their eyes, Icelandic modernity is not an integral part of global evolution, but expresses the spirit of the Icelandic nation and is rooted in the country's history – even the venture capitalists of the early twenty-first century, who disregarded all national borders as they satisfied their voracious appetites for profit, were placed in this nationalist grand narrative. The idea that they were modern-day Vikings rather than players in a modern capitalist game proves, on the one hand, that nationalism is still the prevalent political *doxa* in Iceland, to use Pierre Bourdieu's analytical term, and, on the other, that Icelandic nationalism has still enormous creative potential at a time when it should be disappearing as the world has supposedly entered a post-nationalist age. Thus, while the financial crash altered the Icelandic political landscape in the short-term, causing a drastic shift to the left in parliament ('Apportionment of seats to *Althingi*', 2009), it remains to be seen if it will have lasting effects on the nationalist imagination. The fact that the best advice President Grímsson could give Alþingi as he opened its winter session in October 2008, at a time 'when we sail this turbulent sea' as he put it, was to encourage the members of parliament to remember the struggle for independence, shows that some politicians still consider Iceland as a world apart rather than as an integral part of the world (Grímsson 2008).

This point is of particular interest here, because it reveals how a nationalist interpretation of history works in practice. Without the slightest reservation, the Icelanders – who for centuries were renowned for their lethargy and resistance to change – were transformed into a nation genetically predisposed to taking economic risks and seeking fortunes abroad. Different as they are, what unites the nationalist narratives of the nineteenth and twenty-first centuries is that they are based on the same historical sense and their belief in the Icelandic nature of modernity. This sums up the role of nationalism in shaping Icelandic modernity; that is, it informs the modernist narrative, but the story it tells is constantly changing. As long as people believe in these stories, and are willing to adapt them to new political and cultural realities, nationalism will survive – and with it the nation-state.

Notes

1. The per capita gross domestic product in Iceland was the lowest of the Nordic countries in 1900, and only around half of the Western Europe average; see G. Jónsson 1999: 386.
2. *Fjölnir* was a literary and political journal published in Copenhagen by Icelandic intellectuals from 1835 to 1847, and with 'the nation's assembly' the poet refers to the constitive assembly held in Reykjavík during the summer of 1851. All translations of poems and quotes are mine.
3. In a footnote, Sigurðsson gives this explanation of his reference to Christiansborg: 'Christiansborg, the great palace of the Danish king in Copenhagen, houses collections of antiquities that have been found under the surface and on the ground, in the lands of the Danish king, and they are exhibited there for free every Thursday.'
4. Hannesson was, as one could expect from this remark, a firm believer in eugenics. The ill effects of urbanization on 'racial purity' were among the themes often discussed by the followers of that ideology; see Karlsdóttir 1998.
5. The old adage 'svikull er sjávarafli' – 'treacherous is the catch from the sea' – was commonly used in nineteenth- and early-twentieth-century Iceland as an argument against the expansion of the fisheries; see for example *Tíðindi frá*

Alþingi Íslendinga 1849: 244, 1855: 818 and 1859: 1169; 'Bókafregn' 1836: 157; G. Ólafsson 1859: 96; Davíðsson 1886: 2; 'Fáein orð' 1886; 'Um fjelagsskap' 1880; B. Jónsson 1892; Þórólfsson 1925: 206–12.

6. No thorough research has been done on the social genesis of the early-twentieth-century entrepreneurs, but some of the best-known owners of trawling companies seem either to have been foreigners, like the former shop clerk Thor Jensen, or of poor peasant decent; see Þór 2003.
7. For the strongest case for this argument, see G. Jónsson 1995: 65–93.
8. Lögberg, literally 'the Law Rock', is the place at Þingvellir where the ancient assembly met and the law was announced.
9. The party's most recent general assembly was less clear on the issue, as it called for 'open and democratic debate on the relations between Iceland and the Union' ('Ályktanir' 2009).

References

'Á aldamótum' (1901) *Ísafold*, 2 January.
Aðils, J. J. (1903) *Íslenskt þjóðerni: Alþýðufyrirlestrar*. Reykjavík: Sigurður Kristjánsson.
'Ágrip af ræðum í samsæti 1. febr. 1904. Ræða landshöfðingja' (1904) *Þjóðólfur*, 5 February.
'Aldarhvörf' (1901) *Þjóðólfur*, 1 January.
Álit og tillögur skipulagsnefndar atvinnumála, vol. I (1936). Reykjavík: Gutenberg.
'Ályktanir samþykktar á Landsfundi Vinstrihreyfingarinnar – græns framboðs. Reykjavík, 20.–22. mars 2009' (2009), www.vg.is/landsfundir/ (accessed 20 May 2009).
Alþingistíðindi, vol. B (1944).
'Apportionment of seats to the Althingi, the Parliament of Iceland. Results of the Elections on April 25, 2009' (2009), www.landskjor.is/media/frettir/Results2009a.pdf (accessed 20 May 2009).
Ásgeirsson, Ó. (1988) *Iðnbylting hugarfarsins. Átök um atvinnuþróun á Íslandi 1900–1940*. Reykjavík: Bókaútgáfa Menningarsjóðs.
Bardenfleth, C.E. (1890) *Livserindringer*. Copenhagen: Reitzel.
Benediktsson, E. (1901) 'Aldamótaljóð', *Ísafold*, 2 January.
Bjarnason, B. (1944) 'Þjóðareining um verndun lýðveldisins', *Þjóðviljinn*, 17 June.
'Bókafregn' (1836) *Sunnan-Pósturinn* 2(October): 155–60.
Cheah, P. (2003) *Spectral Nationality: Passages of Freedom from Kant to Postcolonial Literatures of Liberation*. New York: Columbia University Press.
Davíðsson, Ó. (1886) 'Þilskipaveiðar við Ísland', *Andvari* 12: 1–48.
Egilsson, S.Y. (1999) *Arfur og umbylting. Rannsókn á íslenskri rómantík*. Reykjavík: Hið íslenska bókmenntafélag and ReykjavíkurAkademían.
Eldjárn, K. (1961) *Stakir steinar*. Reykjavík: Norðri.
'Fáein orð um fiskveiðar Ísfirðinga' (1886) *Þjóðviljinn*, 15 November.
'Fjölnir' (1835) *Fjölnir* 1: 1–17.
Finnbogason, G. (1907) 'Tómas Sæmundsson', *Skírnir* 81: 97–116.
'Forordning ang. Indretningen af Althinget i Island', 8 March 1843 (1864) *Lovsamling for Island*, vol. XII. Copenhagen: Andr. Fred. Höst, 500–25.

Grímsson, Ó.R. (2006) 'Icelandic Ventures', lecture by the President of Iceland, Ólafur Ragnar Grímsson, in the series of lectures presented by the Icelandic Historians' Society, 10 January, www.forseti.is/media/files/06.01.10.Sagnfrfel. utras.enska.pdf (accessed 25 April 2007).

—— (2008) 'Ræða forseta Íslands Ólafs Ragnars Grímssonar við setningu Alþingis 1. október 2008', www.forseti.is/media/files/08_10_01_Thingsetning.pdf (accessed 12 October 2008).

Hafstein, H. (1901) 'Íslandsljóð', *Þjóðviljinn*, 12 January.

Hannesson, G. (1914) 'Unga fólkið og atvinnuvegir landsins', *Skírnir* 88: 128–48.

Hálfdanarson, G. (2001a) 'Þingvellir: An Icelandic "Lieu de Mémoire"', *History and Memory* 12(1): 4–29.

—— (2001b) *Íslenska þjóðríkið – uppruni og endimörk*. Reykjavík: Hið íslenska bókmenntafélag and ReykjavíkurAkademían.

—— (2006) 'Severing the Ties – Iceland's Journey from a Union with Denmark to a Nation-State', *Scandinavian Journal of History* 31(3/4): 237–54.

Hearn, J. (2006) *Rethinking Nationalism. A Critical Introduction*. Basingstoke: Palgrave Macmillan.

Hermannsson, B. (2005) *Understanding Nationalism. Studies in Icelandic Nationalism 1800–2000*. Stockholm: Department of Political Science, Stockholm University.

Hermannsson, S. (1992). A speech in Alþingi, 24 August 1992, www.althingi.is/altext/116/08/r24134029.sgml (accessed 25 April 2007).

Jóhannesson, A. (1945) '17. júní', in *Lýðveldishátíðin 1944*. Reykjavík: Leiftur, 137–241.

Jónsson, B. (1892) 'Búðseta—þurrabúð', *Ísafold*, 24 August.

—— (1901) 'Á aldamótum', *Ísafold*, 2 January.

Jónsson, G. (1981) *Vinnuhjú á 19. öld*. Reykjavík: Sagnfræðistofnun Háskóla Íslands.

—— (1995) 'Þjóðernisstefna, hagþróun og sjálfstæðisbarátta', *Skírnir* 169 (Spring): 65–93.

—— (1999) *Hagvöxtur og iðnvæðing. Þróun landsframleiðslu á Íslandi 1870–1945*. Reykjavík: Þjóðhagsstofnun.

Jónsson, G., and M.S. Magnússon (eds) (1997) *Hagskinna. Icelandic Historical Statistics*. Reykjavík: Statistics Iceland.

Jónsson, J. (1949) 'Jón Jónsson Aðils' in *Gullöld Íslendinga: Menning og lífshættir feðra vorra á söguöldinni*, 2nd edn. Reykjavík: Þorleifur Guðmundsson, xi–xxiii.

Karlsdóttir, U.B. (1998) *Mannkynbætur. Hugmyndir um bætta kynstofna hérlendis og erlendis á 19. og 20. öld*. Reykjavík: Sagnfræðistofnun and Háskólaútgáfan.

Kjartansson, H.S. (2002) *Ísland á 20. öld*. Reykjavík: Sögufélag.

'Kongelig Resolution ang. Anordning om Althingets Oprettelse paa Island', 8 March 1843 (1864) *Lovsamling for Island*, vol. XII. Copenhagen: Andr. Fred. Höst, 451–99.

'Kongelig Resolution ang. Oprettelsen af Althinget som en særegen Landsrepræsentation for Island', 20 May 1840 (1863) *Lovsamling for Island*, vol. XI. Copenhagen: Andr. Fred. Höst, 614–28.

Kristjánsdóttir, R. (2008) *Nýtt fólk. Þjóðerni og íslensk verkalýðsstjórnmál 1901–1944*. Reykjavík: Háskólaútgáfan.

Magnússon, M.S. (1993) 'Efnahagsþróun á Íslandi 1880–1990' in G. Hálfdanarson and S. Kristjánsson (eds), *Íslensk þjóðfélagsþróun 1880–1990. Ritgerðir.* Reykjavík: Félagsvísindastofnun and Sagnfræðistofnun Háskóla Íslands, 112–22.

Magnússon, S.G. (2001) 'Sársaukans land. Vesturheimsferðir og íslensk hugsun' in D. Ólafsson and S.G. Magnússon (eds), *Burt og meir en bæjarleið. Dagbækur og persónuleg skrif Vesturheimsfara á síðari hluta 19. aldar.* Reykjavík: Háskólaútgáfan, 13–69.

—— (2006) '"Við" erum frábær', article on the website Kistan, 10 January, www.kistan.is/default.asp?sid_id=28002&tre_rod=003|&tId=2&fre_id=39395&meira=1 (accessed 25 April 2007).

Matthíasdóttir, S. (2004) *Hinn sanni Íslendingur – þjóðerni, kyngervi og vald á Íslandi 1900–1930.* Reykjavík: Háskólaútgáfan.

Minningarrit aldarafmælis Jóns Sigurðssonar 1811–1911 (1911). Reykjavík: Hið íslenska bókmenntafélag.

Nordal, S. (1996 [1925]) 'Mark íslenzkra ungmennafélaga' in *Samhengi og samtíð, vol. III, Ritverk.* Reykjavík: Hið íslenzka bókmenntafélag, 190–96.

Oddsson, D. (2004) 'Vandinn við að varðveita og efla frelsið flóknari en nokkru sinni fyrr', *Morgunblaðið*, 2 January.

Olgeirsson, E. (1945) 'Sögusýningin', in *Lýðveldishátíðin 1944*, 381–429. Reykjavík: Leiftur.

Ólafsson, A. (1871) A letter to Gísli Brynjúlfsson, 27 February. The Royal Library, Copenhagen. Nks. 3263, 4°, kapsel V.

—— (1879) A letter to Gísli Brynjúlfsson, 2 March. The Royal Library, Copenhagen. Nks. 3263, 4°, kapsel V.

Ólafsson, G. (1859) 'Um jarðyrkju', *Ný félagsrit* 19: 92–127.

Sigurðsson, J. (1841) 'Um alþíng á Íslandi', *Ný félagsrit* 1: 59–134.

—— (1842) 'Um alþíng', *Ný félagsrit* 2: 1–66.

Sæmundsson, T. (1841) 'Alþíng', in *Þrjár ritgjörðir.* Copenhagen: 17 Icelanders, 73–79.

Tíðindi frá Alþingi Íslendinga (1849–1859), Reykjavík.

'Um fjelagsskap' (1880), *Fróði*, 16 April.

'Utanríkis- og alþjóðamál. Samþykkt á landsfundi 2007' (2007), www.vg.is/malefni/landsfundur-2007/alyktanir/nr/1598 (accessed 26 April 2007).

Zweig, S. (1944) *Die Welt von gestern. Erinnerungen eines Europäers.* Stockholm: Bermann-Fischer.

Þorláksson, J. (1923) 'Frá fyrstu stjórnarárum H. Hafsteins', *Óðinn* 9 (Jan.–June): 8–10.

Þór, J.Þ. (2003) *Uppgangsár og barningsskeið. Saga sjávarútvegs á Íslandi, vol. II, 1902–1939. Vélaöld.* Akureyri: Hólar.

—— (2004) *Dr. Valtýr. Ævisaga.* Akureyri: Hólar.

Þórólfsson, S. (1925) 'Sjósókn og sjávarafli', *Ægir* 18(11): 206–12.

Notes on Contributors

Risto Alapuro was Professor of Sociology at the University of Helsinki until 2010, and the head of the Helsinki Group for Political Sociology. His publications include *State and Revolution in Finland* (1988), and several other monographs and edited or co-edited anthologies, among them *Nordic Associations in a European Perspective* (2010), and *Political Theory and Community Building in Post-Soviet Russia* (2011). His main research interests are collective action, social networks and associational organization in a comparative perspective.

Jóhann P. Árnason is Emeritus Professor of Sociology at La Trobe University, Melbourne, and Professor at the Faculty of Human Studies, Charles University, Prague. His research interests focus on comparative historical sociology, with particular emphasis on the comparative sociology of civilizations. Recent publications include: *Civilizations in Dispute: Historical Questions and Theoretical Traditions* (Leiden, 2003); *Axial Civilizations and World History* (co-edited with S.N. Eisenstadt and Björn Wittrock) (Leiden, 2005); *The Roman Empire in Context: Historical and Comparative Perspectives* (co-edited with Kurt A. Raaflaub) (Oxford/Malden, MA 2010).

Guðmundur Hálfdanarson was educated at the University of Lund, University of Iceland and Cornell University. He is currently Professor of History at the University of Iceland, specializing in European social and political history. Among his most recent publications are *Íslenska þjóðríkið – upphaf og endimörk* [The Icelandic Nation State – Origins and Limits] (2001), (with H. Jensen and L. Berntson) *Europa 1800–2000* (2003), *Historical Dictionary of Iceland* (2nd edn, 2008), and *Discrimination and Tolerance in European Perspective* (editor, 2006). He is the editor-in-chief of the *Scandinavian Journal of History*.

Peter Hallberg is Research Fellow at the Department of Political Science, and Eva Österberg Pro Futura Scientia Fellow at the Swedish Collegium for Advanced Study. Hallberg works at the intersection of cultural history and political theory, with a particular focus on concepts and histories of democracy and the relationship between anthropology and political philosophy. His work is interdisciplinary and frequently crosses the boundaries between the social sciences and the humanities. It has been published in journals such as *Studies on Voltaire and the Eighteenth Century*, *Scandinavian Journal of History*, *History of European Ideas*, *History of Political Thought*, and *Race & Class*.

Niels Kayser Nielsen is Senior Lecturer at the Department for History and Area Studies, Aarhus University. Among his books are *Madkultur – opbrud og tradition* (2003), *Steder i Europa – omstridte byer, grænser og regioner* (2005), *Bonde, stat og hjem – Nordisk demokrati og nationalisme* (2009) and *Historiens forvandlinger* (2010).

Gunnar Skirbekk (b. 1937) is Professor Emeritus at the Department of Philosophy and the Center for the Study of the Sciences and the Humanities, University of Bergen. He is the Norwegian coordinator of 'Marco Polo' 1994–2005, a programme of comparative studies of cultural modernization in Europe and East Asia, established in 1994, at the University of Bergen and East China Normal University in Shanghai. Among his publications are: *Rationality and Modernity, Essays in Pragmatic Philosophy* (Oslo/Oxford, 1993); *A History of Western Thought*, together with Nils Gilje (London, 2001); and *Timely Thoughts. Modern Challenges and Philosophical Responses* (Lanham, 2007).

Rune Slagstad is Professor at the Centre for the Study of Professions, Oslo University College. Among his books are: *De nasjonale strateger* (1998), *Rettens ironi* (2001), *Kunnskapens hus* (2006), and *Elster og sirenenes sang* (2010).

Henrik Stenius is, since 2002, Research Director of the Centre for Nordic Studies at the University of Helsinki. He has previously been acting professor at the Department of History at Helsinki University and Director of the Finnish Institute in London. His fields of research are the history of mobilization and voluntary associations in the Nordic countries, and conceptual history. He is a member of the Finnish Centre of Excellency of Political Thought and Conceptual Change and the Nordic Centre of Excellency of Nordic Welfare Research.

Bo Stråth is, since July 2007, Academy of Finland Distinguished Professor in Nordic, European and World History at Helsinki University. In the period 1997–2007 he was Professor of Contemporary History at the European University Institute, Florence, and 1990–1996 Professor of History at the University of Gothenburg. In the framework of his chair at Helsinki University his research concentrates on two projects: Between Restoration and Revolution, National Constitutions and Global Law: An Alternative View on the European Century 1815–1914 (ERere), co-directed with Martti Koskenniemi; and Conceptual History and Global Translations: The Euro-Asian and African Semantics of the Social and the Economic.

Björn Wittrock is Principal of the Swedish Collegium for Advanced Study (SCAS), Uppsala, and University Professor at Uppsala University. He has published extensively, with eighteen books to date, in the fields of intellectual history, historical social science, social theory, and civilizational analysis. Recent publications include: *Frontiers of Sociology* (Brill, 2009; with Peter Hedström); *Eurasian Transformations, Tenth to Thirteenth Centuries: Crystallizations, Divergences, Renaissances* (Brill, 2004; with Johann Arnason); *Axial Civilizations and World History* (Brill, 2004; with Johann Arnason and S.N. Eisenstadt, 2005); and *Public Spheres and Collective Identities* (Transaction, 2001; with S.N. Eisenstadt and Wolfgang Schluchter).

Uffe Østergård is Professor in European and Danish History at the International Center for Business and Politics, Copenhagen Business School, former director of the Danish Center for Holocaust and Genocide Studies, and Jean Monnet Professor in European Civilization and Integration, University of Aarhus. He has published extensively on political cultures in the various European states, among others: *Europas ansigter* (1992 and 2001); *Dansk identitet?* (1993); *Den globala nationalismen* (med B. Hettne og S. Sörlin) (1998) (2. revised ed. 2006 with a postscript); *Europa. Identitet og identitetspolitik* (1998 and 2000); and many articles in Danish, Italian, German, French, Spanish, English and other languages.

Index

Adelcranz, Carl Frederic, 126–8; writings of, 134
Adorno, Theodor, concept of 'Dialectic of Enlightenment', 31
Agardh, Carl Adolf, 220
Alexander I, Tsar, 3
Armfelt, Count Gustaf Mauritz, 209
Armfeldt, Carl Henric, writings of, 117–119, 123
Association for the Franchise for Women (*Kvindestemmeretsforeningen*), established (1885), 177
Aubert, Vilhelm, 159
Australia, 232, 247
Austria, 56; Vienna, 60

Baltic region 2–3, 55, 240; following fall of Iron Curtain, 64
Baltic states, 3, 23, 92, 95, 199; administrative language used in, 109; Russian control of, 197
Bardenfleth, Carl Emil, childhood friends of, 260; Governor of Iceland, 260
Begriffsgeschichte, 6
Benediktsson, Einar, Aldamótaljod, 253
Bergman, Ingmar, death of (2007), 107
Bergsøe, Adolph Frederik, *Den danske Stats Statistik* (1844–1853), 75
Berlin, Isaiah, concept of 'negative freedom', 29
bildning, concept of, 33
Bildung, 33, 220; vertical dimension of, 221
Bildungsbürgertum, 33, 98; emergence of, 32
Bismarck, Otto von, 56
Bjarnason, Brynjólfur, leadership role in Communist Party of Iceland, 265; member of Socialist Union Party, 265
Bjerve, Petter Jacob, director of Central Bureau of Statistics, 158
Björnsson, Sveinn, First President of Iceland, 265–266
Black Death (1348–1350), 241; political impact of, 172, 185, 240
Boisen, P.O., rectory seminaries of, 75
Bondevennernes Selskab (Friends of the Peasant), established (1846), 55,78; integration with United Left (1870), 78
Bording, Frede, 'Heritage and Race', 85
Botin, Anders af, 130–131; attempted introduction of historical biogra-

phy to Sweden, 128–9; *Utkast till Svenska Folkets Historia* (1757–1764), 129
Bourdieu, Pierre, 176; associates of, 159; *doxa*, 269
Brandes, Edvard, activity in *Kulturkampf*, 57; role in foundation of *Politiken* (1884), 57
Brandes, Georg, activity in *Kulturkampf*, 57; role in foundation of *Politiken* (1884), 57
Brofoss, Erik, Norwegian Minister of Finance, 157
Bukh, Niels, support for Nazism, 84–85

Canada, 232
capitalism, 14–15, 21, 34, 39–40, 61, 73, 89, 146–147, 154–155, 170, 174, 179, 184; agrarian, 17; casino, 230; early forms of, 7; financial, 16; global, 4, 188, 230, 269; social democratic welfare, 158; unrestrained, 187; venture, 268
Catholicism, 9; distrust of, 89; saints of, 89
Charles XI, King, 115; reign of, 95
Childs, Marquis, writings of, 5
Christian VI, King, ordinance of (1739), 74
Christian VII, King, 53
Christian VIII, King, accession of (1839), 55; institution of Alþingi (1845), 255
Christianity, 179, 235; Bible, 118, 126, 172; potential coexistence with Norse religion, 92; spread of, 236
Christie, Nils, 159
Cicero, *De Officiis*, 121
Cold War, 3, 31, 40, 42–43, 230, 232, 247; 'Iron Curtain', 64
Collin, Jonas, 75

composite state, 8, 16, 49–51, 54, 58, 64–5, 70, 73, 244; concept of, 11; *Helstaten*, 55; Habsburg Empire as example of, 243; Kalmar Union as example of, 8; Swedish-Norwegian union as example of, 12
Continuation War (1941–1944), belligerents of, 31
Crimean War (1853–1856), 3

Dalin, Olof, 125; editor of *Then swänska Argus*, 117; Swedish Royal Librarian, 113
dannelse, concept of, 33
Denmark, 1–3, 7–8, 10, 17, 20–1, 25, 29, 34, 41–2, 49, 57, 63, 79–80, 82–3, 92–4, 99, 191, 197, 199, 207–208, 212, 225, 227, 258; Alþingi, 270; Christiansborg, 270; Copenhagen, 46, 50–1, 53, 55, 59–60, 69, 81, 176, 244, 270; Constitution(1849), 59; Constitution (1953), 59; Constitutional Assembly (1814), 173; Danish Social Liberal Party (*Det Radikale Venstre*), 61, 64, 86; *Danske Lov* (1683), 52; Flensborg Fjord, 84; Funen (Fyn), 59–60; government of, 259, 261; Grundtvigian people's church in, 11; imposition of Reformation in, 241; Jutland, 69–70; Left Party, 176; Liberal Party(*Venstre*), 196; National Assembly(*Stortinget*), 173–175; nationalism in, 26, 57, 70–1; Nazi occupation of(1940–1945), 103, 265; *Norske Lov* (1687), 52; North Jutland, 59; population of, 65; Odense, 86; Sealand, 59, 69, 77; Social Democrat party, 61–2, 246; Sjælland, 60; South Jutland, 59; TV 2, 69; Vesteborg, 75
Denmark-Norway, 25, 49, 53, 70, 108,

172; Norwegian secession from (1814), 145, 176, 195; role in outbreak of Great Northern War (1700), 95
Det forenede Venstre (United Left), integration of Friends of the Peasant(1870), 78

Eberhardt, Johan Hartman, 120, 122
Edén, Nils, Swedish Prime Minister, 102
Eisenstadt, S.N., 'multiple modernities' theory, 14
Eldjárn, Kristján, 259–260
Enlightenment, 28; discourses of, 18–19; influence of, 29, 53
Erik of Pommern, building of Elsinore Castle (1420–1425), 50
Eriksson, King Magnus, 89–90
Estonia, economy of, 3
European Economic Community, 89
European Monetary Union (EMU), members of, 89–90
European Union (EU), 2, 268; currency of, 89, 106, 204; European Economic Area Agreement, 268; members of, 90, 104–5, 109, 188, 267; patron saints of, 89; Presidency of, 109
Ewald, Johannes, *Kong Christian* ('King Christian') (1779), 65

Farmers' Friends, *Folketdende*, 175; orgins of, 175; radicalization of, 176
Faroe Islands, 2–3, 50, 59, 66
fascism, 5, 35, 84, 193, 198
Fichte, Johann Gottlieb, 76, 266
Finland, 1–4, 11, 21–2, 36, 42, 44, 51, 73, 79–80, 82, 103, 108, 191, 195, 204, 207–209, 213; acquired by Russian Empire (1808–1809), 195, 212; Civil War (1918), 40, 102, 193–194, 197–198, 200–201, 218, 223;

Fennoman Party, 210, 214, 227; Grand Duchy of (1809–1917), 19, 23, 30, 207, 212, 214, 218, 226–227; Gamla Finland, 72; introduction of universal suffrage (1906), 35; nationalism in, 26, 210; Populist Party, 226; Social Democrat Party, 193, 201–202; *Sockenstämman*, 79–80; view of EU membership, 204–205
Finnish Literary Society, founded (1831), 210
First World War (1914–1918), 2, 4, 57–8, 61, 97–8, 100, 198–199, 224, 227, 252; end of, 254
Fjölnir, 270; editorial staff of, 255; influence of, 255
folk, 86; concept of, 40–1, 63, 83, 202; schools, 148–149, 157
folkedanning, 185
folkhem, 185; concept of, 192
folkehøjskole, 174
folkeopplysning, 174
folkhemmet, 38; concept of, 32
folkhøgskule, 181, 183
folkelighed, 16–17, 174, 185; concept of, 63
folkelighet, origin of term, 149
folkehøjskolen, 32
Foucault, Michel, 187; concept of governmentality, 13–14
France, 31, 106, 171–172, 185, 232; Académie de Sciences, 124; Communist Party, 247; *front populaire*, 39; nationalism in, 70; Paris, 112, 124; Revolution (1789–1799), 19, 208, 212, 214, 216; Socialist Party, 62
Frandsen, Steen Bo, analysis of 'Jutland question', 59
Frederick, Adolph, 127; focus on development of Swedish artistic culture, 128

Frederick IV, *Rytterskoler* provisions, 74
Frederik, VII, King, childhood friends of, 260
Frisch, Ragnar, background of, 157; head of Institute of Economics, 157; influence of, 157–158; recipient of Nobel Prize in Economics (1969), 164

Galtung, Johan, 159
Geijer, Erik Gustav, 220
Gellner, Ernest, 245; analyses of nationalism, 14, 243
Gerhardsen, Einar, Norwegian Prime Minister, 157
German Empire, proclamation of (1871), 57
Germany, 1, 6, 12, 27, 32, 39, 45, 58–9, 84, 149, 171, 185, 215, 226; Berlin, 112; Hamburg, 51, 54, 60; Nazi rule in, 5, 27, 84–5, 103; Social Democrat party, 62; Sturm und Drang movement, 29
Gesellschaftsgeschichte, 6
Ghana, Christiansborg fortress, 50
Giddens, Anthony, 'knowledgeable agents' theory, 144
Gjörwell, Carl Christoffer, 125; attempted introduction of historical biography to Sweden, 128–9; role in translation of Ludvig Holberg's popular biographies 132
Gramsci, Antonio, 176; 'organic intellectual' theory, 149
Great Northern War (1700–21), 3, 9; outbreak of (1700), 95
Great Power era (1620–1720), 94
Greenland, 2–3, 8, 50, 54, 59, 66, 229, 269
Grímsson, Ólafur Ragnar, former chairman of People's Alliance, 268; President of Iceland, 268–270

Grotius, Hugo, works of, 115
Grundtvig, Nikolaj Frederik S., 32, 63, 82, 220; address on The Light of the Holy Trinity (1814), 63; background of, 63; influence of, 63, 83–6
Gustavus III, King, coup d'état of (1772), 11, 96

Haavelmo, Trygve, 158; recipient of Nobel Prize in Economics (1989),164
Habermas/Habermasian, 143, 161, 164, 180; model of types of rationality, 13; 'Technology and Science as "Ideology"' (1968), 161; theories of, 168, 172
Habsburg Empire, 8, 12, 54; as example of composite state, 243; Revolution (1848), 243
Hafstein, Hannes, influence of, 254; *Íslandsljod*, 253
Hammarskjöld, Dag, 109; family of, 102; UN Secretary General, 102
Hammarskjöld, Hjalmar, family of, 102
Hanseatic League, 8
Hansen, I.A., role in publication of *Almuvennen*, 78
Hartz, Louis, writings of, 232–233, 237
Hastrup, Kirsten, 'cultural deconstruction' theory, 241–4
Hauge, Hans Nielsen, background of, 173; imprisonment of (1804–1811), 174; writings of, 182
haugianism, 174; origins of, 173
Hedin, Sven, 101
Hegel, Georg Wilhelm Friedrich, 210, 216
Herder, Johann Gottfried, 76, 148
Hermannsson, Steingrímur, Prime Minister of Iceland, 268
Hernes, Helga, 'state feminism' theory, 160

Holberg, Ludvig, 172; popular biographies written by, 132; writings of, 182
Holy Roman Empire, 49, 95; abolition of (1806), 53–4
Horkheimer, Max, concept of 'Dialectic of Enlightenment', 31
Hørup, Viggo, activity in *Kulturkampf*, 57; role in foundation of *Politiken* (1884), 57
Humboldt, Wilhelm von, 32

Iceland, 1, 20, 22, 25, 38, 41, 50, 54, 194–195, 209, 229, 242, 263, 269, 271; Christianization of, 7, 236–237, 239; Commonwealth Period (930–1262), 266; Communist Party, 265; economy of, 260, 267; Free State, 234–235, 238–240, 248; Home Rule Period (1904–1918), 253–254; Independence of (1944), 265; Independence Party, 267; Left-Green Move-ment, 267; nationalism in, 229, 242–243, 264, 269–270; Progressive Party, 263; Reykjavík, 256, 270; Settlement Period, 267; *Skinfaxi*, 262; Social Democratic Party, 246; Socialist Union Party, 265, 267; UK and US presence during Second World War, 230
India, Calcutta, 50; Serampore, 50; Tranquebar, 50
Ireland, Civil War (1922–1923), 225
Islam, 132; Quran, 133
Italy, 84; Rome, 121
Ivan IV, Tsar, 3

Jaabæk, Søren, 176; leader of Farmers' Friends, 175
Japan, Meiji Restoration, 100
Järnefelt, Arvid, 221
Jesus Christ, 133, 236

Johansen, Leif, 158
Jónsson, Björn, *Ísafold*, 252
Jónsson, Jónas, leader of Icelandic Progressive Party, 247

Kalmar Union (1397–1523), 1, 8, 50; as example of composite state, 8
Kant, Immanuel, 76; *Praxis* concept, 162
Karelia, 72
Karlsson, Gunnar, writings of, 240
Kautsky, Karl, concept of 'centrism', 217; view of role of agriculture in modern society, 61–2
Keynes, John Maynard, influence of economic theory, 39
Kievan Rus, Kiev, 92; Novgorod, 92–3
Kjellén, Rudolf, concept of *folkhemmet*, 28
Kjelsberg, Betzy, supporter of *Ventsre*, 177
Kold, Christen, background of, 75
Krog, Gina, chairperson of Association for the Franchise for Women, 177; leader of Norwegian Feminist Association, 177

Laestadianism, concept of, 218
Landauer, Gustav, *Völkisch* socialism of, 27
Language Movement, 176
Latvia, economy of, 3
Laxness, Halldór, 239
Lazarsfeld, Paul, background of, 158
Lehmann, Orla, 56
Lenin, Vladimir, view of Danish cooperatives, 62
liberalism, 35, 146; national, 55; Nordic, 34; shortcomings of, 212; social, 191–192; supranational, 55
Lindberg, Jacob Christian, 63
Locke, John, *Second Treatise of Government* (1690), 115, 135; translations

of works of, 36, 115–16
Loenbom, Samuel, introduction to *Svenska archivum* (1776), 125
Louis XIV, influence of, 52, 127
Lundborg, Herman, founding director of Swedish State Institute for Race Biology, 38
Luther, Martin, 71; 'Little Catechism', 71–2
lutheranism, 10, 64, 71, 94, 107, 172, 191, 193, 222; doctrines and practices of, 11, 176; youth followers of, 172

Marx, Karl, influence of, 27
Marxism, 35, 40, 61–62, 143, 200; abandoning of, 157; characteristics of, 85, 232
Modernity/ modernization, 4, 6, 13–14, 16, 18, 21, 28, 33–4, 41, 44–5, 50, 83, 156, 164, 169, 194, 215, 220, 222–3, 231, 243, 245, 262; advanced, 230; bureaucratic, 146; capitalist, 39; challenges of, 186; characteristics of, 185–6; classical, 18; cultural, 14, 114, 203; Danish, 16, 63–4; early, 9, 230; economic, 15, 146; Enlightenment, 31; Finnish, 19; Icelandic, 20, 230, 254, 257, 259–60, 263–4, 267; ideology of, 35, 192; industrialized, 259; liberal, 156, 257; Norwegian, 143–5, 147, 163; organized, 156; patterns of, 233, 247; political, 15, 171, 244; process of, 167–8, 170–2, 183, 185–7, 254, 257, 267; programmes of, 14–15, 84, 100, 147, 152; reactions to, 262; relationship with nationalism, 254, 257, 264; relationship with tradition, 245–6; social, 15, 146; sustainable, 187; symbols of, 252; theories of, 13,
167–8; variants of, 167, 187
Mohammed, Prophet, biographies of, 132–133; criticisms of, 132–133
Møller, Aage, 85; established Rønshoved Folk High School (1921), 84; 'Vaarbrud' (1933), 84–5
Montesquieu, *De l'esprit des lois* (1748), 52
Moore, Barrington, *The Social Origins of Dictatorship and Democracy* (1966), 58, 66
Moore, R.I., writings of, 233–234
Mosse, George, *The Crisis of German Ideologies* (1981), 27
Muscovy, 93

Næss, Arne, 164; *Erkenntnis und wissenschaftliches Verhalten*, 162; followers of, 159
Napoleonic Wars, 4, 25, 172, 187, 195–196; belligerents of, 53; Gunboat War (1807–1814), 63
National Liberal party, 55–6
nationalism, 21, 37, 44, 55, 75, 77, 85, 210, 246, 253, 257, 263; cultural, 81, 83, 86; Danish, 26, 57, 70–1; Fennomanian, 211, 223; Finnish, 26, 210; French, 70; German, 1; Icelandic, 229, 242–243, 256–257, 264, 269–270; modernist interpretations of, 245–246; peasant, 82; political, 243; presence in youth organisations, 262; Prussian, 70; radical, 103
Netherlands, 66, 95, 215
New Zealand, 247
Norden, 4, 29–30, 32–4, 38, 44; concept of, 21; liberalism in, 34; Social Democratic-Farmers' Party presence in, 27
Nordic Council, founded (1952), 2
Nørgaard, Anders, 84

Nørremølle, H.P. Hansen, 57
Norway, 1, 7, 17, 21, 38, 41, 46, 54, 58, 79, 82, 99, 108, 153, 163, 183–184, 191, 195, 197, 199, 207–209, 212, 234; Bank of Norway, 182; *Bildung*-bourgeoisie, 149–150; Central Bureau of Statistics, 158; Child Welfare Act (1896), 151; Communist Party (*NKP*), 180; Conservative Party (*Høyre*), 154; economy of, 44; end of union with Sweden (1905), 177; Farmers' Party (*Bondepartiet*), 180; *folkemuseum*, 181; Grundtvigian people's church in, 11; Institute of Economics, 157; Institute of Social Research, 159; Labour Party (*Arbeiderpartiet*), 143–144, 154–157, 160–161, 196; 'Lex Brofoss', 154–155; Liberal Party (*Venstre*), 152–153, 155, 160, 182; Lillehammer, 181; Lutheranism in, 19; Ministry of Finance, 157–158; Ministry of Home Affairs, 145; Nazi occupation of (1940–1945), 103; Oslo, 22, 158–159, 181, 188; Secession (1814), 10, 54, 145, 176, 195; Social Democrat party, 61; Storting, 153–154; Supreme Court, 152–154; Treatment of Neglected Children Act (1896), 150; United Norwegian Workers' Association (*De forenede no-rske arbeidersamfunn*), 180, 182
Norwegian Feminist Association (*Norsk Kvindesags-Forening*), established (1884), 177
Norwegian Labour Party, 18; membership affiliated with Third Communist International, 5

Oehlenschläger, Adam, Der er et yndigt land ('There is a lovely land' (1819), 65
Ólafsson, Arnljótur, 257–258; background of, 257
Ólafsson, Stefán, writings of, 247
Oldenburg Monarchy, 49–51
Olgeirsson, Einar, leader of Socialist Union Party, 265
Organisation for Economic Co-operation and Development (OECD), 97–8
Orientalism, 132; pejorative use of, 137

Paine, Thomas, *Rights of Man* (1791), 227
Palme, Olof, Swedish Prime Minister, 109
Palme the elder, Olof, 102
patriarchalism, concept of, 71; decline of, 72
peasants/peasantry, 5, 8, 10, 16, 27, 29–35, 73–4, 116, 128, 176, 202, 210, 213, 219, 231, 271; communities, 25, 28; culture, 82, 216; Danish, 49, 55, 63, 74, 77, 81, 226; dependency upon landowners, 53; farmers, 49, 55, 57–8, 60–1, 64, 78, 172–3; Finnish, 30, 192–3, 199; foundation myths, 28–9; freeholding, 10, 26, 30, 93, 108, 191–2, 194, 199, 208; Icelandic, 245, 259, 262; libertarian, 62; middle, 59–60; movements, 55, 77, 101–2; nationalism, 82; Norwegian, 32, 70, 79, 172; patriarchalism, 71; political representation of, 5, 75, 78, 135, 173, 175, 197–9; Romanian, 199; schools, 72, 74, 76–7; society, 241, 245, 263–4; Swedish, 29; workers, 197, 199
Peter I, Tsar, 3
Plato, 120

Poland, 11, 93–4, 109, 210
Polish-Lithuanian Union, 8; Catholicism in, 9
Pollack, Michael, associate of Pierre Bourdieu, 159
Polybius, 118; 'pragmatic history' theory, 119–120
Prussia, 1, 9, 26, 51, 56, 187; nationalism in, 70
Pufendorf, Samuel, *De officio hominis et civis* (1673), 115; works of, 115–116

Radikale Venstre, development of, 34
Rask, R.C., research of, 242–243
Reformation, 8, 20, 64, 214–215; imposition in Denmark, 241
reformism, 207; Norwegian, 144; scientific, 146
Rein, Thiodolf, theories of, 216
Reventlow, Chr. D., rectory seminaries of, 75
Reventlow, J.L., reform schools of, 74
Roman Empire, decline of, 91
romanticism, ascendancy of, 229
Roosevelt, Franklin D., New Deal, 154
Rousseau, Jean-Jacques, 76; ' A Discourse on the Arts and Sciences' (1750), 112; criticisms of, 112–13
Royal Danish Society for Peasant Education, influence of, 77
Russian Empire, 4, 9, 19, 30, 51, 55, 194; acquisition of Finland (1808–1809), 195, 212; February Revolution (1917), 224; October Revolution (1917), 31, 102; Revolution (1905), 35, 196–197; role in outbreak of Great Northern War (1700), 95; St Petersburg, 112, 226; territory of, 209
Russian Federation, 58, 92

Sæmundsson, Tómas, 257; editor of *Fjölnir*, 255
Samhälle, concept of, 37
Saudi Arabia, Mecca, 132
Saxony-Poland-Lithuania, role in outbreak of Great Northern War (1700), 95
Scandinavia, 1–6, 8–9, 14, 18–19, 29–33, 35–36, 42–43, 66, 75, 89, 91–93, 95, 108, 155, 161, 171–172, 174, 177, 183, 193–194, 196–201, 203–204, 211, 229, 235–236, 246–247, 259; artistic culture of, 125; concept of term, 21–22; languages of, 21, 45, 185; religious culture of, 239
Scanian War (1675–1679), casualty level of, 51
Scheffer, Baron Carl Fredric, 125–6; criticisms of Jean-Jacques Rousseau, 112–13
Schönberg, Anders, attempted introduction of historical biography to Sweden, 128–9, 131–132
Schweigaard, Anton Martin, 147; background of, 145
Second Schleswig War (1864), 1–2, 16
Second World War (1939–45), 1, 34, 38, 97, 104, 106, 202, 204, 230; Auschwitz concentration camp, 109; operational theatres of, 103, 265
Segerstedt, Torgny, 112
Seip, Jens Arup, 143
Sejersted, Francis, 143
Serbia, 58
Shakespeare, William, *Hamlet*, 50
Sibelius, Jean, 221
Sigurðsson, Jón, 220; influence of, 257
Skjervheim, Hans, *Objectivism and the Study of Man*, 162

Sleswig-Holstein, 1, 3, 16, 50, 58, 72; Altona, 50; Ejderstedt, 73; extension of Law of Succession (1665), 51; Kiel, 50, 55; population of, 54
Snellman, Johan Vilhelm, influence of, 211–212; theories of, 210, 216
social democracy, 17, 30, 39, 58, 61, 64, 83, 86, 99, 104, 106, 191–193, 196–197, 199; Danish, 62; model of, 25; Norwegian, 4, 164; Swedish, 4, 99, 164
socialism, class-struggle, 28, 32; 'national', 28, 32, 39; scientific, 161; utopian, 175
Somalia, 170
Sonderweg, 222–223
Sørensen, Rasmus, role in publication of *Almuvennen*, 78
Soviet Union (USSR), 31, 170, 199–200; economy of, 231; sphere of influence, 203
Staaf, Karl, 34
Stalin, Josef, 5
Stang, Frederik, 145, 147; death of (1884), 164; resignation of (1880), 164
Stang the younger, Frederik, 154
Stauning, Thorvald, leader of Danish Social Democrat party, 61
Stephensen, Magnús, governor of Iceland, 253
Stenius, Henrik, view of differences between Finnish and Swedish mass organisations, 201–202
Stråth, Bo, 197–198, 230
Struensee, Johann Friedrich, attempted reforms of, 53; background of, 53
Sveinsson, Gísli, speaker of Icelandic Parliament, 265
Sverdrup, Johan, leader of Liberal Party, 153
Sweden, 1–3, 7, 21, 23, 25, 34, 41–2, 44, 46, 51, 58, 60, 73, 82, 93–4, 97, 105, 107–8, 111, 134, 191–192, 194, 197, 199, 207–208, 212–213, 225, 227; Age of Liberty (1718–1772), 114, 135; *Allmänna Svenska Elektriska Aktiebolaget* (ASEA),100; acquisition of Norway (1814), 53; 'Age of Freedom', 17–18; 'Age of Liberty' (1721–1772), 227; borders of, 177; Constitution(1719/1720), 113; Constitution (1809), 105; Constitution(1974), 105; Diet of, 29, 79, 114, 128; employers' association (SAF), 101; end of union with Norway (1905), 177; Green Party, 105; loss of Finland to Russian Empire (1808–1809), 195; Left Party, 105; Liberal Coalition Party, 99; Lutheran church in, 11; March of the Peasants (1914), 101; membership of EU, 105; Moderate Party, 103–4; Royal Swedish Academy of Sciences, 112–113, 115–116, 124; Saltsjöbaden Agreement (1938), 103; School Ordinance (1693), 120; second presidency of EU (2009), 109; Social Democratic Party (SAP), 61, 90, 97, 100, 102–4; *Sockenstämman*, 79–80; State Church of, 106; Stockholm, 15, 94–5, 101; territorial acquisitions of (1658), 49; trade union congress (LO), 100; Vyborg, 22
Sweden–Finland, 22
Swedish–Norwegian Union (1814–1905), 12, 19; as example of composite state, 12
Swedish Social Democrats, 28; use of *völkisch* and socialist themes, 27
Swedish State Institute for Race Biology, founded in (1921), 38
Tengström, Bishop Johan Jacob, 209;

theories of, 216
Tessin, Count Carl Gustaf, Swedish Councillor of the Realm, 113–114
Then swänska Argus, significance of, 117
Thrane, Marcus, 174; background of, 175
Thrane Movement, origins of, 174–175; suppression of (1851), 175
Tocqueville, Alexis de, 216
Tönnies, Ferdinand, distinction between *Gemeinschaft* and *Gesellschaft*, 37
Thirty Years' War (1618–1648), Peace of Westphalia (1648), 95–6; Swedish entry into (1628), 95
Tomasson, Richard, theories of Icelandic identity, 20, 232
Toynbee, Arnold, 239; *A Study of History*, 91
Tsardom of Russia, Time of Troubles (1598–1613), 94
Truman, Harry S., Marshall Plan, 159; re-election of (1949), 159

Ukraine, 92
United Kingdom (UK), 6, 31, 171, 218; Labour Party, 62; London, 112; navy of, 2
United Nations (UN), personnel of, 102
United States of America (USA), 6, 31, 158, 167–168, 171, 175; legal system of, 153; military sector of, 97; New Deal, 39, 154; New York, 159; Supreme Court, 154

Vietnam War (1959–1975), opposition to, 104
Völkisch, influence of, 27
Voltaire, biography of Charles XII, 90; *Siècle de Louis XIV* (1751), 129

Wallenberg, Raoul, 109
Weber, Max, 173; identification of origins of capitalism, 173–174; theory of permanent disenchantment, 29
Wergeland, Henrik, 220
West Indies, St Croix, 50; St John, 50; St Thomas, 50
Winter War (1939–1940), belligerents of, 31, 202
Wittrock, Björn, 37–8
Woltemat, Henrik Julius, 130
Women's Movement, 176
Wrede, Hindric Johan, speech at Royal Swedish Academy of Sciences (1743), 115

Yugoslavia, 58

Zweig, Stefan, 251

www.ingramcontent.com/pod-product-compliance
Lightning Source LLC
Chambersburg PA
CBHW072146100526
44589CB00015B/2116